A Select Few

A Select Few

E JASON WILLIAMS

ISBN 978-1-959895-00-8 (paperback)
ISBN 978-1-957582-99-3 (eBook)

Copyright © 2022 by E Jason Williams

All rights reserved. No part of this publication may be reproduced, distributed, or transmitted in any form or by any means, including photocopying, recording, or other electronic or mechanical methods without the prior written permission of the publisher.

Printed in the United States of America

Contents

1: Let the games begin 7
2: The Selection Process 25
3: The Game Plan part 1 41
4: The Game Plan part 2 65
5: The Terrorist Job 85
6: The Mexican Cartel 109
7: Organized Crime 131
8: The Next Global Threat 143
9: With a Little Help from Friends 171
10: The Prime Time Assassinations 189
11: The Domestic Threat 213
12: Second Chances 239
13: The Soloists 265
14: The Major Obstacle 297
15: The Major Obstacle Phase Two 321
16: Winding Down 347
17: The Final Assignment 369
18: Short Timing 387

1

Let the games begin

It was one hour before the polls closed for the presidential election of 2032, Thomas Hardesty had a slight lead over his opponents, but not substantial or by any means a landslide victory. He had not yet announced his Vice President, although they both were well aware of the person who would hold that position, should Thomas Hardesty win the presidential election. His entire campaign was based on something long neglected by the primary parties concerned in the political machine that the United States had become, he presented real issues that the people faced, and how he would like to change it. His campaign was so shunned by his own party, he had to run entirely as an independent candidate. Yet with pre-election polls and other gauges used to try to predict a winner, his previous party had the audacity to demand he select a VP from that party. He had made enemies in both major parties throughout his campaign, and figured by turning down the demand of his former party, a few more enemies was not going to matter anymore than those he already knew of.

He made his announcement of his Vice President forty five minutes before the polls closed. He did this through national television coverage via a video link up with the network. He waited this long, because he thought the other parties would be too involved with last minute maneuvering to question his choice. His first act, would occur before even having a victory party interview or conversation. He was going to seal all the records of his VP for his eyes only, to prevent the other party members from doing research concerning his Vice President. His Vice President had over a thirty year career in the government, but not a single day was spent as a politician in any form of office.

Thomas Hardesty did not consider himself to be anything other than a true conservative when it came to politics, although others considered him a radical, because he wanted to see much needed changes in the political structure, of a once great nation. Government had become so large from all aspects, with 70% of all the people employed, were in some level of government. As a result, taxes of the 30 percent remaining were unbearable. The previous president in his first five years in office, had to derail three attempts to overthrow the government. This did not happen from outsiders wanting to overtake a weakening world power, it came from within, among everyday normal citizens of a nations on its knees, trying to simply survive beyond not having enough of anything, to consider mere necessity. Far too many people could not afford homes, often food to put on the table, all a result of the government at all levels wanting more than their share to operate a government far too large to support. The three failed overthrow attempts became martyrs to a growing concern. Rumors were gaining those following this movement, were gaining substantial numbers, and could quite possibly defeat the government in a next overthrow attempt. Thomas Hardesty sympathized with these people in many ways, but did not want it to end in bloodshed of many innocent citizens, only wanting what was once their right to have.

Thomas Hardesty had based his entire campaign on principles long neglected by the political machine, and was disgusted by that machine sucking the life out of the very people who made them what they were. He was going on the foundation of a government for the people by the people, and the only way that would happen was massive changes in the political machine. The first thing he intended to do, was go to a flat tax system, where business and individuals who earned over a specific dollar amount, would be taxed at a percentage of the entire amount. He would then eliminate all the government ties to an organization that created a taxation system, no person could understand, including those who wrote it. A flat tax under his plan would eliminate all of it, and since he would create a large amount of people in need of jobs, the government would use some of the tax money to retrain these people, for other forms of work. Downsizing government at the same time of a fair flat taxation system, would only be the first steps in having the citizens feel more at ease, with being able to take control of being able to live better than they had been. It would not be overnight, but steps needed to be taken to avert disastrous conclusions that seemed eminent.

Thomas Hardesty already knew he would not receive much support from any other politician in office, and to get around that issue, he was going to put it back into the hands of the people. He was going to use the internet as a voting measure for people to give their yes or no response to his options, to get the government back under control of those very people. He would require it to be a secure site, issues would be posted and the national news networks informed of the time frame in which people could respond. He did not care if they were registered voters or not, they simply had to prove they had the right to vote, and could only do it once per issue. This would need to be done by social security number, which was issued to all people in the country, who had the right to vote. The social security number information would be sufficient to insure voting age was attained, if not, it would be thrown out, as would all multiple attempts to keep it one vote per eligible person.

Thomas Hardesty was going to give the people back what they were supposed to have from the very beginning of the government of this country. He expected nothing but difficulty in going through the normal channels of government, and knew following the political path, would result in nothing accomplished in his term as President. He was going to empower the people with the ability to fire the elected official that stood against the people that elected them. Being fired by your constituents, would be immediate and could not be revoked. He intended to bring an end to a lifelong positions to politicians. Length of terms serving your country, which was what politics was originally intended to be, would be inclusive. No person could hold any office more than 12 years. Did not matter what position they held or how many, the total maximum time would be twelve years. He also intended to have salaries to suggest that it would not by any means, be a method to achieve great wealth, and politicians would fall into the same type of retirement plans as the rest of the population, no longer some special means to insure they received 100%, of whatever the current salary was in the highest office they held.

Thomas Hardesty throughout his campaign, stuck with the issues the people needed to hear. His opponents went about all the usual mudslinging they could muster, to avoid discussing a single issue. Throughout his campaign, he did not retaliate with his own mudslinging, he merely dismissed it to the people, saying his opponents did not want the people to hear issues, because they had no intentions of following through with them to start with. He did intend to bring about the changes this country so desperately needed, to help restore it to the great nation it once again could be. He would have to do it by means never employed before, to give the people the chance to truly voice their opinions once again.

At the same time there was talk of the formation of a world government, it was not intended to be a government of power, merely a tool to get the numerous governments to form a means to work collectively, in a uniform direction in order to achieve a more peaceful world in a global community, rather than a collective of incompatible directions, detrimental to various regions of the world. The only thing the world government wanted to see as a directive, they wished to institute a world currency, to eliminate large numbers of different currencies, and a standard the whole world could work with. It would eliminate the need for exchange rates, to convert one currency to another, and somebody profiting from such. This was the very foundation for Thomas Hardesty selecting Romero Trap as his Vice President, he had a specific task for his Vice President to take, in order to expedite a world government forming. That government would not be responsible for electing members from each country, or paying them, it would be each country whose highest official, whether by election, birthright or dictatorship, to take a place in the world government. It was a means to get all the countries working for the common good of all the people in the world.

The polls were now closed, and it was estimated that Thomas Hardesty had won by five percent over his nearest competitor. Hardesty only needed to hear his competitors admit defeat, prior to taking his first action as President. It was time for Thomas Hardesty to call his Vice President, who was nearby, just not in his campaign headquarters. His call was quick and Romero Trap was on his way to meet face to face. Hardesty had his competitors each admit defeat on national television, and he immediately logged into his computer system to access all of Traps records and seal them for only the eyes of the president. With that actually completed, even he could not look into the files again until at which time, he was sworn into office. Fortunately, this was done by a Supreme Court justice, and not any other politician, in order to remove any doubt in the proceedings.

When Romeo Trap arrived, Thomas Hardesty made sure the Vice President understood his task that had been discussed previously, to their becoming the top two people in the country's government. Romero Trap understood the parameters of it, but needed to know how he would proceed, based on the information he had yet to receive. Hardesty told Trap that he wanted absolutely no details in this task to keep the appearance he had nothing to do with it, but from time to time, input to Trap via untraceable means, various problems to be dealt with, in order for the entire plan to become reality. Trap asked if this was to be kept entirely off the record, if it was possible to get funding from those other countries most in need of a problem being removed. Hardesty said to use whatever means he could have available to him, as long as the goals were able to be met, he informed the Vice President that only Trap and a few he selected would know of the funding in existence, and suggested he use more than a single numbered account in the event one of his entities, became compromised. Since the program would not fall under the funding of the government for obvious reason, it could be subject to the laws of all countries, and funds seized for their activities.

Trap understood the conditions, and said he would start putting together a team of assets specific to the tasks at hand. He did not expect this would be completed for a least one month, and wanted to know if there was a time frame in which to start up operations. Hardesty said around the first week of the next year, he would be expected to give a State of the Union address, which did not take place until his office time was unencumbered. As President elect, he had a few weeks of working with the president nearing his end of official time in office, which usually corresponded with the first day of the year starting in 2033.

With that conversation concluded, the pair went to the place that the campaign officials decide to hold the celebration festivities. It only took five minutes on foot to arrive, and the first thing Thomas Hardesty did was to introduce his Vice President to the group and the news coverage. He told the people listening that although Romero Trap had never before held so much as a council seat in a small local government, he had over 30 years' experience within the internal workings of the government. He did not divulge to the public or even all of his campaign staff, exactly what he did in government. Thomas Hardesty was pretty certain, that none of them would truly like to hear what his longtime friend had truly done in his illustrious career. It was likely too dark for most to comprehend, and in some case, it would be considered an act of treason even for himself to bring it out into public.

Romero Trap had started his young life out in the United States Navy, and after a mere two years, was a member of the Seals, of the most elite group, even among the seals. Trap excelled in several disciplines utilized by elite teams in covert operations, not just a single one. He was an expert marksman in rifle, small hand weapons such as handgun, as well as several other quieter means like blades and garrotes. He was also an expert in close quarters combat situations, and had not once been even slightly wounded by his actions and counteractions. Trap, after a total of six years in the Navy was later a part of almost every portion of the government that incorporated covert operations. After 10 years total, including naval time he spent as the commanding officer of any select covert operations, no matter who was behind it. He never lost his naval commission and attained a very high rank, that would have easily given him a position in the Pentagon, something he refused to do as long as was capable of performing the same duties he had from the beginning. Even at the age of 56, Romero Trap remained a superb physical specimen of the human race. Of course, even with this running through his thoughts, Thomas Hardesty did not utter a single word of this to the public, and turned the podium over to Romero Trap, who had very little experience in public speaking.

He did not give a long and involved speech but he was heard, apparently shouting orders in times of need, prepared him well for that. His short acceptance speech largely entailed expressing his desire to simply do the best he could in his newfound position. He truly hoped never an event occurred, where he would need to move up a spot, as he held the President near and dear to his heart.

After nearly four hours of celebration with the campaign staff, and the news crew keeping every moment on tape, for some time in the future, if it was deemed to be news worthy, nursing several glasses of Champaign, Trap and Hardesty left, and returned to the office they came from. For them it was time to get down to some preliminary business. Romero Trap asked the President if he could use the computer to initiate his first attempt into the task assigned to him. Thomas Hardesty had no qualms about it, and told him to proceed. Romero Trap put out an internet ad so to speak, that read "A Select Few" it was code for any people he currently or previously had worked with in his over 30 year history of covert operations, some were so black, even an overcast moonless night appeared to be bright in comparison. Romero Trap was compared to be as cold hearted as the grim reaper himself, as he did not suffer regrets or nightmares or a guilty conscience about things he had done, for the good of his country. Surprisingly enough, Trap had a moral code he kept, even if it meant the extermination of other people's lives for the good that would follow. It took a unique set of convictions to perform some of the things he did in the service of his country.

He pulled out a phone from his coat, which was called a burner phone or disposable phone, and finished his short ad with COPA and the phone number of the disposable phone. Once his team was assembled, based on the response to this ad, the phone would in fact be disposed of. COPA was code for Commanding Officer Position Accepted, which meant, Trap was in charge of a new assignment, which he already accepted for the team to be selected. Those people available for assignment, would see the ad, and call the number to confirm their availability for assignment to the team. Trap would select only so many of the candidates, based on specific criteria he thought would need to be addressed, for this particular task of covert operations. This was not going to be a short assignment, possibly lasting 8 years. Eight years was the longest amount of time Thomas Hardesty could hold the position of US President.

It was the highest position a person could attain in the government of the United States, and it provided the office holder with the additional title of Commander in Chief, allowing the President to be the person in charge of the entire military structure of the country. Hardesty did not want at any point in his term of office, to openly declare war on any other nation. He wanted all of this handled by his Vice President, through means not military. He hoped he could curb the brewing internal conflict from the citizens of this once great nation, and restore some of the confidence in the government, returning to a for the people mentality. He thought if he could achieve this in his first term, he would in all likelihood get a second, to continue his restoration process at the same time making way for a world government to form. It was a real narrow tightrope he had to traverse, and one wrong move could end it all.

Romero Trap had nothing more in the works for the evening, because in order for him to select a team, he had to know who, and how many would respond to his internet ad. Which was so vague, he did not anticipate anybody other than those who knew what it meant would reply. The wheels were in motion, which was all he could do to start with. He and Hardesty discussed more details concerning the tasks, but it was made perfectly clear to Trap, at no point in the process of this task, did Thomas Hardesty want to know enough details into the task processes, to implicate the President should anything go terribly wrong. The tasks would be entirely off the record of the government, outside of maybe some reference to the task name, and the location of the funds acquired to fulfill the task. It would be up to Romero Trap, as to when and how his people would be compensated for their part in fulfilling the tasks, and even those funds needed to come from whatever means Trap devised to obtain them.

Trap only knew of one means to initiate the entire task, it would involve a government facility first, before bringing into play the various drug cartels to fund his operation. It was not something he viewed without disdain, he abhorred drug usage of any kind, and to make things like this available to the general population, went against his own preference, but he did understand to some small degree how it existed.

It was a means for people to escape reality for a short time, and at this point in time, the government was largely the cause of the effect. Due to the demands of large government taking so much of people's hard earned money, to keep the government merely running, the people were left with hard choices to make. Some people had to decide between a means to escape reality, or bring children into a world that could use massive improvement. Trap had no dissolutions over the hardships the average citizens of this country had to endure. Population growth as a result, was at a near standstill. People even without escape options, could not afford to bring children into the world and raise them, many could not afford homes any longer, and the government had acquired so many across this great land, that they were the landlords of 50% of all the homes available to live in. It created an even larger government entity, than the Internal Revenue Service, and unlike others, it was in the business of making profits. They did this by having high rents, and did nothing to maintain or improve a single property in their possession.

At the same time, utility companies were looking into ways to make energy more affordable to all, and significantly reduce the demand at the same time. The electric companies were well into the process of changing from AC to DC voltage across the country, but the home conversion was an expense most home owners could not afford. So, at a loss to the profit margin, the electric companies, were taking on the additional cost of converting homes to the new power, which made everything simpler in the long run. It would still be up to the home owner to replace the items in their home, with ones that worked on the newer power available. Due to the taxation demands of the governments, the utility companies were at a mere crawl to convert homes, and the government wanted no part of spending money for the upgrades to take place in their properties. The government merely wished to collect funds to grow the government more than it had already grown. The previous government wanted to own every piece of property in the entire country, and Hardesty planned to change that also.

Thomas Hardesty wanted this entire division of the government abolished, and the homes made available to the public once again, at a reduced rate. He was fully aware some homes had been neglected far too long to do anything more than tear them down, and make the land available to rebuild. This would need to be done at the government's expense, but it had to be done to try to give the people back dreams and reasons to make the country great again. He did not see it happening fully in his lifetime, but it needed to be done, and he would get it started and hope the people would elect others holding office, to complete what he started. He would turn over in his grave and haunt whoever tried to reverse it. Of course, he could only vow this to himself.

Thomas Hardesty had wide reaching programs planned, to effectively make the government a role model to follow, as opposed to a criminal offense to pursue the example they set. He was first going to restructure the long time retirement plan the government forced every citizen, who ever worked to contribute to. First, he was going to find out who obtained funds from the program for purposes other than to supplement people's income, once they reached retirement. With those refunds reinstated he wanted monies to be invested in a fashion to gain in the overall fund, to help keep the program in the black as it had become apparent that letting it sit, without any form of growth, was detrimental to its purpose.

He also planned to go over every bill that had been approved in the last 70 years, to eliminate the ones that were not for the benefit of the people; but to have the government hold greater power over those people. These would be beneficial to both people and businesses that continued to operate in the United States. If the government could not set an example for businesses to follow, why would they continue to operate in this country? When the grass was greener in so many other places in the world. Thomas Hardesty knew his vision went against the grain of many long time politicians, who spent their entire lives, filling their pockets with the hard earned money of the people of this nation. It was so epidemic, that he asked Romero Trap during his search for his task, if he could include half a dozen people specifically for the purpose of keeping himself and his family safe. Romero said he could, but wanted to know how these people were to be compensated. Hardesty said they would be paid like any other member of the Secret Service, although they may need to keep it open for those members who were Secret Service, prior to these people being called to duty. Romero said as long as they were started as senior agents, he would include it in his search. Thomas Hardesty agreed that if they were going to put themselves in harm's way, knowing fully well it could come from their very own ranks, it would be done.

Thomas Hardesty felt with Romero Trap as his Vice President, he had no worries from any other agencies or any branch of the military. He did not know where else the disgruntled members of each party had influence, but could assume the outgoing president would have some influence over the Secret Service, as a means to keep that at bay, his salary restructure would exempt those who already received a government pension, although based upon a current salary, it may still prove an obstacle. Hardesty planned to eliminate all means for politicians to take advantage of paid expenses, without political ramifications. A small golf outing for a visiting dignity would be allowed, but the 100 party members travelling to a major golf course in an effort to raise funds for the next election, would be an expense for the political party, not the federal government. It meant the party it pertained to, had best have the money available to use for such frivolity. It was simply immoral to think the taxpayers should be responsible for their irresponsibility, when it came to financial intelligence. These people were supposed to be capable of balancing a very large budget for the government to use to cover expenses to operate. Truth be told, most of them could not even balance a checkbook, if they had to work within the guidelines of the average family. Knowing some of them, it would take all of a week to declare bankruptcy. Thomas Hardesty was tired of politicians lining their pocket with the hard earned money of the people in this country, who made those people who they were, while holding office. Why did they return that, into taking from those who had to pay a large portion of their earnings, to have the privilege to misrepresent them?

Hardesty firmly believed if the founding fathers of this country were here for one day, every member of the Senate and Congress would be hanging from ropes on the white house lawn, for acts of treason against the people. He had plenty of items to put to the people in his first year in the highest position offered by the people of this country. Make no mistake about it, the original concepts devised by the men who wrote the Declaration of Independence and the Bill of Rights, among a few other documents to form the government, were for the good of the people, not the politician. The founding fathers did not expect payment for the services to their country, it was their means of a service to the very people of the nation, who gave them the honor to make the lives better as a free nation. At the time there were still larger powers in the world that wanted them to fail, and be on hand to reap the rewards of the fallout. It did not happen, but several powers were nearby to make every effort to induce the failures they desired.

During the three hours, the two went through these plans, Romero Trap had three calls interrupt them. Romero was quick and concise and simple wrote down the name of each in his small notebook to track those who called. He made sure the number that showed on his burner phone, was a means to contact each, if they fit his requirements for this particular assignment. It was known by all who had the access to the ad as a means to assemble a team, which not everyone would possess the skill sets needed for every assignment, and this was an acceptable risk to all who called, and were willing to take. Trap did not need to again vocalize this parameter to any at the time an ad was placed on the internet. For a select few, had its own little set of guidelines laid out to all, before it ever went into effect.

It was nearing 2 AM, and at some point, as the last night turned into the next day, it was determined they should seek some rest for another busy day to follow. Each with their own agenda to adhere to. Romero would need to be available to take calls from his burner phone, while Hardesty would be making his first entrance into the oval office, as a part of the changing of the guard, in the highest office in the land. Part of Hardesty's initiation to the office of President, was certain documents and secrets were only passed from the outgoing president to the incoming one. It was not something that would take a mere hour, as the list was lengthy as a result from each time the office changed hands, going all the way back to the first President, George Washington. They each headed to what each had for residence in the nation's capital. Romero had a small apartment. It was acceptable to him for the simple fact he was so frequently away for extended periods of time, he felt like it was new to him every time he came into it.

He had the monthly rent automatically paid on the due date each month from his banking account. He did not anticipate getting a whole lot of sleep over the next three days, as it was now about the amount of time for the ad to have been seen by enough members for the different people to be contacting him through the disposable phone. He was home just long enough to get the coffee pot started, like many people in his type of profession, and going back to his military career, coffee was a staple in everyone's diet. For some, it was several days of the only thing consumed. He was one such person on numerous occasions. The first of many phone calls started to arrive, he knew the initial process was simply to see who was available, in some cases the availability list determined the requirements, but that was not true in this case. He needed specific talents to be able to pull this off on two fronts, working in conjunction, and upon occasion simultaneously. Once he had a group more than sufficient to cover his need for 36 people, plus six for the President, he could then find out how many could be available for long term assignment of four to eight years. That amount of time would likely be a contributing factor to some people withdrawing their names from the pool, he knew some people were not ever in the game for lengthy assignments.

Romero Trap did not want to send any child or spouse, the person of their affections, home in a black bag with a large zipper. It was only too common of an occurrence in his over thirty years in convert operations. He was a solitary man, deemed by most of his attempts at relationships to have the emotional range of a teaspoon. He himself had to admit, as a result of the things he did, and was willing to do for the good of his country, it made him void of true emotional passions, which only interfered with what was needed to be done. Exterminating people, who posed a threat to the safety of citizens or even members of his government, required a certain distain toward emotional expression. It was this very reason he was regarded as having all the passions of the grim reaper, and he spent more than thirty years as an assistant commander for the Grim Reaper. He could recall at least two hundred and fifty confirmed kills, and that did not account for a single one of collateral damage, although all of those were just as planned as the target. When a target was a part of a collective, much like a hydra, all the heads had to be removed, to insure it was dead. In many cases, a single confirmed kill accounted for the deaths of up to 18 other members of the targets hierarchy, only once did that include an entire family. Even some of his most elite killers, had second thoughts of killing a five year old boy, even knowing he would grow up to be a more inhumane leader, than his father even could be. Trap was not such a person, and very few people realized just how cold he truly had become. He could use humor as the means to cover up his true feelings, or in reality the lack of feelings.

 After six hours and two pots of coffee, Romero Trap had a list of forty eight names, he did not review it for skill sets needed as of yet. He was debating over attempting to get some rest or making his third pot of coffee. He knew there would be a lull in the phone calls, until it went a full 24 hours, since posting his internet ad. Four hundred people around the world knew what that ad meant, and who COPA was, but considering the amount of people in the world, 400 was miniscule in the sheer numbers of people inhabiting the world, where the internet reached.

 Romero Trap had no calls for fifteen minutes, and decided to take the 2 hour power snooze his training had long used. It was called the power snooze, because he could get as much from two hours, as the majority could from eight hours.

LET THE GAMES BEGIN

Thomas Hardesty would spend the next five weeks in the company of the outgoing president. They would not be short eight hour days, nor would it be merely being filled in on the information he needed to know with the changing of the guard. He was going to be a participant, to the daily rigors of running a huge government. Problems cropped up out the blue for no apparent reason, and they would be presented to his office by any of a number of fashions. An urgent phone call, an impatient commander, or head of department, some even came through his secretary of state. It seemed like an endless parade of people wanting answers yesterday. It was a wonder anything at all got done. The outgoing president, would start the initial meeting by telling Thomas Hardesty that if he had any of his natural hair color when he entered the Oval Office, it would all be gray before his first term ended. The outgoing president also said, no amount of hair color products would help. He further compounded with many have left with far less hair than when they entered office, and worst case scenario was nothing would ever grow there again.

Hardesty was going to hit them all below the belt, by making it so politics did not have a hand in slowing the needed changes to a crawl, by taking it out of their hands and putting it squarely into the hands of the people, once again. The outgoing president told him he did admire Hardesty's moxie for his entire campaign, and was grateful he did not have to campaign against him. He told him, unless he had a good game plan in place, the political machine would stall or stop any attempts to change the way they had long operated. Hardesty did not divulge his plan, but said he thought he had a sound plan to get things done, and quickly. The outgoing president sarcastically stated he wished him well in his naive belief, if the political machine had a will to halt something, they always had in the past. Hardesty only said his plan should bypass the wheels of the machine.

Romero Trap had completed his power snooze, and rose to make yet another pot of coffee. He checked to see if his burner phone had any missed calls, which was a waste of time, knowing it was in the understanding if he did not answer, it was up to them to try once again, and he did not return calls in this point of any assignment. His

A SELECT FEW

disposable phone only displayed numbers from the missed call, no names, so when he checked, he had five missed calls, but two were from the same number. In a two hour interval, it seemed like the next call would be someone's third try. Romero did not own one of those drip coffee maker that annoyed him to no end, he had a commercial grade, which even had two burners and an autofill storage tank, which made coffee quickly, so his wait time was minimal. As he poured his coffee into his mug, the phone went active. He answered after seeing it was indeed the same person who called twice during his power snooze.

It was one of his most elite members of numerous mission together, and Romero asked point blank if the other person was available for long term, for four to eight years. It peaked the interest of the other person, who said they were available but why 4 or 8 instead 4 or 5 or a number in between. Romero said he could not go into an abundance of detail over a phone line, but the time depended entirely on the President being reelected for a second term. That was sufficient for the other person who said Romero had one member on his team. Romero said he would call back to this same number when he had his team selected, but in this case, he required specific skills for specific tasks, and could not deviate from the plan for the safety of all those to be involved. Once again, the vague terms used over a phone, did not give away anything pertinent to the actual jobs each had to anyone who may have a means to listen in on the conversation. Skill sets applied to almost every job in the world, and they were a lot of jobs that required safety measures.

The calls were now coming in from people who were currently in other parts of the world, finishing up with their last assignment, and looking to fill any void. He received two dozen, but went through the same process of the first call since his power snooze with two other members. So, with a list of 72 names, 3 were already selected for the team he wanted to assemble.

Over the next three days, Romero Trap received sporadic calls to bring his list to 96, of which he would narrow down to 33 other people for his teams, and six people for the President. Of the names, he was sure at least twenty would turn down a long term assignment, even if it meant a continual payment. These were people who simply did not want to be tied down to any single location for extended periods of time. It was a superstition among people of his trade who remained in one place too long, would fall prey to the very means they employed. Romero knew it to be nothing but superstition, but he was not ever going to convince people this possibility did not exist.

2

The Selection Process

Romero had his list to choose from, but before he could do that, he needed to arrange a meeting place one month from today for 37 people to attend. He found a restaurant with a full service bar that had a party room, with a capacity of forty people. It would be perfect, so he booked the room with the date he had in mind, which had to take place before the swearing in ceremony of the President and Vice President of the United States. His time was cutting it close, as it only left him three days to spare for the ceremony. It certainly did put a whole lot of new wrinkles into how he had normally operated in the past twenty years of assembling teams, for covert operation and nothing on the scale this would entail. He also got to be a far more active member of the assignments than what his current duties would permit.

With that completed, he started the process of getting all his team put together. He started with making the return calls to the people he first suspected would decline his long term commitment. It consisted of a total of twenty four names and twenty three of them had him remove their names for this assignment. The one who did not turn him down, was a female he always had enjoyed having in his team. Zoe Dubois was without a doubt the most lethal woman he ever had the opportunity to meet, and live to talk about it. Code name Black Widow.

She was unique, and possessed an exotic beauty that allowed her to operate in many countries around the world. At a very young age, she was the victim of sexual abuse from a member of the family, although not immediate family. Like many young girls that had fallen victim to such things, she was ashamed to talk about it when she was young, and something could be done for her and her abuser.

At the age of 15, she got her revenge, as her uncle tried once again to take advantage of her, determined from the start, not to let it continue, she took with her a syringe she had found. She pretended to be compliant in the process she knew was not something of her choice. With her clothing removed and being asked to sit on her uncle's lap, in a fashion not considered typical, she plunge the syringe into his neck with it full of nothing but air, and watched him go through the entire process of dying with nothing in her eyes to hide her disdain for the man, who was her father's brother. When it was over, and she was certain he was dead, she dressed and returned home like nothing had happened. Her parents, worried they had not seen her uncle for a whole day, went to go check on him to find him dead. They called the emergency squad, not knowing what else to do, and discovered he had been dead for nearly twenty four hours, likely from an apparent heart attack.

Zoe had made certain not to touch her uncle in any way to leave finger prints or to cause any bruising to the area the syringe penetrated, as a result, no foul play was ever determined, and Zoe was never even suspected in his death. The damage of seven years of sexual abuse were irreversible for Zoe. She lacked any moral fiber in her entire being. She spent the next three years, researching various means to kill without leaving a trace, all the while taking assignments she could complete with her original method. Poison and drugs of certain types were going to be the tools of her trade, as well as a supply of empty syringes. She learned a few other methods, but they were messy, left a trace and were only last resorts, if it came to that. At 18, without a college education she started doing freelance assassinations for the CIA, and a number of other organizations with a need for her particular talents. Zoe was strictly a one person team, but with her beauty and the lovely form she possessed, was deadly. Romero was not sure how to put her into play, but he knew the people he was going after were already relatively corrupt, and having a beautiful woman take notice of them, would surely be difficult to turn away from even those who were married. They were the type of people who did not concern themselves with such moral conditions, as fidelity.

Zoe had decided at fifteen that her body was simply another tool for the trade she had chosen. Her technique, was to teasingly undress for her prey and before anyone could ever penetrate her that she herself did not desire, they would be dead, and only have seen, but never touched Zoe.

Zoe being a freelance assassin over the last ten years, had amassed quite a nest egg for herself. Romero had on three opportunities with the use of video surveillance got to witness an artist at work. The teasing undressing, she performed prior to the kill, was enough to arouse a dead man. She did not care for explanations about why a person needed to be exterminated, she simply took great pleasure in providing the service she offered at the price she determined. You did not want to pay the price, you looked elsewhere for the job to be done. If you wanted a true professional, you paid the price.

Two other members were from Hong Kong. First was Zi Yang, his expertise in various blades was remarkable. He used short swords, large daggers, small daggers and stilettos with extreme prejudice. He knew points of entry on the human body that caused immediate death. He was quick and nimble, and very accurate in his first strike. He was excellent in close quarters situations, even though long range rifles, were also in play, depending on the number of people involved in a meet. He would come in handy for both sides of the operation, as there were two distinct categories in this particular assignment. His codes name for as long as he and Trap worked together was, Kung Fu.

The second was Shaq Lee, who was extremely good with items from a short distance, throwing blades, required a blade with a precise balance to insure the handle did not make first contact, also darts, which came in numerous shapes and sizes and did not look anything like the ones used for a dartboard. Shaq Lee was code named, Stealth. Darts were the term that applied to weapons of different martial arts, although any of the people he would have on his team were not considered experts or masters by the true masters of the martial arts. Romero's experts, used the martial arts purely for offensive purposes. If they had a move to use as defensive, it was not intended by them to be used in that means, but it did occasional work that way.

Romero Trap decided from his list of 73 remaining names, he should get the six best candidates to act as secret service protection for the new President, Thomas Hardesty. Since Trap did not know the precise moment after election, he acquired the position when he had secret service looking after his every move. He knew that the outgoing president, kept the agents assigned to him, for a very long time and if an agent retired before the family was considered out of harm's way, a new agent would be assigned to him. He knew for certain, as far as the former president and first lady remained among the living, they would have secret service watching over them. He did not know how long it applied to the children of the president and first lady.

The people on his list he would need for the president, would not be a good fit for the rest of the detail, and although their skills may be excellent, it was a matter of the type of work they would be engaged in that would make them turn down the assignment. These people had too high level of integrity to be involved with the dirty work that would be necessary for the other portions of the assignment. It was this very integrity and sense of duty, which would make them excellent for safeguarding the President. Trap hoped he could remember for as long as he had known Thomas Hardesty, to use proper address for talking to the president, especially with more than he and himself present.

He made his calls to the best qualified for the presidential security force, and his first choice would insist on being agent in charge of security. Each was told they would be paid as senior agents of the secret service, all were informed it would take 4 to 8 years before the president would be out of office, and it would be up to them, as to stay on as the president's security, or leave to do other things in their life. All of them accepted the assignment, and Romero Trap insured them that the president was a man of honor and respect from Trap himself. It was the icing on the cake, for the 6 members selected, knowing Trap to be a man of conviction.

THE SELECTION PROCESS

His next part of the process would be the long range rifle experts who may be needed for both portions of the assignment they were about to begin.

One name stood out on his list and he made that call first, might get the best documented long range assassin in the assignment, before going down the list further. Susan Hobart was code named Hummer. It was an easy name to give her, since she had a habit of humming various rock and roll tunes, while in her wait for her target to make themselves available. She once stay perched in a tree for 22 hours humming for the opportunity to take her shot, at 3,500 yards away from her target. It was a perfect head shot kill, and the distance made it so the sound of the rifle firing, did not make it to the target before the bullet had finished the job. Like many snipers, she received her training in the military, before a short career in the CIA, which is where Romero Trap first recognized her as more than a mere government tool. She was too darned good to be relegated to the demeaning works of the CIA. She was hardly the most beautiful woman in the military or CIA, and was fully a tom boy. She could play as rough as any professional football athlete, and in many cases send them home crying to their mothers. Her father was not an abusive man, but provided no slack between his two daughters and two sons. If any one of them took down a six hundred pound deer for food, they had best bring it home, no matter where they got it from.

Susan was not a tall woman or Amazonian, weighing not more than 115 pounds soaking wet. During her initial military training, she like all the others, toted 70 pounds of gear for many of the training exercises. She embarrassed many of a man weighing twice as much and having far more muscular development than she appeared to possess. It was that sheer desire and determination that marked her for sniper training. That and the fact that at two hundred yards with the standard issue military rifle, she shot the center out of it with every cartridge. Her longest recorded successful shot in the military was at 4,000 yards, again with a clean single shot to the head.

For a sniper to make a clean single shot kill from that distance, was no different to the sniper than painting was to Rembrandt. It was a sniper's version of pure art. Not having to be close enough to the target, to see the devastation that resulted from the shot at the target's end. It would certainly change a sniper's viewpoint of artwork.

With Susan Hobart accepting the assignment, Romero Trap was elated, thinking in some assignments he had in the past, with both ladies on board, he had no need of additional personnel. This unfortunately was not the case for this assignment, and he also had to consider he might lose a few key people as the assignment unfolded. Trap did not like having people lost under his watch, ever.

He had two other long range rifle experts on his list, although neither was as good as Susan, but quite good at shorter distances not to exceed 2,500 yards. Trap Johnson, code name Deadly, never missed within his range. 400 documented kills, all in the military, before becoming a member of Romero's group of experts. He also accepted the assignment and looked forward to meeting the feline phenomenon known as Hummer.

His other option was Shorty Johansen, code name Eyes. It was his penetrating gaze that provided his nickname, and he was only short as a child, when he finished growing up, he stood six feet two inches tall, and that was not short in Romero's perspective of things. His name was given at birth, and it never bothered him one bit, anyone who truly thought he was short, was considerably taller and he made sure they got to view things more from his viewpoint when all was said and done. There were not an abundance of words exchanged between Shorty and the other person, it was the things done that made a better point. His acceptance was also provided, but he had no desire to meet Hummer to feel the slightest bit inadequate at his line of work. He simply said somebody had to be the best, even if it was under biased military terminology. He on the other hand had taken out a moving target from two thousand yards, and did not see too many so called experts doing that.

Romero could not argue his point, as most snipers had stationary targets, and required such to make all the adjustments necessary for distance, wind and direction of that wind. There was also the overlooked factor of humidity, which made the air heavier and it had an impact on the velocity of the bullet. All these items and more had to be accounted for in a split second, to take a shot. Technology in the form of a hand

THE SELECTION PROCESS

held device about the size of a cellular phone, was able to instantly gauge all the factors for the shooter. The slightest error would make the target a miss, instead of a clean kill. Snipers, seldom if ever, aimed for any other part of the anatomy other than the head. From those distances, body armor was not distinguishable, and there was no such armor for the head.

Romero's list of close quarter's combat specialists was the longest among his group that responded to his internet posting. By the same token, the assignment required a fairly large number, specifically with the skill set. He need one dozen such specialists, just for the dealings with the cartels, which would produce the funds needed to proceed. It was not one of his favorite means of funding, but it took a large amount of money, and the cartels had far more than any conventional means. He still needed a little more than half a dozen more for the other portion of the assignment, since there were often additional members of any organization or government that had layers of hierarchy, that could easily fill the void with a leader removed.

Romero Trap started with the dozen designated for the cartel group. He got a dozen people from his list to turn down the assignment for the length of time that it would take. All for various reasons, but Romero never begged his people to take an assignment, regardless of his needs for their participation, it was part of the reasons these people respected him, and they were never made to feel it was their duty or anything else, to do so for him. He wanted the best people, but also wanted willing participants, and he anticipated a number of turn downs due to the sheer length of the assignment he was dealing with. His normal assignments previously, never lasted more than six months. It was not common for him to have an assignment going for four year intervals, although it would be a maximum of eight years. He could not guarantee Thomas Hardesty would be elected to a second term, which was entirely within his realm, and how much he accomplishes in his first term.

His list of turn downs did not happen in consecutive calls, but were spaced out between those who accepted the assignment. All of his close quarter's specialists were good with different methods. They could all use small firearms and at least one other means to terminate a target quickly. The dozen specialist he got specifically for the cartel assignment were Jake Connelly code name Blade, L J Daggett code name Stiletto, Chu Fong code name Dart, Al Capston code name Garrote, Tankawa code name Sting, Lee Corbinsk code name Dagger, Brick Morton code name Sharpy, Cory Tolski code name Slice, Johnny Trumps code name Knife, Gordon West code name Edge, Lacy Louis code named Pricker, and Travis Rumfield code name Point. All of these specialists had a minimum of two skills to a person, all were good with handguns or small arms depending on the terminology to best suit the person of interest. The additional skills were varied, but the code names were selected according to their second favorite means of ending a target's existence.

His other group would have an additional eight close combat specialist's, two of which were already on the acceptance list. His next acceptance to the long term assignment came from Howie Short code name Judas. He was not given the code name as an untrustworthy team member. He was given the code name due to his uncanny ability to approach his intended target from the rear undetected, and with various short blades, render his target into the next world without so much as a struggle. Howie was not the only member of the team with stealth abilities, but few could approach from behind totally undetected, the target was down in a hurry, and even with that, Howie could reach another target or two, without so much as a single person knowing he was there.

The next to accept the assignment was Roberto Gomez code name Lucky. His name was a result of his ability to use a blade for a single strike kill every time. This was rather unusual when considering that Roberto never studied human anatomy for such precision in his use of the blade. He did not strike the identical area each and every time his talents were requested. Regardless of the point of attack, he never failed to make a single fatal strike. As a result of his uncanny ability, he was given his codename since he himself always said it must have been by pure luck.

Tron Bosworth was quite good with blades as well, but was also the risk taker of the entire group. He seldom cared if the target saw him coming or not. His first strike was often a throwing blade to slow down his target, so he could go in closer to finish his assignment. He usually carried a dozen throwing blades, which he was deadly accurate with. He still preferred to finish up close with a long razor sharp blade, where he would typical cut throats to finish up his intended target. His code name was Gambler.

Chance Tomlin code name Vicious, was unlike his stealthier members of the blade group of close quarter's combat specialist. He liked prolonging the agony of his intended target. It was often a little messy when he was finished, as he never made a single kill strike and seemed to find great pleasure in delaying the inevitable result for as long as possible. He wanted his victims to suffer for as long as they could withstand the multiple cuts created by his blade, and he never did a kill with a single stab.

His leader of the team was the next to accept the assignment. Jackson Frye was a unique member of any team. He was cold and calculating in the precision of dealing out fatal strikes. He started out in the military like many of his team members, since there was always a need for people willing to kill to survive themselves. He once was placed under monitoring conditions to find out what made him so unique. In a largely outnumbered encounter while monitored by the military medical people, they found he had no variation whatsoever in his heartrate under any circumstances. He remained in total calm, even when he was repelling three attackers simultaneously. He was given the code name Heartless, due to his total calm under any given situation. He admitted he enjoyed killing, but he never showed any emotions in his face or heartrate, or even in his speech. He was quite unique in that respect, whereas most people relied on the adrenaline rush common in survival of combat. Like many of his team members, there were additional skills among them, but Jackson Frye was an exceptional thief. He did not focus on that side of his character, but when a vehicle was required for the team, he would obtain it. His talent would be needed for the first assignment that Romero Trap knew had to be performed, to put them into a position to go further into the long term assignment.

A SELECT FEW

Romero's next acceptance was from the last of the blade experts used in close quarter's combat. Robert Holmes code name Lightsout, was originally a boxer in his initial military training. This is where he got his code name, but he became far more proficient with small blades as he progressed through his military training. He still found his boxing skills useful in his close quarter's combat situations, and frequently knocked out his target prior to using his blade. His code was based upon his ability to render his boxing opponent unconscious in rather quick fashion, and could easily have become a profession boxer, but his fondness of using a blade, was far more appealing to the military than the boxing profession.

That gave him a total of eight close quarter's combat specialist most proficient with blades of some type. They each had their own preference, and Romero Trap never denied his team members of their preference for any type of weapon. It was essential for each team member to be comfortable with their weapons of choice.

He had one other person on his list that could use blades, but still preferred small firearms, using a blade for backup purposes primarily. He did not have an acceptance from this person yet, which wasn't to be expected until the call was made.

Since he still needed his small firearms experts, his next call went to Ty Roberts, who was also the person capable of blades as a backup to his firearm. He was informed as all the others of the pending length of time for this particular assignment, which would certainly entail multiple targets, not a mere handful like assignments in the past. Ty had no difficulty in the length of time involved, since he was one of Romero's most used assets over the last 20 years of black operations, largely in the service of the government and various agencies that had required his particular set of skills, and those of the team he assembled. Ty Roberts was exceptional in rapid fire kill scenarios, where he seldom had to take more than a single shot to any one target. When the ammunition ran out, he carried his backup plan at all times, and usually did not need to use it, but upon those occasions, he was quite capable of finishing what he started. Romero Trap was assembling one of his most proficient teams in his entire career, and was happy to see the quality of his team which allowed for less casualties on his side of the assignment. Certainly, he had to be prepared for such losses, but he did not enjoy the possibility of it occurring while he had his team together. They were all very good at watching the backs of the other team members, and as result losses were seldom. This time was quite different in the length of time the team would be assembled, and his biggest fear would be what kind of trouble they got into on their own. Ty Roberts' code name was Trauma and it fully fit his disposition. Since Roberto Gomez was also proficient with small firearms, although the exact opposite of Ty, as he preferred blade first and handguns as his backup.

His last small arms expert was Sven Turloch, who was also good with a rifle. His code name was Bullseye, which was appropriate as he always hit what he aimed at. He did not need a lengthy sighting in of a weapon, he knew from years of practice exactly how to be in position quickly to be deadly accurate. He was equally proficient with both types of weapons, but never ventured into long range rifles. His rifle was usually kept to 100 yards or less and used handguns in much closer situations.

To be on the safe side and hoping he had little use for his next two experts, he made the calls to see which would accept the assignment. He got two positive and two negative responses in his calls. First to accept was Tom Walker code name Bang. His fourth call produced the second acceptance from Sal Lavetti code name Boomer. If the code names did not give away their area of expertise, the need for explosive experts was always a last resort to any given situation, but a necessary precaution considering the ground they would need to cover over the term of the assignments. If he could take out an entire terrorist group with these two men, then it was worth having them available on the team.

To be prepared for any circumstances that might arise in the little enterprise of the President, he also needed some people good with rifles. These were not long distance shooters, but support to close combat personnel. They would not be far from the vicinity, but not visible either. They were there to insure no single individual was badly outnumbered in close combat. A single rifle shot, could even the odds considerably for any of his close quarter's experts.

A SELECT FEW

First rifle expert to accept the assignment was Harvey Hatfield, code name Bloodlust. He may use a rifle, but he was in close enough to see what damages occurred to his target using 30 caliber projectiles in his rifle. These were the rifles that had magazines cartridges, loads for up to twenty five bullets. Long range rifles were always bolt action and a single bullet loaded for a shot. One of the reasons snipers had to be very accurate, because it took a fair amount of time to reload and by that time, the target would be well protected. Although the rifle used in the short distances were magazine fed, they were not automatic weapons of any sort. Each bullet would require a little time to chamber and allow the shooter to take aim of his next target. Also accepting his assignment was Finn O'Brien, code name Mayhem.

Finn was one to cause mayhem among the targets when they were fairly large in numbers. His first shot was deadly, and he often tried a more rapid fire approach than the weapon allowed. He also created a little concern to the close quarter's combat experts, who often felt the bullet wiz past them to the target. Finn did not require a lot of room for his shots, but it did cause alarm for those team members within his line of sight. He often was asked why he was so close to taking out one of his own, and simply replied he missed them by a mile. In fact, it was often more like millimeters that he missed them.

His final rifle only expert was Joba Ligata, who was trained originally in an African army unit. He learned well how to conceal himself in relatively close proximity to the targets, and found it easy shooting once he pulled the trigger. The targets could hear him, but seldom did any of them actually see him, no matter how close he was to their position.

When dealing with a large number of the opposition, it was always wise to have people proficient in automatic weapons. These people could easily take out a small brigade, when necessary, except for two who accepted his assignment. These two particular experts' preferred heavy automatic weapons over the light weight AK's and Uzi more commonly used. They also were rather large, heavily muscled representative of humanity. They, during their military time served in the same unit, and upon coming upon a wood lined ambush and cutting down four

THE SELECTION PROCESS

team members before getting into a position to return fire, leveled a rather large forest area in less than two minutes, with the weapons they preferred that could fire 1000 rounds per minute. It took gargantuan men to even carry the weapon, much less use it for the purposes they had in mind. They were also quite proficient with the normal automatic weapons, which was by and large what Romero wanted them for. He would get them their preferred weapons also in the event it might be needed to take out a battalion of terrorist troops. It might be good to cover both sides of the coin with this pair of experts. First was Feliz Ramirez code name Turmoil. He and his partner were precisely that when using the heavy guns normally mounted on some type of vehicle. Murray Golic was his second accepter of the assignment and his code name was Cyclone.

His other people to accept the long term assignment were all small automatic weapons expert more in line with what Romero anticipated being required for the duration of the assignment. First to accept was Mitchell Lamb code name Havoc, and he also was good with the short range rifle so his talents could be used multiple ways. The other two were simply automatic weapons experts. Olle Horvitz code name Chaos, and Lonnie Lombardy code name Calamity, and they each brought both to the fight when needed.

With his team selected, and after the members who turned down the assignment there were only 5 names uncalled, and Romero being the leader he was known to be, called each to inform them the team had been selected, but should anything come up to alter that, he would get back with them in the event they were needed. It was also provided they did not find other assignments, but two, after hearing the terms of length of time, told him not to bother, it was too long for them to be in a single assignment.

He had given all of the people who accepted one week to be in the base city of things to come. They would first need to arrange hotel or motel stays, until they found a suitable location to set up as a base camp. Romero was looking into abandoned buildings once used as manufacturing or storage facilities, which would be rather large. His team had the necessary skills beyond the method of killing, to turn an abandoned building into a useable base, and it required sufficient space to house at least one large truck, and mostly likely a number of other vehicles to get around the area. To keep as much attention from the team members as possible, the vehicles would need to be procured by means other than rental. For some reason, it was more difficult to track a stolen vehicle, than a rental one, and unless that ever changes, Romero would stick with what had worked best in the past.

His team had the capability to scrounge up enough materials to turn an abandoned warehouse into a resort, but it would depend largely on the materials found in the nearby vicinity. He would prefer something with multiple buildings, to keep it less obvious of it being occupied by persons not belonging there. Possibly using one building to act as a barracks of sorts, while another to keep the vehicles out of site until needed.

He had already started his search, but the team would need to be present for the final selection to be made, since they were going to spend the largest amount of time in it. With two females in his group, he knew they at least needed separate quarters for sleeping and showering. Although he knew for a fact, neither were overly shy about being exposed for entirely different reasons. Zoe thought her sexuality was another tool to use to entice her victims into their death, while Susan not given the beauty gene, gave no concern about how she appeared to anyone, since her job required nothing of the sort. Her function as a long range shooter, she found makeup and hairdo's did little for her while in a tree for endless hours, and dealing with weather conditions, seldom helped make-up or hair styles. She simply did not care about her appearance in the ways most women did.

Romero had found three suitable locations for his team, but did not venture into the surroundings for the acquisition of material, to transform the location into a more suitable environment for long term housing. The vehicle storage was not a real issue at any of them, unless they would require repair work, which he hoped was not the case. Of course, that was also entirely up to his people, who would be using the transportation that was obtained. They were not looking for vehicles that were certain to attract attention due to their rarity. They required

THE SELECTION PROCESS

inconspicuous transportation, which may have a little more pony power than the normal.

His wait for the team to assemble in the surrounding area would be the deciding factor in what was needed. Additionally, in order to fund the startup of all that may occur, they would need a team ready quickly, to make a raid on another government location that had what they needed to catapult them into the assignment. He wanted absolutely no casualties on either side, since the DEA was considered to be a part of the same team, although in this case rather distant cousins. In order to obtain the immediate funding for the assignment to move forward, the nearly two tons of confiscated drugs were essential to the program. His first consideration after obtaining them, was which of the cartels was most prepared to purchase the quantity. It was also preferred for the first attempt to get the funds, it was a cartel on the elimination list, and once the funds were confirmed to be present at the meet, the money and the drugs would stay with them as the cartel would no longer be a hindrance to the progress of the President. They could then repeat the sale with a lesser cartel, to actual keep the drugs, while they exchanged the funds to acquire them.

In his short waiting period, he made President Thomas Hardesty aware of his team having been selected, and the six security personnel were already in place as requested by the President himself. Two assigned to him, one to his wife and two to his eldest son with a single one to his daughter. The remainder of the secret service detail came from within the ranks of the secret service, but in each case the agent in charge of all four were Romero Trap's own people. Thomas Hardesty had learned long ago to follow Trap's designation in personnel. He knew it was for his own best safety, to go down the path he intended to take. With Romero Trap's people over-seeing the regular secret service personnel, they would insure his safety from within, as well as the outside threats.

President Thomas Hardesty was truly more concerned with the internal threats, with what he was going to do soon into his election as the President. He had already set up the toll free numbers for people to provide a vote, whether registered or not, for what he was going to start doing in turning the government back to a government for the people.

His course of action was already set, he had made it perfectly clear to the people as a part of his campaign. It was now a simple matter of following through, and if nothing else he was a man of his word, something the American people had literally forgotten when it came to politics. They had been deceived far too long, and it was time to show them that he meant what he told them, to be elected to the highest office in the land.

3

The Game Plan part 1

With the team all present, the first part of the equation was to select which of the three sites were most useful for the purposes of the team to use as a home, for an extended period of time not to exceed eight years. He took his team leader, who was most familiar with all the team members at some point in his career as a target killer. Heartless was able to look through each and every site for the best of the three to select. He was far more familiar with the scrounging efforts required, to make the buildings more of a home, and after looking, he selected a single location that had two dozen buildings in the complex. It had the most material for the retrofit, and it might not be a resort, but it would be like a home for the time frame that was expected.

The first part of the plan was not necessarily from the President, but considering all that was required of the team over the next four to eight years, it was essential to establishing several things. First, a place to be considered safe haven for all the team members. A means of income, to pay for their participation was second. None of his people were ever expected to do things out of the kindness of their hearts, it was a job, which specifically required excellent compensation. The mere fact that his people were specialist in a line of work not common to the

A SELECT FEW

general public, they deserved compensation equal to the risks. Loss of life being one of them, and he truly doubted many accountants had to be concerned with such issues. It was possible for politicians, but over the last 40 years, he could in all honesty say, it was a fitting end for most of them. Especially when taken into consideration, all they had stolen from the people in far more ways than mere money. They had turned into a greedy bunch, and would continue to take until there was nothing left. By Thomas Hardesty's own account, that was going to change, and it would be done with the help of the people. Romero was hoping to see something happen in that regard relatively quickly, if he was to go about his own extra tasks as Vice President.

He would need to start making daily appearances in the very near future, but he needed to have a little more in place for that. He would make a trip to the White House the following morning, while he had his best thief in vehicle recon, of the area for both a large vehicle for moving two to three tons of drugs, and a couple vehicles capable of transporting one dozen members of the team, to the nearby DEA facility that had possession of those drugs awaiting destruction. The good thing about lettered agencies, they were never in a big hurry to finish an objective considered completed. The objective being having seized the drugs, once in the possession of the agency there was no longer an objective, therefore destruction was performed as a matter of convenience.

With that completed, he used his disposable phone for the last call to the team members to assemble at the location Jackson Frye (Heartless) deemed the most suitable and had the most materials available, to retrofit the abandoned building to more suitable means of housing for thirty six people, two of which were female. He really had no concerns over sexual harassment taking place, even with thirty four males to two females. The female's reputations were more than sufficient to deter any such considerations. The first rule of all those present on the team was survival. The women were far better at that, than all the men combined, and with Zoe (Black Widow) not a single male in the team was willing to risk finding out just how deadly the spider was. Most of them were content to drool in the distance, because she was very easy to look at. It

THE GAME PLAN PART 1

was a simple philosophy, look but do not touch, since that led to fatal consequences.

It took almost 90 minutes to get the team assembled, Jackson had acquired one cargo van, for the purpose of transporting team members, as well as other gear that may be needed as things progressed. In addition to the van, he took the time to obtain 10 sets of plates, concentrating on out of state ones, to make it a little more difficult to determine they were stolen, and not simply lost. The recently obtained cargo van was almost put to immediate use, one thing Romero did prior to reaching the meeting point, was obtain funds for some items he found made life a little easier, for even the most hardcore outdoors people, those who slept on the ground under the stars type outdoors people. It was hardly uncommon among any of his team members, since most of them did not know from one day to the next, where they would be on the planet. Often notice was short, and most kept a travel bag ready at all times. The opportunity to be in the same base area for four years was more novel to them, than a person on the once in a lifetime vacation trip.

He had two of the team members take the van to obtain 38 air mattresses for the start of sleeping arrangements. The questions were asked on what the spares were for, and it was not intended to be spares, but two members of the team, exceeded the weight capacity of a single mattress, and theirs needed to be doubled, to insure they were not buying them daily to flatten each night.

While the two went to get the materials requested, with more than sufficient funds from Romero to cover the charges, the remaining team members were to start hunting up the materials around, to help make improvements to the conditions they would be living in. Heartless, guaranteed there was enough pipe to make two shower stalls over existing drains, and enough plastic and other materials, to make temporary walls for both of the showers, and sleeping quarters for both genders.

Jackson had three other team members with himself to get power and other essentials back operating in such a fashion that the provider would not know it was done. One of his other talents as a good thief. The two members with the van, returned with 38 air mattresses, all queen size, except for the hulks who each got two king size mattresses.

They all had foot pedal type air filling systems, since power may or may not be ready in time. Also, the lack of outlets to feed so many units all at once. The areas for the different purposes were marked off, and materials started to appear for the putting up some form of rooms. The van was moved to the building next door, and it would be up to Jackson Frye to obtain two more vehicles rather quickly. Romero had funds to operate from his assignment fund, that he also needed to use at the start of any project, but it was essential to establish an income base to reimburse those funds, and run the assignments, as well as pay the people involved. It was decided with everyone in agreement that 1000 dollars a week cash, would be an adequate payment for their skill sets. Since they were operating entirely outside of the government, including their knowledge of the group, there would be only cash payments, and no need to let the self-indulgent politicians believe they were entitled to a single cent. Since all of the people on board had been involved with the government at some point, and most all had military time, Romero just called it duty free money. In essence, he was telling them all it was not to be reported as income, so the governments could steal thirty three percent of it to further grow the size of government, and continue to neglect the reason they increased it in the first place.

During the first day of using the abandoned building, it had water and power working again, surprisingly no water lines leaked, or had burst from lack of use and weather changes. The sleeping areas were walled in, although they could still use some refinements, it would hold for a day or two. With power functioning again, Romero found it had a rather large freezer and a refrigerator, in what may once have been a break room. It made him wonder what the building was used for, but they both still functioned, so he had two people decide what food supplies were best to get for the group, to use while in the building. He also informed them he did not know what time he may be in the next day, as it was time to make an appearance at the White House.

He left them for the evening, knowing they would need to find some means to feed themselves for at least the night. He returned to his little apartment, for a night of rest prior to departing in the morning for the oval office, he thought would be his destination. Soon he and the

President would have to give a speech to the members of government, as a part of normal procedures in the changing of the head of state, as it was called when a president left office for another to take his place.

He needed some time to be able to talk to President Thomas Hardesty in private. Romero Trap needed to know where to get the first of the cartels out of the picture, and who was highest on the President's list. The list was his to decide, Romero and his team were merely the tools to make it happen. He did not know how to inform the president or how he would like to be kept informed, but was under the distinct impression, Thomas Hardesty wanted plausible deniability, while he was in the highest office in the country. If that truly being the case, aside from the president deciding whom he would want removed as obstacles to his path, he wanted no additional knowledge beyond what he saw in the news. His other staff members would certainly keep him up to date on parties no longer posing a threat to the nation.

Romero Trap, seldom got a good night's sleep, but he was accustomed to a least a few hours without his thoughts interrupting the peace of sleep. He was up at five AM and like all career people in the government hierarchy, coffee was breakfast. He long ago could not have a single cup of coffee, to restore his vigor, it took at least three before he felt he had any form of wits about him. This morning, it was more like six, as he emptied the pot before taking care of the essentials to head to the White House.

Upon his arrival and the security people not, sure who was allowed in, and who was not, it took 45 minutes before the marines in charge of security, confirmed Romero Trap was indeed the next Vice President, and had access to the building. It took direct word from President Hardesty, as few had seen Trap, and the security people paid little attention to the election proceeding that already took place. Having been accustomed to following orders, they figured, they would be informed by those who gave the orders normally.

After another 15 minutes of going through various detector systems and emptying his pockets for each, Romero Trap made it to the area of the oval office. He had never been there before, and did not know common due process, to let the President know he was presently outside his office. He did find two secret service agents outside his door, and fortunately, one was the member he selected for the President, and asked him personally. This man knew who Romero Trap was, and just said to wait a moment while he made the announcement inside the Oval Office. It only took thirty seconds before he was informed, he could enter. There were still two presidents in the office, one who he knew he was leaving, and the other just starting to find out what the political turmoil in Washington DC, was truly all about. As he entered, since two were to be addressed in formal fashion, Romero Trap said, "Good morning, Mister Presidents." It was the best he could come up with on short notice. Thomas Hardesty, introduced him to the outgoing president, but that president really did not care one way or another, he simply wanted his time in purgatory to come to its end. He was tired of fighting the political powers of the two parties, and the house and the senate, and especially the war mongers of the Pentagon.

The conversation between the outgoing and incoming Presidents of the United States was centered on the topic of the Pentagon. Largely, the outgoing President told Thomas Hardesty if they kept true to form, every week, they would inform him of a need to go to war with somebody. Every week, it was some different country, and seldom did they present a really valid synopsis of the reasoning for war. Thomas Hardesty was told it was a continual problem of have lifelong warriors in charge of military operations. It was a product of war, being the means to which they earned the right to be among the Pentagon hierarchy. These people knew no other means to utilize, to improve their careers. Romero Trap only got a moment of President Thomas Hardesty's undivided attention to which Trap, said he did need to speak entirely privately with him, when the opportunity presented itself. Thomas Hardesty said, that may take quite some time, but he would get it in somehow today.

Nearly four hours later for a luncheon break, Thomas Hardesty offered to show Trap around the White House, instead of having lunch. It was the most effective way he could speak privately, as they wandered about some of the more historical portions of the White House. Romero Trap asked, "Which of the cartels is the most troublesome for your vision of government during your initial term?" Thomas Hardesty told him

THE GAME PLAN PART 1

the most troublesome was just across the southern border, where they have corrupted government and law enforcement. The cartel had more say in how the government went about their daily business, than any other person or persons in that area. As a result, they wanted nothing to do with the formation of a world governing body, which is essential to his plans. Romero then asked which was least troublesome. It was also south of the border, but also another continent being Peru. Although heavily involved in drug trafficking, the government cooperated with the drug cartels, because it produced income to the country, but the government policies and processes were unhindered by the cartels. During the tour, Romero Trap asked how the President would like to be informed, in the ongoing efforts of his group. Thomas Hardesty made it clear to Romero Trap, he wanted as little information as possible, to make it appear he had nothing to do with the work of Trap's team. He only would provide to Trap, the persons who presented the most problems in forming a world governing body. How Romero Trap and his team went about dealing with it, would be strictly undocumented, and they already knew there would be no assistance or knowledge of their activities from within the government. It was essential to remain anonymous to all of the government agencies.

As Trap had figured, the President wanted plausible deniability with his team of assassins. He refrained from providing Thomas Hardesty any planned moves, even though they were essential to his moving forward. He would also need to establish a line of communications to various other governments, for aid in removing problems from the potential world government, and he was uncertain how to remain anonymous under the circumstances. Romero Trap only knew he needed funds to provide the services requested of his group. Those funds would need to come from more than the drug cartels, which in all likelihood would all become targets, before everything was said and done. He did have his first assignment to discuss with his team leader, and to devise a plan to move the drugs closer to the southern border for an exchange of money for drugs, but termination of the cartel members who made their appearance. With the size of the shipment, Trap fully anticipated a large number of the upper hierarchy of that cartel would be present.

It was also essential to come up with armaments for the type work he was expected to perform for the service of his country, and in particular his friend and president. He did inquire with Hardesty, what would be the best source of getting the required weapons and ammunition to move forward. Hardesty said only the military would have what he needed, and it would require stealth and theft to obtain them, since it was highly unlikely, he could go and purchase them anywhere, without leaving a trail. Hardesty said he wanted no friendly casualties in what Trap needed for his team. Romero Trap assured Hardesty he did not either, but he could not predict the reaction of the places he needed to obtain them. Most that he knew of, were tightly secured by military personnel, who were trained in the use of deadly weapons. His people could try to render those disabled, without fatal consequences, but should things not work in his favor, all hell could break loose. His team's first rule was survival, and they do it instinctively. If his team was placed in that position, he could provide no such guarantees to zero casualties, including his own team members.

Thomas Hardesty understood his dilemma, and simply said to try his utmost to keep friendly casualties out of the picture, it would not do his team much good being hunted by every agency in the country, if it were to be made public. Romero Trap agreed that would not be a good way to start out his assignment. He also asked the President at what point his daily appearance would become necessary to make it look like he had a Vice President in office. Thomas Hardesty let him know during the first week of the New Year, once he was the sole possessor of the Oval Office. It would be the same time a State of the Union address would take place. Being Vice President did allow him more flexibility in his being present as the President could have him out doing other engagements, which did not need to be made into public appearances. Supposedly speaking at a chamber of commerce meeting in some smaller town, would not be newsworthy enough for a national broadcast. Hardesty was making a list of such engagements, just so his Vice President could go about his more important tasks.

The one hour tour of the White House concluded, with the President returning to the Oval Office and Trap leaving the White

House scene. It took Romero Trap another 25 minutes to negotiate traffic to arrive at the team members' location, where upon first notice there were three more vehicles in the garage building. One additional cargo van, one large truck capable of hauling 8,000 pounds, in addition to its own weight. 4 tons should be more than sufficient capacity to move materials they would need to transport locally. The next problem was acquiring a cargo plane, to get the drugs to Texas, close to the Mexican border. Trap would insist on the cartel getting over the border by their own means, although Trap knew they were not going to return at all, with or without drugs. He had no way to determine exactly what the DEA had in its warehouse for destruction, but it was documented as two tons of cocaine, which had a value of 120 million dollars in its current state, distribution alterations and so on, would mean a profit of an additional 500 million dollars. There was also a sedan, which Romero Trap thought was procured for some of the more mundane tasks, like groceries and hygiene essentials.

The building was looking more like a home this time as well, as the temporary walls were given more reinforcements, with additional material found about the premises. Since there were a number of large buildings, most separated by several feet to indicate separate companies once used them. It was not a highly traveled area any longer, like many cities, it was left alone with no hopes of anything more useful becoming of the area again. It did make it easier for Romero Trap and his team to remain in plain sight, without being noticed. One of the qualifications for their line of work for anything used as a base location, for an undetermined duration.

With the assignment from President Thomas Hardesty, Romero Trap called his team to a meeting to lay out the fundamentals of what needed to be accomplished in relatively short order. First the DEA storage location needed to be raided, and Heartless would need to select his people best capable of recon to the location, to see what was best to accomplish the mission. He wanted absolutely no casualties to what was considered a friendly agency, even though no agency knew of their existence, and never would. It required no additional armaments, but it might require some substances to use to in order to render the other agency powerless. He had a number of people in his team familiar with the use of blow darts and powerful sedatives that would accomplish the mission. Most of those people kept a quantity of the material they needed for such occasions. It was still a matter of how many opponents that they would face to complete the mission. Until that was determined by the team, he could not determine the number of team members needed to complete the mission.

His other task was largely for Jackson Frye, and whomever he preferred to help in obtaining a cargo plane temporarily. Romero also laid out the details for phase two of the operation to obtain the initial funding, and in order to keep out of the limelight, he sought a volunteer among his team, to act as the mouthpiece to arrange the meeting in San Antonio, Texas at an airfield capable of having a cargo plane land and take off. His assumption was the cartel would have anywhere between a dozen to eighteen members of their organization present, for such a large quantity of drugs. They would want to test it before making the purchase, but before turning guns on those cartel members that showed up, the money had to be presented. They were to return with both the drugs and the money for the drugs, to be sold a second time to a more docile client that would get to keep the drugs, in exchange for the money. If everything went according to plan, the organization would go from zero dollars to two hundred and forty million dollars, minus what he needed to reimburse his assignment fund, for those funds he used for their arrival and immediate needs. They were all well aware of how Romero Trap conducted his business, and had no issues, knowing they had worked for him before and likely would again.

The final part of the plan was to locate an armory with the weapons they each preferred and those they used as backup. With sufficient ammunition to last at least one year, before they would need to try it again. Since all the people had military experience at some point in the past, they knew immediately the only place to get their weapons of choice was a military armory. Jackson asked if Zoe was up to a reconnaissance mission that would require no killing whatsoever. She first inquired as to what it would be, and Jackson Frye said with her attributes, she was the mostly likely of the entire team to get to see inside an armory, to find out just how well manned it was. Whether she did by teasing, enticing, or offering herself up for grabs, was entirely her own prerogative, but absolutely no killing would take place. Zoe agreed, but it would be up to him or someone else to decide where and which was her armory for such things, if she was seen checking the place out first, they might become a little suspicious. Jackson could not argue her logic and agreed to her terms.

Romero's team of experts were now fully involved into the initial stages of the plan, which all needed to take place before moving forward into the real assignment. He let them work out their own details, knowing that he never once in his career, dictated how the plan would be accomplished. His people needed to feel comfortable with how to carry out the conditions he provided. It was only different, when he was the operative to carry out a mission, and it was usually under those identical guidelines. He had no part of somebody laying down law as to how things were to be done, and only twice walked away from an accepted assignment. Both for the simply reason, the person wanted thing done precisely his way, and had no experience doing any of what he wanted done. It was a recipe for disaster, and Romero wanted no part of it. He was surprisingly enough never reprimanded for either of those failed missions, which resulted in casualties on their side.

Romero Trap did not know the people who lost their lives due to incompetent mission leaders, but in all likelihood, those people would never have made his team of experts. To date, Romero had not once lost a single team member, although he had his share of wounded, but able to recover from their injuries, and continue with the profession they chose. It was largely why his team was always willing to take an assignment from him.

Little did they know, it was their own planning of the details that made that accomplishment possible, for all of them, not just his unblemished record as overall team leader. With all the plans at least laid out to his team, he departed for the evening to return the following morning to see how much progress was made. Romero made it home in time for a chance to go get a decent meal at a nearby restaurant that served wonderful Italian food. He figured long ago, that if the recipes used by the Italians did not kill you, it was good enough for him. He often wondered why the women were so stout, and the men so lean in most cases. It was one of those issues he would never truly know an answer to, but remain something of wonder to him.

He enjoyed every minute at the restaurant, although he figured it may change soon if he became a person of notoriety in the public eye. He really did not want that to occur with his stay in DC as Vice President, he always preferred to be more of a behind the scenes person. He was also worried he would also get secret service persons assigned to him, which would make his task all that more difficult. Although, he did know how to be elusive when required, he did not want to practice it daily, to slip out of the reach of people who believed their duty, was to protect him from harm. It was a wrinkle he never considered when he accepted Thomas Hardesty's offer to be his Vice President. He did know why the President wanted him in office, and he could not use ignorance as any form of excuse. Truly he loathed that method anyway, he could just have his secret service people put into the loop with secrecy being paramount to their continuing to keep breathing on a daily basis. He was far more familiar with this means of communication, than far more would ever have believed of him. Maybe it was possible to simple forego secret service assigned to him, as the President and his family were far more vital than his wellbeing.

The absolute last thing he wanted; was for the country to know exactly what the Vice President did for over thirty years of service to their country. It would cause more panic than good will for President Thomas Hardesty without any doubt in his mind. Assassins do not normally get to hold political office, and although he has been largely in charge of putting the plans into movement, he had done his share of the dirty work before given the opportunity to lead others. Thomas Hardesty insured him, his records were sealed, and could not be opened by anyone other than himself as President, as long as he remained President of the United States, no one else could open those records. The time would come in four or eight years, where the next president would have access to those files. Hardesty needed to have his work done by the time that occurred, for all their sakes. It still was a touchy topic in

THE GAME PLAN PART 1

Romero Trap's viewpoint, knowing other members of government could not resist sealed files concerning another member of the administration. Romero Trap did not want to put an untimely end to some Senator or Congressional member of the house, with enough time in DC to start their own investigation, but if push comes to shove, Trap knew how to finish, with the last push that person would ever know. Trap's face would also be the last thing they ever saw, he would not hide from them. No matter which way Romero looked at his position in the upcoming events to take place, things for him were going to get complicated.

The following day when he arrived at the team's location, at least half of them were out. Jackson Frye had sent them in to looking into armory locations most easily accessed, as well as checking into the security visible at the DEA warehouse. He was certain video surveillance was in use, at least in and outside the DEA warehouse, but needed to know if it was true for the armory as well. The easiest armory would be without video cameras, and if things had not changed in the last 10 years in the military, a reserve base would be the easiest of all, and truth be known, likely far better supplied, since they were largely who went to war for the pentagon chess players.

Bringing up chess was never a good thing for Romero Trap, as it always triggered his memory over his accomplishment in that particular game of strategy. It brought to mind that although he never wanted the recognition of being a grand master of the game of chess. He had been literally undefeated throughout high school and if he had gone to college, it was a game of immense strategy. Often considered the game most esteemed by the war machine, as a means to apply strategy to the world of warfare. Although Romero never once attempted to enter a grand masters match, he viewed all those that were made public through the internet, and found he would have won 95 percent of all the games that awarded the grand master the title. He also remembered how he and Thomas Hardesty had played many games over the years for them to be literally at a 50 percent each winning percentage. Thomas Hardesty, if he were in the covert operations based on his chess playing, would have been excellent in the profession. He was one of the most formidable chess opponents Trap ever encountered, although Trap refused to reveal his master strategy with him. He knew he would have won far more times, but by the same token, Hardesty was so adept in chess, he was one of a very few group of people to solve it, and counter with a win against Trap's best strategy.

Romero looked around once again to see multiple changes in the once abandoned warehouse. All he could do was ask Heartless if any of them ever slept. Heartless answered like many others in the line of work they were in, that he would get more than enough sleep when he was dead, but for now, he was taking advantage of all the time he had until that moment arrived. He said he would be the first to know when his time came. Romero Trap having been there, was certain that last statement was far too true.

One of the many alteration that occurred over the night since he was here, was a rather large room was put together with far better materials than the others. It did not appear any of it was purchased, but it was possible they were dismantling portions of other buildings to obtain the materials used. The actual buildings selected, were those of Jackson Frye, Romero merely presented them with possibilities. The new room addition also had a rather stout door that slid open to at least half the width, and had a rather healthy clasp where the door closed. It was apparent that part of his funds were used for the lock that looked like it would take a howitzer to force open. Jackson Frye asked Romero if he wanted to hold the second key, once the armaments were in place, Romero Trap told him it would be best for Heartless to select another team member he felt most trustworthy, as his position in this assignment, also being the Vice President, it did not allow his direct participation for appearance sake. Frye told him he thought as much but decided to make sure just in case.

Jackson Frye asked if Romero had any preference for the second team member to the key for armaments and ammunition. Romero said Frye should choose the one he felt most comfortable with and to keep in mind, that same person might be his confidant and second in command, should something put him into a position disabling his immediate participation. Frye said in order to keep someone on his good side, he was thinking of Murray Golic, because he wanted no problems from the hulk. Murray Golic was 310 pounds of solid muscle, stood 6 feet 8 inches tall. Jackson Frye also said between Golic and Ramirez, he never saw two people eat so much food. The pair went through as much in a day, as his entire platoon did in a week, when he was still in uniform. It also meant the food supplies were going considerable quicker than originally anticipated, so things for funding needed to be stepped up to keep them fed. He did not want to deal with either one should it come down to food, but it would be nice if they cooked, considering how good they were at consuming it.

By the end of the day, the team members that had gone out to locate an armory and scope out the DEA warehouse, returned with their reports. The armory would be the easiest, it was a reserve base that had ample weapons and ammunition available, and rather young and inexperienced personnel, acting as security detail. Never more than six per eight hour shifts around the clock. First contact should be tonight, after midnight passed, and the last shift was solely in the building. Zoe had asked just how young were these troops, and per person she was told that none appeared more than 20 years of age. She said she would need two bottles of cold sparkling wine of some type like Champaign, but there were other suitable wines, not as dry. She was not looking for the cheap stuff like wine coolers, something with a cork she could use a syringe to induce a sedative. She had a plan that should not take more than 30 minutes, and her signal would be the opening of doors to enter.

Starting at twelve thirty AM, after obtaining two very cold bottles of Champaign, the sedan with only Zoe left and shortly after, one cargo van and the large truck departed, to park close but not on the armory property. Zoe had already injected the sedative into the Champaign, and took them with her, she figured one bottle to share among three young men of the army. Two bottles for the maximum of six army grunts. Zoe wondered if these six boys would ever truly know how fortunate they were to get a bird's eye view of her features, and live to talk about it, once they got over the hangover no amount of alcohol could induce. When the sedative took effect, they would be out for at least four hours, plenty of time to take everything they had, if necessary.

The plan went exactly like clockwork. Zoe said she was there to give the troops her version of a thanks for protecting this country, she gave them the two bottles of sparkling wine and said she had no glasses, but they looked capable of sharing and passing the bottle around while she entertained them.

Once the bottles were handed out, Zoe found one of the support poles suitable for a bit of strip tease, and although it was not a dancer's pole, it would suffice for her purposes. It was a little bit larger in diameter, but Zoe had the strength to use it for her maneuvers, as the bottles neared empty and all six of the boys, as she would call them, had drank enough for the sedative to go to work, she completely exposed herself in a rather sensual maneuver, it had her dress fall to the floor, as the boys got to view the flash of pink with a dark brown patch of well-manicured fur. When she righted herself and slid down the pole for the full frontal view, all six boys hit the ground, under the influence of the sedative. She gathered her dress, opened the large entry door while she put her dress back on.

The cargo van and truck entered in quick fashion, and the crew gathered up weapons. Murray Golic was one of the crew to select the heavy machine guns he and Ramirez preferred to use. No one else in the crew could even pick them up. They found two dozen sniper rifles, and enough ammunition to start a large war someplace. They also obtain the rifles, the automatic weapons and a large number of handgun, mostly 1911's the designated 45 caliber side arm, commonly used by the military, since the war between the north and south. They remained to be the most durable weapons used for hand guns, and ammunition was plentiful, considering how long it had been in use. There were twenty different manufacturers of the type of weapon used for military issue handguns, but each manufacturer had to make some subtle change to make it their own production. Some were so subtle to simply be a different pattern in the handhold of the firearm.

It took the team 90 minutes to load all the weapons and ammunition, before departing to the abandoned base building. Zoe hit the automatic close button on her way out to close the entry door, and make everything appear perfectly normal. The military boys would be too embarrassed to mention her specifically, but none of them knew who she was, so it mattered not, it was also highly likely the military would document the theft and possible have an inventory of serial numbers, but not go public with such an event. Romero Trap had done his homework in this regard many times before, and not once did a military armory get broadcast time on the local or national news. Although all the other government agencies would be well informed, but they still had to have some evidence to work with. His team did not leave any behind, and they were thorough in their assignments.

The next morning, when Romero Trap returned to his team, the finishing touches of their base had been completed, and Jackson Frye showed him the small arsenal that was acquired in the early morning hours. He let Trap know the exact location of the armory, as he was going to find out through government channels in the near future, if not already. Romero Trap had no real concerns over the issue of the armory, he knew his team was professional and left no trace evidence for the other government agencies to find, or following back to his team. The well secured room was now full of all the weapons and ammunition required for a considerable length of time, although it was doubtful it would last for an entire term of the President in office. The team would need to find other supplies, largely ammunition later into the assignments, but the quantity needed, would depend upon how easy or difficult the assignments to follow became. There were no rules carved in stone that would determine those needs in advance of the events to take place.

Jackson Frye also informed Romero Trap, he had found a cargo plane on a nearby base, that although nearing its retirement time for military use, it would serve its purpose for the team. The only problem of taking the cargo plane from its current location, would be where to keep it long enough to change its appearance, preferable in all black to make it stealthier, for what they needed to do. Romero Trap knew of just such a private airfield that had multiple hangers unused, as the airfield was largely out dated and had been unused for nearly a decade. The hangers were perfectly good for hiding the plane from view, as well as giving it a new appearance. It would need to be done fairly quickly, and Trap provided the exact location, and even a hanger number most suited to the size of the cargo plane. Being near retirement age, the military would not make untold efforts to recover it. Before the plane could be obtained, they needed the drugs from the DEA warehouse. Jackson told him that was scheduled for that evening going into early next morning. The team did its best work when it was the darkest hours of any given day.

With everything scheduled, Romero and Frye went over the plan for the DEA warehouse, and did not know if they needed the large truck or should steal the one from the DEA. Time for this type of theft was critical, and Romero knew having to load either truck with two or three tons of drugs, would use quite a bit of time. Romero told Frye he had thought on taking the truck on the mission. If things worked out in Frye's favor, where the DEA warehouse had a truck still fully loaded, he could take it, but if all of it had to be loaded into a truck, it might as well be the one they already had, no point in calling more attention to the team with a DEA truck, likely easily identifiable. If it was a truck with no markings, which were used frequently in transporting large quantities of contraband seized by the government agencies, it would be up to Frye which was easiest for the team. Frye said he was taking half the team, plus one driver for each vehicle. The plan was to sedate, if possible, with blow darts. Should they be discovered too quickly, it could turn ugly, and he could not guarantee a no casualty assault, but that was what was called for, and it truly depended on the reaction of the DEA. Whether they had a large, well-trained detail for security, or, like so many other agencies, felt they had no vulnerabilities, and used lesser trained members and low numbers. They could not get inside to make that determination, but only saw three external persons.

They also needed to disable six security cameras around the warehouse property. The first to go were those on the outer perimeter. Depending on where the security people were at the time, would decide on them being disable before or after the cameras.

Romero Trap enjoyed having Heartless (Jackson Frye) as his person in charge of the team. First, Trap knew him to be excellent in filling in the plan details, and take into account multiple scenarios to be prepared

THE GAME PLAN PART 1

for both, the best and the worst of any given situation. Second was his complete void of emotion, made his plans cold and calculated. As difficult as it may sound to some, it was a necessity for warriors of any notoriety to be precisely calculating. As long as emotions were removed from the details of a plan, the team would be prepared for whatever may really take place, especially since nothing ever went perfect to every little detail. You could not account for the other side to be totally predictable, or every plan would be perfect. Heartless had been in the profession long enough to know this, and plan for as many possibilities he could for any given assignment. With a team of people, he had worked with in the past, he knew what he could expect from those members.

Romero Trap had less than three weeks, before he would need to be on the White House premises regularly and daily initially. Several things needed to be accomplished prior to that day arriving. It still included the DEA warehouse, where two other tasks depended on the success of that warehouse. The cargo plane would be needed to transport drugs not once, but twice. All these tasks needed to been done before his White House time became a major issue. Romero Trap at this point, did not know where else on this planet his team would need to be sent for other assignments, but rest assured, the vast majority would not take place in the US of A.

Of the 36 members of his team, although none held a legitimate pilot's license, five people could fly various aircraft. It covered a rather large array from fighter jets to helicopters, and most anything else with wings. Romero Trap did not believe his team would need to obtain any fighter jets for their assignment, and even if it was called for, they were not easily obtained. The military would certainly go to the extreme to recover such an aircraft, because none of them were inexpensive, and armaments were not easy to find either. Most airbases did not keep aircraft in waiting on the ground fully loaded for take-off. In almost every case, once a sortie was created, it was not armed until shortly before take-off.

That evening starting at 11:30 PM, Jackson Frye started moving his people out for the DEA warehouse. It took both the cargo van, as well as the large truck, that were going to be positioned just outside of the perimeter of video surveillance. He had a dozen of his team members equipped with blow guns and darts, for disabling the opposition. All these people were also proficient with handguns, and they were brought along for backup purposes, in the event something went horribly wrong. Three of his people were also quite capable of rendering opponents unconscious with hand to hand techniques, but these techniques were more effective from and unseen rear approach. He was one of those people, so Heartless took it upon himself and the other two to make the first internal entrance, with the expectations of it being done quietly and unseen. If all went well, not a single weapon would need to be fired, but not knowing the internal layout of the building, he could not fully predict enough materials were present to find good places to hide. The evening attire was in totally black apparel, with face masks and camouflage paint to conceal their appearance. Some preferred the mask, others the makeup, as the mask sometime hindered proper breathing techniques.

Proper breathing was essential to stealth and being unheard, to go with the unseen.

Everyone was in position around the DEA warehouse by 12:15 AM, and the three external security members appeared bored to the point of failing to be attentive. This made his team's job much easier, as all three were hit by separate team members with the tranquilizer darts, and were out for a few hours within fifteen minutes. Next thing to go was the cameras, which only took his people five minutes. With the external portions of the job taken care of and under control, Jackson and the other two infiltrators, sought a rear entrance of some sort to the building that would be least likely to cause alarm. Most everyone on the team at one point or another, had to pick locks to gain quiet access to someplace. It was all a part of the profession they were in, and they were all relatively proficient in this little detail. It took only two minutes to gain access through a rear exit that was locked. Jackson was quite happy, although he would not show it, to find enough material in stacks to conceal them for a quick overview of where the other security people might be located.

THE GAME PLAN PART 1

It took nearly ten minutes to locate the internal security, and everything was falling into place for Jackson and his team. There were only four internal agents or security personnel spotted. One in the office space that was lighted, and the other three wandering aimlessly about. It was hard to determine if it was feigned or real, but they looked like they had nothing to do for so long that they were no longer truly on guard for any type of event to take place, outside of routine. Jackson had each member select one of the wandering guards to remove without prejudice. Jackson took the one farthest away and crept through various cover to keep out of sight, until directly behind the security person. When the security person turned his back to retrace steps, Jackson stepped up from behind, applied pressure to one side of his neck and bent his head over to the pressure point to render him unconscious. The other two had also removed their prey quietly and without fatality. The only issue with doing this type of disable, was everyone had a different recovery rate, and it did not allow excessive amounts of time for the other portion of their duties in this warehouse. Jackson had not had the time yet to determine where the shipment was located, and how much was there, although there was an unmarked truck in the center of the warehouse. If his fortunes were to continue, all the drugs were in the cargo area and all they needed to do was drive off with the truck. He had the other two members see about disabling the office member of the opposition, and it took only a few minutes as the door opened, and tranquilizer dart sent as the person turned to face the door. There were no cameras inside the building that Jackson could locate, which meant they were merely concerned about what approached the facility, assuming all was safe inside. Jackson Frye loved the ignorance of the government agencies he dealt with over the years. The all seemed to act like they had immunity to any possible threat to their agency, and it was not unique to the government of this country. It was a worldwide epidemic. It did make Jackson Frye and his team's job considerably easier for the preliminary needs of any given assignment.

The truck was fully loaded with the drugs, the team intended to take it off the DEA's hands to put to better use, at least from Romero's viewpoint. The DEA even left it on the scale to determine how much was drugs, and how much was truck. Subtracting the gross weight listed on the truck, he came up with a little over 3 and a half tons of cargo, assumed to be all drugs, but of what percentage of what would not be determined until into a more secure location for the team. He had his two companions get the exit door open, while he check for the whereabouts of the keys, figuring they would be near the office, possibly in a key box on a wall. He found keys in short order, and it was quicker than having to change the wiring sufficiently to take the truck by that means. He did not drive one of the other vehicles, so as of now he was the fourth driver. The truck was taken outside, and the two other team members made certain the doors were closed up once again, before boarding the truck with Heartless. He met the rest of the team near the other three vehicles, and in a matter of fifteen minutes from the time they had entered, left and evacuated the scene. It was seldom that a plan went perfectly, but this one did just that. It should still be near time for the unconscious members in the warehouse outside of the office to be reviving, and Jackson and his team needed to be gone and completely out of sight.

The next morning, when Romero Trap arrived it was time to take inventory of the haul from the early morning hours. Trap was unsure of what do to with the extra ton and half, since the initial cartel sales were specifically for two tons of cocaine. He had over two and half tons of that, another half of a ton of morphine, along with an assortment of pills and other lesser drugs, mostly marijuana. None of his team members were user of any sort of it, or they would never have been asked to join him. Most all of them knew the business in which they participated in, was strictly one of mental sharpness. Anything that would dull those senses too significantly, would have deadly consequence for far more than just the individual who indulged in such practices. The additional drugs were off loaded slowly, since there was not equipment to do it in large quantity. The remaining two tons were left on the newly acquired truck, and Jackson having found one of the buildings in the complex to be a paint supply company that went out of business, found enough black paint still usable to change the cargo planes appearance when obtained, as well as enough spray cans to give the newly acquired truck from the DEA, which was perfectly clean, a more common appearance. One team member was a long time graffiti maker in his teens, before leaving high school. Other cans were used for the more common graffiti of lines of various not so straight wiggles, and phony initials. The graffiti wizard did a near graffiti Rembrandt, on the back rollup door. It was not so uncommon to cause attraction, but it was a near work of art, considering it was all done with spray paint. It did give the truck a little character.

That had taken nearly six hours of the day, and Jackson was planning to get the cargo plane that evening, although he did not feel in this case, it would need to be quite as late as the two previous evenings, but still after dark.

Jackson sent three people off to acquire an air compressor, spray guns, two hundred feet of air lines, with connectors for the guns and hoses, masking tape and paper to cover windows on a cargo plane. He would also need a rather tall ladder to get to the top side of the cargo plane. It would need to be 30 feet in height, to reach the top safely. That would also take care of the remainder of the funds Romero had furnished to start things. Most of it had gone on food, and Jackson said to Romero, if he was going to feed a two man army, he would need more before the initial funding would be obtained with the sale of the drugs and obliteration of the first cartel.

That evening, Jackson brought a cargo plane into the airfield selected by Romero Trap, and parked it in the hanger number also provided. The hanger was then locked, and work on the cargo plane would take place in the morning, but this job was going to take a little longer, since cargo planes were not exactly small-scale aircraft.

4

The Game Plan part 2

Romero Trap in obtaining more funds for the team to get through another week of nourishment requirements, also obtained one dozen new burner phones and disposed of his previously used one for the setup of the team. Before handing the 11 other phones over to the team leader, he entered the numbers of the other phones into his new burner phone, and placed his number into the other eleven. It took a little bit of time, but it was something that needed to be done regularly to keep the autonomy of the team preserved, as well as himself.

The following morning when he arrived at base camp for the team, several members were not present, including his team leader. His inquiries into the whereabouts of Jackson Frye were quickly answered, and he went to the airfield hanger with the team's input. Jackson first informed him the meet with the Mexican cartel was set for middle of next week at a private airfield near San Antonio, Texas. The cartel would bring their own truck and equipment to offload the cargo, provided it was acceptable at the price offered. If the quality was pure enough, they had no problems with a 400 percent plus profit margin. But, if it was lesser quality, they would either turn it down or haggle over the price again, based on the quality of the product. The team did not test it, and were a little out of their league for such practices. Romero said it would be necessary to take a handful of additional storage bags with them, the cartel would likely test more than one package before handing over the funds, and since the plan was to exterminate the cartel members who showed up, the open packages would not fare well for the return flight.

Jackson indicated he was pressed for time to get the cargo plane looking less military and more commercial. Romero understood his situation, and handed over the phones to be used by the crew, stating the only number on any of the phones was the one to his. Jackson said once he decided which was his, he would add that to the other phones, but these phones were only intended for emergency use. If the phone rang, it would mean an unexpected development arose in their missions. It was the standard that Romero Trap had kept throughout his career, and his team leader would be following those identical standards. Romero Trap let those present in the hanger continue with their work. He returned for a short period to the base camp, and provided the holder of the extra keys with the food funds, to get additional supplies for the purpose of consumption. It was not to be used for anything else was his only stipulation over the additional funding.

In less than a week's time, the team had obtained transportation, weapons, and the initial drugs for funding, as well as a cargo plane to move the merchandise. They also had managed to make the abandoned building used for home base, more of a home than a resort, but it was not terribly rundown any more. Their efficiency in making all this happen was amazing. They were working like a team that had spent a decade together, as opposed to less than a week, but they all had worked with or under Romero Trap in the past, and knew what was expected of them before they ever agreed to the assignment.

Their profession relied heavily on team work, since no individual could accomplish their missions, even though it should not require every one of them for a single assignment they were going to be receiving. It would allow for some to have a little rest and relaxation time, while others were out performing their own mission. As far as Romero Trap could predict, at no time over the next four to eight years, would the base camp be void of any team members. Romero Trap was only aware of the amount of funding he could obtain for the cocaine, he was not an

THE GAME PLAN PART 2

authority on the current market prices of all the drugs they had obtained from the DEA. He did have a contact who was consider small time by the cartels, and largely dealt with the pill form and marijuana trade. He might also know the value to the heroin, but he was unsure. He would need to unload those items, just to get them out of his control, but he still wanted the normal street value of production not distribution. There was a noticeable variation between the two, but much more work involved in turning it into a distribution product. He wanted no part of that end of a business he loathed to start with. Unfortunately, it was the quickest means to reach his funding for more of the profession he was always in, or so it seemed.

He would wait until the cargo plane was ready, before bringing up placing the other drugs into one of the cargo van to get a street value estimate from his contact, who was more attuned to its real worth in the consumer marketplace of illicit drugs. For some people, it was still a matter of supply and demand, and for a very long time, there had always been a demand for such products. In the meantime, he would make first contact to give his contact first option, if so desired.

With little to do at home base, he left the team to take care of their immediate needs, while he checked on the current whereabouts of his rather infrequent contact involved in the lower end of the drug trade or profession, depending on how one views illegal activities, not from his perspective, did he think he should cast the first stone. He was relatively certain in other countries, he was considered a threat to their way of life, as much as those he removed were by his own government. Another reason why operations were normally performed under the cover of darkness. The exception being for the snipers, who needed light to insure the target was what they sought, they were also far enough from the actual target to not be seen easily. It took roughly two and a half hours to rustle up his contact, but a meeting was set for that evening, and to be able to keep his contact just a bit off guard, he made it like he was looking for a dinner companion for the night, since eating alone was a problem for many, he used that excuse, although he was quite accustomed to eating alone, and often preferred it. His preference was largely to keep a watch out on his surroundings, to be prepared for

A SELECT FEW

anything. His profession made him a little paranoid, but in all honesty, it was for good reason. He killed people for a living, and it did leave things open for retaliation from the wrong sort of people seeking retribution.

The meeting with his contact proved to be more interesting than he anticipated, it seemed his low level businessman in the drug trade, was doing much better than he would have assumed. First, his clientele was for marijuana and various pill form, all for the purpose of pain relief. His clientele all had legitimate reasons for requiring his particular types of product. All the people had medical needs for pain relief of a variety of aliment, from arthritis to sever levels of cancer and osteoporosis, which was the deterioration of bones, largely in females over the age of 40, although some cases were a little younger, his clients were not. Most of the people were obtaining his drugs because the prescription drugs designed for the problem they suffered from, actually cost more and their medical coverage limits were reached far too early in the annual assessments of the insurance companies. In most cases, the annual assessment of insurance companies lowered in quantity rather than increase. They had need for pain relief and whether it became addictive or not was not the issue over relieving the excruciating pain from their aliments. He felt he was providing a much needed service, as opposed to corrupting adolescents. He did occasionally sell some marijuana for recreational purposes, but mostly he supplied pain relief to those denied from normal means.

His contact admitted when he first got involved in his line of business, he was no different than any other provider, who sold to any who asked, who did not appear to be a member of the police. He got busted twice before he learned to specialize. Once he did that, his business flourished, and now he was like any good salesperson, and only worked by referral. "If you were not told by one of my clients to see what I could offer for your specific ailment, you go away empty handed." He told Romero Trap, he did not deal with heroin, but was aware of the street value of uncut product. If he really had half of a ton of uncut product, he could get 200 million for what he did have.

Romero Trap's contact was inquisitive about where Trap had obtained his drug supply, and Trap responded by telling his contact for

THE GAME PLAN PART 2

his own good, he did not want to know, since lack of knowledge would be in his benefit. His contact knew enough about Trap that he decided not to push for more information, because Trap was not someone, he wanted to make an enemy.

Trap did live up to his word, and they did have dinner, but that was not as important to Trap as the information he got; and the fact that his contact, depending on what exactly he had, was in a position to take it off his hands, provided it was what he dealt with. The half-ton of marijuana was no problem, he had locations to keep it that were not likely to be raided. The pills were the point of must see to know, and Trap arranged a place to meet the following evening. His contact was willing to pay cash, which was the only means he would deal with, but how much would largely depend on what he had. The marijuana was worth 25 million to him, as he could double his money in two months. That was his mode of operation, 50 percent out with 50 percent profit. It helped keep his clients content. They were not the kind of people who needed to see prices double every time they needed the product. He made every effort to see that did not happen, and a big reason why he did not deal in the other end of the drug business like cocaine and heroin, which had prices as stable as rubber bouncing balls.

Trap set the time for the meet like always, after dark arrived, and he would bring it in a cargo van. The location was selected by his contact, since he would need to move the product elsewhere. It would also take a little bit of time to transfer it from one vehicle to another, and Trap was surprised to find his contact selected the same abandoned warehouse area the base camp was located. Fortunately, it was a building other than the ones they were using. So at least he would not need to go far with the van.

The following morning, Romero Trap after having his pot of breakfast go juice, left for the base camp to insure a van would be available for the evening, and got help loading up all the drugs they had no other use for, except the heroin, and extra half-ton of cocaine. There were still team members missing at the airfield, but they used the sedan since it could be hidden in the same hanger they were working in, and be far enough away to have no paint overspray reach it. Since it was a rather large plane, one of the team members said it would not be completed until tomorrow, and then needed at least 24 more hours, to insure it was dry enough to use in flight. Cargo planes were not the fastest moving aircraft, but they could carry extremely large loads. And still have room for the entire team in jump seats if needed. It was not a luxury passenger plane, but could accommodate passengers willing to put up with the seating arrangements. You would also not receive meals in flight. For military personnel it was the way to fly, and whether you liked it or not, was never the first consideration for military hierarchy.

With the cargo van loaded after three hours of making the transfer, with lots of assistance, Trap knew it would require help with the next transfer, he simply did not know how much would be transferred.

After dark arrived, Romero Trap with the aid of two very large men, having Murray Golic and Felix Ramirez, he felt he had the best help he could get with a minimum of team members. The trip was not terribly long, and his contact arrived a mere five minutes after he had.

First, he needed his contact to determine what pills were of value to him, his response was it looked like his supplier had a shipment seized or something, because every pill was something he recognized as an item he had clients with those needs. He said it put a small twist in his plans, since the value of his entire cargo was nearly 65 million and he only had 60 million dollars to offer. Romero Trap asked to see the money and if it was all there, he would give him the entire cargo, and be happy to get rid of it, and allow his contact a little extra profit for his trouble. This proved to be worth it for both parties, and their deal was consummated with a large case of cash money. Romero Trap assisted his two behemoths in transferring the contents of the cargo van to the truck brought by his client. It only took an hour with Murray and Feliz handling the largest part of the transfer, with the amount the two could move individually. With the transaction completed, his contact was the first to depart, as was Romero Trap's plan, he did not want his contact to know the base camp was nearby.

Once back to base camp, the first thing Romero Trap did was make payment to all the team members and those at the hanger, who had returned, so the entire crew was present. That took care of 36,000

THE GAME PLAN PART 2

dollars, but it was a small bit of sixty million dollars. He took Jackson Frye aside, and said 30 million was going into an offshore numbered account for the purpose of gaining through interest and investment, for the needs later into the assignments. Jackson had no problems with that, and learned once the account was established, he would get the access information for when it was absolutely necessary to utilize for an assignment.

With the first week one day short of completed, Romero Trap went to his apartment for his last cup of coffee and some sleep. Jackson Frye told him the cargo plane would have the painting completed the following day, and after the 48 hours of drying, it would be ready to go off to San Antonio for the first cartel meet to take place, since the cargo plane was large enough to take both cargo vans, the sedan, as well as one of the two large trucks, his plan was to simply load the DEA truck with its new graffiti paint job. Move the truck out in San Antonio, to make inspection and testing easier, but it would also take a little time to reload it into the cargo plane. He was planning to have six rifles, outside the area to take the first shots, once the money was presented. He would have another half dozen small arms experts on the ground at the point of contact. If the first six shots were all true to the targets, the confusion from the cartel should be enough to create the opportunity to eliminate the remainder, with the handgun experts.

He could not guarantee it would put an end to the cartel, but it should set them back at least six months, before they resume rebuilding from their losses. They would likely consider it a theft of 625 plus million dollars, as opposed to the loss of the 120 million cash. Romero Trap concurred with his second in command that was a distinct probability, but the seed money was needed to get the more profitable assignments from the President.

The following morning Romero Trap went to two locations prior to arriving at the base location of the team. First, he went to a computer store, and obtained three shockproof laptop computers. He also picked up one for his use pertaining to the missions, but it was not shockproof, he had no reason to be that mobile with his. His second stop was to a storage unit that he had always kept for vital pieces of his trade.

One being the satellite link for getting into government and military intelligence, as well satellite imagery. It would take a few hours for one of his team to mount it on the top of the building, and run the cable he brought as well, to make the connection. Although he did not check the building for the roof access, all buildings of this type usually had one, because almost every business in the country, had need to access the roof for any number of reasons. Buildings this size often had roof top environmental systems for at least heat and air conditioning, even if it was not used throughout the entire building.

When he arrived, once again his team leader was at the hanger finishing up with the cargo plane. He provided the equipment, which immediately one of the more agile and wiry members of the team, Zi Yang, took the cabling and satellite gear to the roof and had it mounted in twenty minutes, but took a little longer to get the cabling to the point of the computer systems. There was also the interface box at the computer end, which allowed up to one dozen computers to attach to it, with the cable to the satellite link feeding it. Two hours into his arrival, computers were fully functional and Romero Trap accessed satellite imagery of the San Antonio airstrip the team would be going. Found the location best to serve the teams plan, determined the cargo plane should be away from the transfer site, to insure no collateral damage occurred to it, as a result of poorly aimed gun fire from the cartel. He did not anticipate any such problems from his team.

The building where the truck would be taken was near the perimeter fence that surrounded almost every airstrip in the country, outside of the small privately owned ones for small aircrafts. Just outside the fence, was a fairly good sized tree line that the rifle experts could use for cover, until the time their skills were put to use. The cargo plane would be positioned at least 2,000 yards closer to the main hangers and refueling areas. The cargo plane would in all likelihood need to be refueled before takeoff, and unfortunately the funds for that would need to come from the cartel. Romero Trap could not predict what the fee would be, as almost every airfield did it a little differently, since personnel from the airfield were required to refuel the plane, the costs often involved the labor and equipment charges on top of the price for fuel.

Jackson Frye who was finishing up the painting, knew from past experience that all cargo planes used by the military had a service record in a compartment within the cockpit, the only reason for it not to be in the compartment, was it was being serviced. He made sure it was in the compartment before taking the plane, but did not check it for the number of hours left until its next service was due. He did once completing the painting, and giving it a new set of numbers, that did not exist, but were no longer of the military. He found it had been serviced fairly recently, and he had at least 200 hours of flight time before it would require anything done. He hoped he would not need to use the plane that much, but if they went eight years into the assignment, it would be necessary. The good part was it was not overhaul service, it was fluid changes and checking to see if anything loosened from vibration, although the only way that would happen was if the safety wire used had broken. It was not entirely impossible, but it was rare.

Once he had completed that, he and the few people with him return to base and found Romero Trap going over satellite imagery of the San Antonio airfield. He was glad to see that Romero Trap selected a tree line for his rifle experts, and thought it wise the cargo plane would be some distance from the location of the meet. He also said to Trap is was vital for the team to be on the ground and in place, at least two hours before the cartel arrived, for the exchange that would never take place completely.

The plans were moving forward, and by the end of the next week, the team should be funded well enough to get the more important assignments. Romero Trap asked who his team leader had in mind for making the pitch to other governments and businesses in some cases, to pay for the assassinations, which were the primary objective.

Jackson Frye had asked that of Sven Turlock, since he seemed to be the most knowledgeable member of the team in that type of contact. He had done it several times in past assignments, and always did an outstanding job of getting the highest price for the job per contributor. If it was like any other assignment they had in the past, it was usually for a single bounty to one organization, but often more than a single person needed to be eliminated, to insure the snake had the head completely severed. Romero Trap knew this to be case in most assignments, very seldom did his team have a singular target, which had no hierarchy to take the place of the primary target.

Everything was fairly quiet for the next two days, and like most times for Romero Trap's team, when they had downtime, it was used for the sole purpose of getting fully rested for the assignment that would follow. Romero Trap did not bother his people for those times, and spent a little bit of time at the White House, just to make it appear he was on the job. He also used the time to go over the satellite imagery of the San Antonio airfield, just to make sure he did not overlook any small details that could change the outcome of the plan. The only thing he could foresee as a problem, was if the cartel was planning to do unto them before they did unto to the cartel. It would mean the cartel would have people in the tree line as well as his own, but his people would know to check out the surroundings ahead of time, to insure they were alone. Since the cartels were by and large hunted by many agencies, obtaining the materials of their trade was becoming increasingly difficult. Two tons of pure uncut cocaine, should be plenty of incentive to try to make the deal as best they could, figuring the other party offering, although unknown to them, was legitimately selling their own production.

Cartels were continually needing new providers to keep business moving forward, and as long as they did not lose too much in seizures, which occurred all too frequently in recent years, the demand for their product was high. They would still arrive to the meeting location well-armed, but like many such organizations, they did not have a training program for their enforcers. They just liked to shoot their weapons, and often did it in a haphazard fashion, which got messy, but often inaccurate enough to do damage by true professionals. His team of people, if nothing else were highly trained professionals, and well trained in methods of removing obstacles with great efficiency.

The day arrived for the team to load up the cargo plane and depart for San Antonio. Jackson planned to have the cargo plane refueled, while they conducted their other business, and would pay the costs of

THE GAME PLAN PART 2

refueling before takeoff. It was commonly practiced at airfields and he did not foresee it being any different in San Antonio, although most companies did it with accounts, not cash.

The flight to San Antonio took three hours and 45 minutes, but they arrive three hours ahead of the scheduled meeting time. The truck was moved to the location intended to be used for the meeting, and his rifle people started checking out the tree line surroundings for anything that did not belong there. They were thorough enough to check for both other people not expected, as well as any type of traps or explosives placed to prevent them from using the tree line.

One hour before the meeting time, one of the rifle people reported back to Jackson Frye that the area was clear of any obstacles, and everyone was in place except him and he would be soon. Each rifle expert was to pick a single target, and each would choose a different target. If all six shots were fired in nearly the same time, there should be six less cartel members to be concerned about. Jackson and his six close quarter's specialists would hit the ground with the first shots heard, and be prepared to take aim at those cartel members not targeted by the rifle experts. Weapons would be drawn at the same time they were hitting the ground, and the cartel members were expected to start firing or looking into the tree line for where the shots came from. It should be enough distraction to give his close quarter's combat experts time to finish what was started in quick fashion. Jackson Frye did not know how many cartel members to expect but figured on 18. Although he did not expect all of them would be upper hierarchy members, only a half of a dozen at most, with the others merely enforcers.

Jackson's team consisted of Bloodlust, Mayhem, Terror, Bullseye, Havoc and Deadly on rifle. Kung Fu, Stiletto, Sting, Edge, Sharpy, and Blade for close quarter's combat and himself. Everyone had their body armor under their outer shirts, and although a little bulkier than without, none of them looked overly sized. Five minutes before the expected meet time, a large truck and four other vehicles appeared and were heading in their direction.

At the precise time of the planned meeting, all the members emerged from the vehicles, which came to a total of 24 cartel members, more than Jackson planned on having, but it presented no real complications for his team. He stepped forward as did the cartel member who was the leader of the cartel from what he knew of it. He brought with him one other person with a test kit, but the remaining 22 members were all carrying automatic weapons that appeared to be Uzi manufactured. It meant they were loaded with 9 millimeter ammunition, but in all likelihood the magazines held 25 to 30 rounds each. It was a lot of fire power, but if it was aimed at the tree line, it would make no difference. They entered the truck brought by the team, and the cartel member with the leader, randomly selected three bags of product and test each to find it was all pure and uncut. The leader signaled another member of his group of enforcers, and he brought a very large suitcase and two additional carrying bags that were much squarer and harder covered like large briefcase, but folding top covers. He presented the money, which Jackson merely fanned a fair amount to insure it was all cash, and not filled with blank paper to appear like cash. They both then moved more to the center of the two groups, and exchanged a few words, largely business related. When Jackson turned to walk away, it was the signal for the rifles to take the first shots. The leader was the first down and five others went with him, at the precise moment of the first shot all of Jackson's team hit the ground as planned, and with weapons already in place, the cartel members with the automatic weapons opened fire on the tree line getting off nearly one hundred rounds before his close combat people start picking them off one by one, until there were 24 cartel members down. Not a single shot was fired in the direction of his close combat people or himself, as the noise from the Uzi drowned out the hand gun discharge. Jackson had made it a point for all of his team to take head shots, since it was likely the cartel would have body armor as well. To be entirely sure, Jackson checked each downed cartel member for a pulse, found two and finished them with head shots at close range.

 The team then moved the cartel bodies into the truck they brought, loaded everyone into their own truck, and returned to the cargo plane with 120 million dollars of which 8,000 dollars was needed to cover the refueling cost, although he paid a bit more than the bill was, he did not have the change to do it differently, and figured it could be consider a tip to the service providers. The truck, before being moved had the three bags checked for quality, repackaged into the replacement storage bags that were brought along. The truck was then loaded into the cargo plane, as all the team members got into their jump seats to return to the home airfield. Mission accomplished, although one of the rifle members did suffer a graze from one of the automatic weapons, it was nothing serious, and could be addressed once back into home base. It did produce a little blood, but one other member had wrapped it in order to stop the mild bleeding.

It was one of the hazards of the job, and the rifle expert admitted he did not get far enough behind the tree in time for the automatic weapon fire to be returned. Things did have a tendency to happen very quickly when weapon's fire was involved.

Three hours and forty five minutes later, the cargo plane touched down at the airfield they were using. Since it was no longer in use, there was no place to refuel the cargo plane and that issue would need to be addressed for the next expected flight to South America. Although, distance wise, it would not be much different than the Texas flight. It was still a little too much for the cargo plane to cover both on a single refuel.

The vehicles were unloaded from the cargo plane, and everyone waited long enough for Jackson to taxi the aircraft into the empty hanger. Once the doors were closed, he got into one of the vehicles and the team returned to the home base, although it was late, nobody at home base had retired except for Zoe. Zoe Dubois found sleep was only a portion of the things she was compelled to do to keep herself in condition for the type of work she chose to do. It required the use of a large number of beauty aids and she took care of getting it, since she was selective about which products worked best for her. Although no other team member could comprehend the needs she had, they did not do the exact same type of work she performed. To Zoe, her body and appearance, was no different to her, than most of the others making certain their weapon was cleaned and lubricated, to insure proper functioning when called upon. None of them wanted a weapon to jam as a result of neglect, much the same as men did not find wrinkles and saggy breasts overly attractive. She needed to keep her tools of the trade in as fine of a condition as humanly possible, much like all the other team members. They just used different tools than she, and her body and face were as much of a tool to her, as everyone else was with guns and blades.

The following morning when Romero Trap arrived, he was presented with 120 million dollars, minus the eight thousand for refueling. It was a massive sum of currency, and would need to be placed into another numbered account. Considering they were flying under the government radar, he did not want to risk the government deciding from some other branch, they were criminals to seize funds and equipment from. The funds would be much easier for them, but with his team, it would take an army battalion to get the equipment. He could guarantee the battalion losses would be awfully high to risk so many lives over weapons and other armaments. The cargo plane was certainly not worth that much risk, nor the other vehicles.

Jackson Frye had inquired from Romero Trap where to best refuel the cargo plane prior to going to South America, for the second leg of the funding project. Romero knew of the nearby airfield that replaced the one they were using, and they did not ask a whole lot of questions. He gave his second in command 10,000 dollars back, to have it done in the next day or two. It was also time to arrange the exchange with the second cartel in South America, and they would get to take possession of the uncut drugs for their 120 million dollars, minus refueling cost once again.

Things with the team, progressed nicely for the beginning of the long term assignments. The middle of the following week the South American deal was to be made. The cargo plane had been fully refueled, and was ready to go, with the large truck still inside, and the two tons of drugs inside the truck. The meeting would take place at an airfield in Peru, where this cartel had complete control of the airfield. A part of the exchange, if the drug were as uncut as it seemed, on top of the 120 million dollars in exchange for the drugs, the cargo plane would be refuel without any cost to the team. It was intended to be a sign of good business from a far less troublesome cartel. Peru's government relied on the income the cartel generated, and though drugs were considered to be illegal the world over, it was one of the profit producing crops the country had, and keeping governments and business alike operating, it required money and the cartels in Peru, paid more than their fair share. The cartels wanted no part of defining the government process, as long as they were left to conduct the only business, they knew would produce profits to keep everyone content. From the US viewpoint, it seemed to work well in that country, and as long as no threat to the nation existed, they would continue to let them do business as they saw fit. They could not guarantee the Peruvian government that large shipments entering the United States, if discovered, would not be seized. The cartel knew this to be a risk of the business they were in, and could not stop it from happening, although it would set them back a little bit, it was accounted for in the profit margins.

When Jackson Frye and his handful of team members arrived in Peru, things went much easier than with the Mexican cartel. The cartel was aware of the problems that occurred in San Antonio as it was made public by various news broadcasts. It was labeled as a drug deal that went badly wrong, and the authorities had no clue of what really occurred, but since the bodies of cartel members were found and not a single one was a citizen of their country, Mexican authorities were in charge of investigating the how and why it occurred. They made no real progress, and it was doubtful they ever would. It did keep the Peruvian cartel on guard, but at the same time, nobody in their profession had much use for the way the Mexican cartel operated, and thought it was more of a justice than a tragedy.

With the cargo plane on the airfield, and the truck unloaded, the Peru cartel, the same as the other, randomly testing four packages instead of three. Both parties to the meeting had brought trucks, it was decided easier to exchange plates and keys, than unload and reload the different trucks. The DEA truck would now be in another country and the Peru cartel would take possession of a late model diesel GM truck, of literal the same size and year of the Ford model the team would return with. The funds were checked and trucks exchanges, with the passing of 120 million dollars between the cartel and Jackson Frye. The Ford diesel truck was loaded onto the cargo plane, while it was being refueled. The cartel drove off with the other truck, and not a single shot was fired by anyone of the entourage involved in the exchange. It was a very simple business deal, with both parties getting what they came for in the meeting. Once the plane was refueled and the truck secured in the cargo hold. The team returned to home base, and still had literal half a fuel load left once back in the hanger it was kept.

The following morning Romero had another large sum of dollars to put into numbered accounts. He had broken it up to three accounts to start with, thinking he may need a few more to keep funds always available. The possibility of having fund seized by the government was always a remote possibility, but that would only happen if someone on the team got sloppy, and they were too well trained for that. Still, he wanted to be entirely safe of losing all his funding in one fell swoop by some government want to be. He set up a third numbered account all in offshore banks, all receiving investment and interest earnings for as long as they were on deposit, with the understanding there may be times withdrawal might be required for their business acquisitions. The banks did not really take note of the type of business they were in, and in all honesty did not care. If they did more, identification and procedures to open an account would be required. It was one of the primary reasons Romero Trap utilized these types of off shore banking organization.

He and his business would remain quite anonymous to the entire world. He just needed to keep track of his key codes to each of the banks entertaining the team's funds. He had with the last monies made his second and third weekly installment of the team's payment. He kept so much money in his personal safe to cover at least six months, without a new income from somewhere. He also had to include a rather hefty food bill. The remainder of the funds, were now equally divided among three numbered accounts. Each having approximately 90 million dollars. Before the interest and earnings started to arrive. His hope was the assignments would continue to allow them to grow, as well as make it so he did not have need to make any withdrawals to infringe upon the rather lucrative earnings promised. He understood there was no guarantee of those earning, but past performances were quite good at each of the three banking firms.

It was now time to find out if President Thomas Hardesty had decided on the first assignment on the list he alone kept. He would make an appearance at the White House the following morning, to see if he might get answers for his team of professionals to keep them from becoming too bored or complacent. It was not something that he usually had to deal with, but he also never had assignments for this length of time.

After his typical coffee pot of breakfast, Romero Trap headed to the White House for an appearance, ahead of his expected daily appearances that would start in less than a week's time. The first week of the New Year was rapidly approaching, and being in his profession, holidays were not something he often celebrated. His team was not overly concerned with holidays either, since they were just other work days to them as well.

His modest apartment was never used for cooking anything outside of the use of the coffee maker. He long ago decided cooking took too much time, and to grab food on the run or at a restaurant, was his best means to ensure he had nourishment. He was not sure how that would play out in the White House, but President Thomas Hardesty told him his time would be spent being more someplace else, doing appearances on behalf of the government's primary leader, even though those appearances would largely be false. He also assumed some of the more public appearance would truly take place, he would have to be somewhere, if it was worthy of a national news broadcast, and it would not look good for him to be a no-show with the President's reputation on the line.

His arrival was nothing spectacular, but he did not have to jump through all the security detectors as before. He had pretty much free access to where the President would be found, but he still had to go through the secret service announcement to enter the Oval Office, since Thomas Hardesty was not the only occupant for a few more days.

It did not take long before he was permitted entrance to the Oval Office. It would appear from the topic of conversation; the outgoing president was no longer going over things needed to be known by the incoming president. It was however, a conversation concerning the Pentagon's insatiable appetite for a skirmish, outside of the United States. Once again neither president could find rhyme nor reason behind the request. The general who was present with the proposal was doing his utmost to protest the denial, but since he really could not come up with justification for his request, he left in a huff.

Romero Trap found humor in the entire process, although he did not give it the emotional outburst it deserved. If it were him proposing such a plan to any of his covert people in charge, he would have fully expected rolling on the floor fits of laughter from his upper management. In some ways though, Romero Trap also felt embarrassed for the warrior trying to do what he was best trained to do. Romero Trap still knew a realistic need had to exist, and be presented properly to get the desired results. It seemed to be something the Pentagon big wigs had overlooked for far too long.

President Thomas Hardesty excused himself for the time being, under the guise of needing to use the restroom, after such a foolish proposition and had Romero Trap tag along to avoid his need for secret service. It did not take long for Thomas Hardesty to let Trap know of his first assignment, which would not be easy. It was a terrorist group that had long created havoc around the globe, and appeared to be on every nation's list of groups most needed to be removed from the planet. Romero Trap asked if he could expect a price for the assignment from the US government, as he would be trying to do the same for all the others. Thomas Hardesty said he would need to do some checking, but thought the US government could part with 15 million dollars for the removal of the leader of the terrorist group. He knew there would be a lot more people to remove from the group, aside from the leader, but in all past assignments, it was only the leader who had a bounty. Romero Trap assured him that had not changed, but all things considered for the assignment, he would require a lot more other countries to match his bounty to make the assignment a reality. They would need to obtain a good deal of materials for this type of dirty work, and largely it would consist of ammunition and explosives, that were not available at the armory. He did not know personally where to obtain those items easily.

Thomas Hardesty told Romero Trap to expect a call later this evening, when he had more of an opportunity to look into it. Trap gave him his burner phone number to make the call to provide that information. They both returned to the Oval Office, where Trap remained until lunchtime, when he made his exit of the White House.

Once leaving the White House, he went to the team's base to start the planning and obtaining of additional countries to provide the funding, to remove the largest threat in the world. Per government and maybe some key businesses, the bounty was 15 million, and he needed to see 150 million dollars promised, prior to making the move.

The next thing they did was use the computer system for satellite images of the area in the Middle East considered home to these terrorists, and the government of the United States had long been trying to keep tabs on them. Romero Trap also informed the group he had on three separate occasions tried to find a way to eliminate the leader of this group, to no avail. He could not find a way to separate him from his security detail, but thought this time there was a means to do so. He explained largely to Zoe Dubois, that this particular twisted follower of the Koran, was intent on getting his portion of paradise while still among the living. He had an insatiable appetite for young women, and was doing his utmost to keep himself in paradise on earth, at least from his perspective. He frequented a few places for that exact purpose, but was always surrounded by his security detail entering the establishment. He was a fair bit shorter than those in his security detail, so a clean sniper shot was never obtainable. Nobody else could get close enough to the fanatic but Zoe, she was the most likely to do just what needed to be done.

Zoe told him he would need to speak to her a little more privately on the matter before a decision would be made. That told Romero she would likely do it, but it was worth far more than 1,000 dollars a week in her portion of the profession she was in. He did not know what amount she would demand, but considering her skills and attributes to get close enough to complete the mission, he would likely agree to whatever price she had in mind.

For much of the remainder of the daylight hours, locations and geography of those locations were studied in detail for the assignment. One base was likely to hold the majority of the upper echelon of the terrorist group. It was a rather large base, and outside of the area they actually held, the geography was largely in their favor. The terrorist group was also known to have a perimeter rigged with explosives, to forewarn those in the camp of approaching trouble. Initial details were worked out among his team members, and Jackson thought it would take every one of the crew not involved in close quarter's combat. The dozen members of that group, were not likely to get that close, and there was no point in putting them into a situation where they could not use their best skills. Although they may be useful in taking out the security detail for Zoe to fulfill her mission. That could be worked out later into the mission planning and details.

After nightfall Romero Trap and Zoe had their private discussion. Zoe knew just how dangerous her mission might be, and figured she would normally be entitled to 50 million dollars to successfully complete her end of it for a high profile target. Romero Trap could not argue her point, and it was a condition of her accepting the assignment to start with, she would get paid accordingly to her professional standards. He agreed to her conditions, but the mission had to be completed prior to her payment. She in turn agreed to that, but since she was not the most useful in scrounging and other duties for her 1,000 dollars a week, she would do it 30 million dollars.

The next assignment had been accepted, and from Romero Trap's experience of past work, it would take three to six months before it would be accomplished.

5

The Terrorist Job

Romero Trap's few days before his regular White House appearance went by in a flash. During that time, the outline of a detailed plan was being worked out by the team. In his phone conversation from Thomas Hardesty, he was informed of the best possible location to obtain all the explosives and additional ammunition he would need, and told it would not be easy to walk in and take what they needed. The best approach considering the skills of his team, as he was sure they had not gotten worse over the years, he might be best served to have forged military acquisition forms for the materials required. He provided Trap the name of a high ranking commander, but did not know if any of his people could forge the commander's signature. It would mostly likely require having worked with the commander in the past. He passed the information onto the team for Jackson to see if it could be done that way.

His first day at the White House with President Thomas Hardesty the sole possessor of the Oval Office, was spent doing speeches with the Senate and the Congress as a matter of trying to show appreciation of working with them all in the hopes of a bi-partisan group of elected government office holders. Neither President Hardesty nor Romero Trap made any reference to party names, to show there was no line to draw in the sands of government. President Thomas Hardesty was by far the more eloquent of the two in speech making protocol. Romero Trap was not that experienced in the methods, where he was more familiar with making proposals and personnel requests, for given tasks needing to be done or fulfilled. He did not believe that was a good approach for politicians, so he stumbled through his speech like a first grader, making his first classroom speech as a part of a school assignment.

Thomas Hardesty did try to clear the path for him, by introducing his Vice President to each of the group. With a smile on his face and honesty flashing in eyes he stated, Trap had been a 30-year participant in government affairs from behind the political scene, and his accomplishment were many; but even he did not have clearance to see the classified documents that published his accomplishments. Trap did not know how his friend could outright lie to a body of politicians with such visible integrity.

There were a good deal of questions concerning Romero Trap, and after ten similar questions all worded slightly differently. Trap answered by saying he had taken a sworn oath of secrecy to his deeds long before being in the political limelight. Even if the President asked him directly, the secrets would remain secrets. He was trained to withstand all types of torture methods in order to maintain that secrecy, and it would not change, no matter how many ways they asked the same question.

By the looks on half of the faces of the both groups with that answer, Romero Trap was fully anticipating diaper changes, in the House and Senate. The process between the two groups took all day, largely due to the fact that politicians like to hear themselves speak, using 150 words, when all it took was seven or eight in a simply worded form of a question. Another reason Romero Trap had no use for most them. They spent hours, elongating a simple statement to the point you lost track of the topic altogether. He assumed it had largely to do with spending time on the campaign trail, using this same tactic, to avoid giving a real answer to any question posed to them.

It was not going to be easy to get away to the team's location, if this was how things were going to go every day in the White House. First real day on the job without an outgoing president on board, was totally wasted. They did not return to the Oval Office until 8 PM. Romero Trap told President Hardesty, if he had to endure this too long, his next assignment would be self-inflicted. Hardesty chuckled, and told him his first task would be the President, and then he would have clear reason for the self-inflicted assassination. Hardesty told him that after this day, the advantage was all his, you want to see the president, you need an appointment, and if they give a long winded dissertation over the reason for their appointment, he could have them removed by secret service immediately. Romero Trap replied that there was a bright side to being surrounded by secret service agents, but he still did not need them meddling in his primary task as Vice President. Thomas Hardesty could not argue the point in the slightest, as he much preferred his Vice President work his profession, in the manner he was most adept. Even if it was covert to the rest of government. Tomorrow, the toll free voting lines will go active for the people, the program was written to monitor for anyone trying to vote more than a single time, by using social security numbers, a requirement to have voting status. It would also verify age based on the information used for the social security number, since it had to have a date of birth supplied to obtain. It would further prevent people from using their children's social security numbers, to slant the vote, since age was still a factor in eligibility to exercise the right to vote.

The day after, the first bill to the people reforming the taxation program of this country will go active for one week, using the vote of the people to determine if it becomes law. In essence, although it will be a little wordier to account for the legality of it in the eyes of the Supreme Court, it will set a flat tax rate based on total income to individuals earning 30,000 dollars or more annually at 10 percent. If a person makes 29,999.99, they pay no tax. The 10 percent will hold up to 79,999.99 dollar where at 80, 000 the rate goes to 13 percent and over 125,000 dollars annually to 15 percent, anything over 250,000 dollars annually will be at 20 percent, the highest tax rate in the bill. To start with, businesses will continue under the current program, but the IRS will largely be closed down except for those who only deal with businesses. The business law are bit too complicated to go right into the flat tax program, but it will be in the procedures to complete by the time the second year of his first term goes past.

The next bill, one week after the voting is closed on the flat tax appeal to the people. Will be largely to empower the people to do what they have always had the right to do, but failed to understand they had the right. If a Senator or Congress person is failing to perform for the people by the people, as the constitution clearly states, the people who elected that official, have the right to fire that official, without right of retirement for failing to comply with rules governing his position in the first place. "If I had my way, they would be tried for treason, but I will not go quite that far in the beginning." Thomas Hardesty ended with.

Romero Trap could see the President was fully involved in reforming government and the quality of life of the people, who made all of government possible, but it was far too big to ever get the country under a higher quality of life without major changes. Hardesty wanted the people to truly make that decision, since those who were elected seemed most interested in filling their own pockets, than act on behalf of the people. Romero Trap said he needed to go get something to eat, since all he had all day was his morning pot of coffee. President Thomas Hardesty said he could aid in that issue and they went to the dining room of the White House. The President's wife was already present as was his daughter, who was going to start her first semester in the University of her choosing. She delayed her entrance at the start of the school year with all of the election process, and needing to know where home would be to the family. His son was well entrenched into the west coast, and was in no hurry to return home, since word was, his favorite subject was bedding the opposite sex. With secret service now present for his son, those rumors were confirmed by none other than the person obtained by Romero Trap.

As his father, regardless of whether he was also President of the United States, he inform that secret service member, if his son ever forced his will onto a woman, the agent had his permission to beat some sense into his son. It was possible it may come to that, and he was not one to allow such atrocious behavior from anyone, much less the son of the president. He was not going to act like he had privileges beyond the normal citizen.

He did not inform his wife of this conversation with her son's secret service detail, and did not wish to alarm her, but knew if such an incident did occur, his wife would know. Before arriving in the dining room, Hardesty informed Trap that the chefs of the White House prepared meal for kings and queen for nearly 250 years, so it was obvious to him, they knew how to make some truly fine meals. He told Trap he might get spoiled and want to eat at the White House every night, which as the Vice President, he held that privilege.

Romero Trap could not even pronounce the French name provided for the meal served, although he could identify it had chicken involved. Regardless of what it was called, the meal was absolutely spectacular and Trap stated largely to the president, 'You are absolutely correct, one could get spoiled quickly with meals of this manner regularly." President Thomas Hardesty replied, "I hate to say I told you so, But…." His wife said, her husband says he has known you for a number of years, but she did not recall seeing Trap before in his company, what exactly did he do with the government?

Trap said he simply provide a much needed service that he was not allowed to discuss due to government classified procedures. She tried to ply a little more information out of him. He had to reply about the much overused saying of if she was told he would have to kill her, but in this particular case it was a reality. At which she responded with, "You're not going to tell me you were some type of sniper or assassin are you?" Trap not showing a single trace of his internal feelings said, "That is exactly right, I am not going to tell you that. An oath is only an oath if you keep it. I can say that the government we have, has many things that they do not wish to become public knowledge, which likely goes all the way back to President George Washington. Although they did find out the British government had a very large price on his head for any proof of his meeting his end, sooner than nature came into the picture."

The best thing to come out of the first official day of the new leaders of the country, was Romero Trap was allowed to turn down having secret service for his protection, especial since he knew more about keeping himself protected, than they did. Secret service was not accustomed to having people like Trap holding public office. Most of them quite literally beg for their protection, largely because they served themselves far more than the people or even the government, and needed to be worried about deeds from their past haunting them.

After dinner and his short chat, Romero Trap wanted to return to his far more modest one bedroom apartment, where he knew every inch of the floors, walls and where all the furniture was placed. He did get coffee from the dinner, and even that was better than anything he found for home use, but he truly doubted he would be able to obtain what the White House served from their kitchen, which he noticed was probably three times the size of his entire apartment. His apartment was 1,000 square feet, large for a one bedroom apartment. It had a large bedroom with a walk-in closet. The most unique feature he most enjoyed, was the large bathroom with a large double sink, with a wall separating the two sinks and a door. From the bedroom he had a very large bathroom with the inside door open, from the living area and modest kitchen area, it appeared as a half bath.

Romero Trap managed to return to his own little safe place in time to get some rest. He was accustomed to poor sleep habits during his career, waiting endless hours for a target to appear, and have that clean shot. Hours upon hours of reconnaissance to move forward on an assignment, and untold other reasons, but today was the first time he encountered the problem of wanting to go to sleep while listening to some long drawn out meaningless babble. As a result of the effort made toward not doing so, he was far more tired than spending 48 hours without sleep waiting for his shot. He was expected to be at the White House by 7 AM each morning for the time being, although he hoped he did not need to stay all day long, to catch up on how the team was coming along with the next assignment. He did something he had not done for a long time, he set the alarm to insure he was up in time to get in his pot of coffee in the morning, and all the other essentials to be at the White House in time. He was also used to getting sleep when the opportunity presented itself, so there was not a set wake up time.

THE TERRORIST JOB

The alarm startled him from his sleep, and the only thing he knew was, it did not seem all that long enough. He started the coffee maker; glad it was the kind that had a storage tank to allow coffee made quickly. He did not like waiting for his first cup of instant energy boost. It took him 45 minutes to empty the pot, and be ready to leave for the White House.

Once he arrived, the first thing the President asked was if he wanted breakfast, since that was where he was going. Romero Trap thought he already had breakfast, it was called coffee, but he went along with Thomas Hardesty to the dining area for the first family. President Thomas Hardesty asked the chef to prepare two White House New Orleans style omelets for him and the Vice President. His wife and daughter were late risers and would be in later in the morning.

Romero Trap asked what a New Orleans omelet was, and Thomas Hardesty told him it was a jazzed up Spanish omelet, which told Trap nothing, except he doubted it played music when served. When the food arrived not terribly long after, Romero Trap examined his omelet which had an abundance of green in it. He assumed incorrectly; it was a generous portion of green bell pepper. His first taste told him why you never assume anything, as the saying goes, it make an ass out of you and me. His intestinal fortitude did not take kindly to the peppers that were not bell peppers, but more likely something of south of the border items like jalapeño peppers. The cup of coffee he got did not do anything to curb the unpleasant sensations he felt to his palate or throat. Since he could not decipher the difference in the omelet which green item was which, he left the majority of it on his plate. He was not one of those people who fared well with spicy food, and informed the President the omelet was more head banger than jazz.

Thomas Hardesty was not aware that Romero Trap was sensitive to food with hot peppers, but he did apologize for causing him any discomfort. He said he simply assumed, considering the dangers of his trade, he was prepared to consume whatever was available to keep up his strength. Trap said that was more likely to be bugs and berries than hot peppers, they did not have lingering aftereffects. Although it did upset the bird population of the area. Trap said his diet over the years never consisted of many gourmet meals, but if it came in a pouch, he was more familiar with those items.

President Hardesty only had a short military experience, and eating the rations provided by the military, was one thing he never enjoyed, which led to his early release. He had a reaction to one of the meals in a pouch that nearly killed him, and put him in an infirmary for three months to recover from it. Once he recovered, he was released from service, since they could not prevent him from being in places where that was the only source of food.

After the President finished his breakfast, the two went to the Oval Office, which was completely empty, except for the two of them. Hardesty inquired behind the close doors how thing were coming along with the assignment he was working on. Romero Trap having not seen his team for a few days was not up to date, and said he hoped to be able to change that today. Last he knew the plans were still being worked out, but they had identified a large camp from satellite imagery, that would seem to be the key location for the majority of the upper echelon of the group to be located. There were two smaller location identified as well, but there was no way his team could cover all three in a timely fashion, and the largest was selected as the primary target. Beyond that he was currently as much in the dark as anyone else, because his team needed to be involved for comfort factors in deciding the best way to take care of the problem. Hardesty had no idea that Romero Trap had given his people so much room to operate, but it made sense to let his own people, who were to perform the action, determine the best means they could accomplish it.

President Thomas Hardesty told Romero Trap that he saw no reason for him to remain in the White House after the lunch hour arrived, it was up to him if he wished to stay for lunch prior to departing, or just leave when lunch was started. Romero said it would depend on what was being served, if it was another spicy entrée, he would leave immediately. Thomas Hardesty assured Trap it was not, because his wife and daughter suffered from the same issues of spicy food as Trap did. His only opportunity for such food, was usually breakfast since they both slept later than his job permitted. The President was already considering his position in political office as a job, rather than an honor of the people of this country. Trap did not know what that would do for his longevity in office.

Around 10 AM in the morning, another Pentagon member sought audience with President Thomas Hardesty and since Vice President Romero Trap was also present the audience was granted. It took all of 10 minutes before President Thomas Hardesty had the general escorted out of the Oval Office, with it being the same desire to start a conflict with the same group already turned down for lack of solid reasoning for going into battle. Thomas Hardesty made one point to the general to inform all of his associates in the Pentagon, any more unjustifiable calls to go to war, and the whole group would be banned from seeing the President.

It told the general that if they did not come up with truly justifiable reasons for starting a conflict with any nation, do not bother presenting it. The President was kept well aware of major concerns across the globe, and he would know when and if such actions would be necessary. He was not looking for a weekly attempt for the Pentagon to send boys to their death, so they could play a chess match with American boys as their pawns.

The general returned to the Pentagon to get together with all the major players in matters of war. He informed the group that they now had a President who not only knew how to play hardball, he knew when and how to put his foot down quite hard. The new President will not tolerate unjustifiable calls to action, as he said, any additional attempts would get us all banned from having a conversation with him in the future. It would seem the current president is far more concerned with the state of this nation, than that of the globe, but they still did not realize what role the second in command would play in it. The generals all had some dealing with Romero Trap earlier in his career, before he was a planner, he was doer of actions required for the security of the nation, or at least it was deemed so at the time. His reputation was stellar, and it was quite possible he was placed in his position for behind the scene activities, to keep the military out of the picture. It was also possible; it was done this way to give the president anonymity of actions taken without making the country appear to be behind it. The general's suggestion to all present, was let things play out a while and see where it leads.

At lunch Romero Trap found the aroma of the food irresistible, and stayed for lunch before departing to the team's location. Lunch took nearly an hour, but it was well worth it from Trap's viewpoint. It would be quite easy to eat a couple of times each day with the foods served by the White House chef and staff. He would forego any other breakfasts with the president, to allow him the opportunity to have what he seemed denied most other meals.

Romero Trap arrived at the base camp location at 1:30 PM, and immediately went into getting updates on the progress of the planning. The group had studied the satellite imagery from multiple angles, to determine the best location to place perimeter explosive around the terrorist's largest camp. With two explosive experts, it would likely take four to five nights of setting the explosives in place, and using a remote detonator to trigger all the explosives simultaneously. The camp should think they were being bombed from the air, not the ground. His heavy automatic people needed to be in place for the first explosives, to open fire on the camp and take out as much as possible with the weapons they preferred. Until the dust settled, they could not get into the location for a closer look, but with any luck, the perimeter explosives they set would also trigger all the one the terrorist's had in place, which would need to be located prior to setting their own perimeter explosives. The general concept was the explosives they placed, needed to be inside the ones placed by the terrorist group.

Since most terrorist, use their explosive perimeter as a warning mechanism, the line should be at a similar distance all the way around the camp. Finding a safe passage point between their perimeter and the one placed by the experts on their team, should be marked so they can easily access internally, and place the material they needed around the camp location. Since it will require almost everything done at night, night vision will be needed for the pair, and some form of marking that is only visible with the night vision gear in use. Markings obvious, might alarm the terrorist to activities they are not performing and put

THE TERRORIST JOB

them on alert. Considering there may be as many as 5,000 terrorists inside the location, all precautions needed to be taken seriously.

Calls have also been made to leaders of various governments and a few businesses, and the plan at this time is to collect 50 percent of the 15 million dollar fee up front, and the other upon completion of the assignment. To this point we have 50 countries and businesses to agree, although we have not received a single initial payment, which is to go into the numbered account Jackson Frye had been given. He is monitoring it regularly to see if any deposits have been received, although he was expecting verbal confirmation to insure the right business or country is credited for the first half of the payment. It seems this terrorist group had upset way too many countries and businesses, to allow them to continue to operate.

The satellite imagery also showed the location had a number of vehicles around the camp, although many of them were some form of small truck, there were two transports that appeared to be American. How did they obtain them is the first question? Although there is one thought concerning it, that would explain it without them being supported by some American firm or even our own government. The information for those killed in action never provided the mission they were on at the time, but since our military had attempted a number of missions in and around the area, when they failed and had to evacuate the area quickly, all equipment unable to be taken out, is to be utterly destroyed. It is possible, a mission for that exact purpose was prevented by the loss of troops, and the vehicle taken by those who prevented it being completed. It is only a theory, since records of mission and death records do not coincide in any government reports.

Trap though his theory was the mostly likely, since this terrorist group had played havoc in various parts of their own country, and considering the stance on terrorism internally, he doubted the government, or even any businesses in the country would be supporters of it. The only internal way would be to have a funded cell within the country to obtain such vehicles, but there would be shipping records, unless it went through Mexico.

Romero Trap often wondered why the movie industry often portrait their line of work as all action and no thinking. Like any business, the first part of any plan, started in the mental functions of formation. Trap had spent as much as six months planning for a small assignment, in order to accomplish his assigned task. This task was a much larger scale, and had many minds working out the details. Progress was definitely being made, but there still was no discussion on what materials they needed to obtain in order to go forward in the mission. He realized before the mission was even brought up to the team, they would need to obtain explosives, and most likely a good deal more ammunition to even head to the country this would take place in.

Jackson said as if reading his mind, that they were working on getting forged document to procure additional ammunitions and explosives for the assignment. They were still working on who among them had an idea on which high ranking military commander's name to use for the requisition form, and who knew how to forge a signature to appear like it was from that person. Jackson said although forgery was not entirely unheard of in the line of work they do, most people do not have need to put it to use ever, and some simply do not have it as a skill. At this point we have three people who believe they can do it, and several of the names we knew have gone onto retirement, and we cannot use a retired commander's signature and expect to leave with the materials requested.

Over the next four months, a fully evolved plan was in place, half the payment from 60 countries and businesses had been received, the forged requisition forms were placed and in addition to the explosives and ammunition, a military all terrain transporter was taken, which would seat 24 members and have all the ammunition on board, but the explosives would need to be moved separately. With a vehicle the size of the transporter, the team would not be able to get closer than a mile and half from the base location without being spotted. They needed surprise on their side for the number of terrorists believed to be in the base location used by the upper echelon of the terrorist group. Zoe had her plan in place, and it was decided to have four additional close quarter's combat specialists available to remove the security detail, but after Zoe had performed her mission. They were not going to take it well that their leader died of a heart attack while entertaining a female. To keep her safe from harm, the specialists would be nearby to eliminate the security detail, although there were six to the detail and only four specialists, it was likely at least two would remain outside the building to watch for any suspicious activity potentially targeted toward their leader. They would be the first to go.

The team going to the base location would consist of 24 members, with all the automatic weapons and rifles they could take along. It was absolutely essential to eliminate as many terrorist as possible from a safe distance, and with any luck have some things undamaged to take back to their own location, ideally the other transporter.

They also got all six spare five gallon tanks mounted on the rear of the transporter filled with spare diesel fuel, since these vehicles were not known for their economy and rarely got more than 10 miles per gallon, and with a load, typically less.

Additionally, during the four months his White House time had six supposed week long trips to thank the people of the country for their support, on behalf of the President who sent him, so he could continue to restore the country back to the great nation it once was. The President also got his flat tax bill passed by a large majority of the people who took the time to vote, government downsizing was taking place in areas including the internal revenue service, now only doing businesses. And the people, also passed his bill which was really already something the people had the power to do, and allowed them to fire politicians not working for the people by the people. Five senators and twelve congressmen met that decision made by the people. Additionally, President Thomas Hardesty through the aid of the people put into immediate effect, that there would no longer be expenses covered by the people for any member of the government, where it was not done for the purpose of performing entirely government business. In essence, it brought an immediate halt to aircraft leaving the area used and operated by the United States government, for week long golf outings, and other such nonsense, abused by the political machine of Washington DC. Thomas Hardesty was in some way or another going to get the economy of the government running in the black, before his first term came to an end. The senators and congress people fired, were not replaced, as his next task was to make that smaller as well. Rather than a separate house and senate, he intended to have each state have two representatives, to act on the behalf of the state they came from, and act for those people. The people who each represented, would maintain the right to fire any who were acting outside of the people's interests.

As far as congress and the senate were concerned, Thomas Hardesty had made a good deal of enemies. From the voice of the people, both houses were on their absolute best behavior, and in all honesty to keep their jobs, forced to work hand and hand with the current president. It did not keep the Senate or House of Congress from planning his demise as quickly as possible, to get things back to the way they were, which had become the means they were accustomed to operating. Thomas Hardesty put the secret service members obtained by Romero Trap on full alert, to be wary of any person intent on doing harm to the President, and it included all members of the political machine, as well as other secret service members who were corrupted by the way Senate and Congress ran things before. Make no mistake, prior to Thomas Hardesty in the last 40 years or more, Congress and Senate had been largely the ones to dictate how the president was going to perform in office. Thomas Hardesty was going to let the people decide, who among the Senate and Congress were for or against the people.

With the location of the terrorist base well planned out, Romero Trap in his time at the White House being able to not be present for six weeks, of the four months, requested from the President someway for him to be with his team, when the time came to complete the assignment. Under small operations, Romero Trap had no problems letting his team perform without his watchful eye. This particular assignment was far too large, to not be there for and with them. He might be of some aid in the rifles and automatic weapons, in order to insure the largest number of terrorist were down prior to the team entering the camp location, for a closer inspection and finish off those only wounded. This mission required no survivors, because the hydra must die, to insure the terrorist group could not regroup again. There was no mistake in Romero Trap's

THE TERRORIST JOB

mind, this snake had many heads, and they all needed to be cut off. Romero Trap, also figured his team would be on the ground in the Middle East for two weeks, there was at least five days of preliminary explosive placements, which could only be performed by two of the team members, unless they wanted his aid, since he was at least familiar with setting explosives.

It would take roughly one day each, to fly to and back to the area. In all likelihood it would take another day to get the transporter to and from the location, to use as a station point. Plus, the second trip to get the explosives in the needed location. And if any of the major members of the terrorist group left, and likely to return, they may have some wait time, prior to the optimum conditions for the assault to take place. These were merely some of the conditions Romero Trap could see occurring while on the ground in the Middle East, one of his least favorite locations on the entire planet, because there was always some religious faction at war with another, from the beginning of the world, as far as he could determine. Although he was sure it a least took mankind present to have war among people. The mission had two distinct locations, one being where Zoe would meet up with the terrorist leader, which was a more populated vicinity with lodging, and of course the place in which the leader met up with his paradise attempts. It was doubtful he managed to get to the number often spoken by those of Koran followings in a single evening, but over time he likely exceeded his promised number, again doubtful of the other condition of being virgins.

How any group of people could get so confused over the meaning of a biblical work, was far beyond Romero Trap, but fanatics could change lies into truths, and wine into water, never the other way around. The leader of the terrorist group he sought to remove from the other primary location, was also not too much of a believer in the word concerning alcoholic beverages, as he consumed far more than his fair share, and Trap wondered if this was to get his courage up for the other portion of his intended activities, or a means to prolong the duration. It really did not matter, once Zoe had him, he was history, she never ever failed to complete her assignment, it was the escaping from the overreaction of the security detail, that concerned him most on this particular assignment. Zoe, of all the people in the team was the single irreplaceable element, no other person in the world he lived in, could do what she did repeatedly. Any other woman who did such things, often fell prey to the conscience and overall guilt of what they did one too many times to get over it. Zoe was literally morally void, as a result of her uncle's long time sexual abuse, before she put an end to it for herself, as well as her uncle, she survived, and he did not. She never felt the least bit of remorse for the deed that started her on her path to this profession.

The next morning, Thomas Hardesty informed Romero Trap his two weeks of being unseen were arranged with an out of the country humanitarian visit to the Middle East. The location, although being accurate to his whereabouts, provided very little news coverage concerning anything outside of the number of people dying from some activity or another between the warring religious factions of the region. As long as he remained out of sight of the cameras for the assignment, not a single person would be any the wiser of his true assignment. He could depart in two days, and since the Vice President was going under the radar for this particular event while holding office, he was using military transports to get there. They were a bit less conspicuous than a jet arriving with Presidential markings.

Romero Trap had enough advanced notice to let his team know, and that he would be coming along to give whatever assistance he could to insure the success of the mission. The cargo plane should be loaded with all the equipment they required for the mission, and he expected they would be in the Middle East for two weeks, believing things could not be completed any quicker, without an extraordinary amount of good fortune.

The airfield they would arrive at was a mere 20 miles from the terrorist's main location, but there were no direct roads to get close to the destination selected, and the terrain they would cover was anything but flat. Part of the equipment being taken for this excursion included a number of military issue shovels, since they were not heading into an environment considered to be a tropical paradise. Also, in the forged military requisition form, a towable water tank was included, knowing

THE TERRORIST JOB

none of them could do without drinking water for the length of time they would need to be on the ground. The tank was not large enough to use for showering or bathing, but they could make it with drinking water. Due to the tanks less than all terrain composition though, they may need to take various detours in the trip from the airfield to the planned site, to set up temporary station for the assignment. The sixty countries and businesses had contributed 450 million dollars towards the completion of this mission, with an additional 450 million promised once completed. It would be enough working capital to finance a small army beyond the team of experts Trap already had on hand.

The day for departure to the Middle East arrived, and 29 members of the 37 total people on this team, were on the cargo plane, which had a full tank of fuel, but would require two stops to refuel, before reaching their destination. Trap made certain enough cash funds were taken along to account for the various expenses of the excursion, which would include five hotel rooms for a portion of the time in the Middle East, if not all of it. He could not see any reason for Zoe, and her help to be at the primary location. Refueling a cargo plane would again be required at the landing airfield, as well as two stops between, on the way home. He was not sure how much would be required with the fuel price being so varied in different parts of the world. Trap took a total of 60,000 dollars for the mission, knowing fully well food supplies would be required, although those in the primary location would be anything but gourmet. It was packaged precooked items that were most likely, and his big eaters would likely go a little hungrier than usual.

It took nearly 15 hours of air time, and refueling time to arrive at the designated airfield in the Middle East. Trap had the plane immediately refueled, while the cargo was unloaded, knowing someone was going to need to return to the cargo plane to retrieve the most vital elements to the success of the mission. Considering how much explosives were on the plane; it would likely take two or three people to transfer it in a quicker fashion. He took the return trip duty as his own, and figured the two best supporting member to handling explosives were the two experts. It seemed simple enough to Romero Trap.

It took two hours to cover the 20 miles to the base location, although it was largely due to the number of detours, where the water tank in tow would not make it over the terrain the transporter would, it was not so much of a problem for Trap and the explosive experts to retrace to the cargo plane, and return with the explosives for the assignment that made the explosives the most vital part of the mission at hand. Due to the lovely weather conditions, 25 fox holes were dug in the base station area largely to allow for sleeping less visibly to any who might come across the team, although someone would remain on guard all night, and sleep when the others were working.

It took five days for the explosives and additional fox holes between the two perimeters to be dug. These fox holes were for the weapons people would use during the run of explosives, and be able to start firing onto the location as soon is was safe to raise up out the hole. Most of holes were three feet deep, to allow for either cooler sleeping conditions or no exposure to the debris from the explosions. On the sixth evening, all those with automatic weapons or rifles, went to the designated place between the two perimeters. They had to wait an additional 24 hours, for a single high ranking terrorist to return from wherever he went. Since it had now been a day without any sighting of the terrorist leader, it was assumed it was a result of Zoe completing her part of the mission. Unfortunately, Romero Trap had no way to confirm, since there was no way to have safe communications between the pair of teams. Whatever reason the returning high ranking official left and returned, he appeared highly agitated once he returned. With his return, all eyes were on the cover of darkness to begin the detonation of the explosives. It would be in two more hours, unless the high ranking official made an effort to depart once again. If that were the case, since Romero Trap was highly proficient in rifle fire as a sniper, it was his job to take out the high ranking terrorist and that would also signal the detonations to start.

There was no effort on the part of any higher ranking terrorist and the detonations started as darkness was complete. The commotion in the camp with the explosives going off, and the aid of the ground concussion triggering a vast number of the terrorist explosive devices, was the perfect opportunity to commence firing with automatic and rifle fire. Turmoil and Cyclone were creating total devastation to the terrorist camp, even structures started to fall with the onslaught of high powered automatic weapons fire. Having worked as a team in the past, the two knew to stagger their firing time, to allow for at least one to have ammunition, while the other needed to reload. It was precision teamwork to the likes Trap never needed to teach. After forty five minutes of continuous weapons fire onto the terrorist camp, movement appeared to have ceased. Romero Trap was sure they did not get every member of the group, but there were not too many places left standing to hide in either. Having seen all the explosives detonate between himself and the terrorist camp, he cautiously moved forward ready to fire his weapon. Since he had both a rifle and automatic weapon, he selected the automatic for this. As he closed in on the camp, not a single attempt was made to fire back at him, although he did make himself a little difficult to distinguish from the surrounding terrain. Other team members were also approaching the camp, but since the explosives traveled around the camp, so did the weapons and people using them, so all were approaching from different angles.

They all made it to the camp in about the same time, and the carnage of large caliber automatic weapons was not something most of them had really seen before. It was rather gruesome, but they had all seen bodies before, just typical more intact than some of these were. A body count and check for vitals started and among the 4,936 members of the terrorist group, only two were still somewhat alive. They would not stay that way too much longer, so no more ammunition was wasted to finish what was already going to happen, just it would take a little bit longer. The team being resourceful like always, found a good deal of unused ammunition that they could use, and other ammunition they had no use for whatsoever. Most of the explosive materials, were either used for the terrorist perimeter or went up in the automatic weapons assault on the camp. Romero Trap gave the team 90 minutes to gather all they found useful. He found the transporter had managed to go through the firefight without much damage visible, all the tires were still in good shape, and upon going to the other side, he found the terrorists had a large tank of diesel fuel for the purpose of refilling vehicles. He sent one team member to get the other transporter to refuel, for the trip back to the airbase. As the other team members scoured the remains of the camp, they came upon additional commodities that were never expected. A very large container solidly constructed, had gold bars and uncut diamonds in it, after they removed the padlock.

When Romero Trap was brought to see it, the amount of gold he estimated would be nearly 500 million dollars' worth, but he had no idea concerning the value of the diamonds. He was simply sure it was worth something to somebody more involved in the diamond market, like jewelers. He had the two behemoths, load it onto the additional transporter, and with two now to use, the team could have a little more breathing room on the return trip to the airfield. He did not know if they should bring the nearly empty water tank back to the airfield, knowing with two transporters, space might be an issue. Jackson Frye assured him there was plenty of room, and it may be needed again on future assignment, although he really hoped it would not be to this region again.

Romero told the team to finish up quickly, since it was hardly possible the disturbance that took place did not go totally unnoticed. He estimated the news crews or worse other remains of the terrorist group, might show up and they did not need to be here for that to happen. The second transporter arrived, was refueled and team members started into each vehicle, and they needed to return for the water tank to leave for the airfield. It was all accomplished in 85 minutes, under the time line set originally by Romero Trap, and it was only a momentary stop to get the water tank back in tow to one of the two vehicles. They were actual on the return trip to the airfield, when the ninety minute deadline was reached. It was probably a good thing, because Romero Trap had the team stop the vehicles and kill the lights, as he heard approaching sounds that he thought to be a helicopter engine, and that he had not anticipated, from the terrorists. But from the air, they were too easily spotted moving through the terrain with lights on.

It was as he thought, his ears did not deceive him, and a helicopter was approaching as the flashing lights and sound of the rotors were rather distinguishable. It was not the terrorists, but some kind of news team, and he did not believe it was local. But he was too far away to see which markings it had, with the cover story the President created for him, it was possibly, CNN or other similar networks looking to get a story on the rather elusive Vice President; whom the press had no previous meetings with, and they wondered why. Since almost every major network in the United States, had expanded into the alternative marketplace of televised programming, they all had international news coverage, and teams for that coverage. Once the helicopter was on the ground, it was far more difficult to make them out, as it would be for them. He had the driver start moving again and pay attention to terrain the water tank might not make it through, although with far less water, it would been able to take higher risk ground than when they first arrived.

He did not feel they would have any further chance of being seen, as a news crew would want to get as much of the scene as they could stomach. He did believe, that might be more of an issue for the news crew than his team members, and even he thought the assault was gruesome, and he had seen much over the past 30 plus years. The return trip only took an hour and fifteen minutes, with a much lighter and agile water tank in tow. That was still a long time to cover 20 miles without a single traffic light, but there were no roads either. In the dark, it was highly unlikely they took the identical path they started out with on the way to the assault station location. It did still provide the passengers in the transporter all the same thrills as an amusement park roller coaster.

Once back to the airfield, Romero Trap used a local pay phone to reach the hotel and the name that Zoe Dubois signed in under, certainly would not use her real name for such tasks. All he ask was did all go as planned, she said they were a few sticky moments, but no one was hurt. Unlike his assault team, they managed to have enough return fire from the terrorist camp to have two people wounded, although body armor protects the torso, legs and arms can sometime get in the way of flying bullets. The team had enough members with basic survival skills, which included ways to take care of wounds, and each person typically kept a modest supply of medical supplies upon them when in battle. That was in case no one could get to them immediately. The wounds were not life threatening; one leg was pierce all the way through, but it was not center mass and hit nothing major. The hole was created by 9 millimeter, so not overly large, but it needed to be plugged until better attention could be provided. The second recipient got it in the shoulder, just outside the body armor, and the bullet was still inside likely striking bone mass. He was in a make shift sling after the bleeding was stopped, and he would definitely need more time to recover, and likely be out of team commission a month or more, once back to home base.

His only other statement was to checkout with the rest of her team, and return to the airfield, he could wait for the details when she was back with the rest of the team. One hour later, the team arrived, the rental vehicle they used was turned into the provider and the cargo plane taxied to the runway 40 minutes later.

Romero had to go into the cockpit for the details, because as soon as Zoe Dubois got onto the cargo plane she burst out with, "Damn, it smells like a fucking locker room in here, I will be ill if I do not sit in the co-pilot seat away from the aroma of this sweat box." He truly did not know what she would have expected for 25 men without enough water to bathe or shower for 10 days, in the topical resort they stayed at. Zoe went about her details with saying, "It took three days, nights really, before that ignorant terrorist leader bothered to notice I was even in the room. Granted it was a larger room than the suite he kept reserved, but apparent he is a man of habit, who prefers to stick with the women he has already had carnal knowledge of in his room. Also, during the first three days, while I was trying to get his attention, the man who claims to be follower of the Koran, put down enough alcohol every night, to embarrass half of a dozen sailors on shore leave.

On the fourth night, I final got to meet him, what a pig. Once in his room, I had to listen to an hour's worth of his twisted take on the Koran, where just about every passage he quoted led to killing the infidels, I have no idea what faction of Islam he separated from, but the Koran does not say any of the things that came out of his mouth. On top of that, once I was disrobed for the true purpose of our meeting he passed out from his imbibing. I found not a single reason not to insert the syringe into his carotid artery, loaded with nothing but air. He was dead in five minutes, but it took fifteen minutes for me to maneuver his carcass to appear he was having sex. Then I had to go into academy award mode, and perform my best scream of fear and terror, to rush to the door fully disrobed, and get the security agent outside to verify he appeared to have died from a fatal heart attack. The security guard was a bit suspicious, but he did not see me as threat from my appearance, and allowed me to dress, and leave the room, where the other security guards of his were making their way to the room I was leaving. Once outside the door, I let the other boys in for clean-up work on aisle nine. We have all been spending your money, ever since at the hotel. How did your end fare?"

Romero Trap when over the basic details including two members with less than life threatening wounds, and the number of dead terrorists left in their wake. He also thought he saw a national news crew sniffing around in the aftermath, was his parting statement. He returned to his jump seat to lessen the aroma that had Zoe so upset upon entering the cargo plane. They had one more refueling stop before arriving back, to their home base location and nearby abandoned airfield. With the additional transporter, they had now possessed two rugged terrain vehicles, which would likely come into use again, considering the length of their assignment to the president.

It was still a very long time in flight, and upon landing the first thing to do was get his wounded people to better help at Walter Reed Medical Center. Since they claimed to have a room reserved for him or his people, he thought he should test that theory. The problem here was, by the itinerary set by the president, he could not show up at Walter Reed while also being somewhere in the Middle East, he was not due back for another two days. He asked Jackson Frye if he felt up to the additional trip, using the sedan to Walter Reed. He said it would not be a problem, but he thought at least one of the team was there for a least a few days, to have healing time from the surgery, that would be required to remove the bullet. Romero Trap said as far as he knew, his name could still be used, and that Frye was still performing work under his direction before getting into his current position. Frye said fine with him, but all of the people on his team had earned the right to forever go there for any reason. It was one of the few fringe benefits of having served their country.

Romero Trap returned to his little apartment, where the first thing he did was take a long overdue shower, before going to bed. He had the direct number to reach the President, but that would not take place until he had some well needed sleep.

6

The Mexican Cartel

Romero Trap let the President know he arrived back into DC, but would remain away from the White House until his expected return from the Middle East tour of finding meaningful relations with the region. He was not expected for another two days. President Thomas Hardesty asked if he had seen the news concerning what happened in the Middle East, while he was still there. Trap said he had not had the time, and said he only was aware of some news crew arriving, but did not know for certain which one it was that had the helicopter.

Thomas Hardesty said that CNN had been running the story for the last six hours, they may be wearing it out, but it has had a major impact on the area, largely for the better of those affected by the group's presence. There seems to be little left of the group, in order to return to the form, they had prior to the last 24 hours. He said it seems somebody, had done their country a great service by removing one of the most active terrorist groups around the world.

Romero Trap in keeping with his cover story said he hoped one day to meet the people responsible for such a good deed to the world, as his parting statement to end the phone conversation.

The next thing he did was check on his team, especially those who were wounded, but he still could not go to the medical center to do it personally. He found that one of the members wounded was back with the group after getting stitched up and antibiotics to prevent infection. As well as bandaging that required daily changing. Since his wound was in the leg, it was something he could attend to himself, after the doctors at Walter Reed released him a few hours after arriving. His other member, was in surgery for a number of hours, as the bullet was deeply lodged and required extreme care in removing it, to prevent further damage and issues with the location of the wound. He would be in recovery for a minimum of one week under doctor's care. This was to insure no infection issues arose from the wound, and also to make certain they were able to remove all the fragments that occurred with the impact to the bone, although it was not irreparably damaged. He would still require an additional month of rehabilitation procedures to return him to fully normal movement, and functioning of his shoulder and arm that were affected. It was unfortunately, a risk all the team members faced anytime they went on a mission. They were often outnumbered by the opposition, although in most cases not to the degree of this last assignment. The national network news also brought many of the 60 countries and businesses making their second installment of the payment.

It was largely time for the team to get some rest and relaxation, while there was no immediate assignment to be involved with, but Trap knew that would not last much more than week. The gold was moved into the stronghold room with all the weapons, as was the diamonds. Romero Trap would need to select a few of the diamonds to present to a jeweler to find out what value they may hold for the team. He decided to take care of that little issue that day to determine if he should unload them all immediately, or do it in small batches to different jewelry makers.

Being uncut diamonds, the value was less than those already cut and mounted, but it was how they all started to have a finished piece of jewelry, whether in a ring, or necklace or bracelet, was a matter of how it best presented itself once cut precisely. Trap was no expert in jewelry, but wondered how much Zoe knew, since she was the high priced professional in the group. He asked her if she was busy, and if she had much experience with uncut diamonds in determining a fair value to get for them. She was quite familiar with diamonds, she had received many payments for her services in that fashion, because it was easier for clients to pay in that form than cash. It was also much less bulky. She did have a contact for just such types of transactions, but it was not in the DC area. She did have an idea about how many carats, an uncut diamond could allow, but it was still in the jewelry maker's hands to determine if it would be a single or multiple finished diamonds.

He asked her if she had seen the diamond stash they returned with, and she had not, since she was trying to stay away from all the unclean people he returned with, but the showers were quite busy in the hours after they returned, and the men, once all the ladies were finished, were using both showers. She also said, he failed to have one lady in with the ladies, although she seemed rather used to being in barracks with a large number of men. Lacy Louis if he did not know was also female, and she was one of the close quarter's specialists. We took it upon ourselves to get her in the right room, but she is not overly shy when it comes to being around all men. Granted she is not the curviest and over developed woman she ever laid eyes on, but she had all the right components to be in the female sleeping quarters. Trap had made that mistake with Lacy before, and knew it was largely because partly of the same reason pointed out by Zoe, and the fact she kept her hair nearly in male fashion. He apologized for his error and managed to say to Zoe, it was not the first time he made that error with Lacy.

Zoe said his apology may not be necessary, since it took Zoe, who had considered herself a good judge of gender, three days to figure it out. It was the secrecy to the shower, that triggered her looking deeper into what Lacy really was, and her husky voice did not make it any easier, nor that she behaves more like one of the guys than girls. Romero Trap took Zoe to the secure room used largely for armaments, but now it was the safe considering its contents. Zoe took a look at the rather large container of uncut diamonds, and said there was no way any single diamond manufacturer or processor could take the quantity he had.

There was at least 200 million dollar worth of uncut diamonds, and some of them were 20 carat size, unheard of for a single diamond to be obtained from it. She said it takes a handful of various sizes, and she would go with him to have them evaluated, but she could not say value to expect until she saw what he selected. Using one of the storage bags obtained for the drugs that were opened and repackaged prior to exchanging them for cash with the Peru cartel, he filled it half full and let Zoe examine it. She said it may still be too much for a local jeweler, but they could try, he should not expect less than 20 million for his selection.

Using Romero Trap's own personal vehicle, they went to the jeweler that Trap had in mind. Zoe's estimate was pretty darned accurate, the jeweler told him it was worth 22 million dollars as they were, once cut and polished by a jewelry maker, they were worth five times that much, but there was a fair amount of work involved going from uncut to polished and mounted. He could buy them, but he could only do it with a check, no jeweler keeps that much cash on hand, simply due to the forever possibility of a heist by profession thieves. Most of them were only interested in currency and finished products. Trap took him up on the check, and asked since he had obtained quite a bit more, if he could suggest other jewelers to visit. He said his best bet would be the diamond exchange in New York City, but in DC he only knew of two other jewelers who could purchase similar quantities to that he was getting. Once a purchase like that is made, it usually takes 18 months before a jeweler can make another such purchase, himself included. The absolute best place to get the most for the product was Antwerp, Belgium, which is the world's marketplace for diamonds. It may be convenient to you or maybe not, but he thought he should at least let them know the best place to go.

Zoe said she had forgotten about Belgium, but not knowing how to do that particular venture would present its own problems. Even though they were the best place to go, the quantity he possessed would take a minimum of a full week to get all of it sold, since like all jewelry makers and buyers, it was a collection of smaller groups, and no single company could do that quantity in a single purchase. Also, since Antwerp is more

THE MEXICAN CARTEL

like a wholesale outlet, he would be better off going through jewelers to get a slightly better price, since they would offer what it would cost them to get it in Belgium.

Over the next two days, Zoe and Romero repeated the process for the other two jewelers suggested turning diamonds into cash amounts, all deposited into Romero's working funds account for the time being. All in all, they turned enough uncut diamonds into 75 million dollars, still leaving more than half the diamonds in the safest place they had available in the building they were using.

Once returning to his White House appearances gig, the President made Romero Trap aware of the next assignment, being the Mexican Cartel, that they had once done what was thought to be significant damage, but apparently not enough.

When he had the opportunity to get to the team's location, a team was selected by Jackson Frye for the first portion of any assignment, the surveillance of the primary location used by the cartel. They were able to get the location with satellite imagery, but they needed to know more about the comings and goings of the major players now running the cartel. They were still a little bit in disarray from the loss they incurred four months prior, but it did not completely bring a halt to the operation. They would not get nearly the price from the terrorist group as the cartel, but in this case, many of the largest contributors were the South American cartels and governments. They only got a total of 250 million dollars promised under the same terms as was common for Romero's profession, half up front and the other upon completion. The reason for this method was simple, it cost money for most groups who performed this type of trade, in order to be able to even attempt completing such a task. It made it possible for groups like Romero Trap, to keep the expenses reasonable in order to collect profit, once completed. It also made it so there was incentive from all parties, to finish a job once started. No government or business wanted to expend funds without results, but also understood the cost of doing such business was often rather high, especially for groups, unlike Trap who could obtain many materials without forking over large sums of cash. Other such organization had to go through black markets to obtain sufficient ammunition and weapons, and even though large portions of these materials were stolen by other parties, they had high price tags to be placed on the availability list of the black market. Even the black market, had gone into computerized inventory and sales sites, but it was in a lesser known and tougher area to access on the World Wide Web. It had many different names around the world, the most common was the dark web. It took special passcodes to access it, and unlike other more common internet access, you required an invitation from a member of the dark web, who was considered to be untouchable by authorities.

These safeguards of the deep web were what made it most difficult for it to be infiltrated by agencies of various governments to bring its activity to a complete halt. There would always be some breakdown, but it was considered acceptable losses for the type of business conducted, and also a contributing factor in the high price of goods available. Those goods were seldom found at the local hardware, retail, or grocery chain of stores. You did not purchase heavy artillery or large caliber automatic weapons or explosives ready to use at any of those stores, but on the deep web, they were plentiful commodities for those willing to pay the price for such items. Trap preferred to have his team obtain them in less costly fashion, it insured they got their weekly payment for the assignment. They had no need for additional ammunition or weapons at this time for the Mexican cartel, but they needed eyes on them, to see which people appeared to be performing what function, and just how much product they were producing. Romero Trap fully intended to do harm to the cartel in multiple ways on this particular assignment. First, he wanted to remove any figure in the cartel that seemed to have some form of power, also since the production location was the one selected, it simply seemed at some point all the major players would make regular appearances for whatever reason they decided was appropriate in their line of work. He also knew a number of people working this type of location, were largely innocent of making the cartel what it was. Whether they were forced into service to keep family member alive, or obtained through slave markets, or simply abducted, to be put to work was not his first concern. What concerned him most, was how to spare the innocent, to eliminate the evil.

THE MEXICAN CARTEL

Jackson Frye had selected his team of four members to spend some time south of the border. Romero Trap set down the initial plan, which would be a little time consuming to make the trip, and return. It seemed foolish to him to use a cargo plane for a small group, and be able to have it available for any additional assignments that might come up, before the eyes had seen all that was needed. There were two things necessary to do prior to the departure, both involving a cargo van. First, since they had been used for moving drugs, the one chosen needed to be thoroughly cleaned and sanitized to insure going through the border customs entry and exit, no drug sniffing dogs had reason to detain his people. The second, was to put into most likely the cargo area of the floor, a concealed storage compartments. This was to hold the cash needed for the trip, and possibly weapons, which he did not wish to be used, since they were only supposed to be eyes of the team. A burner phone would also go with the group to update Jackson with intelligence obtained.

It required Romero Trap also providing funds to get the torches necessary for welding the additional compartment into the cargo van, and if they were going to do one, they might as well do both. For the departing members and the other equipment, Romero Trap handed over 40, 000 dollars, which ought to cover all the costs, with some to spare. He did not expect his surveillance team would need to be gone more than a month, and where they were going, lodging and meals were not overly expensive. It was more a matter of selecting people who enjoyed the spicy variety of food offered in the region. Jackson Frye had made that part of his requirements to consider being a member of this particular eyes only assignment. The team members going, all had the equipment required for distance viewing. They did not want to be too close, and it was necessary for them to select different angles of the location, to see all that went on, not just through the front door.

It would take at least two days travel to get to the border from DC area, as long as they drove in shifts. They were entitled to stop for 8 hours rest somewhere between DC and the customs entry and exit of the United States. He had the four members of the team take military uniforms, to seem like enlisted members on leave. They were to answer the customs people with questions, they were there on pleasure, and were trying to find out if they could stay STD free the entire time. It was rather common for military personnel along those borders to do precisely that, although not likely for the length of time they would be over the border.

The final stipulation for those members leaving for Mexico, to leave all military identification behind, not take it, this is to keep it from being pilfered or worse, charged too much for services, because you were an American GI. He also made it clear, this was simply the reason customs was to believe was the reason to enter Mexico. They truly had other duties from the team's need for better information on what would be easiest to make the Mexican cartel go out of business permanently.

Romero Trap made half day appearances at the White House for a full month. It was all for the sake of appearance to the news agencies, who got no information from him other than he was present and accounted for, and never once made a form of a statement to them. He simply smiled and nodded his head, knowing fully well, if he said a single word, it would be misconstrued into something entirely different. He was not going to supply the ammunition of words the news agencies needed, to make a story out of nothing.

Thomas Hardesty was just the opposite, and had no problems giving the press something to work with, but in all honesty, they used his words to make him appear greater than he was, but he was doing something in office never done in the lifetime of most of those in the news agencies, changing government for the better. He was still working with his other staff people on how to implement flat tax for businesses, it was not a simple process, since too many businesses were untrustworthy, concerning the amount they really spent on expenses, that under current tax policy was deductible from the income before taxation came into effect. A flat tax, could simply override expenses as income, or it could be based on income minus a realistic expenses paid policy. What Thomas Hardesty wanted was a system that was policed by its contributors, rather than waste taxpayers money for a large department to insure it was done. He also wanted to eliminate all the loop holes created by politicians of the past, to insure it was fair to every single business responsible for paying taxes. Under his personal taxation plan, it was in the hands of business to insure the correct monthly amount deducted from people's payroll was sent to the government agency of ten whole people, who were more or less accounts receivable accountants. With payments coming only from businesses, it kept the accountants busy, but not overworked.

He needed to devise such a plan for business as well, but it required a large percentage of honesty, something most businesses had not practiced in taxation protocol for decades. It was by and large the government's doing, by wanting more and more to misuse in almost every case. If the monies appropriated were used for the purpose the government made the increase pass, it might be a different story. Instead, businesses and working people watched the government increase in size and expenses, while doing nothing to the massive deficit they operated under the dark clouds of government circles. Thomas Hardesty knew he could not reduce government enough in two terms to eliminate that deficit, but he did need to make a dent large enough, to let the people see he was working in the right direction, with their best interests considered.

If he reduced the size of government, but kept to the current tax policy, the debt would be eliminated in eight years, but the people would revolt prior to that time expiring. He had to balance a double edged sword and not get cut. He also submitted his bill in two parts, concerning reducing the size of senate and congress to a single house of representatives, two to each state, and each would be responsible for half of the state. It would be up to each state to decide the boundaries of the halves. Whether it was an east/west split or north/south split, was up to the people of each state. Largely geographies did not find it conducive to set either as a standard. The voting process was currently in process for this, and his reduction in paid expenses for those people.

The House and Congress, both thoroughly despised him, but they could find no way to disallow his bills with the people's vast approval through his newest voting system, which seemed to be working better than any used before. It was all computerized and no duplicate votes or miscounts came into play. What they truly disliked was he did not check voter registration, which could throw out a large quantity of votes collected, but in all due respect, all these people had the right to vote under the way the constitution was written, and that was never modified to say only registered voters need apply. The President had both the House and The Senate in complete submission, with all of his policy research and bill passage. If they turned down a vote from the people, they would be fired by the people, how was a Senator supposed to make his due interest under this current President?

Romero Trap was getting his intelligence input from Mexico with updates from Jackson Frye on his half day with the team. The location under their watchful eyes, found no time in which the majority of what would appear to be leaders of the cartel, were all present at the same time, the best they had obtained was 60% of the 40 upper echelon members. Romero Trap had Jackson Frye have his people note license plate numbers, make, model, and year of vehicle to see if they could be tracked to a location, to single them out one by one. With sixteen members, removed just prior to the main location being removed of cartel members, it should effectively put the cartel out of business. He would issue other details, which might be required once all of the information was discovered to move forward. Romero Trap did tell Jackson Frye privately, for the individual members his people would need to be prepared to take out any male child age 11 or older, to prevent a next generation cartel leader, making a reemergence in the future. No women were to be harmed, as they seldom became problems afterwards. More typically they are grateful for a second chance at life, without the abuser and criminal in charge. There is often enough money for the family to live quite well for the rest of their lives.

Jackson Frye said it sounded like business as usual to him, so he doubted any of his team members would be unwilling to partake in the activities later into this assignment.

Shortly after information for the vehicles was relayed back to Jackson, and with a little bit of resourceful computer navigating, residences were located using on board GPS tracking on all the latest model vehicles. It was something that could not be turned off or disabled, without distinct knowledge of the manufacturer's computer program. It was sad to see that all these people driving expensive late model vehicles, who made their money from the American population that had need of their product, all drove European cars and SUV's. There were Mercedes, BMW's, Range Rovers, Jaguars, and even one Volkswagen, although the highest model offered by them. No Japanese imports either, and in all likelihood, they purchased their vehicles north of the border. Such lack of loyalty to their primary income source needed no further justification for punishment.

Romero Trap did not believe this assignment required his going with the team, he would let Jackson Frye handle all the little details once they arrived, to encounter the cartel they were to eliminate. The time approached for departure, and once the team was in place, Romero thought it best to take down the separated individual's first, but in a reasonable time to allow the members to partake in the main location. None of the locations found for those individuals was an hour from the main location. It should allow for reasonable timing to complete all the eliminations in a four hour window. He also inquired about the number of workers at the main location, which was largely women, but a single male appeared to be a worker as well, there were 50. Trap gave Jackson a package containing 500,000 dollars, saying no harm to any person not in the cartel, each worker gets 10,000 dollars, to find another means of work, and they can use it however they see fit. Just stay away from the location of the cartel drug processing buildings. Make sure they all understand, if any of this group has to return yet again, there will be no survivors, period.

Jackson said he thought Romero was being rather generous, considering how far that much money would go in Mexico. Romero said he did not know how many of them had families, nor how far away they would like to go to get to a place they would like to call home. Jackson did not give it that much consideration, and Romero told him it was the way the cartel in Mexico operated, that most of the people working there were doing so to preserve the lives of other family members, the cartel did not like to pay any of them, to keep them completely under their control. It was in reality, they used slave trade to operate. One of the many atrocities this particular cartel utilized, to make more money.

Jackson said, since they were supposed to clean the place out, he had both transporters and the large truck loaded on the cargo plane, and the three just fit. They could not use a water tank with this combination of vehicles. The team would be departing soon, and Jackson started getting everyone prepared to head to the airfield, the plane was refueled ahead of time, knowing they would need fuel after landing in Mexico, but since they were landing on flat ground instead of an airfield, he planned to refuel prior to the real point of touchdown. The vehicles would be unloaded, but not moved in closer until it was needed. They would need to find a large number of rental vehicles rather quickly, and get the individual assignment portion taken care of first. He did not anticipate being in Mexico longer than 24 hours to do this assignment. Neither did Romero Trap, the cartel was sloppy in their training methods, but weapons and such things, were only a portion of their business, with moving product being their highest concern.

Two hours later the cargo plane with crew left the airfield, in route to Mexico, Romero Trap did not expect to hear anything from the team until they were all back, including the team sent for the purpose of eyes on the cartel operation. Romero was under the impression they were already on the way back, but driving a cargo van was not the fastest mode of transportation, for the distance between the base location and Mexico.

There were still a few people left in base camp, or home to most of them by now. The place did look considerably different than when they first arrived. They managed to clean it considerably. There were two shower stalls, two sleeping quarters, although one was considerably larger than the other. As well as the armory safe plus other items. The second floor had an equipped break room, which had a normal kitchen. It was kept much cleaner now than previously, and all the appliances, as well as the large walk in freezer also on the lower level, all functioning. Lighting was kept to a minimum, but it was also operating, but the low level of light kept on was to avoid attention to an abandoned building. It was not often any of them heard the sounds of a passing vehicle, but abandoned lots, sometimes become late night drag strips for the enthusiast, with nowhere else to race. Another reason for a large bit of unusable debris, to have been laid out in the lot around the buildings they were currently using.

It did not prevent the movement of any of the vehicles they used, but it did not allow for a straight line race with a two lanes width. The team seemed quite capable of thinking out the details in more than simple assignments. The problems for this type of assignment were uncommon for all of the team members, simply because of the potential length. Most were prepared to go four years with the potential of four more, so they took this into the planning of the home base, to detract from the common street marauders of high powered cars.

Since the flight to Mexico took nearly four hours each way, it took about 30 hours for the team to return. What took place was precise and deadly, but the cartel was ill equipped as far as thinking anyone might take them out, without some form of resistance. Each of the individuals were targeted at nearly a simultaneous time of 9 PM which was after dark fell. Fourteen different individuals with stealth, agility, and silent deadliness, were quick and precise. They were all quite adept in the use of blades, type and size did not matter except to the user. The primary targets were taken with instant death, largely by deep cuts to the throat limiting any sounds to emit to warn others. Each home was further checked for males age 11 and above. The total was two, who were thirteen, two who were fifteen, and one 18 year old male, already to step into his father's footsteps. One ten year old boy, who was large for his age, was grilled before deciding it was safe to let him live.

By midnight the entire team was in place to take out the main location of the Mexican cartel. There were a total of twenty four hierarchy members presently in the building. Each had a car with a driver, suffice to say the drivers were removed first; once again with the deadly silence of blades, as the 24 drivers had assembled outside the vehicles to have a conversation, of what subject or topic nobody knew or cared. Each driver had an assassin prepared to remove the targets. Once again, in was accomplished in short order, the team then spread out into the shadows, and since black everything was the most appropriate attire, it made it difficult for even each of them to see the next closest member of the team. The first thing they needed to discover was where all the cartel members were. Whether they were individually wandering about the production building, or in some sort of meeting room.

The team spotted the workers, but not a single cartel member, both Jackson Frye and Roberto Gomez went inside quietly, without being noticed by the workers, where Roberto Gomez was fluent in the language, got their attention quickly without shouting, of course two automatic weapons were displayed, and the people who worked in the cocaine processing area were unarmed. They were ushered just outside the doors and huddled together, where Jackson Frye stood guard, knowing enough of the language to insist they remain quiet and calm, and no harm would come to them. They were cooperative, but the single male was highly suspicious of the stranger in their midst. The rest of team did a search internally to find there was a rather large room, voices were heard through the rather thin walls, which had no windows. Seemed a strange way for any organization to have that type of room where production was concerned. It made their jobs much simpler though. It was assumed, all the cartel member were seated, so automatic weapons were all held waist high, and they opened fire on the enclosed room. The spray pattern effect incorporated, only went lower until the all the floor was covered. After each weapon had used two full clips of ammunition, one team member closest to the door, got to look inside. They had played it perfectly from the viewpoint that there were no persons moving any longer. It was a little messy inside the room, but it seemed pointless to go and check each for a pulse. If any were still alive, they would bleed out long before any assistance would arrive.

With the sound of gunfire, the group of worker were startled and beginning to think they were next. Roberto Gomez returned in time to keep the panic from getting out of hand. He told them they were all free to return to their homes and families, while at the same time Jackson Frye pulled his bag from under his over garment of black. He had 50 stacks of taped 100 Benjamin Franklins per stack. It amazed him how so much money stacked and held tight with a tape, looked to be so little. Gomez explained that each of them would receive 10,000 US dollars to make a different life for themselves and families if they had them, which was more than likely. They were never to return to this location, because if these people who just freed them of the servitude, needed to return to this location again, there would be no survivors.

Jackson handed each a single stack, and it was not until the moment the male got his stack did his suspicions turn to gratitude. The fifty workers made a hasty departure, most not knowing exactly how to leave to where their homes were located. None of them were from the area, and none had been permitted to see where they were going when they were brought to it. Jackson pointed them to the front where the 24 cars were, and had Roberto Gomez tell them how to reach the closest town only a mile away. The 24 expensive European Luxury cars disappeared in a cloud of dust. The team then went to survey what was really inside. Jackson said to the team, it was a good thing he had all the big trucks brought along for this job. The scale already had a single crate of packaged processed cocaine, and the scale read two thousand pounds or 1 ton. There were 12 identical crates. They could be safely stacked two high in the transporters and the truck, possible three but it had a bit more depth. The transporters were brought up first, the cartel had a tow lift to load them quickly and in a matter of twenty minutes, 12 tons of processed cocaine were on the vehicles, and the team was ready to pull out and head to the landing field.

The surveillance team arrived at base camp two hours before the remainder of the team arrived. It was a real disappointment to Romero, which one of his members of the surveillance team needed to go to Walter Reed for treatment. He decided to follow through on his own accord, with the plan given to the customs border patrol. He had gotten an STD from his little trip to Mexico. The ensuing conversation upon hearing this from Trap, was largely questioning his stupidity about not using any protection, since they were easily attainable. His team member's response was typical of some males that it did not feel the same. He also made it a point that it was not like he had the pick of the litter at base camp, since two of the ladies were more of the boys, or maybe sisters was a better description. The third who was a fine representative of the opposite gender, would likely kill him before he got his noodle wet.

Trap was not trying to make it like as a man, he had no business falling to his urges that would be foolish. It was that fact he was careless about his actions, and now would be making multiple trips to the medical center, which could hamper his participation in the assignments, providing he even had a curable variety of his problem. Some were not, and this fact alone, should result in common practices of using protection among items for sale such as what he purchased.

One of the local vehicles was used to take his less than intelligent surveillance team member to Walter Reed, where it turned out he was at least assumed, he could be cured. He did have a strain of the infection that could not be treated with oral medication, and would require antibiotic injections every three days, for at least two weeks, really 15 days. It may run longer, depending on how long he was with the STD before seeking medical assistance. Romero Trap was not a happy camper, but he was also foolish to believe his team was completely abstinent for the length of time they would be involved in the assignment. It seemed to Trap, there were safer places to indulge in that particular extracurricular activity.

The cargo plane team arrived before the medical trip was completed. It took an hour for Jackson Frye to fill in all the mission details, including the acquisition of 12 tons of processed cocaine. That would require Trap to contact the Peruvian cartel once again, to see if they could accept such a large shipment. Trap figuring prices had not increased significantly from the last time of uncut cocaine, got 120 million for 2 tons and though for the same money he could get 120 million for 4 tons of processed cocaine, although this being product that had everything ready to distribute, was probably worth more, but he did not need to have all those drugs around for his other assignments. It was too risky to keep on hand, and he and his team had no use for it, and did not want anything to do with setting up a distribution network.

It took another day to reach the head of the Peru cartel, who informed Romero Trap although it was in all likelihood worth twice what he could pay for it, he said he could take all 12 tons for 400 million dollars. Trap thought it was fair, since he only expected 360 million. What it was worth was not his primary concern, getting it out of his possession was the priority. Trap knew for this particular exchanged, he would need to be present, and it was arranged for two days later. It would not interfere with his Vice Presidential appearances for half of the day, but might make his sleep time lacking for a least one day.

The cargo plane was fully refueled in the time between, they did take the cartel tow lift from Mexico, as it just barely fit in the cargo hold of the plane. It would come in handy for transferring large amounts of equipment, or other odd jobs that had massive weight to move. In this case, the vehicles would stay behind and the crates of drugs and tow lift would be taken on the trip to South America. The same arrangements were made with the Peru airfield being under the control of the cartel, where it would be refueled without any additional cost to the team. Trap was only going take a total of four people besides himself, since fair trade had already been established with this group.

After his half of a day in the White House and a good lunch in the White House dining room, he headed directly to the airfield, where the other team members were ready for takeoff, as soon as he arrived and got onto the cargo plane.

Another small job was assigned by Jackson Frye to his remaining team members to travel about and obtain two dozen more sets of out of state plates, for the vehicles as some were ready to expire, and there was no possible way to renew them. It would prove stupid to be stopped for such a foolish mistake as expired plate, considering the occupation they were all members. Also, during the time Romero Trap had Zoe been checking out New York for the best place to unload the remaining uncut diamonds, where she would need to know just how much she had to unload, and having the best idea of value, she was the best candidate for the job.

The Peru excursion was not quite as simple as Romero Trap had thought it to be. Upon testing a fairly large number of processed packages of cocaine, he was told it was a higher quality than they themselves normally distributed, it could have come from only one cartel, being Mexican. The Peruvian cartel head man, asked Trap if he had anything to do with the demise of said cartel, and if he had anything to be concerned about.

Trap assured him, he had no concerns for the present, but considering his business had an expiration date based upon the governments of most countries, wanting to put an end to drug trafficking worldwide. He did not foresee his business being around in ten years, but he was a smart businessman, and should see that for himself. Trap said considering his cartel worked within his government's acceptance without corruption, his cartel was the safest in the world for the time being. It would be wise of him to diversify into more legitimate business dealings in the interim. The cartel leader was well aware of the facts surrounding his most profitable business, but was already doing the diversification to more legitimate businesses in his country. They simply were not as lucrative, and made it more difficult for the government to operate without a large amount of tax dollars coming into the treasury. He still pushed for a direct answer concerning the Mexican cartel. Romero Trap decide honesty was the best policy and informed him, his team removed the most notorious cartel in the world, to create room for worldwide improvements to come over the next decade.

Romero Trap did not foresee his cartel being included into his assignments, but it the event it did, he would give the leader of the cartel advanced warning to get out of the business before it was ended for him. The cartel leader had no problems with the Mexican cartel being removed from the picture, simply because the method they used was disturbing, especially when it came to abducting and forcing people into slave labor, to protect their other family members from being killed or seriously harmed. A practice he found repulsive, and his worker were all well paid in order to take care of their families. It was simply a job, available in this country and things being what they were, working for a living was preferred to dying from starvation.

The cartel leader asked since Romero Trap was currently a high ranking political figure in the United States, how it was he was involved in such other activities. Romero Trap having been discovered, was caught a little off guard by the question. He finally replied, he could not talk about specific details concerning his activities, but needless to say, he was not asked to be in his political role because of his politics, The President was trying to reform his overly large government, and

THE MEXICAN CARTEL

make an impact on the way the world was to become in the future. It was his unseen duties, that were having that impact, and he was rather experienced in his secondary duties, to a man he thought was nothing but integrity, in person. The cartel leader said he believed his accountant made a rather large contribution to removing the Mexican cartel, but he did not realize it was Trap behind it until the drugs showed up. As a sign of appreciation to his fair dealings and removing the most loathsome cartel in the business, he included in the transaction not only the 400 million dollars as promised, knowing he would receive nearly 2 billion in distribution prices, but an almost new Lincoln Towne Car, to take on the cargo plane back home. It was his own personal vehicle, and he would get a ride for himself and his driver from another member of his organization. Of course, he would need to obtain another form of transportation, but it was a gift for his complete honesty and fair trade practices when it came to his cartel.

The cargo plane was unloaded with the tow lift to the cartel's large truck brought for just such a need. 12 tons of cocaine all ready for distribution was transferred, the cash payment and Lincoln transferred to the cargo plane, which was refueled during the time on the ground. Romero Trap told the cartel leader he did not know when or if he would obtain any more product in the future, but if he did, he would let him know, also he may have a distribution void to fill with the Mexican cartel out of the picture. The cartel leader was aware of this, but his US distribution was rather small, since the Mexican cartel had taken the largest portion. Trap simply said, it was not unheard of for distribution people to know the competition, and they might help him out in that end of the distribution of his business. It was not something the cartel leader considered, but it did make sense and he would look into it.

The plane took off after two hours on the ground in South America, to return to the home airfield. During the ten hours away from the home base, Zoe had been able to find out the New York diamond exchange had a significant increase in the value of uncut diamonds, and were willing to take all of her offering for 1 billion dollars, as long as she was accurate in her appraisal of carats. The window of opportunity was limited due to the fluctuating market prices. Romero Trap was made aware of this upon his arrival, a lockable case was obtained for the movement of the diamonds, and with the aid of the just acquired Towne Car, and Zoe would go to New York the very next day. For appearance sake with the large vehicle now available, she would get to have a team member of her choosing to act as chauffeur, and security for her trip. New York City was not the most distant location from DC area, but Manhattan traffic could be problematic at the best of times. The Diamond exchange was located in the Wall Street district. It would take a fair portion of the day, but an additional billion dollars was hard to just do nothing about.

Trap had made it home with time for a few hours of sleep, before his White House appearance, and keeping true to form, his breakfast consisted of his one pot of coffee, although his lack of sleep did not bring about the vigor, he normally had with the consumption of breakfast. It was not something he was entirely unaccustomed to, but he was a little slow in his responses to the President, or any other person who entered the Oval Office. The traffic to the Oval Office was rather brisk, but it was largely the President's staff that made the continual interruption to keep the President up to date on issues, pertaining to his office as well as around the globe. None were silly requests from the Pentagon with war in mind.

The Pentagon on the other hand, were trying to figure out what role the president and his vice president had in the events that unfolded over that last three months. It seemed awful convenient to them, that some of the most troublesome groups on the planet were being eliminated without military intervention. They did not mind terribly that the problems were resolved with such efficiency, but it did make them feel less useful, although it was done without any indication of who was responsible. They were well aware if their involvement were required that it would become quite public, as it always had in the past.

The next evening, while Romero Trap was with his team, Zoe and her selected driver who was Turmoil, one of the two very large men in the crew, she returned from the New York diamond exchange with no diamonds, and a check for 1.2 billion dollars as she underestimated the exactly amount in carats for the remainder of the diamonds.

Romero Trap was handed the check to deposit in the accounts he had established, and with the distribution of those fund the following day, the team had 2.5 billion dollars in five off shore accounts, earning interest and investment earnings that were four times what the weekly payroll amounted to. He still had on hand, at least 500 million in gold bars, which would remain in that location, unless they had need of using it for assignments to follow. It was a business that could produce large amounts of profits, but also highly costly expenses, if they had to acquire equipment outside of his usual methods. It was imperative to Trap, to maintain a high amount of profits, since at the end of this long term assignment, he hoped to make it possible for all them to officially retire, with sufficient money to live a life of more than average means. In eight years, should the President keep office for that length of time, Romero Trap would have spent nearly 40 years of his life, removing problems from the government, in untraceable fashion. He was getting too old to keep up with the younger members of his team, and the time for him to leave was approaching. He might as well make it so that 36 other people, could do the same, although none of them had been in the profession nearly the length of time as he. He certainly felt that some of them should be able to live out a more refined existence, and possible have families unlike himself. It was far too late for him to consider the possibility, but it was something he decided to bypass many years before, since his profession could often bring harm to people in his life. He did not want to bring that problem for a wife or child, he could have had waiting for him to return home from wherever the government sent him.

7

Organized Crime

It took a month after the last assignment to receive the President's next directive and Romero Trap was less than pleased with the request from the President. It entailed the removal of 18 Organized Crime heads in the United States, although they were a major factor in the formation of a world governing body, there was virtually no means to profit from the assignment. Romero Trap informed the President, it would be rather costly for his team to perform the assignment, since here was no obvious means to improve the team's net worth. It would cost Romero Trap between two to four million dollars to take care of the problem the President proposed with no government assistance whatsoever. He felt it was expecting too much from him and his team, to risk so much, for absolutely nothing but the appreciation of the President, and what remained of his House and Senate. To this point, the people finding less than satisfactory results from those responsible for their welfare had voted to remove fifty members of the two parties, doing less than satisfactory performance on the people's behalf.

In a way, it was all part of the Thomas Hardesty plan in redistributing the power of those governing the country, and with all intentions of doing it for the people and by the people, as was the expectations of why this government existed in the first place. This was in accordance with the Constitution. He was not so much rewriting the laws of the country, but living up to what was already determined over 200 years previously. He was simply putting into law in far clearer context, what was already the people's given right to exercise.

He still had items to present to the people, ways to streamline government from its current over-grown condition. It was going to take more time to put into words acceptable to the Supreme Court, the proper wording to facilitate it being presented to the people in the fashion of a bill to vote upon. He was working on it with the aid of his support staff, more familiar with exact terminology for both the Court, and the people. Each required far different wording, but had to be identical in the explanation to the different parties, to eliminate loop holes, which allowed other government bodies the potential to incorporate interpretation. It was an entirely different approach to how bills became laws in the past half of a century. The Senate and the House, fully wanted loop holes for the interpretation process to be induced into any law. As a matter of the fact, they often intentionally wrote them into the bills they submitted, to appease other political influences.

Thomas Hardesty was sick and tired of seeing atrocities to the people written into law, for the benefit of a handful of obstinate political members, largely the Senators holding office for the longest amount of time. It was never for the benefit of the people, always for the political party involved.

It was time to bring this behavior from politicians to an end, and he saw fit to be the person in charge to do it. He had already proven he had the authority from the people, and intended to make the absolute most of it. Although, it may seem to be unheard of in political circles, he was going to make it take place against his staunchest disapprovers in the House and the Senate.

Romero returning to the team's location, started pinpointing with satellite imagery the most likely locations the eighteen crime bosses would be found. It was expected to be their homes, but what was around them to place a sniper for a single shot, was more what he was trying to find. Since organized crime was done by division of territory with complete cooperation of the eighteen bosses, there was no profit to be made from this assignment. The best option Romero could see, was to use six long rifle shooters for only the single target. Romero was not taking on the expense of collateral damage that was typically necessary for well-managed organizations. If the President wanted this as well, he would need it done through other government agencies he had at his disposal.

Romero also decided due to the nature of the weapons required for this assignment, he would need to use six rental cars, and absorb the lodging costs for his shooters to stay when not scoping out the target, for best time and location. If there needed to be alternative places, where the target was regularly seen. Some of those selected, would have more ground to cover than others in the way that organized Crime set up the base cities, and no tributary cities were to be included. The way it seemed was population was more behind the location than the geographic position. The eighteen cities were closer in the east than the rest of the country. Those locations were New York City, Boston, Philadelphia, Miami, Atlanta and Memphis, covering the east coast region. Central consisted of Chicago, Detroit, Cleveland, Green Bay, St. Louis, and Kansas City. While the west included Los Angeles, San Francisco, Las Vegas, Dallas, Houston and New Orleans. Whether the bosses of organized crime resided in the major city or nearby suburbs, would have an impact towards getting a concealed and clean shot position. He did not want any of his shooters to be closer than 1,000 yards to allow time to clean up his area and depart before discovery. The distance was determined by the fact that he only had three expert long rifles, which by military standards were no closer than 1,000 yards. This distance was acceptable to Romero Trap of the people capable of performing at that distance, but he did not have enough team members for all of them to work from that distance.

With satellite imagery, they could only determine some details concerning the individual targets, the biggest part would be up to each shooter, as to the best location and position for a single shot kill. It was rather important to keep each target to a single shot, most sniper rifles only had single shot loads that were bolt action. His only question to those he knew to be capable to perform this assignment, was whether they needed a spotter to accompany them.

He got the six selected team members together which consisted of Hummer, Deadly, and Eyes as his true long rifle experts. The other three were capable of using long rifle at the distance of 800 to 1,200 yards but not much beyond those distances, they were Bloodlust, Mayhem, and Terror. All said they could make the shot without a spotter, and were going to study the satellite imagery for potential locations to make the shot, for the primary location of the crime boss in each city. The team was given the three cities they would be involved with, and Hummer was the west coast operative since the distance was going to be the biggest issue between the cities involved. She was also the most likely to make a clean single shot kill from a very long distance, and the closer she was, the more certain of a single shot kill. Although she never missed in her documented time from any distance.

She found for the locations she was going to be in water towers which was within her distance to each of her three targets. All were within 3,000 yards of the location, considered to be the most likely place to find the target, at some time during the day or evening hours. All the long range rifles had scopes capable of night vision sightings, and Hummer had preference to this target set up to a daylight one. Hummer also had custom built her own rifle, requiring a much longer barrel than the standard military issue, this was how she accomplished her truly long distance shots, and it was made to be removed or attached depending on her distance. At 2,000 yards it was not necessary, but she would not go on her excursion to the West Coast without it. She wanted to be prepared for any given situation in her line of work.

After a week of imagery study for his shooters, he arranged the rental cars for them to use for the time on the road. Since carrying weapons into a rental car agency was unacceptable, they would be taken to the rental agency to obtain the vehicles, and return to the base location, to load with the items necessary to complete their individual missions. If was seen on satellite imagery that each boss had a number of other people on the grounds of the primary location. Details were insufficient to determine exactly what those people did, it was assumed they were armed security, which was common among organized crime bosses. Fortunately, most of the bosses' security only carried hand guns for security purposes, and it was unlikely any of them could kill the shooter from a distance of 1,000 yards with a hand gun.

It would take Hummer a week to travel to the west coast solo, needing to stop for rest in areas along the way. Romero Trap provided each shooter with 60,000 dollars cash for lodging and meals, while away from the base location in the DC area. It was also necessary before they departed, to obtain the normal purchases, various gear each shooter requested. All were provided a long rifle storage bag, to keep the weapon safely hidden in the trunk of the large vehicles each had for a rental. Many would be travelling a distance sufficient to find lodging between their starting and destination locations. The shooter who got the Boston, New York City, and Philadelphia run was able to make it to any of the cities without a lodging stop, but would still need lodging while in the cities. There was no definite time frame that could be set for the targets to be removed, simply because each shooter needed to insure his surroundings, and the target was accessible at the primary location. If an alternative location was needed, it would delay the shooter in the city it applied to. As much as Romero Trap would have liked to take out all 18 organized crime leaders in a simultaneous time-frame, it was not possible with the number of people he had capable of making a single shot kill. He only had one other person on the team who preferred a rifle, but long distance shooting was not one of his better skills. Largely because he preferred small automatic weapons over the rifle, but his rifle shooting required multiple magazine loads over single shot.

Romero Trap in determining his team in the very beginning, never expected this type of assignment, and needed the other skills for the jobs he anticipated were more likely to become necessary. It was never a problem in the past, but that was largely because he only had a single assignment, and never the length of time this one would involve.

Hummer had decided to start the excursion in San Francisco, and work southern California second finishing in Las Vegas. Deadly took the Southern East coast circuit of Miami, Atlanta and Memphis, also selected the further location to do first. Mayhem chose the Detroit,

Cleveland and Chicago run. He did not think Chicago would be first, instead he decided to do Cleveland, and then Chicago and work back to Detroit, before returning to home base. Bloodlust got the southern tour to Dallas, Houston and New Orleans and made no decision in advance to which location to start, but thought he would hit Dallas, then New Orleans and return to Houston for the last of his targets. Eye took the Midwest tour of Green Bay, St. Louis, and Kansas City, deciding to take the farther site and work back. That left Terror for the New York, Boston and Philadelphia group of cities, and he wanted to remove New York first, since it presented the most obstacles for choosing a clean shot position.

It took two weeks before the first target was attempted by Terror in New York City. He was able to use an apartment building rooftop for his shot at 1,200 yards from the target, and it was a night shot using the night vision scope of the rifle. Unfortunately, one of the security of the boss, heard the shot, and pushed the target enough not to make a kill, although he did severe shoulder damage, but the target would survive. Terror decided his best course of action for this target, would be to take care of his other two cities before returning for a second attempt.

A week later first kills came from Deadly in Miami, Eyes in Kansas City and surprisingly Hummer from San Francisco. All were single shot kills that had security scrambling, but not knowing where the shot came from exactly. It allowed each shooter to clean their brass and return to the vehicle they were using to depart the vicinity of the kill. As professionals, none of the team needed to get a closer look of confirmation of the kill. It was something the common criminal was guilty of being around the investigating authorities, to get a view of the trouble they may have caused. It was largely more common among arson crimes than robberies, but it did occur frequently enough for criminals to get caught, because they could not resist, looking over the scene afterwards. Professional assassins were aware of the kill the moment it occurred, since good kills were head shots, and there was seldom any dispute of a large bullet entering the target. It showed on the scope, and that was all they needed to see to leave the scene.

Four days later first kills were reported by the other two, who did not take a shot beforehand. It was disturbing that one shot was not clean, but it did occur upon occasion, and it would make the second attempt all that more difficult, since there would be a heightened awareness to the potential attempt. By the time the final two had taken out their first target, the others who already achieved first kills, were in their second city of operations to the assignment.

First to make a second kill was Hummer in the Los Angeles area, at a distance of 1,500 yards which was nearing the end of her barrel range without the extension. The shot was so clean, the target's security had no options to locate and pursue the origination of the kill shot. At close range to the target, it was obvious with the massive hole in the back side of the head, there was little chance of life signs and security people did not bother, besides several became violently ill from what they had observed of their now former boss.

Hummer had plenty of time to clean her single brass and retrace her climb of the water tower for the shot that did its job. Once done there, she immediately cleared out of her lodging location and left for Las Vegas, thinking it would be wise to stop in between for rest, and to be better prepared for her final target. She did not have any idea where she was in relationship to the other five shooters, considering she had the longest amount of time to get to the area she decided on taking. Nobody else had completed a second kill, and she was not given that information in the quick confirmation call to home base over the second boss of organized crime being removed from her list of three.

Four days later, Terror completed his first kill in Boston, the security there did not stay as close to their boss as New York City did, and allowed him a clean uninterrupted single shot kill from his apartment building rooftop, within the 800 yard range of the target location. He policed his brass and had already cleared the motel he stayed at to depart directly to Philadelphia, knowing he would need to return to New York, and wait for a second chance to complete his portion of the assignment. From the appearance of things, the crime bosses were not staying up to date at this point to their associates being eliminated, but that would change from this point forward. It would make the assignments a little more difficult, but not impossible, considering the distance chosen to make the shot from. At 2,000 yards the bullet would arrive at nearly the same time as the gunfire sounded to the security persons involved in keeping the crime boss safe. Over the next week, everyone had managed to complete the second kill to their list of targets, but the last one would take much longer, with the increasing awareness of the crime bosses being the targets of somebody unknown to them. They would never guess it was by direction of the President of the United States, since all of them had voted for him, and thought that was all the support they required. None of them were campaign contributors, since government overall frowned on such activity from organized crime, and it only needed to by suspicion not proven.

The first person to complete all of the three targets was Hummer, as she managed to get her third target, just before awareness increased significantly. It made it so she was the first to return to home base, even though she had the most distant locations. She was back after one month total time away from the team. The southern and Midwest shooters found the increased awareness by the crime bosses to be more of a problem. The people were altering their routines, making it so additional time was needed to discover any type of pattern. Dallas was done, but the New Orleans target seemed totally unpredictable in making a definite pattern, and required a different location than originally planned. Once a location was decided, it still took more time to find an appropriate location to make the shot, without being discovered. The same held true for the final southern East coast location for Deadly to complete the final installment of his assignment. It seemed to the Midwest shooter, that all possible means of deception were being utilized by the target, and his team of security people, it became rather annoying and after completing only a single kill, put out the word he might need some form of assistance. Susan Hobart (Hummer) volunteered to take over the Midwest targets, since she was capable of greater distance shots than any other member of the team. She was given the opportunity, but her other shooter would remain in place for the two to work out the best approach. An additional rental car was obtained for her second shooting event in six weeks.

Before Hummer arrived at her second destination, word came back from another long distant rifle expert, (Deadly) he had completed the three targets, and was returning to home location. The remaining shooters were finding the additional awareness of both the crime boss and security to delay completion, but not to the point of needing assistance. Just would need more time than they had originally anticipated. The longer they delayed in another sniper shot, the more relaxed the targets and their security became, it was partly human nature, and largely the organized crime bossed feeling relatively untouchable, considering how long they had operated within the country taking several generations into the factor.

After three months on the road, all but four targets had been eliminated, five as a result of Hummer, who had to go father from her targets than the other shooters could have accomplished, one being 3,000 yards and the third at 2,500 yards, but the shot were clean single shot kills, and her companion was used as the spotter.

While team's members had exceeded the time in which Romero Trap had figured it would take and provided expenses for that time frame, he did have to overnight ship additional funds to a number of members. Lodging had to be paid either daily or weekly, depending on length of stay. Most of the shooters did not expect to be in any hotel for a month, and planned on two weekly payments before going to daily rates, which were much higher. It was included in his total cash out for the entire cost of start to finish of the assignment. The cost overall were higher than he would have liked, but not quite what he thought would be top end. Still, it was money no longer available for other assignments or interest and earnings. It still managed to keep earning where weekly payroll was met without a problem. The other rather large expense was Zoe, but that was at least capitalized upon for the terrorist job, which produced a good deal of profit over expenses. Romero needed to keep his profit margins high for what he wanted to achieve at the completion of the President's run in office. He still was not far enough into the first term to know if a second term was possible or probable.

So far with the President presenting the people with a say in government, his ratings among the people were quite high according to the national news, which kept track of such information. At the end of the five months dealing with the Organized Crime bosses, he had reduced the Senate and the House to his proposed plan to the people. Each State now had two representative, responsible for fifty percent of each state, and they were to act on the people's behalf, without personal agendas to fulfill. His security people assigned to him and his family, were on high alert, there were a large number of former members of the House and Senate beyond unhappy, about being forced from office by the people's vote in the state they represented. Those members, did not see all the voters as the enemy, they put that tag squarely on President Thomas Hardesty. Many of them had the resources to obtain people capable of removing obstacles from their path permanently. The final addendum to his plans to the people for vote consideration, was to limit the number of years any representative could hold office to twelve years, lifetime. Unfortunately, he did have to reset the clock to day one taking place with the representatives being two by two. Previous time in office would not be accounted for, and should any of them have been career politicians, they would get to add eight more years to their tally. That bill also said that all members of government, were contributing and working toward the same type of retirement plan the people had for decades. The monies in the government retirement fund were redistributed to the other program for all the people, including himself. Government expenses among the representatives were well monitored, and nothing that was not fully government business would be approved by the people, who kept track of the fund. In his first year in office, President Thomas Hardesty had reduced government spending by 50 percent, but it was still running mildly in the red, and needed to get into the black to start addressing the massive deficit over the heads of government and its people.

    His flat tax program for business was nearing a point to present to the people, and it would make government a bit leaner with its approval by the people. Thomas Hardesty was not sure even with this program put into effect, it would allow the government to operate in the black. It was decided with his group of experts the best way to put the flat tax program into effect, would be to allow businesses to be honest and trustworthy in the flat tax program. It would allow businesses to deduct 75 percent of what was currently deductible from the previous tax methods. This would allow business to subtract payroll, benefits, and working expenses such as equipment necessary to conduct business, and interest on outstanding loans. It would not allow them to deduct business purchases of other companies, or capital improvements such as new buildings or additions. It did allow for upkeep expenses in existing buildings and if additions or acquisition buildings were obtained, the expenses of upkeep to those as well.

His plan would be small business would by and large, pay 10% flat tax on the profit margin each month. It did allow for fluctuation in profits. Most small business did not earn over 1 million dollars annually. Over the million dollar range medium business would be accountable for 15% whereas that would go to 100 million dollar annual profit.

Any business in the large scale over 100 million dollars annually, would be responsible for a 25% flat tax, which would be a significant reduction in what the current government tax program demanded. All the same, deductions would be allowed for all businesses, and it required monthly accounting statements and payments to the United States treasury, to get the country back on its feet in the world of economics. He still needed to find ways to reduce government payrolls, by cleaning out the number of people working for the government in unproductive ways. That would take him more time with his staff looking into where waste was, and production failed to meet a high enough standard. It did have the flaw in the program of businesses being completely honest with the deductions, but in the long run they would be keeping a good deal more profit than before, which he hoped was enough incentive to get the honesty of businessmen behind his proposed program. He would still need to keep roughly 200 accountants on staff for tracking businesses monthly information, to insure dishonest practices were brought to a halt. Businesses were already responsible for sending the treasury the monthly tax deductions of their employees, who fell into the different tax ranges for individuals. His flat tax rate for the individuals did not have married or unmarried status taken into account, but did allow for non-working children to be deducted prior to tax rates applied. This was also included by the business that made the payments for its employees.

Although it cost a good deal more to raise a child than the annual deduction, it was always that way and he set it 6,000 dollars per child per year. It meant if a family had two children and earned 40,000 dollar combined, the family had no taxes to pay as the deduction for children would bring their total income to under 30,000 dollars. It was the fairest tax policy the government ever used in recent history, and the people seemed content with how it was working for them. Thomas Hardesty was hoping for the same from business, but knew that some businesses were quite adept at presenting false information to allow for higher profit margins. He was hopeful that was going to be a thing of the past, under his flat tax program. It was also possible, in the future the tax rate could be reduced, once the government was well into having an income, and a major reduction in the deficit, if not eliminated altogether. Thomas Hardesty did not truly expect that to occur while he was eligible to be in office.

The President also had a new assignment for his Vice President, and the time to act upon it was quickly approaching.

8

The Next Global Threat

The conversation between Romero Trap and Thomas Hardesty started out with Romero Trap informing the President, that the organized crime bosses were eliminated; but due the high cost and no means to profit from the assignment, any additional organized crime people were the President's responsibility to utilize his lettered agencies to address. He made the President aware that in all likelihood it was just a small set back to them, until new bosses were appointed to take the place of those eliminated. Thomas Hardesty said he had already considered that, and had his agencies trying to slow the progress they made, but the big bite had been completed and the agencies should be able to keep it from getting too large again.

President Hardesty went into his next assignment which was going to be the most difficult yet to date. "With the removal of the largest terrorist group, a new one emerged that has been reigning havoc on the global community. This group operates entirely differently from the first group. They operate in smaller cells, and spread out over a larger playing field. They have been relentlessly attacking all countries by hitting commercial aircraft that have routes over the area they play in. They apparently have ground to air missiles to target the aircraft and bring them down. These missiles are mobile, so they may move on a regular basis, to acquire different targets from a previous location. To date, since the fall of the first terrorist group, they have brought down over 100 planes from almost every nation including our own, with a loss of life nearing 15,000 citizens who were no threat to the group. I have received approval to provide 30 million dollars from the US, to get the ball rolling on this group of terrorists. Under the circumstances, I can provide that all upfront with your commitment to involve your team in removing this global threat, and you will likely find, most other nations as well as airline companies, willing to provide additional funding to this assignment. I do not know how long this will take, since the small groups need to be located and removed. Keep in mind, all terrorist groups have some location for training their people as well. It would be a great service to the world, to have this threat completely removed. I am sure you will need things different from other assignments over the last year.

Romero Trap knew this was largely another Middle East assignment, but this group covered a number of nations in that region of the world. Finding a location to put a cargo plane down, would not be easy with the terrain of the area. He said to the President, he needed to consult his team prior to giving him his answer, although he knew this was why he was asked to take the Vice Presidency in the first place. He did not want to bring into the fold more trained personnel for a single mission, which Romero Trap feared would take a year to complete. He also knew he could not disappear from the White House for that length of time, without a great deal of suspicion in his whereabouts.

President Hardesty said he would give him until the next day for his response. Romero Trap did not know how useful satellite imagery would be for this assignment. Something had to stand out for locations to start out the assignment, and find a safe place to assemble the team. It would also mean another forged requisition form from the military, as he would need some satellite communications gear for his team members. and one at base to keep abreast of the situation on the ground of another hostile environment.

Romero Trap waited his usual time for lunch before getting his team's opinion of the next requested assignment from the President, who did have validity to the request. His days at the White House dinner table for lunch was certainly beginning to become habit forming. The food was always superb, and Romero Trap had never been accustomed to eating so much wonderful food in his over 30 year career, covering a large number of agencies before going independent. His people were also not familiar with such fine menu items as that served at the White House, although Zoe may be the sole exception.

When he arrived at the team's location, they were aware of the terrorist's activities from news information they ate up from the computer systems, in use at the location. Romero Trap made them aware of the situation from the Presidential point of view; and had requested the team's active participation in removing another global threat to humanity. He said since the President had set a 30 million dollar price tag on the removal from just the United States, to start presenting it to the world and almost every airline as well. The price tag would be 30 million per country or airline, and although steep, each airline had more costs involved for the loss of a plane and its passengers, than the price to eliminate an ongoing threat to their airlines. He also told them since this group of terrorist operated in small cells, they would be in the Middle East for an extended period of time, and various supplies would be necessary to survive in a hostile environment. This portion was both new and old news to the team. They were more than accustomed to the hostile environment, but not the length of time they might be in it.

Romero Trap also made sure that they knew, there was no way he could be with them for the assignment, since his other part time job was to act like a Vice President, and he could not be gone a year as he thought this would take. He could not figure out any way out of the problem other than acquire satellite gear from the military, with another forged document. Trap said to be on the safe side, they should obtain four satellite phones used for communication between the two locations. Three for the team in the Middle East, and one for base location for the origination point. Since satellite phones were quite secure and set to operate only with the group parameters they selected, no other agency or military group should be able to overhear their communications.

One person would need to stay behind for keeping the communication line open for business. It was also imperative that the team destroy any and all land to air missile systems they located, and with any luck, the materials for that will be found within the terrorist cells they locate. Somehow, the group had managed to be financed quite well to obtain the equipment they had, most likely from the black market; but they could be any origin for the country that manufactured such items. Military heists occurred all over the world to supply the black market. Most military leaders did not make such information public knowledge, including their own country. The military mind set did not permit for embarrassment. Romero Trap did not foresee any reason for Zoe to find work in the Middle East, and asked her to stay behind for the satellite phone link that was essential to keep up to date with the team. Zoe said she would need to be shown how to use it, but agreed that her work for this assignment was not required, and she should do something to keep her 1,000 a week payments coming. All the team members were back to fully functioning, which was also a good thing for the team. Personnel shortages from wounds or other foolishness, was something Romero Trap needed to avoid for this mission. Since the terrorist cells operated in small groups, but numbers were not known exactly, he saw the opportunity to use a quieter approach than massive automatic weapon fire intent upon obliteration. They were to obtain what useful materials they needed from the terrorist cells, and it might be a good idea to shuttle the cargo plane back and forth for getting supplies, and may bring back excess materials obtained that had a further use to the team. Ammunition and additional weapons were always good to have as well as explosives, but that may be used as required, once obtained from a cell that has been targeted. He forewarned the team that this group operated in a more multinational area than the previous one, so picking up and moving a base camp was likely to occur frequently.

He believed the group also operated in Afghanistan, which was never one of the best locations for military from any nation to incur upon. Regardless of the exact region they locate, expect to find less than obvious places for people and gear to be hidden. Underground structures and caves systems were abundant in the entire regions they would be entering. The cargo plane would also need to enter the area at a lower altitude than most operations, due to the ground to air missiles, although the terrain variations may keep them above 1000 feet above ground not sea-level, as he did not know what the area was considered in that respect. He did know that all altimeters in aircraft were based on sea level at 0 feet. Many places around the world were above sea level, a few below, but it could make a big difference between flying low and flying into the ground, which produced loss of aircraft as well as people.

Considering the team's active participation, Romero Trap being the consummate profession, asked instead of assuming that it was a go for this mission. His reply was affirmative from all members, no one declined to participate, although they all hated the region they were going into as much as Romero Trap. It was never a kind environment for Americans, whether for peaceful purposes or not, they were all considered the infidel enemy.

He had them study whatever satellite imagery they could obtain from the area to determine a place for first strike and base camp. The team in a mere 30 minutes, located what they thought appeared to be a training location for the targeted terrorists. They found it difficult, but not impossible to put a cargo plane down in the area that would require 30 miles by transport, to set up a base camp still five miles from the target location. Jackson Frye said it would be best to take both transporters, with the water tank in tow. All the gear could be stowed between the two with half the team in one and the other half in the other. Hopefully they could find additional water supplies while on the ground, even if it meant by taking what was available in the terrorists first location on the target map. It might even prove beneficial to take over the terrorist training location once the targets were removed. It made sense to Trap, but it would mean more people on guard duty than normal assignments. There was always someone on guard duty when entering known hostile territory. It kept the team prepared and alive in the event of the terrorists wanting to retake what was lost. Jackson also agreed it would be best to shuttle the cargo plane to and from base once each month, to restock necessary supplies. Largely in the food category, as none of them could go without food or water for that length of time.

It was also decided to obtain military grade cooking devices, to at least set up one transport as a mobile kitchen. This way they could cook foods for the group in small quantities at a time, without attracting attention to a large open fire, typically used when in the field such as this. Just you did not do it where they were going, having learned that lesson long ago from military groups annihilated by terrorists, who discovered the fire visually in the terrain where the terrorists held high ground.

They did operate in groups with the advantage in almost every case, one of the reasons why the team's initial base would be five miles from the target location. It was not impossible to cover five miles of terrain under the cover of darkness, for close quarter's experts to make an initial strike. Using close quarter's experts, often reduced the noise attraction of gun fire. Once again, all black was the attire for the actual attacks to take place. In less stressful times in the environment of the region, as little clothing as possible was often the attire of the daytime hours. The women of the group were more prone to remaining in t-shirts and panties than disrobing entirely, but it was the nature of the military personnel experienced to the area of the globe, they were going to be heading in. Besides that, the women going along for the mission, were quite familiar with how to get by with little clothing.

Romero Trap got to inform the President the next morning his team accepted the assignment, and before lunch arrived, 30 million dollars was transferred to the account being used to fund the mission. While Trap was at the White House, his team started drumming up additional fund commitments and putting together another forged military requisition order for needed materials for the assignment, they agreed to undertake in service of their President. All additional fuel tanks were refueled, as well as the vehicles and cargo plane. It would fall into Trap's domain to arrange a refueling location with friendly allies in the region, to insure sufficient fuel was on board for takeoff and shuttle services. It would require numerous stops, over the time they anticipated being in the region.

It took two weeks of preparation, and during the time, countries around the globe committed to the removal of the terrorist group as well nearly every major airline. The total was over 5 billion dollars and 50 percent was collected up front to fund the operation that was not backed by the US military, or that of any other nation. This was a mission not on record, but the activities would likely make the worldwide news as it progressed. Romero Trap had no difficulty with making news headlines, as long as his people were not identifiable. It was paramount to the means in which he always operated under, to stay far enough under the radar of the news agencies, to provide a service without total recognition of deeds performed. Should he or any of his team be singled out, it meant losing a team member, who could no longer contribute to his chosen profession. It was vital to remain anonymous.

It was also one of the conditions Trap put on a member of his little organization, largely for their own protection, but if anyone wanted to be in the limelight, it would need to be done for somebody else. Once reaching that plateau, the member would never work again for anything Trap had put together.

As for now, every member of his team was well aware of the conditions, and had zero complaints to a continuing career within Romero Trap's primary business. Being the Vice President, did put a rather unusual twist into the fabric of his profession. By the same token, he would never have agreed to it from any other political person other than Thomas Hardesty. He was the single exception to his means of business.

By the time Romero Trap's team had made for departure, Thomas Hardesty had the final pieces to his flat tax for business in place, and would likely have a voter tally before Trap's team made their first attack. Trying to burn the candle at both ends was not something Romero Trap had done exceptionally well in the last decade. Time was becoming an issue in how long he could work for days without rest, while waiting out a target or keep eyes on pattern development for a particular assignment. It was the largest reason for getting younger people into a team of expert to call upon for various assignments. What Trap did know, for the next three plus years, he had no room on his plate for other assignment requests from other parties, other than the President. In years past, his assignments could come from any number of lettered agencies, ill-equipped to do what he and his team were highly competent in performing. It could also come from the Pentagon, and currently that was his biggest concern in how to deny them, while he was involved with something they were not meant to have knowledge pertaining to. It was a rather unique dilemma for him, never having accepted such a long term assignment, although he was quite familiar with off the record covert operations from all mentioned lettered agencies, especially the Pentagon. They were notorious for trying to start a war somewhere with the appearance of total innocence, and lack of knowledge to any such activity involving them.

With the team at last in place, the surveillance started up in 24 hour shifts just to get an idea of how many they were dealing with, and the best time to infiltrate and quietly remove as many as possible, before retreating to safer ground to continue at another time. For the first location, this was the method deemed most suitable to achieve mission results, as well as maybe territory the other cells would prefer to have over his team. It would make the opponents the assailant, and the team on the defensive; but a change up in tactics would throw the scent off of the team for the other terrorist groups they removed from operating status.

It was another one of the means which Romero Trap tried to get his team to understand to utilize to remain under the big radar. If they did not operate in the identical fashion, the terrorist group would not think or discover the team used different tactics for the other, which made this group all the more important in the world scheme. It seemed like an endless cycle in this part of the world, as soon as one group was removed, the next was ready to step in to fill the void. Romero Trap was beginning to believe the only way to truly eliminate such a massive problem, was to obliterate the entire region, but the collateral damage was excessively high, considering the number of believers in ratio to the fanatics, that used terror tactics as a religious shield. There was no simple solution, and the true believer did not believe in war and murder as a means to overcome the problem that existed. To the believer of the Koran, that was entirely against the teachings of the prophet Mohammed. So, it had been for centuries, and apparently so it would be for many more. Every civilized nation, or at least given that title, since that was a debate for scholars, he did not have time to endure, tried to bring peace to the region. To simply fail to get satisfactory results, and eventually give up due to the high costs involved. Every nation since the Roman Empire had to absorb the costs of peace or war, depending on one's perspective of how or what was obtained. At some point, almost every nation to ever try to bring normal relations to the peoples of this region had to retreat, for the simple matter of how costly it was to continue to keep trying.

The team was in place three weeks, performing surveillance of the first terrorist location believe to be a training location. From the distance in which they watched in 24 hour shifts; the terrorist had done an excellent job of concealing what they really had in place at the location. The primary building, assumed to be a barracks, as the majority of people came and went from it, was set into the hillside, as if a natural earth made home. It was seen only slightly from the satellite imagery, and it was still unknown as to how much was in the hillside it was built into. The team of surveillance people had not counted more than eighty terrorist members currently in location, and the first window for close quarter's expert was during the hours after the strike of midnight. The terrorist group was not highly trained, and the close quarter's experts believed they could get in close onto the site, to remove at least 30 people who posed as guards throughout the darkest hours.

It took one more week for the first strike to take place, as all of a sudden there was nighttime activity for five days. It appeared to be a training exercise, not the influx of more trainees into the terrorist's location. The second evening after midnight, twelve close quarter's experts moved into striking distance, and Susan Hobart (Hummer) was their eyes and ears over the operation. Additional headset communications gear was obtained on the forged military requisition, to allow the ground team communication within the group. It consisted of an earpiece with mini microphone so it could be both way communications. The terrorist group on guard, seem too relaxed on their duties to truly see what was shaping up around them, and each of the close quarter's experts closed in on a selected target. The experts each got within arm's length of their target completely unnoticed by the supposed guards on duty. In one quick timed movement twelve terrorist were down and out of action, having blades slice through their throats to keep noise minimal. The bodies were dragged to less obvious positions, although there was nowhere to completely hide the bodies. The experts repositioned themselves for the second targets. The second strike was not timed out so much in synchronization, and Chu Fong was the first to make a move on his second target, Hummer told him he had another approaching from behind, and having his other terrorist in a vulnerable position, shifted to one side, unleash three darts and his got his third down without a sound, before deciding to simply snap the neck of the second target. No need to cover up bodies on this second round. He retreated to a more unseen location, checking if anyone needed assistance. The other eleven close quarter's experts had taken the second victim of undisciplined soldiers, leaving five remaining on the location. The team decided best to return with 25 members of the terrorist's group no longer in commission. They would wait until morning, when the others were more fully active and start locating bodies around the location used for training. To this point, the team had not identified who was providing the training, unless it was done within the building with the sole use of electronic equipment. They also felt there had to be some form of communication between this location and others, but could find no outward signs of how it was accomplished.

The site did present a number of unknowns, and since they only had people in close at the darkest time of the night, looking for anything, was not an assignment for the experts. The second night following, although the terrorist were more alert, they counted only fifteen night time guards, and the best the team could determine the training was poor and inadequate. The close quarter's combat experts went into the terrorist facility to remove the final fifteen guards, which was accomplished rather quickly, as even after the first attack, these terrorists in training had no idea how to prepare themselves for this type of attack. On this attack, with all the guards removed, they made an attempt to infiltrate the building, it was a hasty retreat as they took the single guard at the doorway without a problem, but the interior was far more complex than the outward appearance led them to believe. The building itself was not terribly large, but there was a series of tunnels into the hillside and five entries ways into the building they quickly left. It would require more stealth to traverse a tunnel unseen, not knowing what it might lead to. The plan would be to do one tunnel at time, to see what was at the end, unless they all led into a large open area with more tunnels. It was at least not the kind of tunnel system one needed to get onto hands and knees or belly to travel through, they were large and tall enough to drive a vehicle through, although not the largest vehicle. Small pick-up trucks or Jeep's would easily pass. They did not have the manpower to be overly risky treading into the unknown. It was decided once back to base camp, depending on the number of guards the following evening, three automatic weapons and some handguns were in order to venture further into the tunnels.

Jackson Frye changed the team's plans upon hearing it, he pointed out that in almost every case in dealing with a network of tunnels, there was at the minimum one additional entry/exit on the rear. It would take two days to get four people with automatic weapons and handguns into the back side of the hillside, to find out what they were really getting into on this location. With group communications, they could enter both access points in an attempt to clear out what was left of the terrorists in the location. Careful not to induce friendly fire, and the noise from gunfire should only be heard within the tunnels, as opposed to the outlying areas. The close quarter's expert adept in handguns, would enter from the front location with a total of eighteen team members for this leg of clearing out a terrorist training facility, if that was in fact what this was. It had only been assumed prior to this discovery, but if these people were fully trained terrorists, they were well over matched with Trap's team of experts.

On the third night, the rear side team announced they were in position and found a single very large opening, it was large enough to have the largest of military vehicles enter and exit. This was the point of entry for four members with automatic weapons and handguns. Upon entry from front and rear, neither team found any sort of resistance. They circumnavigated the tunnel system, to find a single terrorist left operating a hand held radio device. He was unarmed, but the team had no call for taking prisoners, although whatever information this person could provide would prolong his life expectancy for a short time.

It took three days, of the terrorist being in all sorts of forms of agony, before he admitted that the remaining ten members, used a small vehicle to leave to other locations, those other location were informed of the location being attacked, although they never expected it at this location. It was not a training facility, although they did use fresh recruits to perform guard duty until they were sent to training. He was left behind, because he was the one to position the missiles for the next hit of a plane. He did not care if it was commercial or military, he was to keep all air traffic out of the surroundings in which they were operating. He believed another location would be coming along soon to retake the communication and vault location. The team did not discover a vault, it took another two days of near death experiences for the sole terrorist, before they discovered its location within the tunnel network. It was hidden by camouflage netting, which made it appear to be a wall in the tunnels. They had no idea, what they would find inside, but the rear entrance had three full sized transporter units fully fueled, with all of its spare tanks full as well. It was decided to send two of them back on the shuttle cargo plane to keep on hand in base, but it would mean expanding the base location to accommodate more vehicles.

Upon the final day of the terrorist's existence, it was determined he had no clue how to open the vault, to find what was inside. In the meantime, automatic weapons experts were kept on guard duty 24 hours a day, in three eight hour shifts, to alert the team of arriving terrorist's intent on reclaiming their location, before all that was valuables was confiscated. They were able to find a large cache of explosives and ammunition, and it appalled the team to find almost everything this terrorist group used was American manufactured. All the ammunition was usable for automatic weapons, including a tripod mounted heavy automatic weapon on one of the three transporters. It was the one to stay behind, and use for guard duty at the rear entrance. If there was a third exit/entry tunnel the team did not find it. They had after finding how the vault was concealed, literally check every inch of tunnel wall for a concealed third entrance. They also anticipated if an assault team were to be dispatched by the terrorists, it would be from the rear, hoping it was not also discovered. The team was on high alert the fourth day after using just enough explosives to crack the vault open. It contained 2 billion dollars in US currency, all nicely bundled in its little wrappers, like it came straight from a US bank. It was loaded onto one of the two departing transporters, but Jackson Frye needed to stay with his team for the expected retaliatory terrorist attack. Since the ammunition was also extremely ample, 70 percent of it was loaded into the second departing transporter, but the cargo shuttle would not take place until after the attack from the terrorist took place. It was expected any day, and the team remained vigilant in watching for any activity outside of the building and tunnel network. Outside of the hill side, there was excellent visibility in the surrounding area. Hummer using her scope for night vision also watched out the rear entrance, while a few other members stood guard at the front, but it would be the back the terrorist were anticipated. The team did not post a single guard outside of the building and tunnel network, seeing how useful it was for the terrorists. During the time of the final terrorist assault and interrogation of the remaining terrorists, all the nearby equipment was gathered and brought to the rear entrance, where they were fully refueled, although there was no need so far to refill the spare tanks.

The terrorists made their appearances two nights later, and Hummer spotted those two miles out with the night vision scope. The team was fully prepared to counter any form of attack, even though the terrorists brought nearly two hundred with them. The heavy automatic weapon would remove a good portion of those, since they would need to approach from open ground to the tunnel entrance. When the terrorist first disembarked, they took up stations nearly 1500 hundred yards beyond the tunnel entrance. The heavy automatic weapon was capable of firing 1,000 rounds per minute and two people were manning it, one for quicker reloads more than to assume the position of firing it.

When the terrorists attacked in the first ten minutes, over 65 percent of the troops were removed by the heavy automatic rapid fire weapon. The terrorist tried to regroup a little bit, and send teams of four, to see if they could close in that way, the team allowed that, just to use smaller weapons to dispatch the first five teams. It left only forty-five terrorists of the 200 hundred they sent. At this point, Jackson decided to take the attack to them, using the heavy automatic for cover fire, he dispatched his close quarter's experts to infiltrate and remove those left. Once again under cover of night and dressed in all black, the experts were able to get behind the attacking terrorists. It would be a little more difficult to get to arm's reach but not impossible, they simply had to tread softly to avoid being heard. The team of close quarter expert's took out an additional 10 terrorists, without a sound to the remaining terrorists. Ideally, Heartless wanted to cut off any chance of the terrorist retreating to their vehicles, to leave before they met their doom.

It took another hour before the last of the terrorists was removed from the picture, he was making an attempt to get to one of the vehicles, when a close quarter's expert sliced his throat to the point of nearly removing his head. It was a little messy for the expert, but it was not like he never had previous experience.

Once the first attack was cleaned up having found excavating equipment in the garage size tunnel area. The bodies were all disposed of in a large gravesite that would not get marked in any way. The team now had the opportunity to survey what they had obtained. Besides the fact within the hillside, it was far cooler than being out in the open, they had a barracks area with 60 beds, more than enough for the team to use. There was a well equipped kitchen area, and large dining area, although comfortable seating was not an option. The walk in cooler and freezer were full of things none of them recognized as real food, but some of it was. All the supplies they had remaining were placed in one or the other. The items they could not identify, were left for the buzzards, although they did bury the dead to keep the smell of rotting corpses from entering into the surroundings that they had acquired. Although Jackson Frye did not know for certain another attempt would be made, he figured he had time to go through a shuttle run back to home base and return. It would take four days for him and half a dozen of his team to make the round trip, and unload the extras they acquired in the first location, which was now the base camp for the team. While he was gone, he wanted the team to find and locate some of the mobile rocket/

missile launchers to remove permanently. The terrorist group brought one vehicle that was modified in such a way, Jackson Frye could not truly determine what it was, outside of ugly. It did appeared to have a small crane mounted on it, and assumed it was to take back the vault in one piece, and drag it a portion of the way from the location hillside tunnel and building complex. It was destroyed, since it would not fit on the cargo plane, even if it was the only vehicle.

The team while remaining on vigilant guard duty, had uncovered three missile launchers of which all were within 30 miles of base camp. When Jackson Frye and his other members returned, since there were five Jeeps in the tunnel garage, he dispatched three with three member teams, to attempt to remove the located missile launchers. These were also items he had no use for, and they were to be totally destroyed, although some explosives, would be required to set the initial charge, the missiles should take care of the remainder, as long as they did not launch, which was highly unlike requiring targeting and use of a firing apparatus. It could be farther away from the launcher than sitting on it to hit a button.

It took a week to remove the three missile launchers, and another three days for all of them to be back in base camp. To this point, there were nearly 300 dead terrorist and not a single scratch on any of the team members. All of this was reported on a regular basis to the main base in DC, where Zoe relayed it to Romero Trap when he was able to be at the base location. Doing his double duty, did not always work out best for Zoe, but she did what had to be done and made no complaints about it. She also liked the fact there was no one else around, she could cook all the best food for herself, and sleep until she felt like getting up. The team did not make more than a single report back to home base in any given day. Things appeared to be well in hand with Jackson Frye leading the team. Romero Trap at one point had to ask Zoe if he had become obsolete, at which point Zoe told him, his detailed planning was still quite invaluable to his team, and without it they might feel they got in over their heads.

He still wished he could be on hand with the team to be more valuable to his own assignment, but knew with his Vice President's duties, he could not have it both ways. He did know for a fact, after President Thomas Hardesty was done with his term or terms of office, he was done with being a political figure. Which Hardesty had all but assured him if it went two terms, he was not allowed to have more than twelve years in any US government office in politics? He wanted nothing to do with local and state levels of politics.

The team was making progress, but he still had no idea how many cells that would need to be dealt with. Some were so well hidden that satellite imagery did not aid in the slightest.

With one large cell and three missile launchers out of the picture, it was just less to deal with in the Middle East region, and still no confirmation on to whether the group had Afghanistan to deal with also. That was totally unknown to the single terrorist they forced to disclose information. With the techniques used by his team to get information, there were no lines that could not be crossed, they had no government backing or sanctions to be concerned with, and intended to take no prisoners. It was how being independent needed to be, with no agency to hold accountability to, and Romero Trap was not going to induce any such stipulations to getting an assignment completed. He did somewhat set the guidelines for the team, but he permitted a good deal of flexibility in his plan. He as well as the entire team, were treading new territory when taking on this assignment, at least in the duration factor. So, things had to be allowed to play out as each situation called for, Trap could not afford to be that rigid in his team's methods to carry out a mission. He had no place for prisoners, and did not need to make it any form of priority in the assignments he accepted.

His only limitation to any assignment was, collateral damage where the lives of innocent's needed to be spared whenever humanly possible. He could not prevent an innocent from stepping into the line of fire from fear or panic, but he did not have his team set explosives to destroy a building housing one enemy and 100 or more innocent people, it was not the means to a job well done, and his team members all knew it.

The team was still using the satellite imagery to locate the next potential target site, and one was believed to be discovered. It was forty five miles from the newest base camp location, and even better conceal than the first location. It was surrounded by large hillsides, nearly mountains, but just short by the standards used to classify such types of terrain. It had a single access point, which although difficult to reach, the same was true for the fools who were within the location, trying to exit it.

The team's new base camp did have its own water supply. It was assumed based on the terrain and the distance from a populated area, it was underground stream or well, most likely stream. Three miles away was a narrow tree line, which in all likelihood was fed by the roots reaching the stream for water to flourish the best they could. At three miles away they could not identify the type of tree, but it did not matter since they could not identify them from the trees, they were most familiar. It would explain some of the excavating equipment located in the tunnel garage. It would seem they originally set a well and ran piping to the tunnel and building complex. It fed the kitchen and showers located inside, although there was no hot water provided. With the daytime heat, it was almost pleasant to step into a cold shower for relief. The team remained on guard duty, but did not anticipate another attack force, since they had more than enough time to remove what the terrorists would deem of value, largely two billion in US currency. That was now within the control of the DC based location. Romero Trap decided to keep it in the secure storage area, rather than dividing it up for the banks. It would come in handy for the upcoming assignment from the President, and Romero Trap was sure there were more to come.

It took the team another month to find the weaknesses in the other location they found. It was not populated by nearly as many terrorists, but at fifty in a tightly accessed area, it was still a more difficult task than the first one. It was found the best means to get into the location would be to use the hills above to scale down into the well-hidden stronghold. It would mean vigilant communications among those who would be top side to scale down, as well as the remaining members awaiting near the single entry point. This assault would require all 35 members of the team, in a coordinated plan to attack and take the whole operation in one move. They also had a tunnel network without any indication of a constructed building. They failed to have more than one entry point.

It was like they never expected to have anyone enter their domain that was not authorized. To Jackson Frye it would be like shooting fish in a barrel.

His initial plan was to use all the rifle people he had from the hillside, they did not need to be long range shooters, merely people who could hit a target from 50 yards with the hillside being cover. The location did seem to have a number of terrorists milling about outside the tunnels, but they seemed rather unsuspecting of an attack, not even having the weapons they carried at the ready. It was not going to be a nighttime attack, more like dusk, where there would still be enough light to make out a target without night vision, while a team would prevent escape from the single access point. It would not make a wise base camp from the team's perspective, and would be completely destroyed upon obtaining anything of value once within the tunnels.

It was not the most opportunistic plan devised, but considering the level of terrorists with military training, he expected no real damage to his team of experts. It went exactly as planned, thirty terrorist were down from the initial attack by the rifles, and it was not too difficult to continue down the hillside to enter the tunnels. Another forty members were within the tunnel networks, and none seemed to be aware of the gunfire that occurred outside the tunnels. They were the most ill-prepared group that Jackson Frye had encountered in his long profession, as a covert military operative. The terrorists may be good at creating panic within a populated region, but had no clue about military tactics.

In the end there were 70 more dead terrorists, no wounded or casualties on the team, and a good load of booty. The caves not only had an abundance of ammunition but the weapons that went with them. All were usable by the team. The transporter was brought in to load up the cache of weapons and ammunition. They also rode off with six more Jeeps, and used explosives to destroy the remainder of the location used by the terrorist group plaguing commercial airlines.

It did take another 24 hours to return to the base camp, formerly used by terrorists. Another shuttle run to the DC location was performed prior to locating the next location. This time two more transporters were returned, and two Jeep's leaving them with a pair of transporter's and 5 Jeep's to get around the region in quicker fashion than by foot.

With Jackson making the second shuttle run to DC, the team took turns trying to locate the next location to hit for the assignment. They found one larger facility than the other two, and wondered what goodies were inside it, but also four missile launcher sites, none were closer than 60 miles. It would soon be necessary to relocate to another base, hopefully as equipped as this one, but none of them held their breath over that prospect.

Once Jackson Frye returned to the ground base in the Middle East, aside from being able to get the cargo plane closer to the base, it was decided to remove the launchers prior to the larger location. It only took three days to take out the four missile launchers using only jeeps, to traverse the distance. They were quicker and more agile for what waited for them at the other end of their destinations. None were over 100 miles, so it was not the longest travel any of them ever faced in enemy territory. Jackson (Heartless) Frye considered their current whereabouts as enemy territory, and would do so for as long as he was in charge of the mission. The only way he would not be in charge, was if something unforeseen occurred, like being killed or severely wounded, considering the training level of his adversary, he did not think that was likely to occur.

The cache of explosives was more than sufficient to set off the first of multiple explosions that occurred with each missile launcher, the detonation did not occur until the team members were well clear of the launcher, not knowing for certain what might take place with a missile over normal explosives. Caution was also one of Romero Trap's conditions for accepting any assignment, it was better to make small advances than loose team members to an assignment. It was rather paramount to Romero Trap since in most assignments, they were going up against much more formidable numbers than they possessed. Take out a few at a time, and wait to repeat was far more in Trap's mindset, than to have an entire team killed by taking on far more than they were prepared to do. In fact, it was one of things that made most of Trap's associates return over and over again for assignments. Trap did not consider a percentage of casualties as acceptable losses, like the military, who those that gave the orders, seldom if ever were involved in the skirmishes they planned out. Romero Trap felt any loss of life, was unacceptable, and was not overly happy with any of his people being wounded. In most cases the wounds were not serious enough to make any of his people unable to continue with their chosen profession, but some were simple stupidity, and he could never account for that in his planning. A single loss of concentration could be the difference between leaving without a scratch, and having a wound requiring medical attention. There were no wounds in this age of technology that did not require some medical attention, even if it was merely to insure no infection arose from a foreign object making contact with human flesh.

Trap also tried to insure his people were protected from major damage with body armor, although to overcome that issue, some of the adversaries they encountered, used armor piercing ammunition and weapons for that use. In many ways technology was become his biggest enemy, as they were developing weapons with the ability to seek out heat, like the temperature of the human body. It would take marksmanship entirely out of the equation, and Romero Trap did not want to be active in the field when those weapons were perfected. Largely because he had no countermeasures to insure the safety of his team members.

It was time for the team to pull up roots and seek closer ground to the next location they had imagery concerning, and now it was time to get up close and personal. The water tank was refilled with the water supply they had in the terrorist location, they decided not to destroy it in the event they could not find another suitable location, so five team members stayed behind, to insure it remained safe. The other location they found was 130 miles away over harsher terrain, although not impassable with the water tank in tow, several detours were required due to the ground being unsuitable for the water tank to traverse, without being damaged or overturned. As a result of the terrain and the detours, it took 3 and a half days to get to a position close enough to observe without being seen in return. They had chosen a longer path to get to the higher ground surrounding the base, and using the hillsides for cover, although to get eyes on the targets, it required a bit of treacherous hiking, but no mountain climbing was needed.

They brought the gear to get down the hillsides quicker if it became needed, but it was not necessary to set hand holds and grappling hooks to make the descent, but the view was much better from the top than the basin where the location was dug into. The location was concealed well, but had multiple access points and was surrounded by numerous hills, although the location had passage points around their camp. The only way they even spotted this location from satellite imagery, was using the infrared imagery available, only by heat signatures did they recognize it as a possible camp location, because there were too many bodies moving around in an area lacking population. It was further decided that no nomadic tribes were that large in number and would only bed down for a night, and move to better grounds.

They set up in the hillsides around the terrorist location for three days doing nothing more than closer surveillance, to see if this group was any better prepared than the other two. If they were, it was certainly not evident, the team in the hillsides were shuttled water canisters to stay hydrated. If would be another after dark assault on the seemingly unsuspecting terrorists, nothing was ever taken for granted by Trap's team of experts, quite familiar with warfare tactics and especially the element of surprise. Food rations were not being cooked in the transporter setup to be a portable kitchen, but meats were dehydrated on flat metal tins, and sun baked into pieces of jerky or similar types of food. It would sustain the team for the duration of this job, but they would need a decent meal shortly afterwards. On the fourth night, keeping both rifle and automatic weapons trained upon the terrorist camp location, the dozen close quarter's experts descended to the basin area, but remained out of plain sight. The dozen were joined by four other members efficient in silent weapons, such as throwing knives, darts and the like. The communications headsets in place, it was kept quiet to avoid discovery too quickly, using only hand signals, they moved about the basin to reach the closest target staying within the shadows of the hillsides around the camp. In fifteen minutes, there were 16 more dead terrorists, and then five minutes later another 10, the throwing weapons were retrieved after using the corpses as cleaning towels. They were joined by the other members with firing weapons to enter into the tunnels, to find what they may inside, prepared for anything, they slowly made their way down seven different tunnels breaking the team up into small groups, but each team had weapons with triggers in the lead.

With a first shot fired, all the tunnels were now active and almost as soon as a terrorist in panic mode ran into the tunnel, he was eliminated. The weapons sounded for twenty minutes before all went quiet. A single team member remained near the vehicles to both guard and insure they were not going to be damaged or stolen by the terrorists, should any escape. After the shooting had stopped for five minutes and the teams made sure it was safe to progress forward, a single large vehicle engine was heard starting up and from the roar of the motor, it left in a hurry. To where, they did not care, if it meant more terrorists returning for this location to take it back, the team was certainly up to the task for what the terrorist offered in fighting ability to this point. Two hours of surveying tunnels and rooms within the network of tunnels, showed this network had four entrance and exit points, the large garage type exit, seemed to be common among all this terrorist's locations. This one also had a number of transporters, jeeps and pickup trucks, which Jackson Frye could not figure out how useful they would be in this terrain. There was also excavating equipment, similar to the first building and tunnel location. After determining the majority of tunnels and some rooms, the body count inside the tunnel was 65 terrorists, with another 26 outside. The tunnels were all wide enough for a jeep to pass through, so using a jeep supplied by the terrorists, the bodies were moved outside the tunnels, the excavating equipment started up and all 81 terrorists were inside the terrain of the Middle East, they were so fond of destroying. This one also had a kitchen with the same amenities as the first, and although it would require more people to guard four entrances than two, it would serve as the next lodging location of the team. Further inspections would be performed after all the team members present had a decent meal, to regain the strength and energy consumed over that last few days.

While checking out the terrorist stores in the cooler and freezer, they found far more food items they recognized than the first time around. It was sufficient to have a grand meal twice each day, for three months without restocking. The members left at the other location, were told to gather everything useable, and join the rest of the team. They would be joining them in two more days, since they had no water tank to tow and enough water canisters to make the trip, along with all the food supplies left. Weapons and ammunition were loaded into one transporter. Food into another, and three jeeps were left for the five, so each had to drive something. All the other vehicles were in the new location that had not been shuttled to the DC base. There were a few more to go this time, and Jackson Frye considered a couple pieces of the excavating equipment to go along to, in case it might come in handy for the DC base location of abandoned buildings. But with the number of vehicles they were acquiring, he would need to make several shuttles runs to DC and back before moving onto the next location, but not necessarily the next target, depending on what they could come up with on satellite imagery. There had to be more missile locations to be removed, to make the area considerably safer for aircraft of non-military use.

After a very large meal for all the members of the team, the rest afterwards only lasted an hour before resuming their search for what was valuable were worth keeping. To be on the safe side, guards were posted at the entrance points to all four tunnels. They did not know what or if to expect company, but one vehicle left with an unknown number aboard. They had to go somewhere and being religious fanatics, it was not likely they were deserting their post. What the terrorists had left as far as reinforcements or real fighters had yet to be seen. Jackson Frye had to believe that there had to be some true warriors among the group, to have amassed a following and the funds for mobile missile launchers. The only other way this type of people operated was to get young children and brainwash them into being fanatics, but usually that was more for suicide missions, than what had been seen of this group.

With the computers and the transporters each having some form of generator to keep the battery charged sufficiently, they did get to keep tabs on the world news, although staying up to the minute was not likely to occur, just enough information to see if they were making any headway in the assignment. The good news was the number of downed aircraft had diminished significantly. Jackson did not know if that was because the terrorist lost a large portion of their missile launchers already, or simply were not in position for a missile launch. Since they were mobile and with the loss of seven, they might be moving frequently to keep from being targeted by whoever was behind the rapid disposal of troops and equipment.

One room within the tunnel network was another motherlode of valuables. Four large locked strongbox were picked to find gold bars inside, it was too heavy for most of them but two people to even consider moving. The two behemoth of humanity were physical specimen's Thor would have been proud of. Although Thor was considered folklore legend, there were enough tales concerning this Norse god, it was hard to believe none of it had any truth to it. The two men each grabbed a handle on each side and without as much as a muscle bulge, hoisted the strongbox onto the jeep, they repeated the process three more times. The jeep looked about ready to lift its front tires off the ground. The pair of hugely muscled men walked behind the jeep, as it slowly made its way to the garage tunnel area. So much as a pebble under one of the front tires was enough to get a rise out of the jeep. It was almost comical, but the two men were too large to sit on the front of it for ballast, and a driver to see where he was going.

Before completely looking over the tunnels room, a communication on the head set gear came from the garage tunnel area. The message started out with it looks like the terrorists communications have gone to hell in a handbasket, you are not going to believe what is taking place 1,000 yards from the tunnel entrance. He did not detail further, so Jackson Frye went to go see for himself.

Jackson Frye was dumbfounded, how could these people have made the assignment list, for how stupid they were was beyond him. The terrorists moved a missile launcher to within 1000 yards of the one of the entrance tunnels, and were putting it into firing position for aircraft. He used his headset communications to get four long rifle people quickly assembled, and told them, the terrorist were too dumb to be allowed to live, he wanted each to pick a target get into position, and take all four out at the same time. He then asked his guard if he could drive that mobile missile launcher. The guard replied to Frye that if it had wheels, he could usually figure it out fairly quick.

Fifteen minutes later four more dead terrorists reached their promised paradise. Jackson Frye, as with most of the team doubted such a paradise existed, and certainly not for fanatics. In took ten minutes to get the missile launcher close enough to the tunnels to determine in its current position, it was not going to fit inside. He was not sure what time it was in Washington DC, but it was time to get some information and preferable from Romero Trap. He used satellite communication gear to make contact. His first question was whether a missile launcher could target longitude and latitude positioning. Romero Trap said since he had computers to look it up on the computer system of the military, he had access to the information, and the computers were quite secure. Frye apologized for asking, but he was running on empty and needed rest so he was not thinking his clearest. Romero Trap asked him why he needed such information, and Frye relayed the details of the stupidity of terrorists they were dealing with.

Romero Trap could not believe what he was told, and asked if he was hallucinating from lack of sleep. Frye said if he was, so were at least another six team members and they were all having the same one. Romero Trap found that more difficult to believe than what he was originally told by Frye, and told Frye to get some rest. He would be able to think more clearly afterwards. Frye agreed, called the team together, asking who felt most capable of guard duty for eight to ten hours, before they got to rest. Susan Hobart (Hummer), Roberto Gomez (Lucky), Robert Holmes (Lightsout) and Zi Yang (KungFu) all took up guard duty, and the terrorist's barracks room had over 100 beds. Most of the people showered first, but Frye was at his limit, he went to sleep no matter if the mattress needed to be burned after he used it.

Jackson Frye slept for 10 straight hours, and upon awaking he realized just how badly he needed to shower. The mattress would definitely need to be burned later on that day. With some breakfast for some people, guards were replaced so they could get sleep, most partook in breakfast before going to the showers and getting sleep. The buzzards were circling over the location where the missile launcher was, and Frye decided to let them have their little feast, while they could.

He searched what he could find concerning the missile launcher, and found out as long as it used missiles of any sort, longitude and latitude coordinates could be utilize for targeting. If it was rockets, that was not as accurate. Rocket were for short range and there were no set distances to go by for the rockets. Most were used to try to target close aircraft, and hope to time the path correctly. It was more shooting a really big gun at an airplane or jet fighter in most cases. Missiles had far more distance, and could utilize a number of targeting methods, including laser targeting done by a person closer to the exact destination. They also could have heat seeking capabilities, but missile were labeled in some fashion to describe what they were best used for, and Frye could not find that information out about the missiles he had, but since all missiles could be used for what he wanted to do, it mattered not if he knew.

Jackson took a poll of his team inquiring how many had experience in using missile launchers, and in particular targeting for where the missile should hit. Of his total of 35 team members only one ever did it before, and it was not by design, it was out of necessity. That member was Chance Tomlin (Vicious), who with the killing of the groups missile launcher crew, while in another foreign land, was the only person left to finish a mission, that was supposed to be easy as pie, according to the CIA and Pentagon for his mission. Upon completion of that very mission, Tomlin was grateful to have been asked to join the growing number of independent contractors of Romero Trap. Never regretting a single moment since, although Romero Trap allowed his associates the freedom to accept assignments from other sources of independent origins, Vicious never trusted anyone but Trap, to insure his survival was at its highest potential. Vicious did know even Romero Trap could not guarantee it, if he did something too stupid or reckless, so Tomlin tried to think out everything in advance of the action to follow.

Frye had Vicious used one computer to take in as much information as he could in using the targeting system of the missile launcher. It was imperative for Tomlin to understand this was to be a ground to ground strike, as opposed to ground to air. He also informed him, he thought it might speed up the process of eliminating the other missile launchers used by the terrorists, at least up to the next eight, since that was all the missiles, they had with one launcher.

9

With a Little Help from Friends

The team was busy trying to locate other missile launcher locations, and seeing if Afghanistan had any bases of operation within this terrorist group. Somewhere in the mix, Jackson Frye (Heartless) felt there had to be some real warriors involved in the terrorist group that to this point, only proved they were poorly trained and largely just plain stupid, at least in military tactics. He knew from experience, Afghanistan had some very excellent people in war tactics and guerilla warfare, since they had turned away countless attempts to invade their country going all the way back to Genghis Kahn. They were always badly outnumbered, and still managed to prevail over well trained military troops for centuries. The country was considered the eastern most edge of the Middle East, and depending upon where within the nation a base might be found, would decide how to best go about that part of their mission, to remove this terrorist group from the planet for the sake of all countries. Jackson Frye did not want to truly enter the country for this leg of the mission, as it seemed the people of the entire country felt anyone entering their lands were invaders and dealt with accordingly. He wanted to avoid losing team members to the harsh stance upon strangers in Afghanistan.

The plan was to locate the missile launchers used by the terrorists and try to take them out with the one they had obtained. Chance Tomlin had devoured all the information he could and practiced using the targeting mechanism for coordinates. Longitude and Latitude would be provided by the satellite imagery system, and it was deemed very accurate from past uses by the military. The missile launcher was capable to adjust to a fraction of a degree in the coordinates, and accuracy for missile launches of this nature had to be exact.

It took nearly three weeks for the team to discover a missile launcher location and Chance Tomlin immediately got the launcher into a position to start the targeting to go for a direct hit. It was decided by Jackson Frye, since the terrorists had increase the movement of the remaining launchers significantly, as soon as one was located to get into strike position, and once sure it was perfectly targeted to fire the missile. Chance found he had a hand held remote firing device for the launcher, so he could get well clear of the missile when it fired off. He was certain he did not want to be too close as it seemed it would do more than singe some eyebrows.

With the location of the terrorist's missile launcher, it took twenty minutes to position their launcher and set the targeting coordinates, and another five for Chance Tomlin to retreat to the tunnel opening. It was quick enough to make sure the targeted missile launcher would not be moved. Since this region of the world had continual satellite imagery feeds, they could use the computer to determine if the missile was true to target.

The missile strike was as true as one could hope making first impact with the missile array on the terrorist launcher, causing a massive fireball explosion of 9 missiles exploding in near unison. The crater left was further proof of the power of the explosion as debris of the launcher was scatter about, but largely what pieces were what, was undeterminable. A week later a second launcher was located, and Tomlin got the missile launcher positioned and targeting set before again retreating to the tunnel entrance. This was going to a little trickier than the first missile strike, since it was found using infrared sighting on the satellite imagery, it was determined by the positions of the four man terrorist crew to each launcher, it could not be anything other than a missile launcher, but the thought of nomadic people seeking a place to sleep was considered and ruled out.

This missile sent from the team's base location was not quite as true, but did destroy the launcher and the terrorists, but the explosions of the terrorist missile launcher were more sporadic, and they only counted a total of seven. It took nearly an hour for the red image on the satellite imagery to die out sufficiently to determine there were no surviving terrorists in proximity to the launcher destroyed.

That put the team up to ten missile launchers removed from the terrorists arsenal, one being the one they were now using to destroy the last two. Tomlin was down to six remaining missiles, but he had not wasted any with a poor targeting setting.

The team was still trying to locate a definite location in Afghanistan, and thinking they might have a large location identified, they needed to monitor it to make a better determination. It was set up largely like the other locations with far more tunnels than out buildings, although this location had two buildings built into high terrain surrounding them, and like the other they were mostly within the terrain. The terrorists seemed to stay away from outwardly visible buildings, likely to conceal as much as possible from prying eyes in the skies. The location was only 25 miles from the western most border of the country, and could easily be a defensive group for the purpose of keeping their lands safe from invaders. The team was trying to better identify its true purpose and determined if they could identify any vehicles entering or leaving their tunnel network, it would give them the answers they needed. Since all the vehicles and equipment, they had uncovered to this point was of American manufacturing, that would be the key they sought. If it was Russian or Chinese, they would refrain from targeting the location.

The team had been on the ground for nearly five months, and it would be longer without the missile launcher to track down the others used by the terrorists. Since they were moving from one location to another in rapid fashion, finding them on Satellite imagery and deploying a team, it would get them to a vacated location and the hunt would start again. With the missile launcher, they could send far quicker and not allow them time to relocate, and not waste personnel on a mission that would fail to produce positive results.

What Jackson Frye did want to find was another terrorist camp, which might have the missile stockpile to keep in the newest camp location, to insure all the missile launchers were destroyed, and to target an Afghanistan base, if one was completely determined to exist? To this point in the mission, it was still speculation the terrorists did operate in or out of Afghanistan. Overall, the entire region had many ways to conceal the terrorist's base locations, but one thing known, it was unlikely they would set up bases in populated areas or cities. The primary means to avoid detection, was using the terrain and tunnel networks they created. It also allowed for a fair survival rate from previously used attack methods, largely targeting from military warcraft of flight. Since it was difficult for any jet to have multiple missiles released to hit the identical target repeatedly, the tunnels allowed for them to travel through hillsides and larger terrain that provide a little bit of insulation from a missile strike, or rocket hit into the earth around the tunnel systems.

For the Afghanistan location, if it truly existed, Jackson (Heartless) Frye wanted to unload a full complement of missiles into the area with the tunnel network. In order to accomplish that he needed to find more missiles, from another location more within the region they were operating in. He had made his several shuttle runs to the DC location while the search for more targets took place, and they had moved the additional gold that Romero Trap though exceeded 2 billion dollars' worth. A number of vehicles, more small than large went, and had the team down to three transporters on the ground with five Jeeps. The one transporter was the one with the heavy automatic weapon mounted, another was still the mobile kitchen, although it could still accommodate 10 to 12 team members for movement to a location for a spell of time longer than two days.

It took two more weeks to locate another missile launcher for the terrorists, as they seemed to be able to keep them a bit better concealed from satellite imagery, but they still managed to be spotted periodically, trying to get into a position to down flying aircraft. The team had no idea how many the terrorist's had at their disposal, but since they were not the least expensive pieces of equipment to obtain, nor the missiles they utilized, they felt they had put a large dent into their obtaining more having removed over 4 billion dollars in assets they previously had. That alone should be a fairly large deterrent from obtaining additional armaments for their supposed religious cause. The team did not believe any religion should operate under the guidelines these fanatics try to disguise through a book considered holy.

The location the team now occupied, was never attacked by the terrorists to reclaim what was lost. It was an indication to Jackson Frye that the numbers were dwindling and considering they had not achieved much in the last six months, getting new recruits to fill the void; it was not occurring as rapidly as they were losing members. Closing in on six months in the Middle East, was starting to wear thin on the team, as none of the team members truly enjoyed being where they were located so far from home base. Information was still relayed regularly between the DC base and themselves, but most of them were feeling a little tired of being in the Middle East and desired to be done with this mission. Finally, the team got the confirmation they needed for the Afghanistan location to confirm, it was part of the terrorist cell they were trying to eliminate. The member who saw the satellite confirmation, witnessed six transporters of the same type found leaving and returning to the base location, while also seeing one missile launcher leave. He called it to the attention of others to confirm his findings, and three team members confirmed he was accurate in his findings. The location however was not going anywhere in the near future, and Jackson still needed to obtain more missiles from a closer location.

A location was confirmed the following week, only 60 miles from their current location; but what treasure it held would not be determined until they made inroads within the tunnel network, now believed to be used by all the location of this particular group of fanatics. Jackson Frye had his team concentrate on that location for the next week and a half, to discover weaknesses, as well as opposition to expect to encounter. As luck would have it, while observing the location, an empty missile launcher entered through the tunnel used for a garage, and an hour later was seen leaving with a full complement of missiles. The team was to track where the launcher went to determine if they could apprehend it with a full load of missiles, or needed to destroy it before it relocated again. The launcher was followed for a day and half using the imagery from the satellite to find the fools were within fifteen miles of their location. A team of six, was immediately dispatched with both long rifle and regular rifle as well as Chance Tomlin (Vicious); to bring back the missile launcher completely intact with eight missiles for the Afghanistan location. It was nearly two hundred miles off and there was going to be the need to get a team much closer to insure as few terrorists escaped as humanly possible. Two Jeeps were used to get the seven people in range quickly. Four people were able to get within 500 yards of the missile launcher, while it was still be positioned for whatever the terrorists had in mind for targeting. They did not appear to have a real game plan for targeting, as much chance encounters with overhead aircraft. Although many airline were required to follow a flight path with only limited flexibility. The flexibility was largely determined by the number of airlines using the air corridor for flights between one location and the destination.

The number of airlines using this corridor had significantly dropped, after losing a number of aircraft, and chose to use safer methods to get from point A to point B. Since the team started the mission, only 20 aircraft were downed since they were on the ground in the Middle East, the largest portion being in the first month, before they made the first assault on the terrorists.

With rifles in position, the team held their place to get four clean shots in quick sequence to limit any terrorist remaining alive, although if more information could be obtained, it might prove useful to have a wounded, but still living terrorist.

The team held for a precise moment and made their shots, and three were down instantly, one was quick enough to being hit but not fatally, although he was not going anywhere in a major hurry. The team approached slowly, not certain of what the terrorist might be armed with; and not entirely sure of how badly wounded the surviving terrorist was in the initial volley. As they neared, apparently missile teams carried no weapons other than a vicious looking knife. They fired missiles, they should not be close enough to the fighting to require a weapon, is what they were told when taking on that particular duty. The survivor had a badly broken arm from where he was hit, and limited mobility as a result. He did not even attempt to reach his knife, as he would have needed the arm that was broken to reach it. He was rather cooperative in providing the team information, this was the only remaining missile launcher the group had left, since there had been none available on the black market, since they had a large portion of their funds confiscated. He had never been to the main base camp, but that was the only place remaining that may still have any funds available. The team already knew of the location the missiles came from, and aside from the main base, only two very small cells were left in the region beyond the base camp. For his cooperation, he was rewarded with a quick death by a single gunshot to the head at close range. The shooter would have done the same for any severely hurt animal, though he did note that while an animal that knew it was going to die and begged for release, a human begged for their life, even if they had no way to get to help before they would die anyway. He consider the bullet to the head a far more humane means than letting him suffer endlessly, until he fell prey to hungry animals or simply bled to death.

It took longer to return to the base location than to get to the missile launcher site. The missile launcher was capable of traversing the rough terrain, but due to its payload it did need to be a slower, gentler pace than what the Jeeps could do with passengers, that were accustomed to holding onto something to keep from being jostled out of the vehicle. They now had three vehicles to return with, and the trip was taken at a more moderate pace covering the fifteen miles over one hour.

Upon arriving to base camp, the team informed their leader Jackson Frye, what they had learned, which meant there was only one more target left to strike before their mission was completed. Leaving behind two small cells which was conceal so well that it was not possible to locate with satellite imagery, was not terribly awful. The best the remaining members of this terrorist group could hope for, was to be absorbed into another group. It would take decades for them to rebuild to the levels they had and the track record they had to show for it; was not very good incentive for new members wanting to join.

With the latest information it was time to decide who would like to be a part of the Afghanistan road trip mission. They would be able to take the mobile kitchen transporter and one other transporter, largely the one with the mounted heavy automatic weapon, and the two who did not get an option, preferred to carry the automatic weapons of mass destruction. There was no way to cover all the entrances/exits of the tunnel complex in Afghanistan, and in all likelihood, there would be some that managed to escape, their mission was to limit the number of people emerging from tunnels, to get away from the hillside coming down upon them. The team of sixteen members would be able to cover at least two exits, possibly three, and all would have automatic weapons of some type. They needed to be in place ahead of the missiles being launched, and now that Frye knew he had the last two missile launchers, he could have Tomlin send a total of 14 missile into the hills of the terrorist camp. The general concept for Tomlin was to target middle to rear, allowing only front exits to be escape routes for the awaiting team members to cut down, with extreme prejudice. Considering the distance between destination and base location, it may take a week for the team to get into place.

While the team was in the Middle East, back home President Thomas Hardesty had gotten his overwhelming approval from the people to put the business flat tax systems to work. The number of businesses trying to cheat the profit margins was found to be quite minimal, as most of them felt it was far fairer than the last decade of continuing tax hikes; and no improvement in the way government spent money they did not truly have. The plan did put the government running modestly in the black, but there was room for vast improvements to have any impact on the deficit. President Thomas Hardesty would spend the next year working on going over all the amendments to the bill of rights; that provided the leaders of government to act without the approval of the people, and try to right the ship that had had listed badly to one side. These measures would further improve the economy, as some of them were just plain silly, to make it law to keep businesses from behaving like the government, when it came to finances. With this in mind, he was truly trying to restore the people right's and force government into acting as a role model for businesses to follow, as opposed to saying do as we say, not as we do policy. It would take some time for his people to work out the proper wording to get into the Supreme Court to agree with, while another wording meaning the same identical thing would be presented to the people for vote.

Thomas Hardesty was successfully bypassing the governing bodies and going directly to the people of this country, to get things done as quickly as it could be achieved. The representatives of each state were hard pressed to contradict the decision of the people, although under the modified members of the government, there were fewer and fewer arguments with those members, even with the long time office holders, who managed to keep their place in government. His secret service team still remained on high alert for any problems to develop, largely with those long time members of the house and Senate, who no longer had government positions. They did uncover one such plot, and put a quick end to it, and although it was done in such a fashion for the person responsible to claim no such knowledge; it did keep them from trying other such means to bring the President to an early and permanent retirement. The president was working with his team of experts to bring about the quickest and most effective means to return the government back to its original identity. A government for the people by the people, was his ultimate goal during his first term in office, assuming if he was successful in his undertaking, a second term was inevitable. It was still like everything else he put into the hands of the people, their decision ultimately.

Back in the Middle East, the team to oversee the Afghanistan location considered to be the largest to date, and ultimately the terrorist group to be eliminated, was dispatched to a closer location. Due to the terrain they had to cover and numerous stops to refuel the members, not the vehicles, it took 10 days to circumnavigate the distance. The farther east they travelled, the more treacherous the terrain became, causing numerous detours for them to work their way through. Although everything they operated was considered all-terrain vehicles, dropping fifty feet, was not in the description of what the vehicles were capable of overcoming. They encountered a large number of impassable trenches along the way. After the ten days of travel, the team reported back they had established a base location, but would need another 24 hours to get into more appropriate positions, to insure the least likely number of terrorists escaping unharmed. There was absolutely no possible way to take out every single member of the group.

With this factor quite literally set in concrete, the team was to remove as many terrorist as humanly possible, without putting themselves into harm's way. This being the last assault the team needed to perform in the Middle East, it was paramount to return to home base with everybody, and none needing any form of medical attention. With heavy automatic weapons leading the assault; it should not be any conflict in interest with the team members.

With the heavy weapons in place for the final assault on the terrorist's largest base, they were made aware of for the region, communication to base camp were sent to commence missile fire onto the location. They were a full fifteen hundred yards from the tunnel entrance, and would not get closer, until the missiles concluded, since 14 was the maximum, they possessed. From their advantage, it was almost fun to watch as one missile after the other hit from middle to rear of the compound housing the terrorists. It took the team ten minutes to get closer to their exit points, but it took 15 minutes for the terrorists to start exiting, none seemed to be prepared to have a ground assault on top of a missile assault. Forty minutes of sporadic heavy automatic weapons fire erupted upon the unsuspecting terrorists, trying to get out of the devastation from within the tunnels. The reason for the weapons to be sporadic and taking forty minutes, was largely due to how the terrorist presented themselves in the escape process. When all was seemingly calm from within the tunnel network the terrorists used for base camp, the team made their wary approach to the three exit/entrance openings that were closest. The rear of the hillside looked like the majority had collapsed, and there should be a large body count under its weight of rock and dirt. The team found nothing in their approach to hinder entering the different tunnels entrances they each covered. Once everything was accounted for, they had exhausted 4,000 rounds of heavy automatic weapon fire and 2,000 rounds of smaller automatic fire, as well as 500 rounds of rifle and hand gun weapons. They still had a modest amount left, but would need to count literally every round as they entered the tunnel systems. One person tried to count the bodies of terrorists outside the tunnel exits they had covered, and after 30,000 he gave up. Since the heavy automatic weapons could pass through multiple targets if it worked out, it accounted for the number of bodies in comparison to the number of rounds fired, since 50 caliber projectiles did considerable damage and traveled a greater distance.

Upon approaching the tunnel entrances of each tunnel, there were still a few die hard terrorist trying desperately to survive the devastation that surrounded them. In all three tunnels there were a total of fifty still alive, before return fire removed them from the equation. The tunnel entrance afterwards were clear of any more terrorist seeking some form of refuge from what was left of their tunnel network and base of operation. After finding most of the tunnels fully collapsed, only making it so far into the complex, the estimate was made based entirely upon previous attacks using missiles for the tunnel network devastated by this same type of attack, they had removed between 65,000 and 70,000 terrorists in a single attack. They were not going to unearth the true count, and were certainly going to use explosives to complete the destruction so it could not be used again in the near future. They had no idea for certain that it could be functional again, but they did not believe it would be done in a matter of months, maybe over a matter of years.

Some of the more forward areas were still accessible, although some debris had to be moved to open doorways and clear passages ways to determine what lie beyond. In their search for valuables, they found a modest cache of ammunition they could use, at least it was sufficient to deal with any other surviving terrorists lurking in the shadows. Additionally, they found a rather hefty sum of US currency and gold bars estimated to be worth 8 billion dollars. It took the two behemoths a little more time to load these on to a vehicle, since the tunnels would no longer accommodate one. They also found that although the center and rear were the primary target areas for the missiles, the garage area of the tunnel was partial intact. They found after the fourth day of surveying the site, half a dozen transporters, one also with another heavy automatic weapon mounted. Five jeeps in useable condition, and the rest was pretty much damaged beyond repair. They did find two damaged missile launchers, and being fully loaded it would make an excellent location for the explosives they brought, to make the location never again useable. The other location would be where the ammunition was found, and those items not useable, would help further devastate the tunnel complex. The timers were set for 24 hours, allowing them sufficient time to evacuate the tunnels with all the valuables loaded, and vehicles moved from harm's way. They retreated to a safer location with everyone and a total of 16 vehicles, and since they only had sixteen people in the team, everyone would need to drive something back to home base in the Middle East.

It would take them another week and half to return, once they made their final departure from Afghanistan, and with only 25 miles to the border, they felt they were unlikely to encounter additional resistance, especially with them heading to the border and not deeper into the lands of a very protective people. The explosives that were set went off and the hillside was turned into a high pile of rubble. There was no way in the next century, these hillsides would hold up to tunnels and rocket or missile attacks.

The team reported back to base location they had accomplished the task they set out to perform. It was decided per team member, to be outside of the territory of Afghanistan, before setting up to partake in a meal cooked within the mobile kitchen they utilized. The area in the last tunnel location thought to be a kitchen and dining area were completely under the rubble of the missile strike, and they were unable to acquire any additional food supplies, and would need to be on a rationed food, until returning to base location. Even with that, most of the team was happy to have food out the mobile kitchen than be using the pouches and cans used by the military, given the moniker of K-rations. One member proudly said the military was also horrible spellers, since C-rations were far more appropriate, since it all tasted like crap to him.

There were no members of the team to argue his observation of military premade foods in pouches and cans.

With the team back to the most recent and final base location, Jackson Frye's first concern was getting all the equipment, and valuables back to base location in Washington DC area, which was really Maryland, but since DC was wedged between the borders of Virginia and Maryland, DC operated in both states, as well as the little portion of land considered Washington DC proper. It remained the only area within the entire 50 states, not considered to belong to any other state or have a state government. Additionally, no formal documents were ever produced to indicate it was a US territory or a fully sovereign city, within the boundaries and borders of the United States.

During the ten-day trip back to the home location of the Middle East, Satellite communications to the DC based location returned some rather startling responses directed to the office of the US President, known as Thomas Hardesty. This small internet based message actually informed the President of the success of the Middle East team prior to the confirmation from Romero Trap. The President decided to show it to Romero Trap when he arrived to confirm the team had all but eliminated the terror threat from the region of the Middle East.

The message read, President, we of the Afghanistan peoples who have long protected this country from all sorts of invading forces would like to extend our thanks for removing a blight upon our nation. We are responsible for having provided safe passage to those who reigned terror upon the world, especially those of the airlines and we fully regret having done so. The people who approached seemed sincere enough to carry out Allah's true work, but we were deceived, but by the laws of the Koran, we were unable to take back what was given. From what was seen of the final assault on the blight residing in our nation, it could have only been carried out by professional of the American military, whether with or without your knowledge is inconsequential, we know what we witnessed. No other troops in the world could have performed such decisive and devastating results. We the people of this nation sworn to protect our lands do not give you and anyone else free passage into our territory, and will continue to repel any and all invaders, as is our sovereign right as a nation. By the same token, we must once again thank you for doing something we could not by the laws of Allah, as the holy Koran so states.

Romero Trap felt he should at least forward a copy to his team that was responsible for the good work to receive a thanks and warning, from the tribes that protected the Afghanistan nation from invaders. Romero Trap, looking at it from that viewpoint, he thought maybe that indeed they had that right, as so many centuries of fighting was merely to keep what belonged to their people.

The President told him he did not need to because he was releasing the statement from the Afghanistan's with an addendum of his own thanks, to the unknown parties who achieved such service to the world, without any knowledge or backing from the US government and in particular his own. Thomas Hardesty told him he could inform his team where to look for it if they so desired. Romero Trap said it would explain the influx of profits arriving in the last day and a half from countries and airline alike.

Once Romero Trap made it to the team's home base, he was informed of the immense profits taken from the last terrorist target, and it would require multiple shuttle trips to and from DC, until everything of value was removed from the Middle East before the entire team could return.

It required another month and half for the shuttle service to be completed from the Middle East, and the teams was getting dangerously close to nine months in a region of the world they would all like to avoid if ever possible. The good news is the terrorists were very poorly trained, and the team suffered not a single wound to any of its members, unless they wanted to consider the scratch one member got trying to determine if a certain vegetation of the area, had thorns or not. They all decided from his reaction and slight seepage of blood, that they did indeed have thorns.

It was later confirmed, when one of the team members provided some minor first aid and had to remove a thorn lodged into his skin at the point of the scratch he encountered. He said he had never been treated as a result of some dead looking plant or weed before. He also said he had bullet wounds that did not create such tenderness to any part of his body like that did. His first aid applier told him that was because it was infected, and she cleaned it properly, and used a gauze wrap to keep it covered. Also informed him to prevent any additional infection; to keep it clean and change the wrapping daily, if he needed assistance he only needed to ask.

On the last day of the tenth month away from the other team members, being largely Zoe and Romero, the team had everything they had left for supplies and clothing, as well as weapons and ammunition loaded, and ready to go with the single remaining transporter left in the base camp after shuttle runs. It was a little cramped, but it was not a horribly long ride as the cargo plane was able to get considerably closer in a more secured area, than when they first arrived.

With the plane taking off, at reaching six hundred feet above the ground a flash appear in the close vicinity and it first concerned Heartless, but it turned out to be fireworks, the first flash was followed a flurry of eruptions of colored flashing lights and a few loud booms. Jackson did not know if the people of the region were celebrating the latest terrorist group's demise, or their leaving their homeland. He was never certain about anything when it came to understanding the people of this region, who all claimed to be true believers in the words of Allah, and they had too many interpretations of those words, which all came from the same book. So, to be on the safe side of things, and leave in a gesture not to be confused with aggression, he did a tip to each side of the less than maneuverable cargo plane of the wings as a goodbye gesture. He started from there to get more to the altitude planes of the size of this cargo plane, got better economy from a fuel on board. So far with all the shuttle flights and short trips he had spent over 200,000 dollars on fuel, and there was at least two more refueling to be done before taxiing into the hanger in the DC base, at which time, the next maintenance would need to be performed. It was still a rather long time to be seated in the jumps seats of a cargo plane, the manufacturer of this one, did not take its seat design from Pan AM, or any other major airlines, if anything they got it from a police interrogation room. It required most every member of the team, to make several attempts to get up, and stretch the legs around the space left in the cargo hold of the plane; at least with what was left to bring back, it was not nearly as difficult to do as in the original trip, where the hold was quite full.

The refueling stop took place in the eastern most point of South America, as it was the most direct means to cross the ocean with fuel to reach a destination. The leg home was not so much of a stretch to be thinking it might have just enough fumes to reach land.

When the team made it back to home base, and the last of the equipment was off loaded from the cargo plane, Romero Trap gave them all one month off; to get in some activity other than murder and mayhem around the world. He did say if it involved sexual activities that required payments, to use common sense, although he knew for some men the two activities were never in the same plane of existence. As he thought about all the mentions of male anatomy in relationship to other things, he came to remember one in particular. In general, it stated God definitely had a sense of humor, why else give a man two heads, and only enough blood for one of the two to fully function at any one time.

For the next month, Romero Trap made a few changes in how things would progress over the next few years. With nearly five billion in gold, he needed to convert some into currency to earn interest and investment earnings. He also decide to see since the properties they were using were abandoned, what funds he would lose trying to obtain them. The county in Maryland informed him that the only thing of value was the land, as the buildings were so far out of code, the only thing to do was tear them down and rebuild, which was out of reach for most businesses and the county it belonged to. They would sell the whole lot of buildings on the forty five acres, for 25 million dollars, but all improvement were at the new owner's expense. Romero Trap decided to give the team a true home and made the purchase, under the name of a shell company they all were a part of. The shell company was not traceable beyond some dummy account he set up long ago as a member in the CIA, for a short period of time. Even the CIA did not know it was under their shell company names. But the property that encompassed all the buildings and grounds the team currently used, now belonged to them. He was sure the team would continue to use the utilities in the same fashion already utilized.

Romero Trap also had a load of lumber and other materials delivered to the main building, to be used by the team to make it much more a home. And for the final touch of home, he had a large flat screen for television or cable or whatever means of transmission was used; in the ever changing world of entertainment, along with enough comfortable seating in sectional and lounge chairs to seat all the members of the team comfortably, as long as the two behemoths used the lounge chairs. He also had some plumbers come in and update and modernized the pair of lavatories for each gender. He did not know about having plumbers do anything with the makeshift shower stalls, and considered having showers put into the lavatories, but thought he should hear that from the team. All of this was completed before the month of rest and relaxation came to an end, and the President was made aware of it the moment the team arrived. He was not willing to except another assignment until the team had some time off, they had been working for almost two years, without too much time to themselves between assignments.

The President did not mention any other assignments while the team was taking a break, and spent the better part of his time with Romero present, going over all the bill of rights changes with his small team of people who had been with him for many years.

Thomas Hardesty did not get into politics like many others, having a degree in law, he had a degree in economics, which seemed fruitless with the ways the government was increasing taxes and the economy was bottoming out in the country. When he graduated, he was asked to take a position in the local county government to help it get back into a more desirable position with the funding they had available. There was too much waste, and no regard to where money was going, and it had to stop before the county became insolvent. His term was two years, and he righted the ship so well that he was asked to run for the mayor of a larger city, within the state he lived. He accomplished the same thing as mayor, which pushed into a run for the US Senate, where no matter what he tried, the internal bickering among Senators, was the only thing that seemed to get done. After two full terms in the Senate, and not indulging in the excessive expenses generated by those Senators and Congress folks alike, he made his pitch for a Presidential run, seeing that the people had enough. And that was where he was now, but his team of people were much more eloquent in the use of words acceptable to legal people. The Supreme Court being a part of the legal people, required wording that only legal people took to enjoy. He thought it required an 18th century dictionary if one even existed. It seemed, in the term he called legalese, such documents said a whole lot of nothing, with an abundance of antiquated phrases. In people talk, a fifteen page document could be reduced to four sentences.

10

The Prime Time Assassinations

The team was back and noticed the changes while they were away. When Romero arrived after making massive deposits to the five accounts, he had found that enough funds were available for all of them to have a decent retirement program at the end of this assignment. If nothing else changed, as of this moment they had about 400 million dollars per team member; and it would clean out all the accounts, except for Romero's working assignment funding account which he had prior to the assignment. Team members were informed that the lumber, tools and supplies were to be used as they saw fit to make the buildings more like home. He also informed them that as of three weeks ago, the entire building complex and Property of forty-five acres was now owned by them. Whatever they wished to do for improving it could be arranged, but the county stated the buildings were all too out of code to be considered for anything other than destruction, so the cost was largely just the land, it was really not a bad deal.

It meant the team could use all 12 buildings in the complex if they needed to and they were already using three, although two were simply to keep all the vehicles they obtained from the terrorists and the military. Since they obtained the military issue equipment by forged requisition, a requisition form was under the guidelines of no return was

A SELECT FEW

expected. If it was an acquisition form, that was military terminology for short term lease. And just to keep everyone on their toes in the military, they changed it every 10 years approximately. So next time the forms could mean the exact opposite, from the ones used this time. Once it was obtained, based on either form, the terms of the form remained in effect. This was largely so military supply personnel from the top brass to the new recruit, did not have to pour over past documents to make the change, and put it into effect. The paperwork trail alone would keep them busy for the first five years of each change, and they did not want the headaches associated with government changing policies.

 The team decided since they now had the entire complex to explore for useful items they would start there, it was determined, with the amount of debris and garbage filling the lots and some buildings, dumpsters should be obtained to clean the property up. If they owned it, they might as well improve its appearance. With thirty-seven people in and out of the complex, there was enough additional skills to make repairs and improvements, although whether it was within code or not, was really not a concern, but water leaks in the roofing, or plumbing issues, as well as erecting more solid walls around the sleeping areas, these skills were well within the groups capabilities. The first discovery was a building four structures away from the main building, which was only perused for useful items, but not explored fully. It was a former laundry service and all the equipment was still in place. It would take three of them a week to determine how much was useable and how much was spare parts to keep the working ones running. It did mean they no longer had to find someplace else to do the laundry, as each took care of their own, and after nine months in the Middle East, they all needed to do laundry, most of them, as pointed out by Zoe Dubois, stunk to high heaven, and were left in the garage area with the vehicles to limit the odor in the sleeping quarters. They found out of the sixty commercial washers and dryers that 75 percent of them were still functioning, and as soon as one pair was made available, somebody in the group used them to get laundry done. A jeep was used for all of them to get the laundry supplies each preferred, and this expense was from their 1,000

THE PRIME TIME ASSASSINATIONS

dollars a week payment, but none of them expected to go the four years without some out of pocket costs.

Two weeks after the team had returned, and got the base a little more in shape, during Romero Trap's half day in the White House, the President posed the next assignment for the team, although he did not believe he would need to dispatch the entire team for each of three targets. He would prefer it done quietly, by long distance rifle, something the President knew Trap had at his disposal among his selected team members. The assignment would be a little more openly public, than any of them would like; but three of the world's supposed leaders were major obstacles in the formation of a world governing body, and this was still part of his overall plan to make it happen. One being the biggest obstacle was the latest leader in South Africa, who is bent on having slave trade resume as a means to produce government income. He was also fully in opposition of any governing body that might interfere with his idea of the future of his country. He was not yet labeled a dictator, but he was operating like he was. The simple fact of his wanting to reestablish slave trade as a government sanctioned export, was more than enough to get most of the world's leaders in a foul mood.

As much as he hated to ask the next one, knowing Trap and his team's love for the Middle East, the latest religious and political power in Iraq, had once again started to rewrite the meaning of the Koran, and wants to remove all the infidels from anyplace including the United States; to return the lands to the people of Allah, who he feels are entitled to it all. He cannot be allowed to raise another group of fanatics true to his cause. Both of these leaders are relatively new in their positions of power within their own countries, but world leaders around the globe, are really tired of this type of behavior from that region, and would like it brought to an abrupt halt.

The last piece to the President's problem came from the area of Eastern Europe near the Russian border. That leader is a renegade of the past, and want to bring back the communist power from the past; and really wants to take over all the area that was once under the likes of Stalin; when he held domain over the entire region considered the Soviet Union. He is even being viewed as an enemy of the state by the Russian government, and they specifically asked for assistance in this matter, as it would be considered an act of war, if they make any attempt to curb the problem growing in that area. Since it seems like the names of countries in that area change regularly, I will need to delve a little further into which he considers to be his at this time. He seems to be moving between two currently, and also has support from both. Although, he is only considered the leader in one, he holds power in the second, since they are without any leadership currently.

Romero Trap said he would let his team know, but he did not see needing more than three people in any given location, but it might not be wise to take action on all three in short order, but to spread it out a little, allowing the same team to relocate to the different locations. Of course, there is always the time it takes to establish patterns and points of vulnerability. Something his experts are more equipped to perform than he, but he was never a long rifle expert beyond 1,200 yards. He also preferred to have more than a single round in case things went wrong with his shot. But with a rifle that only takes single rounds, he was not the best person for that type of work any longer.

The day concluded with his lunch in the White House dining room for the first family and Vice President, and he had reached the point of looking forward to the daily meal that was always superb. From lunch, he had to report the latest assignment to the team, although he did not really expect it would be necessary for too many people on his team to be leaving for parts of the world that were not their homes.

Upon his arrival, the first thing he noticed was the team had located gates to place at the entrance of the building complex; to be installed to keep unwanted trespassers away. They were simply, resting against the exit fencing that went around the entire property, and although aged the chain-link fencing was completely intact and holding up to age. Two large debris dumpsters were now in the rear area of the buildings and much of the debris, but not all, was inside of one of the two dumpsters that once filled, would be hauled away for a mere 1,200 dollar fee per dumpster, and a replacement in its place if deemed necessary. Romero Trap was sure there was at least five to six full dumpsters worth of debris and garbage littering the grounds, and 12 buildings. The team had also uncovered a cache of new brooms, the commercial type used for the flooring and other hard surfaces on the property. As a result, the concrete surfaces to the main living quarters, were all swept and looking much nicer than previously. It seemed to Romero; his team was keeping themselves occupied around the base camp as long as it was possible.

There were thirty six people chipping in, to take care of the property, so it was taking place far quicker than he would have thought. Upon his arrival, there was not a single person resting or taking a break within the main building, so he had to wait until they noticed his arrival. Fifteen minutes later, most of the team had started to appear within the entrance to the building. Since they now owned the property, lighting was no longer required to be kept minimal, and the majority of lights were illuminating the place, there were a few that required replacement, and being the long tube type and rather highly placed, they would need to be able to get access to them at some point. Since these were all commercial buildings, it was likely one of them had a maintenance room that may provide the needed items for replacement. The problem with the type of lighting was until a bulb was replaced, and also failed to light, was the most practiced means of discovering a faulty ballast. A maintenance room, would also have some of those on hand as was common. After 25 minutes, the entire team had assembled, and Romero Trap told them of the next assignment. His thoughts were and he decided for this, their input would be most important, as to how to achieve the assignment. He thought a three person team consisting of surveillance, spotter and long rifle expert would be all that was required. The primary input was whether three separate teams be sent, or a single team to cover all three targets, allowing a bit of comfort zone in the potential targets, if they felt they were possible targets. Certain leaders felt above such attempts, since they had nothing to hide, even if it was against the laws of nature and revolting to the rest of the world. Power did strange things to some people, once they obtained it.

Susan Hobart (Hummer) said she preferred the single three member team approach, although it may require more than a single cargo plane flight, depending on the three locations. If Hummer was the shooter for this assignment, no one else was arguing her opinion on the subject.

Romero Trap asked if she was volunteering for the assignment, and she wanted to know where before giving her answer. Romero Trap stated the three locations, although for the Eastern Europe a more definite location was to follow, at this time he only knew it bordered Russia and had raised their attention considerably. The Russian government also pointed out if they did anything at all pertaining to this situation on their borders, it would be viewed by other nations as an act of war and have asked for outside assistance. Since this team operates entirely independent of any government, and the team was also working without their knowledge, they could do many things and the governments of the world could all claim to have no knowledge of it, even if they helped finance it. Their financing was entirely off the books to all governments and businesses alike.

Susan Hobart stated it was possible to cover the Middle East and Russian border assignment without another cargo plane being involved, but crossing a large body of water to South Africa whether first or last, would require a cargo plane. It was not possible for her or any of them to get their weapons of choice into other countries through commercial air flights or even charter. Romero Trap was already aware of that fact but it was good to know his people knew the rules of engagement as well. Romero Trap asked again if Hummer was volunteering, knowing that few others wanted to be shown up by a woman in marksmanship. She smiled a proud little grin, and said she knew nobody including her that wanted a return trip to the Middle East, but someone had to do it, so it might as well be her. Shorty Johansen (Eyes) volunteered for the spotter assignment since he hoped to learn a few things from the reigning long shot record holder. The good thing about most long rifle experts is the weapons of choice could be quickly broken down into small pieces to allow them to be hidden better. Carrying a small bag as opposed to a long narrow rifle bag, which did stick out for what it was inside, was the most common method of transporting such weapons. Each shooter took extreme care in how it was done, so as soon as it was assembled, it was ready for the shooter, of course the shot adjustments needed to made when the time came. After a shot, the first thing all shooters did was reset the adjustment back to a zero discrepancy for scope and barrel.

THE PRIME TIME ASSASSINATIONS

It was done this way because the time frame between assignments may extend to a point where adjustments left would be there on the next, and if a shooter failed to remember to zero his/her sights, the shot would miss horribly, and the shooter would be left wondering why it had happened. It would require resetting everything at a target range to insure accuracy for the next go around. There were not many target range that had 3,000 yards or more distance between firing position and target placement. The longest military range was 3,500 yards and Hummer surpassed that and it was on record for the feat.

Hummer said it would be best to finish with South Africa and take the other two out first, although she thought it would take a month or more for the pair, before going to South Africa via the cargo plane. They would need a trio of headset gear, as well as a satellite communications equipment to keep home up to date. A single jeep ought to be able to cover the distance, and depending on which location is the easiest to get a cargo plane in, should go first. Romero Trap saw that Hummer was taking charge of the needs and how the job should be completed, so he did not need to do anything outside of sit back and observe.

Romero Trap still needed the most likely location for the Eastern European leader to be found. Most of Hummer's details were laid out and the items not set in stone, were variables only the shooter could perform, at the time the shot was taken.

The following day Hummer was given the two locations of the Eastern European leader of Latvia and Belarus and Belarus being the far larger, was likely the target site. Hummer said it would be best to work from there back, with South Africa being the last leg of the assignment. Jackson Frye agreed and was the only primary cargo plane pilot having the most experience flying that type of aircraft. There were others who could fly helicopters better, as well as jet fighters, but they had none of those. Departure for leg one of the assignment was set to take place in one week, with all four people at the ready. They all had a new vigor after a month off doing whatever pleased them, some, not many had their own families, and seeing the wife and kids was always a great pleasure to those. Others simply went away and had a good time with friends and drinking buddies, but those times were short and often far between. Although none had an assignment go two years without a break before.

The President in the meantime, had a large percentage of the details worked out for the revamping of the bill of rights, to get it much more in line with how it was originally meant to be; removing a large portion of the President's power over the people, instead of the other way around, as it was meant to be. The President of the United States was intended once upon a time, to be the voice of the people, who accounted for the country existing. Over the years since Lincoln was President, most amendments seemed to override the people's say and place it squarely into the president's hands, and in more recent years, it was to avoid dealing with the majority of people in the country. It seemed to Thomas Hardesty, that voting no longer meant much in what the people wanted, if such things were a done deal without the peoples consent. His first mission as the President of the United States, was to empower people with the right's they were originally given as citizens in this country. He did not know where exactly it got off track, but it needed to be fixed, if the United States was going to return to being a trend setting country in the political arena. A model for other countries to follow, instead of seeing if there was a better, more efficient way to hold power over their people. With the bill of rights documents to present to the Supreme Court, it would take another six months to get into the proper wording they find acceptable, and a week prior to that, it would be presented to the people to vote upon.

His next task was to remove a very large group of people under the government's payroll for being thieves, as far as he was concerned. There were thousands of people involved in the housing market of the United Stated government, and they were now playing landlord, more like slum lord, to 50 percent of the population. When people reached a point of being unable to maintain a mortgage with taxation. The government often acquired the property. Upon removal of those who occupied it, the rents were set exceedingly high for the type of property it was, and the government made absolutely no attempt to repair or update those dwellings, to justify the high rental price. Admittedly, they were a modest profit leg of government, but without them at all and making those properties available once again to the general public at a more reasonable rate, taking condition in as a factor; the government would go much farther into the black, and start working on reducing its enormous deficit. With the sale at a more than fair price of the properties currently control by the US government of every property; it would reduce the deficit by over half. This was his next goal, although even with a flat tax system in place, it was unrealistic to expect this to be completed before his first or even second term was completed, if he got a second go around as the country's leader. The approval ratings as of this moment according to the national news network that was most involved in the political structure, had him at ninety percent satisfactory. A major milestone over the last three people to hold the highest office in the land.

Even Thomas Hardesty knew you could not please all the people all the time, and those most dissatisfied with him, were those wealthy people who figured out how to cheat the government tax program, with all the loopholes plugged into the former program. Those loopholes no longer existed, and those wealthy people who previously figured out how to get away with a five percent tax on all their wealth, now paid twenty percent and were upset by it. But it did make the other ninety percent pleased with how much more of their hard earned dollars they got to keep. Thomas Hardesty considered it an extremely fair trade-off, if it would improve the nation's economic standing in the worldwide global market it had become. With the last deficit numbers, if the United States government became insolvent, it would become a Chinese territory by default on the monies owed them, by the government most responsible for helping them join the world economy.

Thomas Hardesty did not truly understand that process at the time it took place, and if loaning the government money to keep operating was the reason behind it, it made even less sense; considering the hardships it put many American workers, and was the kick off point for the program, he next wished to remove from the government's responsibility. Who ever said politics always made any sense to those who made the laws?

The team of three people and a pilot were in route to Belarus, with a jeep that was from the terrorist group, since it did not have camouflage paint, but a simple tan color that was just as effective in their environment. It would not be an out of the ordinary vehicle in any of the locations the team was destined for. They had done enough research into the targeted leader to find he made their jobs quite easy, as long as Hummer could find a reasonable perch with a clear view of the area, she needed to take her shot. The newest leader did a weekly town hall type speech in a center that had enough open space for a few thousand people to gather, and listen to the leader's speech. It was largely rhetoric about his direction the country was heading in, and it was not an open questions and answers forum to the people or the press coverage. It was merely a means to give regular speeches, instead of arrange television coverage that would require payment to schedule each week. By having a town hall meeting, press and television would be present, as it was considered news worthy for the population of the country. It was true in most countries around the globe, but most also preferred a higher degree of security and control in a press conference in an enclosed location, not out in the open.

The team took the first night in hotel rooms to get a good night's rest before finding a location to occupy. The town hall meeting was at the identical time and day each week. The next was the morning after they arrived, and they would be in Belarus a total of nine days if all went according to plan. Hummer and her spotter were able to find a perfect location before the start of the first town hall meeting that would take place. The jeep was in an alleyway next to the building they had found, and it had a fire escape they were able to use to get to the rooftop, which had a former bell tower, which no longer served as that purpose, but the enclosure was still present on the rooftop. It made the perfect cover in the event of any air surveillance. The pair made it to the former bell tower long enough prior to get an idea about what preparations were done before the speech and the appearance of the leader. From the bell tower, it was 1,600 yards and a perfectly unobstructed view of where the podium was placed. Because this was a weekly town hall meeting, none of the items such as speaker systems and microphone were removed, including the podium. Everything was securely covered to avoid weather damage to any of the items that remained in place. The first activities to be ready for the town hall meeting started one hour prior to the speech time, and it took about the same time to secure the items after the speech.

They stayed in place during the speech, and the afterwards portion of taking care of podium and equipment to allow for another week of town hall meetings. They noticed how many news crews were on hand for the town hall meeting, and it seem a number of press people were taking notes as well. Hummer and her spotter had not understood anything that was said, not being familiar with the dialect of the country. During the entire time on the rooftop, the driver was trying to remain inconspicuous by leaning against the wall of the building, occasionally take a small stroll, but not venturing out of sight of the jeep, to insure it would be there for the team's departure. A week later they would get a little earlier start to check out of the hotel for all three rooms, and be fully prepared to depart for Iraq after the shot was a confirmed kill. It would take five minutes for Hummer to assemble her rifle, and verify the sightings had not changes in the movement and unpacking. She would also be in position to take the shot, although she figured it would not take place until 45 minutes later. Patience was a large part of being a long rifle shooter and assassin for the most part.

The week had passed without any suspicion of the trio, as they wander a bit around the area for meals, and seeing what, if anything this part of the world had to offer. The meals were acceptable from what they had tried, but none of them thought it was gourmet food to die for. The plan was in place on the morning of the weekly town hall meeting, and they were all checked out of the hotel hoping not to have to find another place to stay in Belarus, if things went awry, which even for Hummer was possible, but she had not encountered it yet. There was always the first time, and she did not wish it to be today. The hand held device was checked before making the climb up the fire escape, but it might be different on the rooftop. It was simply something she always did to determine if it was going to be a good day to shoot. The breeze was steady at 10 miles per hour and humidity on the ground was

76 percent. Direction would be best ascertained from the point the shot was to be fired. Largely with buildings of any size, wind direction could be altered by the buildings to give an inaccurate reading at ground level.

Upon the first building check before leaving the rooftop, they found there was a rooftop exit and entrance from the building, the door was open, and it would be the best egress, to stay out of sight after a shot was fired. There was a door at the ground level near where the jeep would be waiting. The driver upon hearing the shot, would return to the driver's seat to have the jeep ready to leave as soon as the pair got into it. They were not to make a noticeably hasty exit to bring attention to themselves. It was to try to blend in with others who wanted to get clear of the shooter who killed a world leader.

At forty five minutes prior to the expected start of the town hall speech, Hummer and her spotter (Eyes) were fully in position. Eyes did need to do a few check of wind, direction and speed, as well as a humidity check higher in the air, but also on a rooftop. They never were identical, and it could go either way, but it needed to be accounted for to pull the trigger. Wind speed remained 10 mph on the rooftop but humidity dipped to 72 percent, the direction of the wind was south east and she was firing northwest so the minor adjustments were made for the shot with her sighting adjustments that were separate for up and down and side to side. In this case, she only needed to alter up and down shooting into a mild head wind.

The Belarus leader made his entrance to the podium, and started right into his little speech, knowing the sound check was already completed and everything was in order. Five minutes into the speech, with a final check on conditions remaining unchanged, Hummer gentle squeezed the trigger, and with the bullet in flight a wind gust which swirled in a different direction hit and the amount of time was not enough to change the outcome for the Belarus leader. It did alter its path mildly, and instead of a clean head shot which was considered centered on the forehead, it shifted to the leader left side and he was hit with a large portion of his head on the left gone as he went down. It was a confirmed kill, just not a clean kill. Her first but still a kill, and she quickly broke down her weapon after resetting the sights to zero. The

THE PRIME TIME ASSASSINATIONS

pair were in and down the building to ground level within five minutes to leave the scene. Hummer was a little peeved it was not a clean kill, but there was no sign of wind change or gusts, prior to it occurring after the trigger was squeezed. It was rare, but not unheard of and definitely affected the shot, just insufficient to keep from completing the mission.

It took a while to get to the Iraq location, but it was completed in less than a day. The first thing to do for any team was to get a full night of rest, before starting the surveillance on the next target. This one might not be so easy, but once they found the mosque he frequented, it would be better determined if it could be done from a building within Hummer's range. It was just some of the building designs of the area around a mosque, also interfered with a clear view of the target location. The one thing they saw as beneficial, was the number of times each day a believer prostrated themselves to Mecca, the supposed holy land of the faith. It could be determined by surveillance of which direction that was from others in the vicinity, but whether this leader did it in a public viewing or confined to a building, was yet to be seen. They did know he would enter a Mosque daily for whatever ritual they performed while within. It took a month to find the most common place the Iraqi leader frequented, but he was not entirely set to a schedule, if his political duties took him away from his preferred location, he would use the closest one he found. It was also the same while he was within his normal domain, but had to go elsewhere. It was not considered out of his area, simply that there was a specific time of day for certain events within the religion to take place. It meant the team could not check out before a shot was taken, because it might not occur with the leader's scheduling of daily events.

They were not going to blend in so easily once a shot was fired, and just because they were obviously not part of the people, they might be held accountable for every moment they had been in Iraq. They did not have any type of cover story as aid workers or doing humanitarian mission work, that was only something available to people sanctioned by the government, and they were flying under those radar guns. In order to achieve some means of quick egress from the area, they chose to use weekly rates and pay in advance, the worst thing to occur from that was to waste six days of paid hotel space to depart quickly. Advanced payment would make it so they could pack and leave without going through a checkout process, unless they were foolish enough to use materials that required additional funds. So that was deemed not to be done by any of them while within Iraq or the hotel.

They did find the leader of the Iraqi people did frequent the same mosque each day of the week regularly. The shot would be taken on that day, if all went according to plan, the cargo plane would need to be ready for a quick departure, and if the plan failed to produce the desired results, it would cause a delay in the cargo plane leaving. All of this was relayed back to home base with the cargo plane expected to arrive the evening prior to the day of the shot attempt on the leader of Iraq. The pilot would get rest on the plane during the ground time, instead of getting a hotel room to stay at. Hummer did not like having so many variables in any plan, but it was going to be required for this assignment with the erratic routine of this leader, and high ranking member to the religion he belonged. Susan could not be any more precise, since nothing was guaranteed to take place by the target at the designated place and time, although there were patterns, none were without fail. She had to take a shot at a predetermined location, and would prefer for this type of assignment, it be done within a one hour window, to allow for a safer retreat from the shooting location to another destination beyond Iraq.

The evening before the planned event for the leader of Iraq, Jackson Frye, the pilot equipped with a local headset, informed the team in place, he was on the ground at a nearby airfield approximately 10 miles east of the hotel they were staying. He was on the ground a full eleven hours before the shooting time, and it would allow him plenty of time to rest, having brought two sleeping bags to pad him from the cargo plane floor to get some rest.

It would take 20 minutes to get to the building selected for the rifle shot at the leader, and the weather conditions were largely hot as hell, with almost no wind. Nothing to truly effect the trajectory of the bullet itself, although the area did get occasional windstorms that caused low visibility, today was not one of those days. She would be on the rooftop one hour before his scheduled time to be at the mosque, allowing time to reassembly her weapon and be in position. It took them ten minutes to gather their belonging and get them to the jeep, without going through check out proceedings, they still had three days left on the weekly rate, so it being empty early would be no problem to the hotel staff.

While Hummer was reassembling her gun on the rooftop, which always took much longer than break down, she started up with her humming. Eyes having time to not be a delay to her shooting, asked her why she hummed whenever she was preparing and waiting for her shot. She answered with, when she first went through her training, the instructor, than current holder of the distance record at 2,300 yards for 30 years, told them all, it was not unusual for all long distant rifle shooter to do something that helped them stay focused on the shot. Humming was her focus, everybody does something, humming was her thing. She said it must help for distance too, since she was the longest recorded clean kill by military standards. Eyes thanked her for that little bit of definition, because his longest kill was at 3,000 yards, but it was a moving target and nobody kept track of those. He thought it should at least get some type of recognition, but his satisfaction was he completed his mission. Hummer though it was amazing that anyone could take out a target moving at that distance, considering all the additional parameters you would need to make for when to pull the trigger, for the bullet to be the exact same point as the target. She hoped it was at least at a steady rate the target was moving. She had her weapon assembled and double checked at the end of the conversation. The reason for a weapon of the precise nature as an assassin's long rifle taking so much longer to reassemble than breakdown, was really quite simple. Any failure in completely securing a single piece would cause devastation to the shooter and the weapon. There was no room for mistakes, and most pieces made a distinct click when locked into the secure position. Other items did screw on such as a noise baffle, like a handgun silencer, but nothing truly silenced a rifle, such as the long rifle. She also had the barrel extension she custom made to increase the distance range. She herself did not make it, she had help from machinists in the military that followed her design to the letter.

The pair were in place 40 minutes before the expected arrival time of the Iraqi religious and political leader was to arrive. In previous surveillance, the shot would be most successful as the leader was entering the mosque, although timing his deliberate steps up the stairway before the flatter surface nearer to the entrance. His security were more concerned with what was close by their leader, and one would enter the mosque prior to the leader, to insure it was safe inside, and another would take his eyes off the surroundings to open the door. The remaining two, were more concerned about what was in proximity from either side of their leader. At no point in time during the prior surveillance, did his security people appear to scan the higher buildings or farther out beyond a 100 yard radius. It was merely a matter of timing the squeeze of the trigger to his final step, before the flat area serving as an entrance, it would mean the Iraqi leader would not enter the mosque. And even for an assassin, it was a bad omen to make a kill on holy ground, such as within the entranceway to a church, synagogue, mosque or temple. It needed to be completed prior to crossing that threshold.

The Iraqi leader arrived right on schedule, and at 1,000 yard with a clear view, Hummer got fully into the zone for her one shot to remove yet another obstacle to President Thomas Hardesty plan, to bring the world closer to a world governing body, to attempt to achieve a more peaceful world. She was keeping her sites directed at the moment the Iraqi leader was making rise to the final step, as the top of his head just came into the sites, the trigger would be squeezed and as he rose, he would walk right in line with a clean kill shot. The Iraqi leader was very deliberate in circumnavigating the 10 steps to the top flat entrance, some fifteen feet in front of the entrance door. She went into a counting process while humming, and at the precise moment the top of the leaders head made view in the bottom of her scope, she squeezed the trigger so gently. The shot rang out, but not long enough ahead of the bullet to prevent the leader from walking directly in line with the projectile speeding his direction. He went down in heap and barely cleared the last step with his momentum being pushed forward by the impact of the shot. The Iraqi leader's security immediately went to check on their very dead leader, before trying to figure out where the shot came from,

THE PRIME TIME ASSASSINATIONS

and Hummer already had her rifle dismantled and packed, as they made their second clean getaway out of two of three assignments for this leg of their mission.

The jeep arrived at the airfield some thirty five minutes later with the cargo plane ready to load the jeep and passengers, before closing the cargo bay door, starting the engines and departing to South Africa. They were in the air one hour after the Iraqi leader was removed. For an assassin with a 4,000 yard clean shot kill on her record of accomplishments, a 1,000 yard clean kill was a walk in the park, but she was most proud of her unblemished record of every single shot she took, resulted in one less obstacle in the world. To date, Hummer had never missed, and she wanted to retire with that achievement in her pocket. No blemishes, had ever been accomplished under military standards, and she desired to be the very first, and it only added insult to the male population, it took a woman to achieve it.

The airtime between Iraq and South Africa was not exceptionally long, but sufficient to require another refueling before the pilot (Jackson Frye) returned to the home base in DC. Hummer and her other team members could not give him an estimate about how long they would require to be in South Africa, as this particular leader was far more erratic in where he would be on any given day. They needed surveillance time to determine if there was any pattern to his routine overseeing a country bent on returning to times long past. Before Heartless left for the DC area, he did inform Hummer and her pair of companions, that the Russia government made good on the one billion dollar bounty on the Belarus leader, and there was an expected 3 billion total for the Iraqi leader, but the South African had an estimated 10 billion dollars committed, with the largest portion coming from the black business leaders around the world, who wanted no more slave trafficking to ever come into the activities of the world again, ever. It seemed the direction the South African leader wanted to go, was highly against the judgement of the rest of the world, which brings to the equation, who would buy slaves from their government if it came to be. A ten billion dollar bounty was pretty steep in anyone's financials, and it seemed nobody liked the South African's idea in the slightest.

Hummer just took the information as more incentive to make good on her part of the bargain, since she, as the team were made aware of Romero Trap's plan after this was all over. None of them could figure out how to spend five hundred million dollars in a lifetime, although there were some among the team who would make every effort to do so. She was not one of them, although still young enough to have a family, considering what she did for a livelihood, did detract considerably from going through with the attempts. She knew she was hardly the most glamorous female in the world, but given a little makeup, and a new hairstyle, she could at least be somewhat attractive. She was hardly voluptuous, but she did have some form to indicate her gender over the other option. Besides, it was said for every woman there was the perfect match somewhere in the world, the problem was, it was a very big world for that type of search. She knew many female friends that never found it, and took what was available, only to have it end miserably.

As was the first thing to do with any trip into other countries, was to get the hotel room once leaving the airfield with the jeep and the gear loaded. It was also time to get some of the clothing cleaned to be a little more presentable in public. That was taken care of the first two days in South Africa, with the next chore to start the surveillance on the final target of the mission, which Hummer had undertaken in the name of a more harmonious world than currently existed. Hummer actually considered herself a more proactive peace keeper, than all those who only made the vocal effort and kept a hands off approach to obtaining what they wanted. They were simply unwilling to do anything to actually achieve results, in order to keep their hands clean. There were far more people who followed the Pontius Pilot way of dealing with things, than people willing to perform the actions.

After the first two days, it took nearly three months to find a defined pattern to the South African leader's activities. He preferred to frequent a particular restaurant about once each month. Unless weather altered his normal means to go to the restaurant, his preferred method was to enjoy his meal in the seating outside the restaurant doors, where there was a relatively large patio type seating arrangements. He normally received a specific table, and that only occurred to regular customers of esteemed value to the restaurant. Obvious to Hummer, he frequented this restaurant long before he obtained his latest position as the country's leader, to be giving the identical table each month when he arrived. He was pampered by the people of the establishment, and that did not occur in a six month time span, regardless of who you were as of today.

It gave Hummer and her team nearly a month to locate a building for the shot, with a clear and unobstructed view of the arranged table for this dignitary. As far as being a man considered a dignitary, Hummer felt scum of the earth, should have no such titles bestowed upon them. It was totally unjustified in today's global economy and marketplace that had fueled the global improvements over the last three decades, although some countries, still prospered far better than others. By the fact that her country had gained enormous debt feeding a world economy, at the cost of those within, she felt a bit slighted. Thousands lost the means of employment with their jobs being sent to other countries, and the company they worked for, made larger profits by doing all the labor processes in the other country. Although, it was also a larger percentage for the government to absorb from the company that complied with the governments wishes. There was no advantages any longer to follow the example of the leaders of government in any of the fifty states, and Thomas Hardesty the current President, was trying to undo all the wrongs of government for the last forty years. From what Hummer had already witnessed, he was making major strides forward in that quest. Her fear was that some old ways politician or politicians, would try to bring it to a quick finale.

Romero Trap was not a person that Hummer or any of the team wished to see have to fill the shoes of a president assassinated, while holding the highest office in the land. As much as they all had grown to respect Trap, he was not national leadership material. He was excellent in covert and black operations, especially in what to anticipate in opposition, as an assignment went deeper into the primary purpose of what the job was to accomplish. To the person, not a single one of them would have taken an assignment for this length of time, if it were not Romero Trap in charge of it. Many including Hummer, would work with no other person in charge of any assignment requiring multiple experts. With over two years into the assignment, not a single one of the team did not participate in some part of the assignments, and for nearly one year every single one of them had participated in the terrorist assignment in the Middle East, although Zoe was the only one to work it from DC base. Hummer did not really envy her for that, since communications could come in at any point of a twenty four hour day and she was always there to respond. Hummer also admired Zoe for what she did, Hummer did not believe she herself, could kill a target looking directly into their eye at an intimately close position. Admittedly, she did not have nearly the shape or exotic beauty of Zoe Dubois, but it took a soulless individual to do what Zoe did for assassinations.

Hummer had made the communications back to DC for the time and place of the next attempt to complete the assignment. She could not guarantee the cargo plane's arrival would not be in vain, due to the unpredictable nature of the final target. Out of the last three months of observation, this was the only location the leader had gone to at the same time each month, and weather could also be a factor in whether the assignment was completed or take an additional month to try again. The building selected with the least obstructed view of the table location always given to the leader, was 2,300 yards away. South Africa being the country on the tip of the continent, seemed to always have some wind being ocean surrounded the majority of the country. The seat of government was quite near the very tip where the land was at its narrowest. South Africa had created its own problem by demanding excessive taxes and fees from shipping companies and traders that for centuries, used its ports to dock for unloading cargo for the entire continent. South Africa in its need to fund the cost of a growing government, started to impose fees and taxes far beyond what had been common practice for centuries. As a result, other African nations with coastal ports, made improvements to harbors for larger ships, and far more modest fees, to attract more shippers and traders to their ports. This was where the leader of South Africa, who considered himself a historian of South Africa, discovered the time of slavery was the most successful time of the nation, with an abundance of money in the government treasury. Even with inflation and cost of living taken into account over several centuries, the country seemed rich beyond its needs.

Hummer was determined to get this 10 billion dollar bounty collected by the team, to remove the biggest thorn in the world today.

On the day of the leader's visit, it was a little higher wind than Hummer would have liked and it had a fair share of wind gusts to add to the problem. In her determination to accomplish her mission, she insisted the team be fully in position two hours before the shot was to be taken. She wanted her spotter to take continuous readings, so she could try to time the gust intervals to take her shot. She could make the adjustments necessary for the shot, but it had to include everything, since she knew how fast the bullet would reach its target from the time it left the barrel. She could account for the drop in velocity based on the wind direction, or the angle to fire for the wind to bring it true to home. She needed to know how many gusts, at what speed to include into her adjustments, and the only way to do that was be in position. For two hours, Eyes and Hummer went over the details of this particularly tricky shot, the gusts varied but she got the timing down to two gusts between the bullet leaving the barrel to reaching the target. The variable was the wind speed and she had two different gust miles per hour in the readings. One at twenty seven miles per hour and another at thirty five miles per hour. It took fifteen minutes for Hummer to calculate her needed adjustments. She also had to account for the steadier wind at 15 miles per hour. What the weather conditions told her if she was at home, was a storm was brewing. It was still a matter of when it would arrive, since it could take as much as 10 hours of unsettling conditions, before the storm really made its appearance. She on the other hand, did not ever live in a place this close to an ocean, or surrounded by ocean.

The time was approaching for the South African leader to arrive for his luncheon at this same restaurant for however long he had been, to get such special treatment. Since the weather did not turn to rainy conditions and there were no visible signs in the sky above, the leader would be eating in his usual place. Hummer did not think a little breeze, although it was more than a little, was enough deterrent to have him decide to go inside the restaurant seating area. If he did, the day was already a waste of effort and they would need to find another location to stay for yet another month. She truly did not want that, they had been away for nearly six months, and it was time to go home.

The leader arrived and did take his regular table outside on the dining patio. From prior surveillance, Hummer already knew that while he ate, his head would bob up and down like he was raised by swine. Chewing his food, and taking another bite before the first was done, and continuing that process until his cheeks started to bulge slightly. She had already determined for this shot to go center mass on the neck, that way if his head was down, it hit center of forehead, if it was up, it removed a large portion of the center of his neck. She was poised for the shot, making her adjustments for the two wind gusts and the steady wind speed. All from the side as opposed to a headwind. It would definitely alter the trajectory of the bullet, mentally noting the clicks to undo with the disassembly of her precious rifle. His meal was served, and he went right into the bobbing of the head, she squeezed the trigger with Eyes still taking continual readings of the wind conditions. The first gust hit 30 miles per hour and the second 40 miles per hour altering her shot more than she accounted for in her adjustments. It told her the storm was approaching, for such a change in gust speeds. The shot did not hit center mass as planned instead his head was up and it removed one entire side of his neck. From the geyser effect of the blood loss, she knew the carotid artery was severed and from the blood loss, the leader would not survive. There was no way to stop that much blood loss in time for medical attention to arrive, much less save him, although since it did feed the brain, he was likely already brain dead.

Hummer undid her adjustments to bring the scope back to zero and dismantle her weapon and put it into the bag. Once again, it was not a clean kill, but it was still not a blemish on her kill record. Eyes said it was amazing she could adjust for all the variables, and still be good enough to hit the target, with the sudden change of wind speeds. He was impressed, and thought it rivaled his moving target kill he was most proud of. They made it to ground level for the awaiting jeep, and as they were moving out, the sirens were wailing to indicate emergency vehicles were nearing the vicinity.

From the target location it took forty five minutes to reach the airfield, and upon arriving, the cargo plane was waiting to load a jeep and three passengers, to close up and take off for home.

11

The Domestic Threat

Eyes had spent a week telling everyone individually what he witnessed in South Africa as a kill shot that rivaled his own, but he had perfect conditions for his moving target, whereas Hummer made the shot in rather unstable wind conditions. Five and a half months away was enough time for a few things to change at home base.

The team members remaining had transformed the building complex into a much more pleasing environment. The grounds were completely free of any debris. Entrance gates were in place at each side of the complex for the long wide loading and unloading area behind the buildings. The lumbers and other materials for the main building complex made the internal rooms look far more like real rooms with lumber studs used to make walls, which were insulated largely to cut down on external sounds for those who were using the sleeping quarters. The building used for a garage was thoroughly cleaned, and vehicles were neatly parked in a useable fashion for a quick exit, although it was not likely it would be necessary. They even took the Lincoln Town car to get a complete wash and wax to make it look like new again.

With the three person team out of the country for five and one half months, the President had finalized his bill of rights adjustments, and in some cases revoking a bill that only gave the government control over the people. It had overwhelmingly been approved by the people, and it did include one new addition to how government would operate into the future. Since all businesses were required to have an annual report showing where the company stood, as far as assets and expenses, the government of the United States, would file an annual report, showing the people just exactly how their hard earned tax dollars were being used. It was time to set a more exemplary example to the people and businesses, as how to go about wise spending, and have the annual report show a profit or margin of gain. Thomas Hardesty decided to go back to when he first took office, to show just how badly the money was being used, and that government before him continued to operate at one trillion dollar a year deficit. In his first two and half years, he had transformed the government to being 100 billion dollars in the black, all of which was used to reduce the massive deficit, but at the rate of money going towards the deficit, it would take a hundred years to delete it completely.

Thomas Hardesty also got the federal government completely out of the real estate market in the United States, which accounted for the big jump in the government working within the black, for the first time in two decades. He kept a mere two dozen people to keep track of rents received as he reduced all rents to 25 percent of what the government was collecting. There were not enough people to pursue missed rental payments, or attempt to start any legal process. With people keeping more of their money, they erased 25 percent of the homes rented which were in poor condition, but the renters were given first purchase right on a fair price. This further reduced mortgage amounts and how much each month would go into to a house payment. The value for each property was based on what it would take to have it returned to fair market value, with only a 5 percent overall profit to the owner. The only way for owners to truly make money from the sale of the home, would be if they were able to complete all the repairs and the improvements to current codes, without a contractor and do all the work themselves. This to Thomas Hardesty was simply fair business practice, something government had forgotten about over the many years they abused the budget.

President Thomas Hardesty was still very much in the peoples favor as his approval ratings remained at 89 to 90 percent. There were other things to be concerned with over the other 10 or 11 percent who disapproved of him, and the rumblings from Wyoming were not what he truly wanted to hear. He was sent an e-mail from a citizen, who had not voted in twenty years, until Thomas Hardesty ran for office. The person found few politicians that were honest enough to admit things needed to change, and Hardesty took the bull by the horns. He completely approved of the president's methods, and even voted to oust a long time useless Senator from Wyoming, who had previously influenced business leaders to insure he remained in office. The former Senator appeared to be amassing a small army of staunch supporters, and what he overheard was, they were planning to remove the President from office with extreme prejudice. He though the president should know, and be prepared to do something about it. President Hardesty was not willing to jump to any conclusions concerning this single account from one citizen, although the former Senator mentioned had absolutely no good things to say concerning President Thomas Hardesty, he had no proof of the Senator being ready to take power by force, if that was the plan. He asked Romero Trap to look into the potential issue in Wyoming with the help of his team. The president did not want any action taken at this time, merely some means to uncover what or if the former senator was up to, causing a citizen to write him an email, making accusations that there was trouble stirring on the horizon.

President Thomas Hardesty knew the former Senator had a very large ranch and horse farm to raise racing thoroughbreds, to run in the high stakes races. His means of having become an important political figure from that area of the country. He also failed to obtain the office of president in his defeat from Thomas Hardesty, but again he, like most other politician's in recent years, spent large amounts of his campaign funds to smear the name of the other contenders, and completely avoid a single issue to promote his being president. The Senator from Wyoming was a little more than upset by his being removed from office by the people of his state, which cost him his political retirement fund, and he was now collecting it under the same means as any other citizen. He also still held some sway among the legal members of the federal government and petitioned the latest bill of rights changes as unconstitutional.

The Supreme Court ruled against him, saying the bills amended were returning the people the rights that previous made a mockery of the bill of rights, when entered into the bill. If anything, he was restoring the injustices to the people's rights, back to the rights they were entitled from the very start.

With what the team of Romero Trap had accomplished during President Thomas Hardesty's first term in office, other countries were making strides forward in combating the illegal drug trade, and for those people who were in need of assistance in getting away from drugs, programs were being established in lieu of prosecuting them as criminals. This lessened the need for illegal drugs, further reducing the immense profits of those whose trade was in that arena. They were also more watchful for the formation of terrorist groups to try to put a halt to before it became a larger problem. The globe may not be entirely at peace, but there was a definite reduction in the amount of strife countries were faced with.

Thomas Hardesty also tired of the annoying Pentagon war mongers, put into effect policy stating their primary function was to defend their own nation from those wanting to do them harm. In effect, it told them to quit concerning themselves with the troubles outside their own borders, and prevented them from bringing any such issues to the President. It had created nearly nine months of peace in the Oval Office, allowing the President to address the issues of the people. He had made major strides forward in returning the government of the people to once again, be for the people.

He even got a congratulations from the Supreme Court on his method to bypass the Senate and House of Congress, which would have prevented him from making a single accomplishment during his first term, and possibly prevent a second term. Giving the people the right to have a say, which was supposed to be expressed by those in office, was a truly brilliant way to bypass all the bickering that would have resulted with not any single bill he presented to those in the houses of power, going beyond one of the two.

The information from the President occurred at the point of time for his third State of the Union speech, to the one hundred members of the reformed House of Representatives. It was Romero Trap's duty to not only be present, but provide his own input on his activities as Vice President, which for the last year were very little. There would never be any mention of his extracurricular duties directly from President Thomas Hardesty, since it was never to become known to the public. Romero Trap was simply glad he could help the president progress towards what the president foresaw as a potential, for a world far more at peace with each other. He had been a major aid in that respect to President Thomas Hardesty.

After the State of the Union address which took only 90 minutes, even with all the press coverage, the luncheon was served in the first family dining room and Romero Trap made his exit to talk to his team.

Since this was only to be a surveillance assignment to start, he was unsure of the number of people needed to be sent to Wyoming. The purpose was to gather as much information as they possibly could, concerning what was going on within the former Senator's home state. According to records, the Senator had a 3,000 acres piece of Wyoming with a number of buildings for the horses, as well as his estates, and a place for farm hands to reside. Since the Senator also bred thoroughbred horses with his successful horses that were turned to stud duties, the horses required a good deal of attention. As a result, there were trainers as well as caretakers to attend to the needs of the thoroughbreds. The large ranch also had its own track, to provide the horses with training, as well as determining their capabilities on a racetrack of high stakes. The former Senator had a very lucrative business that involved some of the finest race horses in the country. His primary goal concerning his horse business, was to produce a Triple Crown winner for the second time, before he reached an age where it would remain an elusive dream. It had never been accomplish by anyone involved in thoroughbred racing.

He let the team decide how many wanted to be a part of this assignment, and no single person would be taking more than a handgun, which was for self-defense purposes only. The President just wanted confirmation on whether a potential problem existed in his longevity as the United States President, before the people decided if he deserved a second term. Romero Trap could not see anything that would prevent that from the people's point of view, but being assassinated in office, would certainly bring a quick end to his chances. It was always in this country's history, to come from within its own citizens or politicians with too much at risk personally.

If the previous regime were to regain power, there was no chance government would continue to operate in the black, everything Thomas Hardesty accomplished would be undone, and the people would be back to starting the next US revolution. It would also prevent the formation of a world governing body to oversee that the globe worked towards harmonious interaction.

Ten people volunteered to go to Wyoming, it was considered a pleasant experience to actually do something within the borders of their own country, and not go to somebody else's part of hell on earth. The initial plan was to first discover all they could concerning the large 3,000 acre compound that was home to the former Senator. It was certainly a place to hold some sort of meetings among people, who he convinced a change was in order for the resident of the White House. First the team would discover if meetings were taking place, as indicated by a concerned citizen, and whom was among those attending. The next part of the surveillance would be to find what public places these people frequented, whether a bar, nightclub, restaurant, social club or even a pool hall. The theory here was if there were enough people attending meetings on the former Senator's ranch compound, somebody among those attending would be unable to keep their mouth closed over the agenda discussed at that meeting. It was almost human nature for words to slip through loose lips, when more than three people had a secret to keep. The team was to make discoveries concerning what the Senator was planning, if there was a plan. A regular meeting would be the first sign of something to be aware of, what information could be obtained, would only come from someone in attendance of those meetings. Based on the number of people attending, would also indicate if active recruitment was taking place to generate more numbers to take part of whatever plan was being formulated. If the meetings kept consistent numbers and the same people, there was nothing to indicate the meetings did not deal with his horse businesses.

The team did not know how long it would take to discover the true nature of the Senator, and whether or not he was planning something to disrupt the President's term in office. They could have the answers in weeks or a number of months, but the one thing clear from Romero Trap, was no action was to be taken, without his additional decisions once the President determined what to make of the information they obtained.

The surveillance team would consist of Ty Roberts (Trauma), Tron Bosworth (Gambler), Howie Short (Judas), Shaq Lee (Stealth), Zi Yang (Kung Fu), Al Capston (Garrote), Travis Rumfield (Point), L.J. Daggett (Stiletto), Chu Fong (Dart), and Lacy Louis (Pricker). All information obtained would be relayed back to the DC base of operations and COPA (Romero Trap), would relay it to the President to determine if or what other action might be necessary, to prevent problems arising within the White House. This group would take five jeeps on the Cargo plane, and Romero Trap discovered another large ranch compound within 10 miles of the Senator's ranch, that was converted into a Bed and Breakfast, when the ranch fell into hard times and in order to keep from losing the property, the conversion was made. The monthly rental for a stay was less expensive than a week in a hotel, and Romero Trap arrange for his ten team members to stay for three months, all prepaid through his working account and reimbursed from the other accounts. With the last bounty collected and interest and earnings the other five accounts were at 40 billion dollars total. Romero Trap did not know how the numbered account banks achieved such a good rate of investment and interest, compared to banks in the US, but he did not care enough to investigate. He suspected it was done by money laundering, but since his business activities were not exactly legally sanctioned, he had little room to cast any stones. He simply knew his team would be able to retire from the lives they led, in comfort when the assignment came to its conclusion.

A SELECT FEW

The first day after the team arrived in Wyoming, and got the initial check in process to the bed and breakfast completed, they made their first observations of the Senator's ranch compound. There were seven large buildings on the property. One being the Senator's large estate, another for the hired hands, which appeared large enough for 30 residents with amenities. Two large stables for horses, which appeared to be one for the thoroughbred for racing, and the other for breeding. The other two buildings were used for the equipment required for the ranch property, and the last a rather large feed storage, considering there were approximately 100 plus horses to attend to on the ranch.

It also had a very long road or drive to access the ranch property, which appeared to be a mile long marked as a private drive, but it was not all within the property of the Senator's ranch. The layout had far more of the property owned by the Senator rear than forward. There was still 1,000 yards distance from the fence line to the first of the buildings, which were not entirely clustered together. Behind the buildings was the practice track for the thoroughbreds. It was not the largest track, but sufficient in size to give the thoroughbreds a good work out, and time the distance of the oval. There were areas used exclusively for the materials planted for the horses feed, as well as pastures for the horses to roam freely when not in the stables.

After the initial check out of the ranch, the team returned to the bed and breakfast, which really served all three meals of the day, included in the monthly rental fee. The only thing the team members would need to purchase while in Wyoming, was to keep hydrated for their time in surveillance mode. Each member had a pair of high powered binoculars with night vision capabilities, and for the team to take eight hour shifts, allowing twenty four hour coverage, and rest time for all the members. It was determined not to get closer than a quarter mile for the first portion of the surveillance, until they had some idea if and when meetings were taking place. It was also discovered during the initial checkout of the ranch, the Senator did not have a group of people for security purposes, but a large number of video cameras around the property. It would require stealth and agility to avoid detection, only after darkness fell. It could not be done in daylight hours. Three team members excelled in that area, and one was the risk taker, who was not in charge of the group mission. That responsibility was given to Ty Roberts.

Trauma would relay to the team all guidelines provided by the DC base, which would be from Romero Trap, either personally or by those at the home base communications center. He was selected, because he would not deviate from those parameters received from base. He was also very good in following procedure, although he could still think on his feet, if a situation arose prompting a change in plans.

The shifts were selected and the first three returned in a single jeep to the Senator's ranch for observation during the daylight hours. Using the binoculars, the team found the only activities going on within the ranch property, were related to training and taking care of the horses. There was an occasional vehicle to enter the long drive to the ranch, but it seemed to be a delivery of either stock for the horses or the hired hands. No vehicles had its occupants approach the Senator's estate. The first few days provided no real clue as to anything abnormal taking place on the property until the fourth day. A delivery vehicle arrived around 3 PM and unloaded a large stock of alcohol at the Senator's estate. The team relayed this information to those still at the bed and breakfast, and it was then relayed to DC base of operations. The team noted that no single person could consume that much alcohol in five years, so something was going to take place soon.

On the fifth evening after dark had arrived, the pair of observers witnessed and counted 150 vehicles enter the estate property. A fair portion were on the ground around the estate, but many of them also lined the roadway on both sides leading up to the ranch property. The pair were in positions to observe from front and rear, but the estate itself had all the window coverings completely drawn closed, and outside of a glimmer of light here and there, nothing could be seen within the estate's main residence of the Senator. It was deemed without any band or loud music being played; it was not some sort of a party thrown by the Senator. Unfortunately, nothing could be heard to indicate what was occurring within the large estate home.

The information was relayed back to DC location later that evening, and for the next week nothing else occurred, until the same two events they noticed different the week before took place again. The large liquor delivery followed by a gathering of vehicles this time numbering 160. Whatever was taking place within, was growing in numbers. Each vehicle that arrived had a single occupant. None were chauffeured and almost all were luxury vehicles of some type or another. The few exceptions were rather expensive sports cars of foreign manufacturers. The second week proved to present no more additional information than the first, and it being after dark, night vision did not provide sufficient detail to get a good description of any who arrived. The meetings were taking place on the same evening of each week, but whether the pattern would continue or not, was yet to be determined.

The third week produced the same findings and now the count of vehicles was up to two hundred. The difference being, after they had all gathered within the Senator's estate and would be within the home for at least two hours, Shaq Lee (Stealth) entered the property being cautious of the camera placement, and concealed himself in the bushes around the large front porch of the estate and waited. Stealth was trying to achieve two things, overhear any conversation that resulted with the exit of those in attendance, and to see if he could identify some of those attending. He could not use any form of camera to make visual confirmation, due to the close proximity to the estate. Any sound emitted might prove to be his undoing, and he was unwilling to take such a risk. When the people within started making their departures, he noted many were armed with handguns, being Wyoming, it was perfectly legal and common practice. The conversations were typical of people exchanging their departing pleasantries with the host, and not a single word was said of what the gathering pertained to for so many people, Shaq Lee was able to memorize faces of a dozen people, all of whom seemed to be prominent business leaders in the Wyoming area. The Senator, was the only politician among the entire group.

With descriptions of the dozen people the next thing to try was visiting the closest town, to see if any of them showed up regularly at some public place. The purpose was to see if a conversation could be overheard that might indicate what was occurring each week at the Senator's estate. It was decided that Shaq Lee would go through a shift change to spend time in the closest town of any size, which was 8 miles from the Senator's estate. Admittedly, with the large number of ranches and farms, the towns were relatively far as part of Wyoming. So, eight miles, seemed much better than the next closest at fifty miles away. Shaq Lee would have at least one other team member with him to at least appear to be having a meal with a friend, or other ranch hand, since that seemed to be more appropriate.

Shaq and the team also noticed that virtually everyone in the area wore a large hat, considered to be a cowboy hat, but there were a variety of styles. At least there was nothing they noticed to indicate that ranches all wore the same type of hat, like a form of a uniform for the ranch. So, the first thing needed by Stealth and his teammate, was local garb to blend in better with the crowds, likely to be found in the town. There was a ranch and farm supply store in town, which catered to every need of the farms and ranches in the surrounding area. The clothing including footwear more to those found on ranches, was only about a hundred dollars each, but the cost of hats took them by surprise with the least expensive being about 300 dollars for one, and they needed a pair. Once that was obtained from the funds supplied to the team for local expenses, the pair returned to the bed and breakfast, to dress like the locals, and then went to the only diner and restaurant in town, which also served as the local bar. There was a walkway to the pool hall next to it, and it seemed it also was a part of the business they entered.

Shaq and his teammate, L.J. Daggett were in the restaurant for two meals each day lunch and dinner, which was nothing extraordinary in foods, but being ranches and farms surrounding it, the prices were more than reasonable as all the food was obtained through the local associations, such as Cattlemen's and Poultry. All the vegetables were locally grown as well. It was a standard farmers and ranchers dinner every night and lunch. They needed to frequent the restaurant every day until the three month timeline had just about expired, before overhearing for the first time what the Senator was up to, and it was via a recruiting effort. The pair overheard the conversation, it was between a person seen by Shaq exiting the Senator's ranch during the meeting he was able to conceal himself in the bushes, and the potential recruit.

A SELECT FEW

The Senator was assembling a team to storm the White House, and take it by force, considering he knew well enough how well guarded it was. The Marine barracks at the rear of the White House property was on the next adjacent lot, but it had direct access to the White House ground. A team of 48 marines, whose only duty was to guard the perimeters of the building housing the commander in chief of all the military branches. They did not have any other responsibilities in the Marine Corps, and the President's politics were not to be an issue, it was their sworn duty to protect and serve the commander in chief. It made it so there were 16 marines posted around the White House grounds, 24 hours a day and seven days a week. Those who were not on guard duty, had their time to do whatever needs they had personally to take care of including sleep.

The Senator was trying to assemble a group four hundred strong, and at the last meeting at his estate, there were over 300 hundred vehicles to arrive. It would seem time was now of the essence, in order to stop it from reaching Washington DC, although from Wyoming, the team did not see any simple means to get four hundred armed people from Wyoming to Washington DC, in a quick fashion. Even if it were possible to charter 3 aircraft for the trip, it would mean transportation would be needed to be acquired in Washington DC, and it was highly unlikely that many vehicles would be available in a short time frame at a singular location. Dulles International would be the only airport to land a plane the size of the charters they would need, and the Wyoming location was a long ways off from an airport, the size needed for passenger jets, like the charters they would require. All the information was relayed back to the DC base of operation. The following morning the President was informed of the situation brewing in Wyoming, and his decision was immediate to Romero Trap. Remove the problem before it ever left Wyoming, by whatever means necessary.

Since the team did not have any such electronic devices to place into the Senator's estate, nor the skills set to employ it if they could, word of mouth was the best option in finding out if a threat was imminent. The Senator also seemed to be the type to prefer being pampered to his every need or wish, and had staff to take care of his every need, so he did not need to make the effort. With all the windows and glass doors

THE DOMESTIC THREAT

completely covered, determining the number of staff, was something the team was unable to accomplish. In all likelihood a number of innocents, would perish in an attack as well. It would be considered collateral damage, but it appeared to be unavoidable. Verbal warning was not possible, and also the staff's loyalty was an unknown quantity to the issue.

After the White House luncheon, Romero Trap had devised a plan to send the heavy automatic weapons to eliminate the problem in Wyoming. The cargo plane would have both transporters with the Heavy Weapon mounted, and both the behemoths would take their personal weapon of choice. It would mean abandoning a couple of jeeps in Wyoming or sell them quickly. There was not enough time as far as Trap could demise, to have the first team shuttled back, to send the heavy weapons into Wyoming. It would need to be done with a singular return and the Cargo plane did not have enough room for all the vehicles. The team had enough funds left to cover the daily charges of the bed and breakfast before everyone left to return to the Washington DC area base location.

Romero Trap (COPA) was well up to date concerning the time and place of the large meeting, and there was enough time to get the cargo plane loaded, and the team going for that portion of the mission, in Wyoming, before the next meeting. Since the fence line to the buildings was 1,000 yards, which was only half the accurate distance of the heavy 50 caliber automatic weapons, the plan was to get the transporter up to the fence line without entering the property. The hand held weapons of Turmoil and Cyclone would be stationed alongside the transporters out of the path of the mounted weapons, and all four would open fire on the Senator's estate. With the power and quantity of ammunition each could fire within a single minute, it ought to bring the house down like a Broadway play. With four weapons at 1,000 rounds per minute, they should eliminate the risk rising from Wyoming in a matter of minutes. No survivors would be expected, and as long as the Senator perished, the matter would be closed. The only restriction was no horses or farm hands should be removed by intention. It was primarily the senator that needed to be removed, as the rest had no real purpose without the senator directing it. The ranch hands, needed to survive to tend to the livestock, and the horses were entirely innocent of being a part of the anything other than racing or breeding.

The day of the team arriving and the other members checking out of the bed and breakfast, had produced the sale of three jeeps at 6,000 dollars each. A bargain for the vehicles, which were considered excellent to have around ranches and large farms, such as those around the area. Since they could travel over all types of terrain, they would largely be used to cover that vast area of a farm to get cattle back to the stable areas and horses as well. The ranchers who obtained them were very pleased about the deal they struck, for such useful vehicles for the farm or ranch, while the team did not have to abandon them outright. It was all arranged by Stealth in the town restaurant over a two day period. The two remaining jeeps needed to make a couple of trips, to get all the team members to the landing location of the cargo plane, which was a private air strip used by another rancher for his planes, since it was the easiest means to travel about the entire state as he needed to frequently. The plane was refueled prior to landing at the airfield at a larger airfield, not privately owned, and this was to insure take-off and arrival to DC area without another fuel stop.

The cargo plane landed at the airfield five hours before the planned time to be on the Senator's front porch. The transporters with heavy automatic weapons mounted needed to remain less visible, until time to leave around dusk. The twenty mile drive should be covered well within the time for the meeting to still be in progress, when they pulled into position with lights completely off. They did not need to draw more attention than necessary, and in the dusk hours, the mounted automatic weapons could just as easily look like a small crane, or similar piece of equipment, found around ranches and farms. In order to allow the transporters to be unloaded after putting the cargo plane into a safe location off the runway area, which was entirely lawn and pea gravel, the weapons were covered with tarps to disguise what was beneath. It also allowed for the two jeeps to be placed side by side in the rear of cargo hold, (which from a plane was forward), and allowed room for the transporters when they returned. If need be, the sixteen team members could find more comfortable seating within the transporters, after they started their return to the DC area airfield. There was enough 50 caliber belts to bring the Chicago Tower down in a heap. 100,000 round were available, half of the belts in each transporter and 250 rounds to a single belt. The heavy automatic weapon were auto fed by the belt, once the first round in a belt was in the chamber of the automatic, the belt would feed the next round, until the belt was emptied and a new belt loaded. The belts were typically too damaged for a second use by the force and the rapid feed capabilities.

In all total, there were now seventeen members of Romero Trap's elite team of experts in Wyoming. The ten original members for surveillance, four heavy automatic weapons people, two on the mounted units of the transporters and the only two men capable of toting them around without tripods and mounts as hand held, more arm's length, nothing but sheer muscle was the main ingredient. Darkness arrived at 9:45 PM and dusk started at 9:30 PM. The transporters were having the tarps removed at 9:25 PM, and should be ready to get under way exactly at 9:30 PM, to go the 20 miles to the Senator's large ranch estate. The three remaining team members were the pilot and the two drivers of the transporters. The transporters were all terrain vehicles, with six independent drive wheels, and a two wheel idler axle for stability and weight distribution. Being a relatively large vehicle and all terrain capable, it had a top speed of 70 miles per hour. It could however, do that over any terrain, although it was not likely to be a pleasant experience for passengers over rough terrain. It was manufactured for that purpose, in the event it was in a hostile environment requiring high speed maneuvers, to avoid large gun fire such as from a tank or similar gun, that was towed into position.

The transporters did not arrive to the Senator's ranch until 10:15 PM. The roads in the immediate area were not highways, and most had speed limits to prevent fast travel from point A to point B. They also had to pass directly through the little town, and of course the two stop lights worked against their benefit. The only thing in their favor was the town was not heavily lit, being rather rural in nature. Within visible distance of the ranch on the normal road that ran perpendicular to the ranch property, the lights were doused, and they went to the off road means to pull right up to the fence line. There appeared to be 350 cars around the property, but nobody took the time to do an actual head count. With the transporters in place, both heavy weapons peoples using the muscled version, emerged from each of the transporters, with enough ammunition belts around the torsos to look like a walking armory. Before the firing was to commence, each weapon carried was set on the ground and the belts carefully laid out for quicker reloading. Once they had completed that and raised the weapons off the ground, and into position, firing commenced upon the large estate of the Senator at 10:35 PM. The noise of four heavy automatic 50 caliber weapons was horrendous, and got a bit of a stir from the ranch hands building. The door opened, and three of the hands emerged with hand guns, fired off a shot or two before deciding it was too far to have any effect, and with the weapons that were being used, they retreated quickly, hoping they did not attract the same attention as the Senator's estate.

Gun fire to the estate was heard for six minutes, although with reloading time and the heavy weapons no longer firing in sequence, each had really fired off five minutes of ammunition or 5,000 rounds per weapon. 20 ammunition belts each. During the firing the front door of the Senator's estate managed to get opened by a single person, who was cut in half by the heavy weapons. After the guns came to a silence, thirty seconds of dead silence, then a loud heavy creak was heard from the house, followed by an even louder wood groan, and the porch roof fell to the ground followed by the entire estates roof collapsing onto the remaining estate, until it was nothing more than a large pile of rubble. The heavy automatic weapons were a bit unique from most other weapons, having a dozen barrels rotate in time with the chamber mechanism to account for the number of rounds it could release within a single minute. The team could not determine if there was anyone who might have survived the onslaught of 50 caliber projectiles, but they were not going to go through the pile of rubble left in the wake. The collapse of the large structure, should have finished off those who managed to avoid the weapons fire.

THE DOMESTIC THREAT

With the noise and attention, it likely received, the team quickly got the gear they needed, leaving all the spent and damaged belts behind. The two muscle men were the last ones into the transporter but at 10:58 PM, the transporters were back onto the road and leaving the Senator's ranch estate. There was one horse lost in the gun fire. Since there were no eyes on the estate for the day, as it was deemed unnecessary, apparently, one horse was still running the open pastures, and it was not normal from all the observations previously provided. In its panic from the excessive noise of gunfire, it ran directly into the line of fire and was immediately down and did not suffer a bit. It was an unavoidable loss, although horses were not to be harmed, the team with weapons had no idea of its presence, until it was too late. You simply do not just stop a large weapon of the nature of these.

The time to retrace their route to the private airfield was shorter on the return, largely due to the lights in the town going from fully operational, to merely flashing caution in the path they followed. As soon as they were on the airfield with the cargo plane in ready mode to receive the two additional transporters, the drivers slowly and carefully drove into the cargo hold, one after the other, but only one at a time on the door that was also the ramp. The transporters with the mounted heavy automatic weapons needed to go slow, since clearance in height was marginal, and too much speed might cause damage to the cargo plane if there was contact. Once the transporters were completely within the cargo hold, the pilot, Jackson Frye made certain the door would close properly, before entering through the rear cargo hold door to get to the cockpit, to use the lever that closed the rear hatch. With that completed, the cargo plane started its engines, made sure they were all running at the normal high idle speed, before it taxied into position for takeoff, to return to the DC area abandoned airfield.

Once the cargo plane was airborne, Jackson Frye reached an altitude that at 18 miles from the Senator's ranch, could see that flashing lights of numerous emergency vehicles, and also spotted a helicopter circling to find a safe landing location, for the news team that was investigating the scene. He did not need to go in for a closer look, knowing what had taken place an hour before. The return trip to the DC airfield would not be a problem for the fuel, but it would require refueling, before another assignment required the cargo plane to head into another direction, also it was now time to perform some routine maintenance of the cargo plane, once back to the hanger it occupied at the airfield. Largely like any road vehicle, although planes went by hours of use as opposed to miles, fluid changes were due. Using engines that were based on the same principles as the automobile, oil needed to be drained, and replaced with fresh oil. Hydraulic fluid reservoirs needed to be checked for levels to insure there was no minor leaks, which could result in insufficient fluids for components of the plane to properly operate. If such were the case, the leak would need to be found and resolved. Most typically from vibration, a fitting would loosen enough to cause minor seepage, and a simple tightening was all that was called for. It was part of the 400 hours of operation maintenance check, standard by military policies to prevent a plane becoming a falling object from the skies. For the most part, it was seldom necessary, except for the oil replacement, but it was a good practice to keep, if you relied upon such an aircraft.

Jackson Frye and two other members of the team were those most familiar with the maintenance needs of aircraft of any sort. As long as the maintenance log was kept in the plane, it was a simple procedure to follow, if you knew about maintenance. Those unfamiliar, would be clueless without some form of training in the process of aircraft maintenance. It was seldom if ever, a one person process, as there was simply too many items that needed to be checked throughout the entire plane. Hydraulic lines ran throughout the plane to reach every piece that had movement from the landing gear, to the rear tail, as well as the length of the wingspan. There were numerous reservoirs within lines to prevent multiple items from having simultaneous failure. A single item failing, crippled a plane, but did not make it impossible to overcome. Multiple failures as a result of lost hydraulic fluid, could have disastrous results. Therefore, there was at least one reservoir for each hydraulic line, the lines were hidden under panels within the main hull, or torso of a plane, and access panels also were available to the areas not accessible from within the planes main body. Some wings were large enough to have crawl space, many had panels on the outer skins, which

THE DOMESTIC THREAT

required fastener removed to access. Also, during maintenance, virtually every inch of the outside of the plane was inspected. This was to make certain none of the fasteners used had loosened, and fell away from the plane during flight. It was not entirely uncommon, as most were quick connect type fasteners, which had a locking point with a half turn and pressure applied downward on the fastener. Also, all the external panels were checked for stress fractures, that would appear as hairline cracks in the metal used for the outer covering of the entire plane. These fractures required entire panels of metal being replaced, which could have resulted from metal fatigue from age, or having been in very turbulent air for a length of time, such as a severe weather patterns that covered a large area.

The plane set down at the DC airfield at just about the hour of dawn, it was nearly light, but not quite. The plane was taxied into its hanger, before unloading the vehicles on board. As well as allowing all the team members to disembark from the cargo plane.

Once everyone was out of the plane and the vehicles had been unloaded, the team members returned in one of the four vehicles for the trip back to base camp. Jackson Frye was in the lead vehicle, but not driving, to get out and unlock the gate, open it for all the vehicles to pass and then closed and relocked the gate. His vehicle was pulled to the side so he could get back in, instead of walking back to the main building a fair distance away. Once all the team was back in the main building, the team members who stayed behind, informed them they had made the national news and turned on the large flat screen, as the coverage had been pretty much non-stop since 2 AM in the morning DC time. They provided a bit of a recap that the news considered a mass murder, and had the Senator still been holding office, it would have been deemed a terrorist attack on US soil. The investigating authorities actually collected and counted the spent rounds of ammunition and came to nearly 20,000 rounds of high powered machine gun fire. They have already questioned the military about some rogue members attacking a former Senator, and the military could account for the whereabouts of every single member during the time the attack took place. The authorities had a few witnesses to the event, but could make no identification from the distance, and said they each fired at least one maybe two rounds from handguns, but saw the futility in it and quit immediately, to return inside their own building, hoping they did not draw the attacker's attention, for like events to take place on their building.

The authorities can only determine the weapons used were military grade, but origin and country were unknown, as the type of weapons used, were not something they had in their databases. The witnesses had said there was 6 minutes of heavy gun fire and it halted, they then heard the Senator's estate collapse onto itself. It was almost as loud as the gunfire that preceded it. Investigators were still going through the rubble left it the wake of the attack, but did find one person to survive, although both legs were crushed beyond repair from the weight of the house falling in on him. Somehow it left enough space for the survivor's upper body to be free of the collapsed structure all around him. He was in surgery for most of the night, and the legs from the knee down were amputated from the extent of the damage, with no chance of saving either leg. He was unable to say who was responsible, as the only person to reach the door was cut in half by the large caliber weapons firing into the house. There was no place to really hide as the bullets passed completely through the estate. The Senator had fifteen bullet holes through him, and was dead before any emergency personnel reached the scene.

Investigators did not have enough information at this time to give any idea of who was responsible, and feared it may even be retribution from when the Senator held his seat in Washington DC. He did make more than a few enemies from foreign governments over some of his policies. The investigation would be ongoing, but the possibilities were too many without enough information to pin point any party to hold accountable.

The team members returning from Wyoming, after hearing the news report were all overdue for some sleep, and all seventeen people went to the sleeping quarters to fulfill that need for rest. They were aroused much later by the aroma of food, another thing they had neglected the last twenty four hours. Jackson Frye was the first to leave

THE DOMESTIC THREAT

the sleeping quarters, to find Romero Trap was present, and had been for nearly five hours.

Trap informed him, the President was glad to have the obstacle removed, and Romero Trap said if the news was disturbing to Frye and the team, it was next to impossible to perform any domestic assignment, without it becoming a major news story. For jobs within the borders of the United States, it was part of the hazards of the profession. They did a marvelous job and it was time to rest for a bit. Jackson (Heartless) Frye told Romero Trap, it was not possible for too much rest, since the cargo plane was due for maintenance, and it had to be completed prior to leaving the hanger again.

Over the following two weeks, the three people familiar with aircraft maintenance went over the plane with the maintenance procedures, most commonly used within the military programs used by all the branches that flew aircraft. Helicopters had a few difference, but items like fasteners were relatively common to all aircraft including commercial. They were however not something you would obtain at the local hardware store. The items needed were purchased in quantity, and only available from the manufacturer of the aircraft. The minimum quantity was ordered through Romero Trap, and were to be delivered to the main base building. The team did not want anything to draw more attention to the abandoned airfield the cargo plane was utilizing, and a delivery would compromise their location. Also, two cases of the correct specified oil were ordered, having four engines and half a case per engine. They held more oil than the standard automobile. On the other hand, automobiles did not travel at 30,000 feet above land. It was not the ideal place to have engine failure due to a lack of oil.

The President was into his final 9 months of his first term, and once again it was time to hit the campaign trail, although he followed the same path, he took the previous election. He refrained entirely upon slinging mud at his competitors, and concentrated on first, his accomplishments during his first term, and what still needed to be done to make the government leaner and more capable of paying towards it enormous deficit. He ended his speech with telling the people not necessarily he was the best person for the job, but should they feel, another person could achieve the goals in quicker fashion to vote for who they felt was most likely to continue the progress, he had made in his first term. His approval rating were still holding near 90 percent, and it would take a miracle worker to oust Thomas Hardesty from office.

His things still needing to be completed were listed for all the people who listened to hear. It consisted of one area that needed more people to provide a better service to the people of the nation, being the Social Security Administration responsible for all the people who were receiving their income from years of hard work, or on the list considered unable to continue working. It was the mandatory payment they made during all the years they worked, to form what was also the retirement plan of the vast majority of citizens, who had reached the golden years of their lives. He also planned to consolidate all the different agencies under a single agency. It was to provide a full cooperation among all those who worked in agencies design to protect the nation. It also would allow them to better utilize the manpower available, for whatever need was most required at the time. Analysts would all share information, since there would no longer be agency boundaries to cross. It would also allow for those least effective, to be removed, and either nothing in his or her place or obtain less costly help. Just another measure to streamlining government, but all the major ways were already addressed, so now it was down to going through literally each department for a means to streamline the excessively large payroll of tax payer's dollars, to make it more efficient.

It was easier to remove unnecessary groups of people performing tasks the government had no business being involved with. Streamline the remaining government offices and agencies could be a little trickier, since every one of them think they are irreplaceable. It would also mean delving much deeper into the records of those people.

With campaigning being a major portion of Thomas Hardesty time in each day, the assignments would not be quickly forth coming. It was really a matter of his reelection that would determine additional problems to face as a President, and a nation trying to achieve the goal of a world governing body, to bring about a much needed cooperation of nations, and maybe even some resemblance of peace. This had been

Thomas Hardesty's ultimate goal from the very beginning, he simply did not add it to his campaign or make it a public event. Too many things needed to be in place, many of which had already been done by Romero Trap's team of elite experts. It was still a matter of one hurdle removed to merely be replaced by a new one, which to this point had not happened, but the Organized Crime people were working towards that goal. It did take a little time to replace so many bosses with new ones, who had the confidence of those under him. It was after all, considered family by such people, and extremely important to keep family bickering to a minimum, although all families have some, which is really unavoidable. The biggest difference to Organized Crime families and a normal family, is organized crime often used guns to settle their bickering, bringing about a more permanent definition to the dispute.

With the campaign in nearly full swing, the President and First Lady were away from the White House more than within, leaving Romero Trap to spend more time confined to the White House, although he did not occupy the Oval Office while the President was out. He had another office not far away, and anything that needed to be addressed by the President, went through his door. It seemed to be rather like a revolving door that seldom stopped, and Romero Trap was not enjoying the time as secretary to the president one little bit. He was continually needing to reach the president through his mobile device, due to the urgent nature of everyone who passed through his door. Romero Trap had a very difficult time believing so many things on a daily basis were that urgent. President Thomas Hardesty on the other hand, was all too familiar with the over used word of urgent within the White House staff, and often had to put things into a more correct order of being addressed. Ninety percent of all the urgent items that went through his doors, were hardly urgent in any way shape or form, the only truly urgent item he had in the last six months, was there was no toilet paper in the stockroom and it seemed someone forget to reorder it. It was not his duty to check such items, but made certain the order was placed on a rush by the appropriate staff member who failed to do it in the first place. He was also ordered by the President to obtain enough locally to satisfy the needs of the staff, until the order arrived.

Upon hearing this from the mouth of the President, after his moment of laughter, he inquired at how the president wished him to proceed, until life in the White House was more to the normal variety with the President in residence. Thomas Hardesty informed Trap to decide which of the items truly needed the attention of the president, but to make sure the staff members understood the president had a campaign to complete, prior to his being available again. It did not deter his staff one bit on making urgent requests, but the vast majority would be put in the hold file box, to deal with at a later time. They were as the president had said hardly urgent, people simply wanted to get thing out of their 'to do' box and onto someone else's, and all the bucks stopped at the Oval Office. There was no place else to send them.

Over the next eight months outside of an occasional week long stop in the White House by the President, there was little accomplished beyond the campaign. One month prior to the election, Thomas Hardesty had completed his rounds throughout the country. His closest competitor was a young upstart in politics, and under the current method of holding office, it would always be, but he had a few good ideas that Hardesty made note of, rather than dragging him through the mud, like many of the longtime political office holders would have done. When the election came to a vote via the old fashion method of going to the polls, the turnout was larger than it had been in the last forty years. Thomas Hardesty was reelected to serve a second term as President of the United States by a landslide victory, of 89 percent of all the votes.

Life in the White House would return to the preferred method of Romero Trap. He had been unable to visit his team for any length of time during the entire time the President was on the campaign trail. By the same token, the President was too busy campaigning to provide Romero Trap with any new assignments to give his team. They were each allowed to take time off, but this time to be spread out among the members instead of all at once. Each member was allowed 30 days and no more than five were to leave at the same time, and no more than ten in overlap time. Over the nine months, it was more than enough time for everyone to get in a 30 day break from the ordeal of their profession, and have a little fun.

The investigation of the death of the former Senator of Wyoming fell into to the cold case files, as no additional information could be obtained to pursue any suspects in the death of so many people in a single estate, although there were never any questions raised over that matter either. The only survivor was closed lipped about why he was there in the first place, and in a foul mood trying to adjust to life without legs.

12

Second Chances

It had been nearly one year since Romero Trap had any of his team out on a mission. They had kept themselves fully occupied by taking 100 dollars per member of the team as a fund to return all the buildings on the formerly abandoned commercial property into useful buildings. Since it was now owned by all of the team, they made two other buildings into more reasonable sleeping areas, and turned the restroom facilities into large scale bathrooms, including two shower stalls per restroom, in both buildings. All the roofs were checked and fixed of any leaking, which had occurred since it became an abandoned property. In a year's time it looked much closer to the resort they all pictured it could become. The main building from the start, was still the only one with the large flat screen television and home to the armory and safe. Beds were acquisitioned from the military, and although it was not fancy, it was better than sleeping on air mattresses upon the floor. The air mattresses were still in use, but now they were above the concrete floors. Two other buildings were used to house the vehicles in a less confining space. Transporters in one, and jeeps and Lincoln town car in another. Another building was converted entirely in to a materials and tools storage area. During the looking into what really was left behind by companies who left the properties, they found six decently supplied maintenance rooms. All the fencing of the six were used to create a much larger storage area for all the tools they were able to locate, within the 12 buildings.

President Thomas Hardesty was now into his second term, trying to lead the country into a more prosperous nation, businesses were growing again, and the flat tax program and reduction in government, was allowing the deficit to be lowered instead of increased. Departments were being analyzed for efficiency, and further reductions in staff of those who were merely collecting a paycheck. Without the need of going through the voting of the people, departments of the various government functions was streamlined into a more productive and business like function. 30,000 more jobs were removed by and large, those removed were merely taking up a space, and pretending to have a position of importance, as opposed to performing at an optimal level of efficiency.

The wording for the Supreme Court and for the people to consider for a vote was completed on the combining of all the agencies the government used. Instead of a separate CIA, FBI, ATF, DEA, Homeland Security, and US Marshalls. All of it would be combined into a single organization to be known as The Marshall's Services. There were no longer to be interagency bickering over who did what, who needed to take charge, or any of the other arguments that had bogged down the efficiency of these agencies. It would allow any and all resources to be used where it was most needed, at any given time. Instead of multiple department heads wanting the most power among the agencies, a single agency head would come from those already in place. The President also wanted a department head who used a hands on approach, instead of sitting back and directing and watching those who did the work. Those who were not selected could take a reduction in pay, and be a group manager, but it also had to be a hands on approach.

He was going to get static and was prepared to meet it head on. It would further reduce the government payroll at the same time, making all of them combined far more efficient in the duties to their country. Some of the current department heads would in all likelihood opt to go into private security for larger companies. This was acceptable to the

President. He did not want anyone left in any of the current agencies to create problems for the newly formed Marshall's Services. It was the final reduction the President found within the now downsized government of the United States. With businesses and families all receiving better wages and growing, the surplus to aid in reducing the deficit was growing. The combination of the agencies was the final step, and the size of government during his first five years, would have been reduced from over 70 percent of the jobs to just under 30 percent. It meant an additional 40 percent of people were now contributing to the treasury, instead of taking. It would be considered a major accomplishment by the people of the country, who had been supporting far too many government employees.

To further enhance what Thomas Hardesty had done at the federal level of government, many of the states were doing the same at their level. The trickle-down effect would fall to cities, then counties, and finally at the most local level of government. It was the second chance of the forefathers, who founded the nation, based on principles that remained sound even 250 years later. He had nearly returned the government of the people, back to the people, and it would be up to his predecessor to continue down the correct path. The one thing President Thomas Hardesty could not guarantee would follow. He had done his part, and hoped the people were wise enough to know how to keep it on that path.

Once again, the Middle East was raising concerns, but it was much different this time. The terrorist activity against the world of infidels, as they like to refer to all those who did not follow Allah and the Koran, was not so much making attacks as gathering. Thomas Hardesty wanted to know what they were up to more specifically, and see if it could be brought to a close in whatever means necessary. He presented Romero Trap with a new assignment, which was only surveillance to start with. He did not know if any of Trap's team understood the languages of the Middle East, but it would certainly be helpful in determining what needed to be done.

Romero Trap was back to his half day sessions in the White House with the President back in the Oval Office. Additionally, a large portion of the so called urgent issues received during his campaigning trips, were resolved, many by means of being discarded. Romero would present the latest assignment to the team, and see who wanted to go back to the Middle East for mere observation. He also had decided that the 2 billion dollars in currency still in strong boxes in the secure storage, would be deposited into a 6th account, but not a numbered account. It would go into a US bank under the shell name employed by the group. It would serve as an expense account, but also collect a modest interest common in the banking industry of this country. It would still have a little growth when considering the amount of funds going into it. The remaining 1 billion in gold would stay in the storage area. It would serve as a fall back should any of their accounts be seized, although nothing, had occurred in that area as of yet. With the agencies being combined under a single agency, it would reduce further that possibility, but it was best for the team to take precautions.

After his White house luncheon, which he did not miss for the last four plus years, he went to the base complex that was now more like home to his team. His first question to the team was who among them knew the lingo of the Middle East. Only one person among the team was familiar with some, but not all, but knew enough to get the general idea of the discussion, regardless of which language they employed. That person was Zoe Dubois, who among her skills was able to pick up dialects relatively easy, and in her profession, it was extremely helpful. She volunteered to be a part of the team going to the Middle East, since she had not been called upon for her own skills, but the one time. It all honestly, she said she was a little bored, and did not want to be sitting around for communications to come in this time.

A team of eight people would go to the Middle East for surveillance and observation of the terrorists, still active in the area. Although recruitment was all but extinct with their last successful mission, rumors were the terrorists were all merging under a single banner, and if that were the case, they could be as much as 70,000 strong. If they were to become active in what they had been in the past, it could pose a major threat to any harmony in the world. They needed to know more about what they were doing and why, before progressing into a more defined approach. A team of 35 experts may not have been what they wanted before to remove over 8,000 terrorists, but 70,000 was a bit too much for his team of professionals.

Jackson Frye knew his job was to take the recently maintained cargo plane into the world's void to get the team in place, and thought when he was in base camp, he would take the communication responsibility. Romero Trap let the team decide who was willing to go, knowing fully well, none, truly enjoyed going to that part of the world. Jackson would take the list of volunteers, and four jeeps would be used in the process, allowing for two person teams. Arrangements would be of their own choosing, since hotel accommodations were not an option, where they would need to be going. The first location previously used during the terrorist attacks may still be somewhat useable, and it did have a water supply. The last two were destroyed, and not likely to be of any use unless they felt like digging through all the rubble.

Zoe was already on the list and seeing as to how women were looked upon in the Middle East, she would need to wear what was deemed appropriate. For the most part, women were covered head to toe, and Zoe was quite familiar with the process she needed to go through, having been there before, and having the items as a part of her own gear. Lacy Louis, also decided to go as did Joba Ligata and Roberto Gomez. They were going because they felt they would not stand out so much as foreign devils. Cory Tolski, Gordon West, Harvey Hatfield and Mitchell Lamb would all need to do a little makeup, but could fit it when required. The intentions of the team was to try to blend into the locals, although that it was not likely they would be visiting large cities, with tall buildings and deluxe accommodations. The satellites imagery system were actively being viewed by the following day when Romero made his daily appearance. They were trying to determine how many bases were established, and the area they could get the most accomplished in a short time. The good thing was this trip would not involve Afghanistan, as the country was no longer providing safe harbor to any outside groups. They were only going to protect what was rightfully theirs, and do as they had always done to any who invaded their lands.

It was still a large area to cover and the terrorists were employing different means to disguise their locations. The only way the imagery was helpful now was to see a few too many people in a general area; which appeared void of any buildings. Once on the ground with definite locations to observe, they would learn more about how the terrorists were operating. From what it appeared from overhead is they were either using exclusively tunnel systems, or disguised buildings to appear to be natural hillside formations. It was going to be the head count that would provide the most insight into the locations to observe.

They did the satellite imagery for a week, before the team was ready to depart to the Middle East. Romero Trap hoped they would not need to be gone more than three months, and by that time, have a clue what to provide to the president in more information.

The cargo plane was loaded up with the jeeps and gears for the eight people as well as a large number of cases of bottled water, until the team found a better location to gather. Romero Trap really did not want the four pairs to be working completely independently, and left without any support. Only handguns were taken by seven although Zoe could use one, she did not find it a needed part of her normal gear and stuck with empty syringes, to be safe. The other team members were making the vast number of calls for financial support promises, and were including a very large number of businesses such as airlines, oil companies, and others with invested interests in the region. When all was said and done, they had a promised 45 billion dollars collected with another 45 billion upon completion. The team fully expected to go into the Middle East to bring the terrorists down with extreme force, but a call for more arms would need to take place if they had to deal with 70,000 strong, in the Middle East. The President was now in a position to welcome the formation of a world governing body, and beginning to make it known publicly. He accepted a meeting with those members already in the formation group, but it was not complete and the governing body was not officially in operation. It had taken over four years to get the United States leader involved, although Great Britain and a number of other countries, were formally within the group forming the governing body. Ideally, they wanted every nation on the planet to be a part of the governing body, which would serve as a means to establish far better communications, involving all the world's leaders. A place to voice concerns as direction, but not to dictate how the world should be run. It was largely a move to create a more peaceful world, and small disputes and aggressions, could be settled within the governing body.

The countries most behind the formation of the governing body were tired of war being a solution to the world's problems. It was time for people the world over, to find harmony with all peoples, not just a select few. Forming a world governing body for all to participate in, trying to overcome the issues nations faced, without a violent conclusion. Those countries not directly affected by other nations problems, could act as arbitrators to those countries problems, and hopefully find a solution other than war. As the world governing body now stood, it was still too weak to be effective, and required many other nations to find this a more viable answer, than what they current employed.

If the world was going to continue to survive as a species, more peaceful methods needed to be employed by all the world's governments, whether democratic, ruled by royalty or dictatorship. Something needed to change, to put the world into a more harmonious state of being. The long overlooked possibility of not being the only species in the universe, needed to be addressed, at least from the standpoint of survival and defense of their world. It was hard to believe that for as vast as the universe was made to be believed, the only people in the entire universe, was on the planet earth. This compounded with the fact that as a world of intelligent beings, they had not even achieved reaching all the planets within their own solar system, much less explore vaster regions of an infinite universe. Granted there was no such proof of other life forms in the universe, but it did not make sense for such a vast universe, to only have a single planet with life. What would be the point of all of that space, and limit it to a single intelligent species.

The team was on the ground, once again in the Middle East, satellite imagery had helped identify 30 different locations that were likely used by the reforming terrorists. The four teams each selected a single location to select for a 24 hour period of surveillance, and were to meet up at the former base location, they had control of when last in the Middle East. Surveillance revealed a major difference between this formation and combination of remaining terrorist cells still operating in the Middle East. It was already known with the destruction of the largest terrorist problem that recruitment of new members was not going well, since the only thing accomplished was being wiped out without much to show for it. The new terrorist groups were definitely more in a defensive posture, than a one of creating havoc and terror. Each of the four location observed had buildings well disguised, as if belonging to the hillsides they were holding. Each had a heavy automatic weapon that had teams of three manning it, the entire 24 hour period they observed.

The former base location was partially destroyed by the blast of explosives. The garage tunnel entrance was only partial damaged, and had room for all the jeeps. Tunnels were collapsed to some areas but the water supply was accessible. They had decided to keep all the empty water bottles from the cases they brought for the purpose of refilling them for subsequent locations to observe. Sleeping was not going to be the most comfortable, but it was something that could be done within the garage area tunnel using sleeping bags.

In the first communications back to base in DC, Zoe inquired if they fulfilled the mission in a more peaceful means other than trying to kill 70,000 terrorists, did that accomplish the bounty for the mission? Romero Trap was not present at the time and he would need to provide that specific answer. The team tried to get some rest before going onto the next four locations. The distance between the location used for water and sleep, would be ever increasing with each trip, and they had not yet identified the largest and likely home of the overall leader, to the reformed terrorist organization.

The answer came from Trap during the time of sleep and Zoe was informed the concern to the majority of the world, was activities that resulted in innocent people being killed for little reason other than they qualified as infidels to the terrorist group. If an agreement was obtainable to insure all commercial aircraft could pass overhead unharmed, and the group did not attempt to do anything more than defend their own borders, like they now did solely in Afghanistan, the terrorists might even work in conjunction with their own government, as defenders of the nation, from intruders wanting to take what was rightfully theirs. They would be left alone, as long as they complied and made no attempt to disrupt the formation of a world governing body, which they would actually benefit from. A single violation of these terms, would insure retribution from those they offended, and it would bring the lives of many of the people responsible to a quick end. Romero Trap said it was very likely the new leader of the terrorists, would reply to the effect that he was being offered nothing for him to become subservient to the Great Satan. Zoe said she had already considered that, and had ample verbal responses to contradict that very statement. Communications concluded, and Zoe tried to get a little more sleep, before the teams went about the next observations of another four locations. Zoe was unable to return to the sleep process, so she rose from her sleeping bag, and used some water to give herself a little washing without anything other than water, which was cool but not cold. It would have to do for the time being.

The location for the former shower area was a little difficult to reach, with a partial tunnel collapsed, but with a team effort, it might be made accessible, although in what condition would not be known, until other efforts were made to gain access. It might be something the 8 team members considered before going to the third group of locations to observe. Zoe did not want to go two or three months without a good cleansing, and doubted any of the others were willing to wait that length of time also.

The second day of observations brought about similar findings as the first, again each location had buildings disguised as part of the surrounding hillsides. From any distance in the air, it would not be visible, even at ground level it was not easily discernable. Night vision was the most effective means to identify the buildings from ground level as heat sources of human beings were visible, not true from the air as enough hillside coverage, prevented those findings. They were primarily working from the satellite imagery that identified too many people about in the open to be a mere tribe taking refuge for a night, or day in the heat. It was not totally uncommon for the nomadic people of the area, to travel at night and rest during the hottest part of the day. It had been practiced for a millennium, and remained the way to travel from one area to the next, in search of either food or water to stock up on. During the day water was used far more due to the heat, and for the tribes, it was as precious as life itself. They could go days without food, but not water.

It took a little longer for each team to return to the location of the water source and a place to rest. Zoe decided to see about attempting to get to the shower area before everyone went to sleep, and in a matter of five hours, of moving rocks from the partially collapsed tunnel, they made it to the doorway where it had been. Some of the shower area was also caved in, but there remained four showers that appeared usable enough to allow for cleaning. Considering the team had worked together for over four years, cleansing took precedence over morals. Four showers allowed for half the team in one shift, and the other half in the other. It was more important to remove the dirt and grime from seventy two hours of observations and travel, than to check out the others equipment. One lady to each shift, is how it worked out the first time they were used.

The entire team felt better going to sleep after a thorough cleansing, than sleeping with the odors of bodies needing a good washing. Sleep was far more pleasant and much deeper as a result. When they had all awoke, they all felt much more their normal selves, than ghosts of the people they were. Although it took nearly three quarters of an additional day to leave for the third group of locations, it was much easier to go about their twenty-four hours of observing another group of terrorists. Once again, the results were the same, the terrorists were far more intent upon defending their little piece of territory, than trying to achieve random acts of terror that would affect other countries. As they observed to this point, 12 different terrorist locations, they had yet to spot a single missile launcher being moved or even in use. What was apparent, was the newly reformed terrorists were far more intent on defense, to hold out against any type of attack, like those that took out the biggest contributor to the world's chaos. It only fed Zoe in her determination to bring about a more logical solution of peaceful negotiations, than reign destruction upon the terrorist groups, which now formed a group working more in unison.

The natural order of things said the time was right to convince these terrorists that peace with their own governments, would be far more beneficial to all parties involved. The government would have people familiar with the use of weapons to defend their borders, and the terrorists should benefit with both the government's support and provisions of armaments for that very purpose.

It would take two months of surveillance before locating the primary location that the current leader of the combined terrorist factions would be found. It was the largest in number of buildings and personnel, but also the most elusive to spot from air or ground. Due to the ever increasing distance from the base location, twenty four hours of surveillance, took 48 or more hours to return to the base camp, they were using. As a result, the showers were getting more workout than the sleeping bags. But since people were returning from their surveillance at various intervals, it was more two to the showers, than splitting it into two teams of four. Not a single team member complained in the slightest about the shower arrangements. Mostly they were happier just to have them, although the showers were also getting used as a laundry as well, since that was entirely under rubble and not accessible in the slightest as were the barracks. Several had gone to starting the showers fully clothed, to get the clothes a little more in line with smelling clean before disrobing to clean themselves. As a result, the showers ran far longer but it was necessary, unless they wanted the terrorists to smell them approaching.

It took almost forty eight hours to negotiate the terrain and distance to the location and camp of the leader of the terrorists, which had formed under a single banner. Zoe had the driver of the jeep drive to within 100 yards of the main building, and insisted he stay in the jeep, and make no overt moves to be misconstrued as aggressive in nature. She got out and walked directly toward the building like she owned the place. The terrorists all had their weapons pointed at her and she ignored them, until she reached a point where others were there to impede her progress. She announced immediately upon being halted, she wished an audience with their leader to discuss terms they could both agree upon, to bringing about a more harmonious conclusion to the events that could take place. They took her to a place to search her for weapons, and although Zoe had her syringe well conceal within her attire the search proved fruitless. The leader was Ali Bin Uddin. First Zoe needed to find a common dialect they both knew and could have a conversation without losing the real meaning.

It was quick to come about as the leader greeted his guest in a language, she was quite familiar with. She greeted him in return and said, "I have come on behalf of my own leader, who wants to help bring about a new world order. As you are probably aware, the terrorist group responsible for bringing down numerous commercial airlines and killing thousands of innocent people is no more. What you are not aware of is the over 8,000 members who lost their lives being members to that group of terrorists, died at the hands of a mere 35 members of an elite team of experts. I come to offer a better means to bring this to an end, without further loss of lives. It will take specific objectives for you and your people to meet, as a sign of your intention to honor this agreement, as well as spare you and your 70,000 members a similar fate of those before you."

Ali bin Uddin simply said he was listening, and had Zoe continue. Zoe said, "I bring you a condition of peace among nations as long as you and your people make no further attempts to disrupt the peace. It would mean instead of going about acts of violence against other nations to generate fear of your power, you concentrate in defending your own borders, and nations from intruders wishing to take away what is rightfully yours. Become more like the Afghanistan nation, and you will be left alone by other nations. You might even make amends with your own government, to act as defenders of your nations, and in good faith, be given weapons and other provision to be used for the purpose of defense. I can assure you, if these terms are not suitable to you and your people, the same fate of those before you shall befall you as well. The Great Satan has never sent weapons of mass destruction at any of your nations without being provoked into a call of retaliation, for atrocities commit upon their soil, and those who claimed responsibility, came from this region."

Ali bin Uddin said she was offering him and his people absolutely nothing and why should he believe her. Zoe replied, "For the believing portion of what I offer you to consider, since I knew how to find you, I could have just as easily brought 1,000 elite warriors more than capable of bringing this entire location to ruins. The pair of heavy automatic weapons on the hillsides to protect would be no match to ten or twelve identical weapons mobile and trained people to eliminate those weapons you hold, before wiping out every living person in this location, without receiving so much as a scratch in the process. I chose to come talk instead of taking the other action, which can still occur, should I not be able to leave here unharmed. As to the peaceful methods I ask you to partake in, they are simply the true words of the Koran. I may not be considered a true believer of any religion, but I am quite familiar with most of its writing which include the Koran as well as the Bible. Mohammed is referred to by Islam as the thirteenth prophet, and not a single believer of the Koran, can tell me who the other twelve are. Yet all of Christianity know the twelve, and it means the Bible and the Koran are based entirely upon the identical principles and teaching. No person will be received into paradise by violating any of the conditions set forth in the Koran, which are the same principles of the Bible to the Christian faiths. You say I offer you nothing, and I say I offer you everything. Follow the agreements set forth, and you will have a much better chance to see paradise, when your time comes more naturally, not as a suicide or death in a battle you cannot win. Just so we understand one another, and you have time to consider joining a new world order of things, where every nation will have a seat to discuss the effects of agendas concerning their own nation, I will give you 96 hours to think about it. At which time, I shall return to hear what you think you consider is best for you and your people." At this, Zoe waited for no reply, and turned to walk back to the jeep awaiting her.

The return trip took 42 hours, it was quicker, but it was like a good roller coaster ride as the jeep went airborne a few times, and kept trudging forward with its landing. Zoe told her driver if they planned to get any sleep, for the return trip, it would need to be exactly like this trip back to the base. They both showered and went straight to the sleeping bags to get some rest to cover the next 48 hour excursion. Sleep came quickly for Zoe but seven hours did not seem to be enough after 48 hours up. It was all the time she allowed for sleeping, though and soon after the pair were back to the roller coaster trip to the terrorist leader's base location. This trip was even more exciting than the previous return trip. Zoe on two occasions, was tossed high enough into the air, to nearly get into the rear seat from the front, without making a single move of her own. It was a good thing she was not one prone to motion sickness, or the ride would also have been messy.

Upon arrival, the identical parameters were used and she waltzed right up to the point of being searched, without any concern of the weapons pointed at her from other terrorists around the front and hillsides of the buildings. She acted like she was untouchable, but deep down inside she knew she was taking a risk with her own life, if things did not go as she had planned. She was once again ushered inside to see the terrorist's leader, Ali bin Uddin. As was customary greetings were exchanged, whether they were done in honesty or vile, was never obvious.

Zoe opened the conversation with, "I hope you have decided to follow the true meaning of Allah, and the holy book of the Koran, instead of the twisted version many of your predecessor's have taken, and possibly influenced you as well. Please keep in mind that the vast majority of true believers, understand the true meaning, and fail to see the interpretations of those who would see the entire world as Allah's territory."

Ali bin Uddin replied, "There is some wisdom in your words concerning the Koran, this I could see from our first conversation. I have concerns that even by complying with your offer, the Great Satan will strike anyway. I need some assurances this will not occur. I have seen the truth in how some of the true believers use the Koran as a book of war, and you are correct, that harming others was never a part of Mohammed's writing or the will of Allah. The Great Satan has often come and brought destruction upon our lands, and this we wish to bring to a complete halt, so our people can begin to thrive, instead of rebuilding over and over again."

Zoe said, "If you look upon the history behind every single attack on your lands by the Great Satan, you will find in each case, the destruction you speak of, was first set loose in the lands of the Great Satan. As an honorable people, the only response of an atrocity committed upon their soils, is one of retaliation and a means to inform those who brought death to innocent people, it will not be tolerated. I cannot give you every example to diagnose for yourself, which you needed to do, as proof to the commitment the Great Satan has towards its own people. The Great Satan will maintain it eyes upon your lands to insure you keep your end of this bargain, but I can assure you, no attack upon you lands will be initiated by the Great Satan, unless some other attack occurs from within your lands. Using missiles to destroy overhead planes over your skies, would be one such attack. Commercial aircraft must follow a specified flight pattern, set forth by governments and aviation authorities, with only a slim margin of deviation. Typically, there is a mileage range in width, as well as altitude parameters that must be maintained to be considered in a safe passage of all countries. Flight patterns are continuously monitored by aviation towers of all nations, to insure the commercial aircraft stay the correct course."

Ali bin Uddin stated he did not realize the flight paths of commercial aircraft followed strict guidelines, as he would need to look into that being the case, but he did not intend to use such methods seeing what it brought upon those that did. He asked for another forty eight hours to determine what was true and what might be false to coerce his decision. Zoe told him he could have five days, since the time it took to reach him and return had not allowed for adequate rest, but a decision needed to be reached by that time, to keep greater forces from acting out their intended plan to remove yet another obstacle to forming a world governing body, where all nations would be allowed to participate, instead of those who met the correct criteria.

With this final concession to Ali bin Uddin, to have time to see the truth for himself, Zoe made her departure to the awaiting jeep, oblivious to the guns trained upon her every step. No shots were fired and she entered the jeep, and the awaiting driver for another return to the base location they had established. She really wanted to be done with this entire ordeal in the Middle East, but preferred a more philosophical approach than outright elimination. Even though they did not have the personnel in place to accomplish such a mission, she did not believe for a second, it could not be done. Although it would require the President authorizing military action, against a troubled nation. Zoe believed she would overcome this problem with peaceful means, instead of complete destruction of another group of terrorists who stood in the way of the overall plan of a world governing council. In five days, she would know if or if not, she was successful in her negotiating skills with a believer of Allah. She did not want the ultimate solution to be the elimination of another 70,000 plus people in a region her country had no business being in the first place. It had been at war from within for over two millennium over religious beliefs, more than any other purpose among these nations. Interference only further fueled the radicals and fanatics among them. Bringing more of the same would only make matters worse and prevent what the President was truly working towards, in the ways of a world governing body where all nations would have a say in the future of their own respective countries. She could not afford to fail in getting the terrorist leader to come to the agreement she proposed. It only served all parties better than any alternatives.

The return trip was a little less eventful allowing more time, which would equate to getting more rest for the two, who had already made two other round trips.

When they arrived at the base location some forty eight hours later, the pair again showered and dried a little better and went to get some sleep. This time it allowed them twenty four hours of time for rest, another shower, maybe some chat time with the other team members, before making another 48 hours of traveling to get the decision, made with the last attempt to offer a better way for all. They both slept for a solid nine hours of much needed rest, and intended to get another round of sleep, prior to the time to depart for the final time to the terrorist's largest location. It was one of the last four visited by the group during the time of observations. Only two locations were not visited of the thirty, they were able to find using satellite imagery. The two were even farther away from base location the team of eight observers used for rest and water, as well as cleansing. Food provisions were running low, but all of it was package foods, requiring little or no preparation. Anything that required preparation was done over a small open air fire, just beyond the tunnel entrance.

After the nine hours of sleep and feeling a little less like walking dead, the other team members were joined for a little bit of casual conversation, and communication to DC base were also done, to have the cargo plane in place for the team's departure. Either way the decision went with the terrorist leader, Ali bin Uddin, the observation team was done observing. They knew enough about the terrorist locations and defenses to call a major incursion if it was required, or leave the region to find their own peace between nations, with far more in common than they had as differences. Although they followed a number of factions concerning the Koran, they all followed the same religious principles. Instead of using their minor differences as a means to wage war among themselves, they should find what they all held in common, to work towards finding more harmony within their nations. Negotiating and discussion always seemed more difficult than going to war, it was time to change that. Bringing to light that the remaining terrorist cells were from different nations, and religious factors, but found common ground to work together for a cause, should be enough evidence to the various governments, that it could be achieved. Zoe decided, if the leader was still undecided, she would bring these points to light for him to make a more beneficial decision concerning the fate of his people.

After four hours of small talk and contacting the DC base, Zoe went to take another shower, this time she was alone, and used the privacy to perform a more thorough cleaning and made certain her attire was in more useable condition as well. It would dry easily just outside the cave entrance, before it was time to put them back into use for the last round trip to the leader of the terrorist group. Zoe did not think terrorist was a good term to use for this group of people, who assembled under a common cause, and were more prepared to defend against the Great Satan for another attack, than to raise havoc upon the rest of the world.

It was still a matter of perception of the leader as to which event led to which, and if he did not make the attempt to find the truth in what Zoe had told him, the decision to follow would be based upon the wrong perceptions. Zoe put her clothes out to dry and stark naked returned to her sleeping bag, to be as fully rested as she could for another four-eight hour trip over rather inhospitable terrain for most vehicles. Although the jeep was capable of covering the terrain, it was not like there were any highways for high speed travel between locations.

Zoe slept for another eight hours, and this time upon waking without any assistance, she felt better than she had since first arriving to the Middle East. She and her partner would need to leave in three hours, so it allowed her time to take another cool shower to take away some of the heat that was present in the region, although with forty-eight hours of travel ahead, she did not think it would hold up. It simply made her feel better and that in itself, was helpful. She needed to be at her absolute best to reach an agreement with the leader of the terrorist group, which posed a concern to the President and the world.

Zoe was not normally any type of negotiator, considering she killed people while staring into their eyes, but this particular assignment needed a better solution than the annihilation of seventy thousand people or more for being in existence, having not shown themselves to be a threat to anyone. It was merely assumed they were up to the same old tricks as those who preceded them. From what Zoe had observed, they were nothing of the sort, simply trying to be prepared for the same kind of attacks that killed over 8,000 others in a short time frame, with a mere 35 person team of elite warriors.

Her driver timed his sleep time better, rising only an hour before departure time and went to shower before making the trek over the rough terrain, although the extra four hours did make the trip not quite as brutal on the body, as it bounced across some of the rough areas in the transit. Zoe dressed in a mere t-shirt and panties got her dry clothes and dressed in quick fashion, she would not be in the Miss Universe pageant with her current wardrobe. It was not something she found to be highly attractive herself, but it served its purpose, for the climate they were located.

The forty-eight hour journey was almost leisurely in comparison to covering the same distance and terrain in six hours less time. Upon their arrival this time, she had the jeep get closer to the buildings, but still twenty five yards of safe distance between her driver and the weapons that would stay trained on him, after she went inside.

Customary greeting were exchanged before Ali bin Uddin said, "I have found you have spoken the truth concerning every instant concerning the Great Satan, except for one. A major city was bombed as retaliation for an incident that the responsible party claiming to be the planner of those attacks did not reside in, or was he permitted to. It seemed this city was targeted for unfinished business from a previous attack, which did not resolve anything. What do you have to say about this?"

Zoe knew from her history of only one such incident, and explained what she understood of it. "The city was believed to be hiding the arbitrator of the horrendous attack on the soils of one of Great Satan's most populated cities in all of its lands. Those words were from people within that very nation, who claimed to have seen the person responsible, and even indicated which building complex he could be found. These reports came from multiple sources, all living in that very city. These reports did not come from US citizen visiting, or offering aid to the people of that nation. Whether it was not fully verified, or whether time was of the essence to bring this person to his deserved end, is not clear, but afterwards, it was discovered not only did he survive, he was never where citizens of the very nation attacked, informed people he was there and they had seen him. Bad information led to a retaliatory strike against the wrong target. It was unfortunate, but as a warrior, you yourself know how difficult it is to insure not a single innocent falls victim to aggressions. It is always the plan of the Great Satan, but the reality of it, seldom if ever, is such action 100 percent free of error. Politicians who never participate in these actions, but often demand such actions be taken, call it collateral damage. It keeps them from having to deal with the reality of the actions they seek taking place."

Ali bin Uddin said he had no way to verify her explanation, but he could see the truth in it having been as she said. The person responsible was considered a criminal in most countries of the region, and had evaded all of them for years. He could also understand why citizens who were poorly treated and cared for, would wish harm to come to those in charge of the nation, as a way to improve the nation's way of life. He then asked, if he agreed to her proposal, what guarantees he had, as proof such an agreement existed. Such an agreement would go a long way in allowing the governments to support their efforts, instead of hampering them.

Zoe said, "Once I have returned to my home location, I can have it drawn up and sent in a digital format. I believe it will have the United States Presidential Seal as the top heading of the document, and will be signed by the current President of the United States. Since you most likely have computers to use, but I am unsure of how to have paper documents sent to a location without any address. In order to do this, I would need an email address you can access, as I am sure you do not wish to use anything too personal. Once you have viewed and read the documents, as long as you fully agree nothing other than what we have discussed, is within those documents, you can merely reply to the email with the word CONFIRMED. That will serve as your signature."

Ali bin Uddin said, "There are two other items that need to be addressed. First if we become the defenders of these lands, you yourself stated, that over 8,000 lives were taken away by a mere thirty five elite warriors. How do we train our people to become such warriors, as it will certainly be required, if any strife occurs within the lands we must defend? Second, should some other faction develop that we do not control that is bent on destroying anything that comes into the space above, or they go out into the world, how can I be assured we will not be targeted for these others actions?"

Zoe replied, "It is easier to answer the second first in this case. To be assured you will not receive retaliation for the actions of others, the simplest solution is to understand the oath all people in the United States military must take. To defend our nation from all hostiles foreign and domestic. The Great Satan had never asked nor will they ever ask for aid for problems originating from within their own lands. We police ourselves in those circumstance. The Great Satan will never deny aid, to those who can justify a need for such aid. In order to best serve you own concerns, should such a separate faction develop, you must become aware of it, and offer information to their whereabouts in order to prevent retaliation. The Great Eye in the sky is not so wise as to know which faction is located where. Your help will aid you and your people, if this is an acceptable explanation to you."

Ali bin Uddin nodded in agreement that it was acceptable and made sense in more ways than he would have thought. He did state he also wanted it in the agreement. Zoe confirmed it would be included. She continued with his first concern. "To be honest, the elite warriors are elite by the fact any good group of warriors are seventy-five percent planning, twenty percent preparation and believing in the plan, and five percent skill. It is often achieved by allowing all the warriors to be involved, also included into the formation of an executable plan. Using multiple experiences and different viewpoints, minor but important possibilities are brought to light, and addressed to create a plan that see as much about what could go wrong, as to a plan that goes without a problem. From my experience, seldom does a plan not have obstacles to overcome, but with the foresight of all the warriors involved in making the plan, those obstacles are foreseen, and an action to overcome them is available within that plan. You can become just as elite as any warriors, by employing these tactics, which all start with having a well-formed plan to expect as many obstacle put in your path, as you can image. It can be learned, but having our warrior's train you on lands you are far more familiar with, may not lead you on the correct action to take under all conditions.

There is one more item that allows the most elite teams of warrior to understand what everyone else is doing in their assignments, and that is communications. Every nation in the world at this point in time, has wireless communications available, in the public forum. Computers and cell phones are the most common, but there are certain frequency levels reserved for government and military usage, not available to the public. Using such devices for your people, allows them to stay in communications with one another even over fairly long distances.

It serves many purposes from a spotter informing a small group what hostiles are heading their way, to being able to know precisely where each and every person is, and what they are doing during a skirmish. These are all the secrets of elite warriors, they are the means to employ for your people to become elite as well, but it also take many hours of practice, for each to know how the other will react or behave in any circumstance."

Ali bin Uddin no longer thought he needed outsiders coming in to train his people, he did need to get the document to take to the different governments, to become the protectors of the lands.

Zoe did ask one question of Ali bin Uddin. Zoe asked, "If it is not too much trouble to ask, how did you come to form as a group, since it is obvious from our observation, all of your people are not from the same nation or identical religious beliefs?"

Ali bin Uddin said, "With the destruction of the most radical of the groups, it was a means of survival. It was apparent to all, and the single person who got away that without forming as a unified group, we would all perish with the Great Satan upon us. It was decided to put aside our difference, and work together as a single team, and it has worked surprisingly well."

Zoe said, "That being said, you could fuel the government's fires in trying to achieve that among all your nations, as you are proof it can be done. If you succeed, maybe your nations will learn to become tolerant with their neighbors, and the world could come to a more peaceful place for all of us to live in. It will take ten days to two weeks before you will receive your document in the email address you have given me. During that time, I suggest starting a training program to get all your people to understand each other, to better prepare to be the defenders of these nations. If this is all you do until your document is received and you reply with CONFIRMED, no harm shall come to you from the Great Satan. I cannot however provide you with such guarantees from other nations, so it is best not to offend any who will retaliate."

Ali bin Uddin and Zoe had an agreement, which was all she needed to achieve while in the Middle East. It was time to return to the local base, to gather everything up for when the cargo plane would arrive. It was still a two to three hours trek to that location, if it was the same as when they first arrived, but there were not that many places to land a plane in this terrain.

The first forty-eight hours was the trip back to the Middle East base. Again, it was shower and sleep time before doing anything else. Upon rising after ten hours of sleep, she established communications to the DC base and informed Romero Trap what she accomplished. When she returned to DC, she would give him the full details, and what needed to go into the document to be signed by the President, and sent to the email address she would provide. She did not know if the bible was written in his language, but if it was, a digital copy should be included so he could judge for himself, how similar the Koran and the Bible were in the teachings and principles, between the people of Islam and Christianity. Her first mission upon returning was to get a hotel room of the finest standards, where she could subject herself to all the female pampering, she could endure. Then she expected to dine at a fine restaurant with Romero Trap, to give him all the details for the document. Romero Trap gave Zoe Dubois all the room she required to get back to being herself. She was still after all, one of the most unique assassins in the entire world, and it took a truly cold heart to completely expose herself for the purpose of killing a man looking into his eyes while he died.

After the entire team got in a good night of sleep and again showers were used in groups of four. All the supplies and equipment were loaded into the jeeps. The team left for the airfield where the cargo plane was located, and after a two and a half hour drive over the rough terrain, they arrived at the airfield. The jeeps were loaded one at time in two by two fashion. After an hour and half of loading, a double check of everything being secured, Jackson Frye started the engines, closed the rear door. Made his last walk through from the pilot seat to the cargo door to insure it was fully sealed and everything remained secure. Upon his return to the pilot's hatch, strapped in and started to taxi the plane into the takeoff position, to start the return trip to the DC airfield. The team was in the Middle East for two and a half months, and not a single life had been taken.

As soon as the cargo plane was on its home airfield and placed into its hanger, the team took the four jeeps out of the cargo plane, waited for the doors to be closed and Jackson got into his own jeep, and the five jeeps returned to the main DC base of operations. As soon as Zoe entered the building, where she was located with all her gear and personal belongings, she changed into a more becoming attire, took an extra dress and other garments that went with a dress. Got to the garage, and took the Lincoln Town Car to find the best hotel she could on short notice. She had noticed the team had no difficulty in taking the 100 dollars a week for improvements, which seemed there was little left to do. Although it was looking far more like a home, it did not offer what she desires as far as certain luxuries she had grown accustomed to having in her own home.

She found one very luxurious hotel with all the desired special featured she sought. Once checking into her room, her first need was a long hot bubble bath to remove any and all remnants of the Middle East. After completing that, she dressed and went to the masseuse that was in one of the many concourse shops of the large lobby area of the hotel. It took an hour and half to feel all the aches and pains slip from her entire being. From there it was a trip to the hairdresser, and then a manicure and pedicure. Her final stop was for the full treatment facial that took another four hours of her time to complete all the female pleasures, she had her heart set on getting. It was closing in on dinnertime with Romero Trap, and before returning to her room, she found the lobby shops also had an exclusive shop for women's evening attire. For an additional 300 dollars, she found a dress she thought was perfect for her and sensual enough to entice most males. Although that was not her plan, it would be at some other time when she was back to her own specialty.

Dinner was at the hotel restaurant which was rated as five stars, the highest rating given to food establishments. The feature was largely of the seafood variety, but the very best in lobster, crab and shrimp dishes were the main menu items. It also included caviar for those who fancied such exotic foods. It was only the finest available in the world, and the prices matched the items.

Dinner with Romero Trap was for Zoe strictly business, detailing to Romero every word needed for the agreement to be written by the President, and signed by him as well. She told Romero Trap no deviations could be used or additions included that would cause Ali bin Uddin to refuse to agree. She provided Trap with the email address to send it to, and the language to use in the interpreter software conversion, so it would be understood by Ali bin Uddin. She also said, if it was possible to attach a copy of the bible converted to his language, for him to understand just how similar it was to the Koran. Dinner was superb and Zoe willingly parted with another 400 dollars to take care of the exquisite feast the two enjoyed. Romero Trap assumed he was to pay for it, but Zoe said since it was, she who insisted upon having to indulge her need for a night of luxury, she felt it was her obligation, and besides she had the money to do it. She also explained to Romero Trap, when she was in her own home as an independent contractor, this was how she lived. Her particular skills offered certain rewards and luxuries, that she had enjoyed taking part in.

The document from the President was sent to Ali bin Uddin and received CONFIRMED after the tenth day of her night of luxury. An accord had been reached and the President of the United States had made the public aware of it, through a news conference, which had national and international press coverage. The results of the news conference brought about the remaining half of the bounty from all who committed to it. Although it was not under the conditions, they all had anticipated, it did fulfill the expectations of the bounty. Having the first peace accord to the region, was far more beneficial than annihilating another group of terrorists, which only seem to raise more of the same.

13

The Soloists

President Thomas Hardesty had spent the last three months slimming down government departments, removing those who failed to participate in making those departments functioning at optimal proficiency. What he found, was most of the highest paid department personnel were the ones most prone to sitting back and watching, while others performed the job. Those people were removed, putting a lower paid official in charge of the departments, but also contributing to overall performance. For those who moved up, it was a pay increase, but not at the level of the predecessor for an overall cost reduction in the government payroll. Thomas Hardesty looked upon it as a win-win situation for the departments involved. There was far less strife among its members, and everyone remaining felt it was still an excellent position to hold, considering they did not have the skills to earn as much in the business world. Government still operated in a slightly different mode than business, largely because so many of the departments were for citizen's welfare, which businesses did not address. There were still offices that were mostly the watchdogs of business and the public, than positions that equated to job skills in the business world.

The President was also looking into what other problems existed that would compromise the full formation of a world governing body, which was his ultimate goal to complete prior to the end of his term as the leader of the nation. He had identified five such people within his own country. They were very vocal against the reformed government, although they were subject to nothing but criticism and ridicule from the national press, and general population according to public polls. It seemed the best thing would be to silence the fools, before they generated support. One was a former Senator who wanted nothing more than to return government back to the leaches of the taxpaying citizens of the country. He still believed a larger government would better serve the people, and he failed to see how people's approval had any bearing on the way government should operate. This Senator would bring back the citizen's to the brink of another revolution within the nation, and that would most definitely be a deterrent to a world governing council. Currently the formation of the world governing body now had 50 percent of all the nations of the globe, on board and formally committed to its process.

He had not yet identified the sources of such drawbacks in other countries, although he knew there were two in Russia, but not whom specifically. What the vast majority of the deterrents had in common, is they obtained large amounts of wealth, through means vastly of illegal activities, many sold weapons on the black market, but disguised their wealth through businesses that appeared perfect legitimate. A third was located in Japan, and was a major concern to the people of that nation. He was the largest among the crime networks in that part of the world.

As a result, they held political influence, although within his own country that was limited to the representatives holding a seat from states within his House of Representative. They had absolutely no influence over the president, vice president or Supreme Court. Such was not the case in the other countries, where they held influence over some of the highest ranking officials within the respective countries. President Thomas Hardesty was still compiling his information over the other countries, and it was only a matter of time before he would pinpoint it to a single source.

It was made apparent to Romero Trap, while in the Oval Office on his typical half day sessions, it would be at least another three months,

THE SOLOISTS

before he had compiled his list of remaining targets for the team to take care of. How Trap went about that end of his business as Vice President, and care taker of the problems that prevented the complete formation of a world governing body, was up to him. Since these were going to be individual deterrents to progress, there would be no government funds for the issues discussed. Trap would need to address the issue himself. He had done a marvelous job of funding to this point, and saw no reason he could not continue in that line of obtaining bounties for targets. The problems were not the President's alone, the impedances were shared by other governments and business factions around the globe, but largely within their own country. In order to reduce the deficit, the nation had amassed over the last 30 plus years, every spare dollar was being applied to that. Leaving the government at the end of each fiscal year at zero, in order to start without as much deficit, but having to watch every dollar spent, during the upcoming fiscal year. It was working, as he had reduced the time for the deficit to be eliminated from one hundred to fifty years. He did not foresee it occurring prior to his end in office, but it would be going in the right direction, and hoped with the last round of deductions on government payroll, by the end of his term, seventy-five percent of the deficit would be paid off. He unfortunately could not guarantee his successor would continue down the same path, which would be highly regrettable, but outside of his control. So far, he had reestablished a confidence in the government from the people that had not existed for at least twenty five years and far likely longer. He simply could not induce his will upon those who would follow, and would make no attempt to do so. His hope was the people having tasted more prosperity in their lives, would vote accordingly.

It would also depend largely on those political person's running for office, as to whether they would continue to present issues to the people, or return to the mudslinging common prior to his election. Thomas Hardesty believed in all his heart, if people were given real issues to consider, instead of who the least was concerned about the people's interest, they would make wise decisions. Upon hearing this from the President, the first thing Romero Trap did was give his team sixty days of paid vacation. He did not care what they did during that time, but did not want any of his team to be found at the base location. It allowed Zoe to return to her own home, and the life of luxury she was accustomed to having. Romero Trap also realized he may have some of his team reconsider the continuance of the assignment, but he did not foresee too many leaving, prior to the end of the President's final term in office. The funds amassed in the six accounts was more than sufficient for each member of the team to have a life of luxury beyond the rigors of their profession. Even Romero Trap could not conceive of any way to deplete 500 million dollars over a lifetime. His team definitely deserved it, for all they had done in the name of their country, even if the country did not recognize their contributions. It was part of the deal, and it was best for his people to remain anonymous to the general public, as well as other government officials, including the Pentagon. It was in everyone's best interest to go unrecognized and not be put into the spotlight.

Romero Trap, during the 60 days continued to visit the base location every day, largely to insure everything was untouched by outside intruders or vandals. Although he had not encountered any such activity in four and half years, he still stayed vigilant to the needs of the base and the team. He did not spend vast amounts of time at the base, being the sole member present, but he did make it a daily checkup that usually consisted of an hour to two checking each building, and the property for signs of anything out of place.

Zoe was truly enjoying herself within her own home and having cooks to prepare her gourmet meals, as well as other people who took care of the house, while she enjoyed a large number of days in her Jacuzzi; which did a wonderful job of soothing her muscles and body tone, while not doing a wonderful job of taking care of her skin which she did afterwards. Zoe considered bringing her agreement to an end, but in the end decided it was in her best interests to fulfill her commitment to Romero Trap, as no other person had ever given her as much credit for her skills, or number of assignments that paid quite well. She was after all a professional at her purpose in life, and it would only harm her reputation to leave an assignment before it was done, although she never would have thought a President would do so much in such a short time, to get an overwhelming second term. She truly only thought about it being a four year assignment, not eight years. Thinking back about it, she was warned it was a possibility.

The rest of the team was rather private about their personal lives and even kept it from the other team members. Whether it was superstition or simply for the protection of those close to them, they shared it with not a single other person, including those they worked with on regular basis. Romero Trap could understand this behavior, since it was his profession that brought him to the decision, not to be personally involved with anyone. He did not want his family being the target of retribution for his deeds. Keeping his profession in mind, and knowing fully well, that there were many factions in the world who get their revenge by going after innocent people important to the person they sought. It was a cruel but effective way of drawing out the real target, and disrupting their piece of mind in order to create enough distraction in the person, to make that fatal mistake. His profession not only made him aware of this method, those who gave the assignments often employed it, because they were invisible to the actual events that were to take place. It was not the profession of highly emotional or mentally challenged individuals. Decisions had to made, often in fractions of a second, and you did not have time to consider the consequence of your action in the process of taking those actions. If you let your conscience interfere with your job, it was time to consider another line of work.

Romero Trap did get all the information he needed to obtain, concerning the five people within the borders of the United States, and they were spread out fairly well. The former Senator considered Wisconsin his home base, and owned a rather large home outside of Milwaukee. It was close enough to the larger populated city area to indulge in all the luxuries of a large city, but far enough outside to be considered almost rural in nature. He was a man in in late sixties, and prone to all the male problems associated with having reached a certain age. He knew Zoe would want a very high price for this assignment, but she was the best choice for this particular target. He wanted it to be very public, like in a fine restaurant, but it would also need to be done so discretely to disallow any suspicion placed on Zoe. He knew she could do it, and her academy award would be her payment. No trophy other than a large amount of cash. He did not know what she had in her bag of tricks, but knew she had done something quite similar previously.

The four other highly vocal businessmen were in Miami, San Diego, Kansas City and Phoenix. He was trying to figure out how to best take care of these, not wanting to use the same approach for all four of them. The good thing about all five of the targets were they were all creatures of habit. They frequented certain establishments on a regular basis, and remained highly visible. The four businessmen were quite wealthy, but their money came from criminal activities disguised under legitimate business fronts. One in San Diego had an import and export business, that appeared perfectly legal on paper, but his largest business dealing were in black market weapons, sold to the highest bidder. He himself did not perform the acquisition of those weapons, he had people for that specific task. His primary source was military thefts, but his people did not go into take all that was available, they took a small quantity, which made it more difficult for military logistics to discover.

Another businessman in Kansas City was a nightclub owner, which seemed to be exceptionally popular among the younger crowd. It also served as a front for illegal drug sales, largely stolen pharmaceuticals, which were in high demand. His prices were a bit steeper than others, but he always had what was in demand. He also did not sell or obtain the drugs; he was just the person to call all the shots.

The Miami businessman was a liquor distributor. His means of high profits came from his own distilleries, which he used to take one bottle and make four of several brands of highly popular brands, diluted with his own illegal product. He also did the only recycling of bottles in the whole state, paying a small fee for every empty bottle collected from his distribution. Even at five cents a bottle, it was more than any seller could get and the alternative was to discard the empties in the trash. He had a means to produce his own sealed caps as well as labels of the brands he altered. His other means of high profits came from the number of illegal aliens he employed. They did get paid, just not at the standards of legally employed people, and it was still better than what the illegal aliens had before working for him. His businesses were hidden in plain sight, and yet he never drew suspicion of the authorities into his moonshining practices. Like all the others, he had a hands off approach to his illegal activities. He did have an office in his distribution center, and was normally present at least five hours of each day they operated. Romero Trap thought this would be best accomplished with the use of explosives, at the primary distribution facility.

The last member was in Phoenix and he was a person who enjoyed the nightlife. His activities were a bit more unknown, but he obviously had a source of income to have a lifestyle of expensive nightly partying. He thought this would be perfect for an apparent robbery that turned fatal, and he had a number of people who could pull it off. Since this businessman carried large sums of cash on his nightly excursions, it was the best means to make his death appear to be a robbery gone badly wrong.

He was still awaiting his targets from outside the US, which would have a higher degree of expense involved. He only knew of two cities to this point, and three targets, but not specifically whom his team needed to eliminate. His team still had another 30 days' time before returning to the main base of operations. Romero Trap would use that time to decide who was best for each of the targets, and he was sure he could do it with solo acts to each target. Romero Trap also knew in order to transport any weapon, it could not be accomplished using commercial airlines, and flying the cargo plane back and forth around the country for a single person was illogical. Outside of the Lincoln, the rest of the vehicles were more military grade, and not really the best option to use for traveling across the country. Rental cars would be required for the long trips across national highways, and two cities were on the opposite end of the country. They would not be short leisurely drives. It would also mean hotel arrangements in each of the cities, since it was highly unlikely any of the targets could be removed upon entering the city they were located. It would still require time for his professionals to determine the best location for their job, and time to observe their habits for a pattern best suited to the task. Romero Trap always allowed his team members to make those final decisions, it was important for good relations between himself and each of his team members. It was also his professional trademark, which kept his team returning time and again for new assignments.

Romero Trap left the base location, and returned to his quaint little apartment for some additional research into his assignments. For the targets of this assignment, there would be a fair amount of public information available, through social media and internet browsing. They were after all visible in the public's eyes, and most of them fed the frenzy, with their own little sites and social media pages.

He decided Howie Short (Judas) was the most effective person to bring about the demises of the Phoenix businessman to appear to be a robbery. He would allow Howie to keep whatever cash he got from the job, as long as he made it appear robbery was the cause of death. He was extremely efficient in taking down his prey from behind with his expertise in blades. He could do that in a dark alley or a parking lot with poor lighting. He was certain Phoenix had such locations, and his assignment would frequent one such location.

Sal Lavetti (Boomer) was an explosives expert, who could perform the Miami job perfectly. He could get into the building during hours unoccupied, and set the explosives to bring the building down on the target. He could do it by timer or remote trigger, but he would be able to make it appear to be an accidental cause, since liquors were highly flammable, and one small error could result in just such an accident.

It still left two cities that needed to be done in different methods, one could be long rifle but the last was a bit of a quandary. His only other means that came to mind would be with a hand gun to appear like a gang related kill. San Diego would be a location where such killings were often in the news, and the most common method was a single shot to the back of the head at close range. It was more a matter of if his target had stepped upon enough toes of the local gangs in running his business. He was sure between the two cities left, one of them had, but he needed to know which was more likely to find his demise in that fashion. All the targets were singular, which meant there was no needed to be concerned with hierarchy in which the problem would continue with a new leader. It made the tasks much easier to coordinate among his chosen professional for each of the tasks. The problem he did foresee, was the Japanese target who appeared to be like a ghost. Seldom seen and without ever being identified, he posed the biggest problem. It would take a very specific professional from his team to remove this particular threat to the formation of a world governing council. He had one person in mind who came from the country and lost his parents to the acts of violence affiliated with the crime syndicates in Japan. Romero Trap knew he was of age when he lost his parents, and originally got into the team for the purpose of removing those responsible for his parents deaths. Unfortunately, the assignments they received, did not aid him in his quest. He was a little bitter, but always did his job like a true professional. He would jump at the chance to get his retribution for the loss of his parent's, even if this was not the syndicate leader he truly sought, he would get some satisfaction from removing a similar threat.

Tankawa (Sting) was a martial arts offensive expert, and well versed in the use of the tools of his trade. Expert with darts and blades, he could invoke a great deal of pain to his target before finishing with the fatal blow. He would do it in the Japanese way, which had the most effective means of informing others they were next. The removal of the head with a samurai sword, was considered to be a longer reaching warning to all others who might seek revenge upon the death of their leader. Considering the meaning of such a death, his hierarchy would be overly cautious in getting the revenge they sought, and by the time they reacted, Tankawa would be long gone. All martial arts people possessed a great deal of stealth in their movements, in order to get close without being discovered too quickly. It was something inherent in the formal training, something Romero Trap never participate in, but regretted from time to time not having done so as a youth. It would have made him a little more lethal than he already was as a long standing professional in the assassination trade. He seldom called upon himself for an assignment in the last ten years, but under circumstances, other than serving as Vice President to the nation, he would have found use of his own skills over that last four and a half years.

The best thing about his new position of Vice President is he was heading downhill now, to a government position that had a time limit equal to his time served. It was too far into this assignment to consider acquisition of a helicopter; the only thing Romero Trap knew how to fly. He was aware of military aircraft of that nature that had two or three rocket launchers for attack purposes. Only the Russians used a larger helicopter, capable of mounting as many as seven rocket launchers but it was like flying an ocean liner. Simply too large to go undetected under radar. He had the opportunity to do that once, and it was like fighting a raging bull in the air, and he did not feel like subjecting himself to that much exertion to merely fly from one place to another.

Romero trap continued his research over the next thirty days to discover as much about his foreign targets as humanly possible. He was still coming up way too short on information for his Japanese target, in which the President only was able to provide a single name of Matura. His name was used in many threatening documents to political figures and authorities, and he did his research to find out about each member he targeted as to family and people close to those, he wished to serve him. He always used the same person for his affairs for such arrangements. Ugi Osaki was a rather well known lawyer in Japan. He did not get paid by Matura for his intermediate council. His family was threatened in ways that Ugi could not discuss, but he did his work for Matura out of fear for his family's wellbeing. Matura had a reputation of being truly brutal, but never once did Matura perform the act. It made him all the more unpredictable and faceless to the recipients of his rage. He took revenge upon any who offended him, and always started with the family first in a most brutal fashion. Apparently, those who did the tasks for Matura had no inclinations towards empathy towards the victims.

Somehow Romero Trap needed to narrow down the options for Tankawa, Tokyo had an awfully large population to have to examine, and observe every citizen of Japan within the Tokyo area. Unfortunately, he was not finding anything useful in his research, Matura was for all intents and purposes truly was a ghost, and there was no photos of him anywhere on the internet, or even in the authority's records, which he could access. He was reaching a solid brick wall in every turn of his research, and he did not like asking a team member to go into a situation completely blind, even if that member had an overwhelming desire to get justice for acts committed upon his family. Romero Trap

THE SOLOISTS

had reached a point of exasperation concerning Matura. He was familiar with single names for some people from the nation, but most of those had a long history of honorable standings within the Japanese people. Matura did not seem to possess those qualities. If anything, he was among the dishonored known as Ronin.

The remaining thirty days had passed and Romero Trap was totally frustrated by the fact he was unable to discover any more prudent information concerning Matura. He had exhausted every avenue in his research, to find absolutely nothing more than his name, and President Thomas Hardesty was no more successful in his findings either. What was the most frustrating concern to Romero Trap, was whether this person truly existed or whether It was a pseudo name used for intimidation. With the team all back, he had those not selected for the assignments, make the bounty contacts which really was a disappointment at least among the national problems within their own country. Even with all the ridicule and distrust these five people created among the general population, they did not earn the outright ire of major businesses or governments at a local level that wished the persons removed from the public limelight. They were deemed mere nuisances unworthy of assassination. A total of 100 million dollars was all that could be raised for the five residents of the United States. With Zoe, the best he could hope for was a break even on costs involved with these five individuals.

Romero Trap had thought it would earn considerably more, but having accepted the assignment from President Hardesty, he had to move forward. If the team lost money on it, which was the one thing detrimental to having accepted this type of assignment, lasting eight long years. There had to be more than enough left in the profit reserve, to allow these people an excellent retirement for all they had provided for their country, knowing fully well the government would not see to their needs. They had no problem asking young men to give their lives in the name of their country, but to reward them for such a sacrifice, was never in their game plan. They viewed it as the cost of freedom, and that was all the reward they were willing to provide.

On the other hand, competitors of the foreign targets were chomping at the bit to get in the removal process of the person responsible for taking away so much of their business. At last count, it was up to five billion dollars and climbing. The time to dispatch the chosen was approaching rapidly. Between Kansas City and San Diego, Kansas City was the better choice for a hit from gang members, San Diego was a long rifle take down. Since the San Diego business was import/export, he spent some time in the docks insuring his shipments were on board ships to depart from harbor. There were more than enough large ships in port at all times, to get a clean distance shot, although it would still be within 1,000 yards, and he had a number of competent people at that range. Since Eyes wanted to prove his worth over Susan Hobart, he was selected for the San Diego job. It left one person, expert in hand guns to take the Kansas City job and that person would be Sven Turlock (Bullseye). Information was still being compiled for the two Russia and single Japanese targets, and it all likelihood they would not be dispatch until after the completion of the domestic targets. Methods for those targets did not need to be all different like the domestic problems. The domestic problem makers had to all look like random acts or accidents, whichever applied most for the situations.

Romero Trap arranged for four cars to be delivered to the base location from the same provider, the only one he knew that brought the car to you, although it did require a trip to return the person that brought it. He select all four of the models as Mercedes, not sure if all the hype was true, but thought with the distance some had to cover, if they pushed too long and too hard, a vehicle capable of stopping itself was better than having a member of the team not able to reach the destination.

Zoe had requested 50 million dollars for her high profile target, indicating the risks she had to take to remove a Senator in a crowded restaurant, with her being present for his demise. Romero Trap had to do some serious negotiating with Zoe making it perfectly clear that her high profile target, did not have a single penny contributing to his removal. This Zoe was unaware of, but still thought she was the person taking the biggest risk among the domestic targets, and she was well worth every cent. Romero Trap said since she was not going to be involved with the foreign targets where the biggest bounties were coming from, she was not entitle to rewards from there.

He also had to disclose that the primary reason of insuring a maximum of profits maintained, was to insure at the end of the assignment, every team member had sufficient funds as to have a retirement to live a life of luxury. Although, he also admitted she might be the only one among them to be able to spend every penny, before facing her human fate. Zoe asked if that was being old and wrinkled, in which Trap replied was the more permanent fate reached after that. Whether she planned to be planted or burnt made no difference, at that point she would no longer feel pain. He also went into specific detail that all the traumas you subjected to your body during your youth and prime, returned with a vengeance once you turned fifty, some people before that. Even with Zoe prodding him for an amount, he maintained his composure and did not give her the believed amount. This was largely due to the fact some unexpected expenses could change the amount. The biggest concern was having to replace the cargo plane by means of purchase. It would be a large sum of money, but the need was still present with another three and half years left in the President's final term. President Hardesty like all politicians currently in office, would revert to the retirement program that was used by all the citizens of the nation. Unlike his predecessors, who remained among the living, they were paid at the same rate he was currently, although he did lower it across the board to provide more money for the deficit repayment process, he had established.

President Hardesty had reduced his government considerably, but could not find any additional means to reduce the deficit in a quicker fashion. If everything stayed the same course it would still be fifty more years, before the nation was debt free. He highly doubted his plan would stay the course with at least 7 other Presidents to follow in his footsteps. A more exact number would require him being clairvoyant, and he was not in the least.

Romero Trap had all the Mercedes arrive at the same time the following afternoon, he selected four other people, not departing, to return them to the rental agency while last minute discussions were done with the five who were departing. Boomer should have the shortest drive, and be able to reach Miami in less than a day. Zoe and Bullseye were considerable close to identical distances, it was a matter of which of the two had the heavier foot. The most direct path might also come into play. It would take at least three days for the other two, to reach their destinations depending on how long they could hold up under the extended drive. Not everyone held up to the rigors of driving across the width of the entire country, and although Phoenix was closer than San Diego, it was a mere 8 hours between the two cities.

Once the cars were back to the base of operations, the drivers heading to the different cities had their luggage and gear ready to go, and were all off before 3 PM in the afternoon. Communications from this adventure for the five would be done through burner phones, one for each team member and the final one for Romero Trap. The rule was once the job was completed, and they made their call to Trap, the phone was to be discarded. He would not discard his until all were back, but all had reported in with completion of their assignments. Each person was given 20,000 dollars to cover expenses, although all the hotels were arranged and paid for in the city they would stay in, he could not predict where and whom may need to stop for rest in their travels.

Romero Trap did not envy Boomer in the slightest for his trip to Miami. He remembered making the grave error when he was much younger, to take a week of vacation time to go to Orlando, and visit Walt Disney World amusement park. He went at the end of June beginning of July, and was never so miserable in his entire life. Temperatures were in the nineties and so was the humidity. The only thing to get a workout for the entire time was his sweat glands. His clothes were soaking wet within an hour, and it rained for one hour every day. He even stayed in the rain for one day for the entire hour, hoping it would bring him some relief, only for the sun to come out afterwards and be overwhelmed by the stifling humidity. He vowed to himself to never return again in any month other than the dead of winter. To date, he had not been back at all.

The rest of the team was still working on bounty for the two Russians and single Japanese targets, and the Japanese threat was obviously disliked by far more than the other two. He alone accounted for 6 billion in promised bounty with his removal, while the pair of Russians were only at 3 billion dollars combined. Romero did not try to determine, who was leading in that race. He would call it off as far as bounty was concerned when it reached 10 billion dollars total. He still had the task of getting people there with weapons, and the only conceivable means he had, was to put the three team members on the cargo plane, although the jeeps would not be so out of place in either of the two cities or countries. The plane would need a total of three refueling stops round trip. First leg would be refueling after crossing the Atlantic Ocean somewhere beyond the actual coast, refuel in Russia with the delivery of two jeeps, and team members. It should be sufficient fuel to make Japan, and return a fair amount of the distance back towards the coast of the Atlantic. He did not know if it would require a fourth refueling before returning to the hanger. He would have to clarify that with Jackson, who knew more about how far fuel would take him than any other person. He would be carrying a fairly light load in his trip, and that made a huge difference in the distance it could cover before refueling.

Boomer was the first of the team members to arrive at his destination of Miami and let Romero Trap know he arrived, immediately after checking in to his hotel and getting to his room. He drove non-stop and was going to get a long night of rest, before determining anything concerning his target. In Romero Trap's internet research, the one good thing about public forums on the World Wide Web, was all the domestic targets had recent photos posted. His team members on the individual assignments, would have no trouble identifying their targets.

On the following day, both Bullseye and Black Widow arrived to their destinations, each decided to stop during the trip, for a sleep period before resuming to the destination. Bullseye reach his hotel and was checked in only 30 minutes before Black Widow. Black Widow on the other hand, was going to immediately make contact with her target, while Bullseye needed to do some closer observations for a good location to give the correct appearance of his target's demise. Boomer had determined the hours of operation for the Miami distiller business, and since the business primary closed down after five PM until the next day, he used the evening hours to place his explosives in hidden but locations to cause the most destruction. All of it was set to a single remote detonator which only required him to point toward the building and press the button. After three hours he relocked the door, he picked and returned to the hotel for sleep until the next day.

Zoe and Romero Trap had gone over how Zoe planned to accomplish her mission and Trap thought it was brilliant. Zoe Dubois (Black Widow) went to a local watering hole also called a nightclub, although it was only late afternoon. She located a payphone within the establishment, and used it to place her acting call to the Senator. Her story was she found his number on the bathroom stall and being totally new to town, she was looking for some company since she hated being completely alone.

After the quick introduction without using her name Zoe said, "I do not normally take much stock in things written on bathroom walls, but seeing THE SENATOR intrigued me, are you really a Senator or if it is just a name they gave you?" The Senator said, "I was a Senator for the state if Wisconsin for 34 years, until the sly son of bitch President managed to find a way to work around the political circle long established. He campaigned by telling the people how he wanted to change the government for the betterment of the people, but never went into the details on how he intended to achieve it. His means caught everyone off guard, and we were totally unprepared to combat his method. Whom do I have the pleasure of speaking with by the way?"

Zoe told the Senator to call her Catrina, and she truly was hoping for some companionship over a fine meal and drinks to see where it went from there. The Senator had a penchant for young women, and like most men in his later years of life had all the failings of his age, but he still liked to try, and used his position to his advantage for many years. A time and place was set, and the Senator said she would recognize him with the Stetson he wore. He was born in Texas, but at an early age, his parents moved to the Midwest, and this is where he had been ever since, but he still liked to think of himself as a Texan. Zoe said she would meet him at the restaurant, and hoped he had a good Champaign in mind for the start of things to come.

The Senator agreed, and Zoe went over all the details she had concerning her target. As a man in his late sixties, depending on his physical condition would determine how the long the venom she acquired for just such a target, would take to have its effect. She had only one source for this particular method, and although difficult to obtain, it was colorless, odorless and tasteless. She thought with the Champaign, it would not take long for the Senator to need to make one of his more and more frequent trips to the men's room. She would then pour the small vial into his Champaign, and wait for it to take hold. The unique way the venom worked, was the initial symptoms would seem like nothing more than the light headed effect of one too many drinks. It was untraceable after one hour in a person's system, and when the hour was up, so was the time for breathing. It would immediately stop the heart and lungs, and without immediate assistance, death came within three minutes. For people in extremely good physical condition, it took a little longer, for poor physical condition it only took 45 minutes.

When the Senator arrived, Zoe was still in the waiting area not being told if he had a table reserved or was simply given the next available one. She saw the rather large hat, and approached the potbellied old geezer she thought was her evening dinner companion, and said she was Catrina, and thought she was here to meet him. He was quite pleased to see such a beautiful woman wishing his companionship for the evening. The restaurant host ushered them to the Senator's table, always reserved for him where the Senator immediately ordered the bottle of Champaign. He had already had a few drinks, largely to get up his nerve to meeting an unknown woman, who only sounded intriguing; but he had learned that voices and faces do not always have the same pleasing affects. In this case it did, from the Senator's perspective.

The two chatted for fifteen minutes and had two glasses of Champaign each, while Zoe told the Senator all the practiced falsehoods she came up with for her character of this evening. She told him how she was a well-paid bartender at a very popular nightclub, and behind the bar mixing drinks for clientele, she was considered by the owner to be the main attraction for his growing business. She was asked to come to Wisconsin from Cincinnati on the riverfront nightclub, to get the new location going. She had not even been to the place yet, and did not believe it would be opened for another week. She hated being totally alone in a strange new city and not knowing a single person. Fifteen minutes into the conversation and the Champaign, the Senator excused himself for a moment to take care of a pressing bladder condition.

As part of her attire for the evening was a revealing evening dress, Zoe had worn a large bracelet to conceal the small vial tucked into it. With the Senator heading away, she told him she would refill his glass while he was away. Once out of sight, Zoe made sure her arm was upright to remove the small stopper to the vial, and with a well-practiced maneuver, she reach over the Senators glass spilling the vial contents into the Senator's glass, while reaching for the iced bottle of Champaign, to refill their glasses. It took a mere 30 seconds.

When the Senator returned, they continued a bit more conversation while they each had another glass of Champaign. It took only 20 minutes for the initial effects of the venom to hit the Senator, where he suggested they place their orders. The server took their orders and the food was served. The Senator managed to get in a few bites of his food before keeling over onto the floor, twenty-five minute later. Zoe went into academy award acting, and cried out for help and acted entirely innocent of having anything to do with the Senator's collapse. Emergency crews were fifteen minutes in arriving, and the Senator was pronounced dead as soon as they started to examine him. Zoe acted entirely distraught over the whole scene unfolding in the restaurant, and was asked only a couple questions which she sobbed her answers. It took the emergency crew another twenty minutes to get the Senator wheeled out of the restaurant, but the scene had disrupted the evening business. Zoe was told, she may leave, as the restaurant in light of the events would need to close for the evening.

Zoe did not know from her source, of the contents of the vial what type of venom was used. Her contact produced but a single product, and only he knew the process used for creating the final product, which he had turned into a very lucrative business. Zoe had no idea how long her contact had been in business, nor any clue about his age. She did know that the contents of the vial was one of her most effective methods, although she used it quite sparingly. With her leaving the restaurant, she returned to her hotel and made the confirmation call to Romero Trap. Trap merely asked if he was to deposit her fee into the same account as previously. Zoe confirmed, as it was also a numbered account, one she used largely for deposits to be redistributed to two other numbered accounts, which received excellent earnings. She only kept six figures in her deposit account, which was kept open for the deposits and redistribution. The six figures were still more than sufficient to have no concerns raised by the bank that held it.

Once again Zoe was the first to complete the tasks, and two of the people were not even at their destinations yet. Zoe would stay at the hotel for two more days, before starting her return trip to the DC base location. She discarded her burner phone in a dumpster behind the hotel the following morning.

That same morning Boomer returned to the Miami liquor distributor/moonshine facility and noticed how many vehicles were present. A very expensive luxury sedan was present in a place marked president and with that simple confirmation, he took cover and pointed his remote detonator and pushed the button. The facility went up like a bomb blast, largely fuel by the moonshining distillery utilized by the Miami business mogul. Boomer stayed long enough to know not a single person managed to leave and quickly departed before emergency crews arrived, he could hear them in the distance, but had plenty of time to leave the scene without so much as a single person to give him a glance. He made his confirmation call and checked out of his hotel to return to DC, tossing the burner phone out in front of an eighteen wheeler screaming past him. The big rig was moving so quick the phone did not clear the front bumper of the truck and shattered upon contact.

Two days later, Bullseye had found the perfect location for his target. His target frequented an establishment, where he liked to park his exotic sports car in the dark alley adjacent to the building he would enter. You would think for a man of wealth, he would put it into a more secure environment, such as any number of parking garages in the vicinity, or even put money in a meter on the street, but he preferred not to pay for such things, if he could use someplace with no cost involved. There were a number of places to conceal himself in the alley, to await his target returning to his sports car. Bullseye was certain the local hoodlums would have removed items from his precious sports car, but it appeared they avoided it like the plague, being concerned to some degree of just who he was dealing with to instill such fear in the hoodlums, who had seen his sports car and cleared away from it upon recognition of it. He was a professional after all and he had dealt with many foes considered way too dangerous to mess with. He was going to be a little more on guard for this particular target, considering the strange circumstances he had observed.

His fourth night in Kansas was the time he selected to bring an end to his target in gang like fashion. He waited for several hours hidden between two large containers in the alleyway. When his target came out of the building, and went to his nice little sports car, he came up from behind, unseen and unheard, clubbed the businessman in the back of the head with the butt of his 45 caliber weapon. Attached a silencer, turned him over on his belly and fired a single shot to the back of his head. Removed his wallet which contained nearly 20,000 dollars in cash, dropped it after removing only the currency. The silencer muted most of the sound of his weapon producing only a spitting sound. He then walked away for others to find the businessman who met his end. He expected to see it on the news by the time he returned to the hotel.

After seeing the news report, Bullseye used his burner phone to make the confirmation call to Romero Trap. Upon completion, he stepped out onto the balcony of his hotel some 20 floors up, and threw the phone as far as he could while keeping his balance on the small balcony with only a three foot railing around it. He heard the phone explode upon impact, and went back into his room for a night of rest, before starting his return trip to the Washington DC area in the morning.

Phoenix and San Diego members had only arrived to their destination in between the time Zoe and Bullseye had completed their tasks. Eyes was the first one to determine a distinct pattern to his target, and only on his second day in San Diego, he was prepared for his target to meet his fate. He was a creature entirely of habit, which made the job simple. He went to his office, parked in a reserved place in the garage on the fifth floor of a nine floor garage. Like most parking garages, it had two halves, separating the up level from the down level. In the center on the rear wall of the garage was the elevators, to make it easier to get the garage levels for those that used it. Many of the spaces were reserved with names painted on the parking stops placed to keep vehicles from going too close to the concrete barrier, which was the wall. Open parking started on levels seven through nine. He had parked his rental on the eighth floor of the garage, and walked down the stairwells to the fifth floor where his target would be heading in for his evening run at the office. Eyes figured he did his legitimate import/export business in the day, and since he was the only one at night, that was for the more illegal portion.

He did not truly need to confirm his assumptions. Once on the fifth floor stairwell landing using the butt of his rifle, he knocked out the light on the level in the stairway. He selected a normal rifle instead of the long range, since it was only 250 yards from the end of the ramp where a vehicle would exit onto the floor, and the back wall where the stairwell was located. He already knew how long the vehicle would take from entrance to the garage and exiting onto the fifth floor level. The security cameras were mounted above each side of the elevator over the stairway doors. He cut the feed cable from the partially open stairwell door, to insure his act was not on camera. Although he did not believe the barrel of his rifle would extend far enough from the stairwell, the muzzle flash might be visible. The elevator structure blocked the cameras from seeing into the separate sides, until at least half way between the two points of egress. One camera to each half of each floor. He took his rifle out of the bag once he was on the correct floor landing, and took out the only light. He knew the exact time his target would arrive at the garage entrance, and timed his opening of the door to when his target's vehicle was out of the garage ramp. One fourth of the distance from the ramp to the rear exit stairwell Eyes opened the door fired two shot at the drivers glass on the front of the vehicle, the second shot was more assurance, but the first shot hit center mass on the target's face and head. He knew it was good clean shot, as the car took a wicked turn and drove into and through the concrete barrier that acted like a wall. The vehicle plummeted five stories landing nose first, onto the pavement below turning a relatively new luxury vehicle into a pile of scrap metal. The cars weight from the height it fell crushed the front end into the rear, the motor slipped under that car, the fuel tank and line ruptured and the heat of the motor caused it to ignite and burst into flames. Eye retreated up to the eight floor of the parking garage, putting his rifle back into the bag as he made the ascent.

He arrived to his rental Mercedes, put the rifle into the rear of the trunk, and made his way down to the parking attendant at the exit to pay his fee, and leave. Upon arriving at his hotel, he made his confirmation call to Romero Trap. He would be leaving in the morning, but not to expect him for at least five more days to cover the distance without trying to cover too much in a single day. Long distance driving at a steady speed was something he had problems with, and he needed to be alert. He could go eight to ten hours before he was lulled into the idea of going to sleep. Romero Trap had only two remaining domestic target.

The total cost to this point was 60 million of his collected 100 million, and he knew it was going to climb higher with the Phoenix target. He also was unable to obtain any more information concerning Matura in Japan, and did not want to send Tankawa in blind. Tankawa was ready to go regardless of how much information Romero Trap had, even in the fifteen years he had not been to Tokyo, he knew the places used by the criminal syndicates were not likely to have changed from the subterranean portions of Tokyo. Even fifteen years prior, it seemed everyone knew about them except for the authorities. He would find Matura, he guaranteed it. Romero Trap asked if the person did not truly exist what then. Tankawa said it was the long standing last name of a Ronin whose ancestry was long tied to the criminal network. He did not doubt for a moment the person he sought was using only the last name of his ancestors. Much like my ancestry only gave me a single name at birth.

Romero Trap had not decided who was going to Russia, and knew he had best get that over with soon. That evening Boomer called from Miami to confirm his explosives in the distillery location went up like a nuclear bomb blast, and his target was inside at the time. He would be back sometime the following evening. He called from the burning building and tossed his burner phone into it for disposal and left to his hotel room.

The Phoenix target was a little more difficult to get into a preferred location for the type of method deemed most suitable. He liked spreading his time around for the nightlife and his business endeavors, it did not offer too much opportunity for his purposes. Judas decided after finding no true pattern he would need to tail his target for the proper place to bring his target to meet his God. That occurred on the second night of his following the target at a safe distance not to be spotted. His target went into a club that offered a parking lot for its clientele, but it was very dimly lit, and the target parked in the darkest corner of the lot. Howie Short would simply wait behind the nearby vehicles and wait out his opportunity. It took nearly two hours, but none of the other vehicle owners emerged to leave. When his target made his appearance, he appeared to have a bit too much of the spirits and was a little staggered in his gait. Paying no attention to his surrounding, the Phoenix businessman fumbled with his keys to get the car started, while Judas snuck up from behind and plunged a long blade into the man's liver. It was a certain death for most anyone as it was the one vulnerable organ, which could not be repaired quick enough to overcome the damage. As agreed, as his target started to collapse, Judas removed his wallet before his target fell completely to the ground. He was surprise to find the target had 30,000 dollars in his wallet and the credits cards and everything else for identity were tossed on top of the dying man. Judas left the scene completely unseen and unwitnessed.

Upon his arrival to the hotel, and it was rather late in Phoenix, it would be even later in Washington DC, Judas made his confirmation call to Romero Trap. He went straight to bed afterwards, and had no conscience to bother him in going to sleep. He would return in three days to the Washington DC base of operation, and with everyone else already back and rental cars turned in, his was the last of the domestic problem that the President wanted silenced.

While the team members were out on the domestic assignments, it was suggested to give the three jeeps going on the foreign mission a coat of flat black paint like used on the cargo plane, to make them a little less conspicuous in the areas they were going. It was not uncommon for jeeps that might be used for off road travels or even city use, to be painted like suggested. It would make them more garden variety than desert terrain jeeps. Jackson Frye asked if he could be one of the pair going to Russia, since he had to fly the cargo plane, it would be safe on the airfield until the time to leave. He wanted to do a little more than be the team's mouthpiece and shuttle service. Romero Trap had no arguments to counter the offer, so he was left with choosing one other candidate for Russia. Romero Trap decided on Al Capston (Garrote) as his code name implied, it was one of his favorite methods to employ in close quarters. Romero Trap did not give any specific means to remove the foreign targets, as little would be questioned in how certain people met their maker in two countries, at a large distance from their base of operations. It was just imperative the people were removed from the potential threat list of the President.

Romero Trap's only concern would be how long it would take for Tankawa to find his target, while the Russian jobs would likely be completed. He really did not look forward to a cargo plane resting at a Russian airfield for three or four months, but he thought it might. The Russian's could get a little strange over some of those types of intrusion upon their turf. They most certainly had in the past, and it raised a problem he did not want to face and make his activities known to the Russian's, even though they contributed to the removal of two of their own internal sources of conflict within the government hierarchy. It was silly to move the plane to Japan until Tankawa was done with his assignment, but his would be the most time consuming. It would definitely mean changing hotel arrangements for the two left in Russia, awaiting word to go to Japan. He decided the best thing to do was ask Jackson Frye for his input, because they did not need the plane impounded by the Russian government, before going to Tokyo for the final pickup to return home, with now four refueling stops as determined by Frye, even with a light cargo load. Frye had already informed him he could make the trip with three, but would be on fumes getting to the hanger they kept it in. It might not even have enough fuel to take off afterwards, and he did not like putting it in the hanger with nearly a full fuel load, as the type of fuel was susceptible to expansion from heat and could overflow while in the hanger. It would create a potentially flammable situation, which would be bad for the whole team. Frye much preferred only having a half fuel load on board when in the hanger.

The next day it was decided that Jackson Frye and Al Capston would leave Russian soil after completing their missions and wait in Tokyo, since it would not be anything the Japanese would get overly concerned about. It would mean setting up different hotel arrangements for the pair, and preferable a different hotel than Tankawa would be in, to further reduce suspicion. Long layovers in Tokyo were not terribly uncommon, especially for a cargo plane awaiting the arrival of the goods to transport out. To be on their best behavior in the eyes of the Japanese, the pair would go to the hotel in a single jeep, and the second would remain in the cargo hold.

As to Russia, there were still some who wanted the country to go back to the old ways, this was largely for selfish reasons, as they had amassed some wealth taking advantage of the general population and preferred living like royalty. The numbers were dwindling as age was taking away their numbers, and the general population was making too vast of improvements in the way they got to live. They preferred ruling by the iron hand of fear, over the wellbeing of the citizens. They also enjoyed the wealth they had gained and now had to be more economical. The members of this group were slowly disappearing as fate would have its part in human life. Death was a part of that cycle, as people reached ages that came to an end by nature's methods. Some simply succumbed to too many years of abusing the vodka Russia was famous for.

This was a large reason that Romero Trap only came up with a generalize plan that had his team inject their own knowledge of certain countries and procedures, they needed to concern themselves with. His team often knew more about the idiosyncrasies of places he did not know so well. It was what made a plan better, instead of doing what you were told and where you were told to do it. Romero Trap had also been open to the idea of his team members providing input to reach a better conclusion, he felt it was only fair for those who were risking far more than he. It was also something he learned the hard way when once left out in the cold, to find his own way out or die.

Two days later, the foreign team of three people were on their way, it was decided to go across the US continent to reach Tokyo first, and then head to Russia from there. Tankawa had the most difficult of the three assignments, and would definitely require the most time to complete his mission. No matter how Frye looked at it, he would have to circumnavigate most of the globe for the cargo plane. He figured going this route out and coming back over Europe and the Atlantic Ocean, it was nearly the same distance. No matter how Frye looked it over, it would require four refueling stops to leave him with fuel enough in the hanger to make any other trip, even if it was merely to get more fuel before leaving DC again.

Tankawa was the first to arrive as was the plan, and it was estimated six to six and half hours later, the two going to Russia would be in their hotel rooms. The Russian assignment had the pair staying in different hotels, each closer to his designated target. Although Romero Trap had informed them both, the Russian mafia means of a hit was two close shot to the chest, he did not tell either of them the method they needed to employ. Neither member discussed with the other the method they intended to use. Romero Trap had made it perfectly clear, the best method possible for each was all they needed to concern themselves with, and even if it was identical, there would be no additional suspicions raised over the pair of targets, especially since they had amassed a three and a half billion dollar bounty on the pair. Refueling the cargo plane would be the largest expense for Russia, with Japan being in the equation. Hotel accommodation were quite reasonable in comparison to the United States for finer hotels.

It took only four days for the pair of Russian businessmen, if one chose to call them that, to be removed. Both Jackson Frye (Heartless) and Al Capston has removed their targets. Jackson Frye found it advantageous to use the Russia Mafia method of two bullets at close range to the chest, whereas Garrote did use the piano wire to garrote his victim. Each appeared to be quite personal, and placed suspicion on other parties, not outsiders to the Russian population. One day after the calls on burner phones to Romero Trap, the cargo plane was back in Tokyo waiting for Tankawa to fulfill the final individual on the list.

For the next two months Tankawa searched the subterranean parts of Tokyo that most residents of Tokyo knew of, and avoided like it contained the black plague. To those normal citizens of Tokyo, the criminal syndicates were quite the same to the plague and fear of contagion of bad things happening to them, they stayed away. Tankawa used all the stealth he possessed to get close, but unseen, for any conversations he could overhear concerning the syndicates that brought fear to the Tokyo people. He heard many names in his time in the dark, but never Matura. He would continue searching until the name did get mentioned, and then he would know where to be more regularly. As for now, he searched every underground passage forgotten in the passage of time, as well as the sewer systems that traveled throughout the metropolitan area. His search came up empty until he found bomb shelters not used since the Second World War, when Japan was in conflict with most of the world, including the dragon slayer known as the United States. This was where he heard Matura's name repeatedly in conversation among several of his assumed underlings.

He listened intently to the conversation as all of his language skills in Japanese were returning from his two months of listening to every conversations he overheard. He had come as prepared as possible in his entirely black attire, bringing within the little pouches he lined every reachable place with darts, throwing blades, and strapped in quick release sheaths, his pair of swords of the samurai. They each had different names and originally served two separate purposes. The true samurai sword was a curved kitana blade considered to be a long sword, the second blade was much shorter and far straighter in nature. The kitana blade was used for combat of the samurai warriors long removed from present Japan. The short sword was for the purpose of a ritualistic suicide called Hara-Kiri. Even when it was practiced, it was a gruesome and some called it a barbaric ritual. It was for the samurai who brought shame upon his shogun, who he served, although the shame was not great enough to be cast out and dishonored to be Ronin. The ritual was only practiced by Samurai warriors, and it involved getting in a kneeling position opening the robes, thrusting the short blade into one's abdomen area pulling from one side to the other to remove one's own intestines, as much as possible. A relief samurai stood behind posed to strike should the person accepting the ritual as his forgiveness of his shogun, be unable to complete the rest. The rest was to sit and wait until blood loss brought on death, but it was an excruciating painful wait. Very few Samurai were that stout to wait out the entire time in took to bleed to death, while his intestines lay around him. Most had their heads removed when they asked for it. Some simply asked for it at the onset of the ritual, to at least have more intact for the next lifetime they were to embark upon. In modern day, the use of the pair of swords was entirely for offense and defense.

The samurai warriors also did not have the advantages of modern day technology, such as body armor to prevent bullets penetrating, so even as sharp a sword of the Samurai that could cut clean through bone, it was not going to cut through the Kevlar armor. From conversation he overheard, he was under the impression that among some of the lowest levels of the sub terrain of Tokyo, largely the bomb shelters which were numerous, Matura had converted one into a private paradise, he considered to be home. It would be one way to be heard and not seen, having his underlings take care of business in his name, while he made all the plans to continue to grow their illegal business practices. As Ronin ancestry, there was few other means to achieve notice outside of illegal activities. It simply meant he had to be invisible to the authorities to thrive as a criminal syndicate leader. It was also helpful to be invisible to the other syndicate leaders, as it was not uncommon for one to start killing another to grow their own syndicate. Something Matura preferred to be on the giving side of, instead of the receiving. It was still unknown as to the age of Matura, and whether he was in the syndicates fifteen years prior.

For the next two weeks with every minute Tankawa could manage in the subterranean Tokyo, he returned to the same general area until he could get a more exact placement for Matura. His underlings did do a good deal of conversation concerning their syndicate leader, but none had presented his exact whereabouts. During his long hours in the underground tunnels of Tokyo, he learned with his face mostly covered with the mask that only allowed him vision, about once every hour, he would need to lower the mask for a better air supply, to take away the mild light headed effect of lack of oxygen. He did not know nor care about the component designation for his exhaling, but he knew it was hardly the same as the normal oxygen intake he got without the mask. After an additional week in the tunnels, he finally got his break. The tunnel he had been in had four widely spaced doors in the tunnel. His assumption was each was a bomb shelters capable of having ten to twenty thousand persons within during the bombing raids of World War Two. There had to be dozens more elsewhere, due to the large population of Tokyo even during that war. An underling went to the very end of the hall and knocked upon the steel door, which opened to reveal a man in his mid-forties dressed in what he would call geisha robes, as they were what he remembered them being used for while indulging in the pleasures of the geisha houses of Japan. His assumption was an underling, and it seemed to be the case, by his subservient behavior towards the man on the other side of the door. He waited patiently for whatever was being said as it was not loud enough for him to overhear from where he was concealed in the wide tunnels. Tankawa was simply happy the tunnels were so wide, and the lighting poor to light every inch of the tunnels. Once the underling was gone and no other persons were seen within the tunnels, Tankawa approached the very same door, mindful of any noise or sound he heard coming from the tunnels behind him. He removed two darts from the pouches in his black attire, and knocked upon the heavy steel door, hoping it would be answered. It was, and as soon as it was opened, Tankawa unleashed his two darts striking Matura with sufficient velocity to weaken him and send him farther back into the room, but hardly did he disabled him. Tankawa entered, close the door behind him and latched the lock in an extremely quick fashion. In his best Japanese, he demanded from Matura how long he had been the leader of this syndicate. Matura was not in the answering mood and Tankawa removed his short sword as well as a throwing blade. He told Matura he could make this extremely long enduring pain, or make his misery quite short, but he needed to answer the question.

Matura had no weapon at his immediate disposal, never expecting a solitary man to enter his domain undetected. Matura asked him how long he was observing his movements unnoticed. Tankawa told him three weeks, but he poise his throwing knife ready to send it in Matura's direction if he failed to answer his first question. Matura was eyeing his own swords in the stand, but knew he was too far from them to make any use of them without some form of distraction. He answered with eighteen years, but it took a little time to build up to true syndicate standards. Tankawa asked only one more question concerning his parents small business fifteen year prior who were killed, by asking Matura what area of Tokyo did he concentrate on in the beginning. Matura not thinking this question was harmful, answered Tankawa and it was the same area his parents business was located. It was all the proof Tankawa ever could have asked for, in the blink of eye he had his samurai sword in hand, and swung it so fast Matura had no chance to react before Tankawa had removed his head with a single blow.

Tankawa was satisfied he avenged his parents, and made sure the tunnel was still clear. He left the heavy steel door partial ajar when he left, so the syndicate leader would be found with the message he felt it would leave behind. The type of killing of a syndicate leader of the nature Tankawa left in his wake, was a warning from other syndicate leaders of bringing shame upon their way of doing business. It was to serve as a serious warning, to the next leader to remember, once he took charge. All divisions of the Japanese criminal syndicates had a hierarchy in place in the event of someone becoming careless or stupid, or worst of all, caught by authorities. They had been entrenched into the city since the days of the shoguns, and they were not likely to go away any too quickly. Tankawa decided to get his belongings from the hotel and check out, grabbed a Japanese take out meal, since he had not eaten all day, hoping to get the opportunity he needed. He made his burner phone call while he stuffed his face sitting in his jeep, with all his luggage and gear already in it. He confirmed his target was no longer going to be a problem. He did not provide all the details or the satisfaction he felt concerning the loss of his parents. After finishing his quick take out meal, he left for the same airfield he was delivered to upon arriving. Tokyo had long ago used up all the lands they could expand to, and all building was skyward for many years. Tankawa did note in fifteen years the city had changed in height, but not in the tunnels.

On the way to the airfield with oncoming traffic, he discarded his burner phone distinctly hearing a vehicle run over it completely destroying it. The jeep driven by Tankawa was on board the cargo plane 35 minutes later. Everyone had checked out of their hotels, had all their belongings stowed onboard the cargo plane. It took fifteen more minutes to start up the engines, taxi to a position to enter the runway for takeoff. There was incoming aircraft, which kept them holding at the point of entering the runway for the takeoff for another fifteen minutes. With most active airports and airfields, timing was in control of those in the tower. There were some lulls in the planes landing, but insufficient to allow two planes within the same airspace for safety factors determined by higher air control authority agencies. Once enough clearance was considered safe for the cargo plane to takeoff, and safely reach an altitude that would not coincide with inbound planes, the team was allowed to enter the runway and takeoff.

They had to make four fueling stops between Tokyo and their final destination, this time flying into an eastern direction. There was one stop before reaching the second, which allowed the plane to reach the coast of the European side of the Atlantic Ocean. The final stop would be near Philadelphia before going to DC from there. They had to follow the preferred flight determined by the FAA in order to avoid restricted air space. It took with refueling and getting takeoff clearance at the three other locations used, eighteen hours before the cargo plane was back in its own hanger. Belongings and three jeeps were unloaded and driven back to the operations center, for the team and three people immediately went to showers and get some well-earned rest.

It was not until the fifth day the reports from Tokyo took place indicating the criminal syndicate leader believed to be Matura was found dead, from what appeared to be a rival syndicate style killing. Authorities were unsure, since no other syndicate was claiming responsibility which normally occurred, although not by conventional means. The syndicates still operated outside of the local police's visibility, and so was their communication methods. One week after the news reports, the bounty was paid in full and Romero Trap's three foreign targets netted nine and three quarter billion dollars. It also left the team with nothing more to do for the time being.

14

The Major Obstacle

President Thomas Hardesty had reached a bit of an impasse in the progress of aiding in the formation of a world governing body. Although it was the result of illegal endeavors from a single country, the groups involved had far reaching monetary holds on many of the surrounding countries, affecting a majority of South and Central America. It presented too many governments keeping from progress going further on the global scale. After giving the State of Union speech with his Vice President Romero Trap also expected to give the public words of encouragement, they completed five years in office as a team. Once back to the Oval Office Thomas Hardesty informed Romero Trap of the growing concern in South America, involving the Columbian drug cartels.

The problem had grown to epidemic proportions in the surrounding countries on two different scales. First there were at least a dozen different cartels that appeared to be working in cooperation of one another. With the loss of the Mexican Cartel, the Columbian cartels moved into control of the largest drug operations in the world. Even with losses of product being seized, the cartels seemed to have unlimited resources for corrupting the political structure in most of South and Central America. In order to maximize profits from their production fields, they had started abducting young adolescent and early teenagers to work their fields under armed guards. They traveled throughout all the countries to obtain their own slave labor camps, and in the event of a single individual attempting to escape, anywhere from six to two dozen children were killed in the prevention of the single individual. It was not to be tolerated any longer by the President, but again he would not take it to the military for resolution. He needed Romero Trap and his team of experts to eradicate the disease the Columbian cartels were spreading.

Romero Trap informed the President that the information he could obtain for the region was limited due to the time the Satellite imagery system passed over the region. Unlike the Middle East where the eyes were ever present, it was not the case over Central and South America. In order to determine where the cartels operated, imagery was vital to his means of inserting people into the region for safety to his team. Romero Trap did not like putting his people into harm's way, just for the sake of having intelligence on the operations of such people. His team had been working together for five years and it was a little late in the process to obtain additional members to compensate for the cartels. It was also likely since the cartels have spread out over a large area, they in all likelihood had also done so in the fields, they grow the crop used for their production. He would not give the President acceptance of the new assignment until he had more substantial intelligence on how the cartels were operating in such a vast area. They may even have taken up operations in the former Mexican cartel region to increase their distribution network. President Hardesty was empathetic to Trap's concerns and would give him whatever time he needed, but ultimately it had to be addressed if a world governing body was ever to become reality. It was his ultimate goal, and he never hid it from Romero Trap when he asked him to become his Vice President.

Romero Trap said he would look into it, but since the President was never fully involved with how Trap and his team had to operate, in order to insure all his team members returned home from a mission, he should be aware of the unpredictable nature drug cartels presented, as opposed to other military forces. Drug cartels were entirely out of

THE MAJOR OBSTACLE

control when it came to weapon's fire, there was little if any concern towards innocents in the line of fire, and they were erratic in how they utilized those weapons. Unfortunately, it seemed they all had automatic weapons, and in using a spray pattern in most case, they finally got what they wanted accomplished. His team were precision experts. Long range shooters used a single bullet, his heavy automatic weapons people were still going for a specific target, even if it looked otherwise considering how many rounds it could fire in a single minute. The cartels were likely all spread out across many countries they paid to be overlooked, while they operated outside of the legal parameters of most. Lack of satellite imagery on a twenty hour basis, also seriously hindered him having a good plan to work with and the locations he needed to concentrate on. Additionally, if the cartels are working in some form of cooperation, removing one, will put all the others on alert, which only increases the dangers to his team members inserted for each mission. For nearly twenty years Romero Trap operated in a precise manner, that made it so all of his team came home, although upon occasion damaged but repairable. He would not compromise his team even for the President, or Thomas Hardesty would need to seek assistance outside of his Vice President and Trap was the absolute best at what he did, for the sake of his country. There was no animosity between the two, it was merely to point out the president was asking him to endanger the well-being of his team members over something best handled by military intervention, considering the large scale of operation with less than admirable intelligence information.

Military hierarchy had no issues over loosing lives over the welfare of the nation. They actually include a percentage into the overall plan for such an endeavor. Since they have no real accountability in what occurs when a soldier dies in the field of battle. They provide a letter to the parents and a burial, provided there is a body recovered. Short and precise and then forgotten by the people who give the orders. Trap refused to operate in that fashion, as every single team member was important. As was their welfare, when asked to go into a weapons active environment. With the State of Union address being earlier, it was a full day in the White House, instead of his half day sessions, so he in all likelihood he would not get the team looking into things until either late that evening or the following afternoon. President Thomas Hardesty's request would be reviewed first, prior to any form of a commitment from Romero Trap, and most his team who would be the people most affected by the assignment. President Thomas Hardesty was not happy about the answer, but based on what Trap had told him, he did understand, he merely thought since Trap had repeatedly pulled off impossible missions, he could just add another to his list of accomplishments, that few people would ever know about.

Romero Trap was not enthused about turning down the President's request, but he would if there was no possible means to overcome the intelligence he could obtain. Without any idea of where and in how many locations the dozen cartels may have operations, he refused to put his people into circumstances against their survival. It was after all, why they repeatedly accepted assignments from the planning of Romero Trap, even though his team members had input into the plan before it went into effect. His success rate was more a result of his team, than what he deserved credit for when it came down to the final analysis. Unfortunately, like many things that involved the government, it was much easier to give credit to a single individual, than an entire team of experts in their profession. Even when the actual documentation was so classified that only a very select few could view the documents. Unfortunately, it was why it was always labeled covert operations, with the highest level of classification within the government documentation group. It was so secretive, that no single individual could input more than a single document, pertaining to a mission, for the need to know basis that surrounded the entire mission.

Any individual who knew too much about any given mission of covert operations, was classified as a security risk, and the surveillance from government agencies would drive a person into reclusion or suicide. Those agencies did not care which it was, as long as the threat was minimized. Working for the government was not always so much of an advantage, as many would believe. In more cases than not, it really put you at a higher risk, than many jobs that required participating outside of sitting at a desk.

THE MAJOR OBSTACLE

Romero Trap decided to go to the base of operations to establish a watch on all of South and Central America until the time pattern for the satellite being in position over the region was established, he requested 24 hour coverage. The satellites since there were more than one, had to be over the region at least once every 24 hours. Assuming there were at least three, although the imagery may only last one hour per satellite, it might provide enough on locations to get some idea of how many they would have to deal with. He pointed out if only infrared was useable at the time of the coverage, a single large structure would emit a large field, for all the teenagers being held as slave laborers. He let the team know what they were looking for, and the possibility of an assignment, but there was no point in details unless it was something they could possibly pull off, without losses. He thought with the erratic behavior of most drug cartels, he was asking his team to go into a situation where the odds, even with surprise, were not in their favor. He was unsure if the slave laborers were used for both harvesting and turning the product into the street substance, or simply harvesting and another group transformed it from crop to street value product. One thing he did know for certain, the Columbian cartels never sold pure product, as it was far less profitable.

The team of 36 would take one hour shifts at the computers used to monitor satellite imagery. This way, no one would be exceptionally tired and miss something, but when a satellite was over the region, the time of day and duration would be recorded for everyone to see and know. Recording methods were simple and old school by Romero Trap's terminology, paper and pen or pencil kept by the computers. Anyone who took a seat for the hour, would see if anything had been seen. The initial imagery was simply to find locations to be suspect, the region was quite vast and Mexico was not to be overlooked, the Columbian cartels may very well have taken over for the void left as a result of their previous work. In all likelihood, these cartels would not be so foolish to think they were untouchable. Especially with governments around the globe putting programs in place to effectively combat the growing drug problems. Many did not stop with the mere seizing of the drug shipments, they were putting programs in place to aid those with a drug problem, instead of jail time for having an addiction. It was helping some, but time was needed to provide more in depth care and pattern development to determine the actual results. Not every drug problem, could be treated identically and this presented issues, as they were still learning how to become efficient in providing positive results.

Once Romero Trap had set the initial parameters of what they were looking for, he told them he would be back the next day more in his normal time frame. He did not have another State of the Union for another year. He went from the operations base to a little quaint restaurant and deli near his apartment, for his evening meal before it was too late to get food. He was no longer in the habit of missing meals after five years near the Oval Office, although he still only did the White House luncheon, and had his dinner at any of two dozen restaurants nearer to his apartment. It was not like he lived extravagantly, but he had too many things interfere with his day to ever take up the cooking skills needed for the nightly nourishment. His cooking skills were limited to making his own pot of coffee each morning, before heading out for the largest part of the day. He was also sure since he learned that in the military, his idea of coffee might harm a fair percentage of people who had milder forms of the brew. In his military days one person tested the coffee each morning, to see if a spoon would stand straight up before drinking any. He did fail to notice which way he preferred it, as it was always a fifty-fifty proposition for military coffee. Some was quite stout, even for Romero Trap.

For his evening meal he decided not to go too overboard and got a Reuben on rye, with a small five bean salad. It was a bit later than he would like for his evening meal, but not so late as to skip it altogether. He decided to just have the ice water for his drink. Once home to his little apartment, dealing with politicians all day took more out of his energy levels than 48 hours in hostile territory. Romero Trap thought that had to do with wanting some sleep, with how long it took some to get to the point during a conversation. He went to bed shortly after arriving home, to regain his vitality for the next day.

After his normal half day White House session that included lunch, which Romero Trap thought was superb, he arrived at the

THE MAJOR OBSTACLE

operations base to see what may have been discovered. Over the time from his initial visit to start the team on the satellite imagery, they had four satellite times that provided a total of six hours of imagery from overhead. Four hours of it was during hours of darkness, which only confirmed five locations thought to be where the young people were held for performing the labor of harvesting. It was also discovered that the Mexican facility was being used once again, but from the imagery it did not get used for anything other than a processing location. It meant harvested crops were brought to it, for the processing, primarily for US distribution. It seemed the US was still the location where the products were most in demand, and the Columbian cartels were doing everything possible to make it available.

There was still far more research necessary in determining how many locations were being used and for what purpose, since it seemed to Romero Trap, with up to one dozen cartels, they would not restrict their processing to a single location. He needed far more intelligence into the number of hostiles he would find in the different locations, as well as how many were there against their will, under armed guard. Based on the distance Mexico was from the rest, that was the most logical starting location if he decided to accept the assignment from Thomas Hardesty. It would likely put a major wrinkle into the cartels' US distribution, which would be the primary source of profits. Romero Trap would also require the President getting some form of agreement with the Mexican authorities to insure the location was not active again. His team was never, nor would they be, responsible for policing areas after removal. He and his team would not go to Mexico for a fourth time over this same issue. Without an agreement, Romero Trap would refuse the assignment and let it be handled by other governments and military personnel more responsible for having done so in the first place. It was largely corruption that allowed drug cartels to operate in the first place. The Columbians had their fingers into far too many politicians and higher authorities' pockets. It was the only way the cartels could have become so large, to cause fear in the majority of people. That and the reckless abandon used in enforcing their business practices. Drugs to them were big business, it did not matter if it was illegal, and it produced massive amounts of profits by the simple supply and demand conditions of any business.

Over the next two days, the times for the satellite imagery system to be overhead in the region they needed more information about, were determined as a certainty. It meant over a twenty four hour period, only six hours needed to be monitored, and now it was a matter of concentrating on how many locations, and the possible numbers of armed hostiles were present at each. Since four of the six hours were using infrared vision, it made it difficult to do a true head count. The number of people confined to a single large structure were likely the innocent, but were armed guards within the structures, as well as outside of it. Romero Trap also informed President Thomas Hardesty of the additional condition of his team entering Mexico a third time, and the President would require time to get an agreement, as well as some type of story over how he became aware of it.

Romero Trap informed the President, since it was no secret the world over, the United States used satellite imagery as a means to monitor for hostile activities that posed a threat to the nation, he could say it came from one of his agencies. As to how the problem was eliminated originally in Mexico, the unknown assailants did most of them a big favor, but could not rely upon them coming back, unless it was a rival cartel.

President Hardesty took Romero's input under advisement, and let it sit there until he could get an agreement with the Mexican authorities.

It took nearly a month just to identify the possible 30 locations in Central and South America and they were spread out quite well. Even though this was the Columbian cartels, only three location were in Columbia, with approximately another dozen in bordering countries, although no more than 50 miles from the Columbian border. Even though Costa Rica was not a large country, it held three locations used from the imagery, as merely where the crop was planted and harvested when ready. Another three were found in Nicaragua, which told Romero Trap the cartels were prone to use the poorer nations, to take advantage of the governments easy to corrupt, and turn a blind eye to the activities used, to get laborers for their production fields. The other nine were

THE MAJOR OBSTACLE

spread about the rest of South America and of the 30 locations found, ten appeared to also be involved into transforming crop to product, ready for distribution. These thirty locations did not include the processing location in Mexico. Romero Trap looked over the large area that needed to be covered, and knew the cargo plane would not be invisible in a number of the areas. As much as he hated the idea of adding yet another piece of equipment to the list, a helicopter would be the more logical approach to moving his team in and around the region. It was going to be easier, if it could be acquired closer to the region, but he doubted he would find one with armaments to use.

Additionally, Romero Trap needed to find out whom among his team besides himself, could pilot a helicopter, since he could not go on an extended mission with his White House duties. The problems of this particular assignment were definitely mounting, and unless Romero Trap and his team could find solutions that would provide the safe return of his team members, the President would have to live with disappointment on this one.

He did not even have his team members making bounty contacts, because the assignment posed enough problems initially, to not immediately accept it. The intelligence being gathered was less than promising, the large distance between locations, presented another unique set of circumstances to overcome. Even if he were able to acquire a helicopter, the cargo plane could not hold it without repositioning the rotors and that required tools, he was not sure they had. If they overcame that problem, there was insufficient space for anything more than the helicopter. It meant multiple trips to get vehicles in place as well. He did have one additional thought that might aid in this whole situation. He would need the cooperation of the Peruvian cartel for a safe haven for the cargo plane, and possible refueling location, as well as a helicopter. Until the helicopter was obtained, he could not acquisition armaments without knowledge of the specific type and model of the helicopter. Not all helicopters were capable of holding armaments, as the weight would affect the helicopters ability to stay airborne. All armaments posed some handling issues with a helicopter, as it could make it front heavy and less responsive to the controls. The biggest advantage to having a helicopter with armaments, is they could get much closer to the ground for the use of the weapons. The disadvantage, was due to the close proximity to the target, it could be damaged in a number of ways, including return ground fire.

Romero Trap was not in bad terms with the Peruvian cartel and made his call to the man in charge of the operations within that country. The conversation did not go entirely the way he had hoped, finding out the DEA had seized most of the product sent to the states for distribution, allowing the Columbian cartels to move in right under their noses. His price for using the private airfield and all the fuel he needed, was to reacquire his lost product so he could move the product elsewhere, to recoup his losses. Should Trap obtain more, he would consider it, but funds with all the losses were not the best he ever had in the past. Trap informed him the operation was not definite at this time and would only try to obtain his lost product, if the decision was made to go ahead and except the mission, which would be useful to the Peruvian cartel for a little while. Should he successfully complete his mission, it was time for the cartel to expand into other business endeavors, as the crack down on drug trade would only heighten. He also informed his Peruvian friend it appeared the Columbians were hedging into the borders, although not terribly far from their own borders, it was still they had held half a dozen locations within the borders of Peru.

Romero Trap was not overly accustomed to the one step forward, two steps back approach in putting together a basic feasibility plan to any potential assignment. This far into any of his other assignments, even those of the President, he had far more accomplished in one fourth the amount of time, and knew within days whether to accept or decline an assignment. He did not have quite the advantage with the President, as he had as an independent contracting service, even if it was for other government entities. Nobody else ever would have questioned his decision to decline an assignment, largely because they had never had to plan details for what was wished. The president did not plan details either; but his nomination to hold the Vice Presidency, was hung upon Romero Trap's more covert abilities. He was dealing with a whole lot of guilt, he never experienced prior to this assignment. He had to either

THE MAJOR OBSTACLE

put his crew of experts into harm's way, or disappoint the president of the United States. It was not such a simple decision. He decided the best way to at least get to the decision portion, was to have an open discussion without any set plan among all the team members. Since without a real basic plan, he did not have the team members narrowed down to who needed to go, although Trap did not believe any more than one would remain behind.

The meeting with all the team members lasted for four hours, during which time the team came up with a number of feasible ideas, but it could not be done in a time frame that did not put other locations on high alert. High alert, meant the possibility of fatalities, which to date, Romero Trap limited to a few wounded, but no causalities. He had no desire to ask any of the team to put themselves into that position. He did have two people other than himself who had piloted helicopters, as a part of their military training. Admittedly it had been some time, but felt they could refresh quickly, just like riding a bicycle. It would be necessary to obtain one in some fashion, and have it fitted with armaments to cut down on the number of people he would have in a position to receive serious if not deadly wounds. At this point, they all understood all the issues of an assignment covering the vast area that would be required. It was decided the best location for a run was Mexico, if the assignment went no further, it could be passed off as a rival cartel, reclaiming their territory from the Columbians. It was also conceivable some of what they would need to acquire would be there, after all, the crop to turn to production grade had to arrive there in some means quicker than using trucks. A helicopter was far quicker, and could hold a good deal of unprocessed crop, as long as it was packed properly. This was in all honesty not something Romero Trap had considered, but it did make good sense. Overall, it had to be more economical for a helicopter than a large truck going a less direct route, in order to follow roadways suitable for a semi-trailer with large truck to pull it. He did not have an immediate answer and any deployment would be on hold, until he got some agreement from the President concerning Mexico. Also, the President's understanding going into Mexico a third time, did not mean the assignment was accepted. It was only one of many hurdles to address.

The meeting in the morning with President Thomas Hardesty at least produced an agreement made with the Mexican authorities, to police their own territory if the removal of the Columbian cartel happened to take place. Hardesty had hoped for a more concrete commitment to the entire assignment, as opposed to pick one and see how it went. Romero Trap fully explained the reasons behind it, and the potential of finding needed equipment, prior to committing to Central and South America. Even if a helicopter were obtained in Mexico, it would take at least three possibly four refueling stops to get it to DC. They simply did not have the tank capacity of a winged aircraft. Most had a flight range of 300 miles or less, which is why they seldom venture too far from a home port. Those used by news crews, local police and emergency life care, had specific time durations they could fly in any one direction, to allow enough fuel to return. They had rather strict guidelines to follow to insure a helicopter did not run out of fuel while in flight, this was due to they fell like rocks without rotor power.

In the event they did obtain a helicopter from the Columbian cartel, a number of other things needed to be done prior to it returning to Columbia. It would require new paint and fictitious numbers. If it were to be loaded into the cargo plane, tools needed to be obtained for the rotors as well as to move a bird with stationary runners, instead of wheels, some type of wheel aid to slip under it. Not always the easiest thing to accomplish since the helicopter had to hover, in order to put the wheeled device under both runners, and the rotors had to have sufficient clearance from the cargo plane. It could easily result in not one but two unusable aircraft.

The first hurdle was cleared at least as far as Mexico was concerned, he still only had a vague idea of the number of people at the location, but having brought a plane and vehicles in once before, it was going to be a quick hit and run. Since there was no slave labor structure in Mexico for harvesting, it was going to be assumed all people present were Colombian members of one of the cartels. The entire team would go except Zoe and Trap. They would hold down communications in

THE MAJOR OBSTACLE

DC, with the rest of the team in Mexico. Before going through with guns blazing, Romero Trap would give his close quarter's experts the opportunity to do things a little quieter, and hopeful have someone to provide a little more information on the number of cartels involved, as well as which locations were primary. The means in which his team could inflict pain to get information were wide and varied, but always effective. The other thing, is it seldom took a lengthy wait for the subject to speak without pause. He did not want Zoe involved in this portion of Mexico, but there were few people who could watch the methods Zoe could use to inflict pain on the opposite gender. Romero was present for all of one minute once, before specific male anatomical parts revolted against his continued presence with what Zoe was doing. Romero Trap only knew if observing created phantom pains, he wanted no part of the real process employed by Zoe.

It was going to take a few more days to try to determine if a helicopter was indeed in Mexico or not, as well as how many to anticipate. The advantage to most structures put together in this type of location, materials were not cut to size and were hardly close to being airtight. There were often gaps of various sizes, and even the smallest was more than enough room to get in a well-placed dart with either a powerful sedative or poison. Five days after giving the president his answer only for Mexico, the team was on their way to Mexico. As far as the cargo plane was concerned, both heavy weapons mounted transporters were on board, and all the gear the team could carry. With 35 team members on board with the two transporters and gear, the only room to move on the cargo plane was between the two seats where the jump door was located. There were no parachutes. Refueling took place in the State of Texas, to allow plenty of fuel to leave Mexico when their job was completed.

The plane landed on the same private airstrip used the first time in Mexico, all the gear was unloaded, and half of the team split into each of the two transporters. It was still a bit crowded with the gear, and Jackson Frye figuring it would not be terribly long in Mexico, stayed as part of the team. The plan was to get the transporters in fair proximity of the processing location of the Columbian cartels, and the close quarters experts would move into closer positions around the processing structure. Until darkness arrived, they could only get so close without the risk of being spotted. Depending on how well the group did in quiet removal of the cartel members in and around the structure, would determine if a run with heavy automatic weapons would be necessary. The heavy automatic weapons run could not be performed until the close quarter's specialist were out of the immediate area. The structure was not likely to keep the large caliber bullets from going completely through the structure, especially since the Senator's home, which was far more heavily constructed, and it did not stop all too many.

They only had a couple of hours from touchdown until dusk. Unloading and moving the transporters closer took one hour of that time, and the close quarter's people would need the rest to get into position. Everyone had the communications earpiece with mini microphone in place, in order to insure how successful stage one was from the close quarter's specialists. All of them had some type of throwing or blow dart weapons to use initially. If they were entirely successful, there would be no need to bring in the transporters with the mounted heavy weapons. As standby, six others were moved into close range with small automatic weapons. They were not as noisy, and could be used if any of the close quarter's experts were in jeopardy.

With looking into the surroundings, the close quarter's specialists confirmed a helicopter in a clearing some 500 yards from the processing structure. It appeared to be armed with heavy automatic weapons, one on each side and a third front mounted. It was armed to allow for unimpeded movement in the air against other small aircraft, and would be more than sufficient in protecting the helicopter from local authorities, but not against large aircraft. Although it was quite difficult to take out a helicopter with fighter jets, it was not entirely impossible. That type of aircraft was seldom available for use in the fight against drug trafficking. It would need retrofitting once back to the DC base of operations. The front mounted heavy automatic weapon could stay, but the two side mounts needed rocket launchers for what was planned, if indeed Central and South America became an assignment. The team found a group of 30 people within the processing structure, all appeared to be working the product. There were 3 small automatic weapons members also within the structure, although they did not appear to be there as a threat to the workers of the product. Another dozen and half similarly armed cartel members were wandering about the area, as lookout for potential problems.

The close quarter's experts were in concealed positions, but not close enough to the structure with fading light. All the whispers over the communications would go quiet with the fall of darkness. Two of the dozen and a half cartel members wandering the property got too close for comfort to two of the specialists', and they were dispatched quietly and permanently. The time frame should not have been long enough before dark for them to be considered missing by the remaining cartel members.

When darkness fell the close quarter's specialists moved into closer range of the structure still occupied by 33 people. The specialists' decided to remove the outside cartel members before going to the structure, for the attempt to keep a survivor for information. With throw weapons of a variety of types, it took 30 minutes to take out the fourteen remaining cartel members. None of them would be the information provider, and weapons were retrieved prior to reaching the structure. A closer look through the gaps in the haphazard construction, showed all the 30 members of the processing people had hand guns. Proficiency in the use of them was largely questionable. The three cartel members with automatic weapons were dispatched with two poison darts and one strong sedative. That got the attention of three of the remaining 30 to draw their handguns but could not see a target. The small automatic weapons people had also moved in closer to the structure, and all of Trap's team members wore body armor. Automatic weapons were in semi-automatic mode, allowing for single shot activity. The three cartel members poised to shoot, were still looking for a target when they were each shot a single time from the automatic weapons. The other 27 members threw down their weapons, and dropped to the ground. It seemed apparent; the weapons were more for show than proficiency in the use of them. The sedated cartel member was tightly bound to a chair to await his coming out of unconsciousness. It took almost an hour. In the meantime, not a single person on the ground made a move. All the team members were now within the structure, and having enough people proficient with languages, questions were asked of those face down on the ground. Most knew nothing more about the cartels operation other than the single location they worked. Most were from South America and very low level members, only used in the processing of the product to turn it into a street value commodity. Outside of their job, they knew nothing more in the operation of the cartel. All the weapons were placed in an area out of reach by anyone other than a member of Trap's team. It was guarded in the event a cartel member managed to get away undetected.

Among the group was one who like to finish his accomplished missions with the lighting of a rather large cigar. It required by his standards, a trimming of the end to get the most out of his one vice, used as a celebratory means to his missions being completed. He carried two such cutting instrument upon him at all time, one was never used for cigars. He used the second one for the purpose of interrogation, by less than acceptable ways among any form of a military code. Since as an independent contractor, he was not held to those standards. As much as the opposition thought otherwise, although they did not feel such standards applied to them as well. When the lone survivor of the armed cartel member was more coherent, his talents were put to use. The surviving member held out for nearly 45 minutes of having his fingers shortened with the use of the cigar trimmer, one all the way to the knuckle. After he took as much excruciating pain as one could endure, he spilled what he knew. The cartels cooperation was among eight of the dozen Columbian cartels, as a means to prolong their business practices. With government's the world over cracking down, they needed to be more prepared to prolong the businesses they had for nearly 100 years. The other four cartels were smaller, and the point of impasse was the mean of obtaining labor for harvesting. The smaller cartels were more prone to providing income to the poorer regions they came from, and did not need to bribe local authorities for the jobs they had available to so many without. They did not try to influence the local government, merely to coexist as business people in the way of providing jobs. The

THE MAJOR OBSTACLE

largest portion of these smaller cartel were on the Columbian-Peruvian border, and might be on both sides of the borders. All were small and poor communities, with little authority to oversee things.

Only the cooperative cartels had expanded into more of South and Central America to keep production optimal and losses minimal. The vast majority of their profits were accomplished by transforming the harvest into street valued product. The team decided to do something different with their single survivor, and bring him back to DC operations to pinpoint the locations of the cooperative cartels fields and processing locations. After that was accomplished, he would be turned over to authorities for prosecution and a long time in a maximum security prison. He was one of the six people put on the helicopter, although with a lack of full sized fingers on one hand, he was not going to present much of a threat. Fire was used to stop the bleeding, which only made the cartel member pass out, once on the helicopter. They had found two strongboxes full of cash and gold and did not count the value, it was time to leave with all that could be salvaged including all the weapons used by the cartel members and ammunition they has available. It still made the pair of aircraft a rather tight space with all the team members and equipment aboard. Departure time at the airfield was three hours after everything was loaded from the cartel location. The gold and currency were on board the helicopter and it went directly to the Texas border in order to refuel for the first of five stops, before the final one at an airfield near DC closer to the hanger location.

Even with the extra time for departure, the refueling put the helicopter three hours behind the cargo plane, arriving at the abandoned airfield used by Romero Trap and his team for the aircraft they had available. The hanger was large enough to accommodate both, but the helicopter could not be flown into the hanger for clearance sake.

Instead of killing the remaining twenty-seven processing people, they were told to return to their homes and never again venture into the cartels businesses, as they were also going to be eliminated, and there was no future in their line of work any longer. None of the twenty seven people were from Mexico, and they had a long way to go to return home. They were left to their own as to how they would accomplish it.

It was figured by the time any of them made it home, the Columbia cartels would be either already be under attack, or about to be attacked, to remove any future obstacles from the business they had endeavored in for many years.

The team had already decided to go ahead and let Romero Trap know when they arrived, the assignment was a full go, and even though they knew they had a much higher degree of risk, they were all in as a team.

With Romero Trap being given that information, he had the team start the bounty promises and get the helicopter retrofit acquisition going from the military, using forged documents. With two rocket launchers, they would need a very large number of rockets to destroy 26 fields and the locations of the Columbians processing locations.

The team also had the additional responsibility to obtain the seized product for the Peruvian cartel, to have access to the airfield and fuel. It was all accomplished within a week of returning, with a promised 50 billion in bounty monies for the removal of the Columbian cartels. The largest portion was from the South and Central America countries, disappointed in the ways they operated within their different countries. Although they were willing to permit the crop and processing of the drug, the abductions were beyond the original agreements, and it was beyond tolerance. A large number of large businesses also contributed, as did a good deal of the other countries who were affected by the drugs entering their borders. The same rules applied to the DEA warehousing facility, there was to be no friendly casualty, incapacitate, but not to kill any of the agents held accountable for the guarding of the product within. The exception to this would be after getting the cartel member brought back from Mexico, to pinpoint on satellite imagery which location were a part of the cartels in cooperation of the others, he would be left bound and gagged, with a computer printed note indicating what to do with him.

Six tons of processed product was removed from the DEA warehousing facility, no agents were harmed aside from the nasty headache they would have once outside of the influence of the sedative, used to incapacitate them. It was taken directly to the airfield hanger in the transporters that had mounted heavy automatic weapons. The cargo plane would make the first trip with only six people aboard to Peru. The arrangement were set for Jackson Frye to hand over the processed product for an undisclosed price, since the cartel was somewhat short on working capital. Romero Trap also in his conversation with the Peruvian cartel leader made sure he understood with the sale of the product being delivered, he had two years or less of business time left, before all governments would end his drug business.

They needed to acquisition 208 rockets for the 26 fields they were going to hit with the helicopter. Sufficient damage to the growing fields could be done with eight rockets per field. It meant with two launchers mounted, they could take no more than two fields per trip. The distance between the Peru airfield and the other countries was far greater than the fuel capacity. The helicopter also had a jet booster engine for increasing flight speed, or countering the rocket launcher, when fired to maintain a hover position. The Peruvian cartel leader provided locations for refueling with a minimum of questions, although with a helicopter armed as such, it may still raise suspicions outside of Peru.

President Thomas Hardesty was informed of the team's decision to go forward with the assignment and was quite ecstatic to have everything going the way he hoped. In a total of 10 ten days from the time the Mexican location was shut down for a third time, the first part of the team was in Peru. It still required another cargo plane flight to get the rest of the equipment and team members to Peru, and this time Zoe was going and Lacy West was left to take care of communications with the help of Romero Trap.

There was only one Columbian location and Peruvian location used by the cartel cooperative. They would be the first removed. The helicopter would be first to go in and used eight rockets for each of the growing fields, before the team in transporters arrived. It was to be total destruction using both heavy automatic weapons transporters to eliminate everything in the structure, not used to hold the forced laborers of the cartels. Not being able to determine the armed guards' reaction concerning the laborers held captive under armed cartel members, it was assumed there would be casualties not desired by the team, but for their own safety, it was the best they had to go with. The best they could hope for was all but one armed cartel member, would check on the noise caused by the rockets destroying their growing fields, and limit the number of casualties as a result of a panicked cartel member, with an automatic weapon. It would still take 15 to 20 minutes to get people into the location after the rockets did their damage. The two structures were not close enough to the field to receive any damage, but to get the team in too close prior was not a wise decision either. It was finally decided to have an armed transporter with top and rear by means of the two behemoths firing after the top mount was past. A single individual of the close quarter's group would be at the slave labor structure, to take out armed guards quickly. It was also decided to teach the individuals to say in Spanish 'stay on the ground until the noise stops' at which point that individual would depart as fast as possible, to a safer position. The rockets would follow within minutes, and the armed transporter would clear the processing structure with extreme prejudice, trying to avoid the slave labor's structure being in the line of fire. It had to be quick, precise and very accurate, for the cleanup team to get into place.

The first locations were not terrible far from the Peruvian airstrip, so no refueling would be necessary. The Peruvian cartel was informed of the location not selected to hit, as the small cartels who operated, primarily as means to provide jobs to the needy members of the region. If anything, it would seem like a cooperation among them and the smaller Columbian cartels, would be in order as long as everyone was in new business endeavors before the two year expiration passed. At that point, Romero Trap could not provide them with any means to protect their drug business, or their people from getting killed or incarcerated. Romero Trap thought it was as fair of a deal as he could offer for a business that appalled him personally. As for his view on obtaining confiscated product for them to conduct business, it was merely a means to the goal.

Romero Trap really had very little in the ways in conscience to conflict with his true objectives. Whatever was necessary for an assignment, was done in order to obtain a successful completion of the mission. He did much prefer the short term missions he completed for so many years, but this was his last hurrah in a long covert operations career. He had easily dismissed all his actions past and present, for the good of his country and now the world. He felt no guilt about all those who lost their lives at his hands, for that very same reason.

First mission went about without a whole lot of fight in the Columbian cartel members, who were accustomed to guarding young children who were overmatched, and easily swayed from trying anything stupid as they called it. As a result, the five guards inside the laborer's structure were all dead in mere seconds, with poisoned darts fired from the gaps in the structure. The close quarter's specialist was quick to dispatch them and inform the laborers in Spanish what was expected. He fled to cover, away from the rockets and heavy weapons fire and this was identical in both location, and took place with a mere thirty minute differential. Each transporter had approximately 15 members of the team unloaded away from the target area, to close in after the heavy weapons were finished.

When the cleanup team went in to verify there were no survivors in the processing structure, all the people were checked for valuables which by and large was currency. There were a total a fifty cartel members in the Peruvian location used by the Columbian cooperative cartels. There were a total of fifty children used as harvesting laborers. The currency collected was equally distributed to the children to use to return home, by whatever transportation was available to them at the nearest city or town. Most of them had been abducted from other countries and brought to the location. Fortunately, the majority were not excessively far from their origins, and told whether their family thought them dead or not, they would all be greeted with overwhelming joy by their parents. None of the young stayed long to see about anything else, they wanted to go home where they belonged. The aftereffect would linger, but subside with being near the people that cared about them.

The Columbian location was a bit larger having nearly 100 children as slave laborers, and nearly two hundred guards and processing people in the other structure. The process there was the same as the Peruvian location, although the close quarter's experts had a larger number of armed cartel members watching over the laborers. It was sufficient for at least two shots to be fired in a general location of where the close quarter's expert was believed to be, but he was not there any longer in either case. There was a good deal more currency, not useable by the team to distribute among the children used as harvesting slaves. There were also four strong boxes with US currency and more gold bars. Since it seemed all the cartels were keeping gold bars as did the terrorists, it was assumed it was one of the means they used for investment. Even though gold prices fluctuated on a daily basis, over a year's time value increase roughly 10 percent annually. It meant if the bars were obtained ten years prior, the value was twice what they paid to start or 100 percent profit. The helicopter did not have time to stop with the two fields destroyed and returned to the Peruvian airfield to refuel for the next mission. A total was not counted until the entire team was back to the airfield where they also had to setup a camp base of operations.

When the product was retrieved and brought to the Peruvian cartel boss, although it was worth nearly 20 billion with an estimated street value of 150 billion dollars, the cartel boss could only come up with 5 billion for Romero Trap. Since he did own the private airfield which had a hotel and restaurant, he would cover all the cost for his team to stay there, in lieu of being unable to give him the proper amount of funds, even though most of it was his to start with. Seizures were a part of doing the type business he was in, but not usually to the degree of his attempts to do business within the US borders. As a result, he would be more than happy to sell his product to US distributors, but would not venture into its borders for delivery. That risk would need to be taken by the distributors, to get the product once purchased into the country from the closest part of Mexico he could get it located. If the demand was high enough in the US and the product more difficult to obtain, distributors would take that risk. He was also shutting down his own growing fields and planned to use the profits from the sale of the 5 tons of processed cocaine, to move into other legitimate businesses although his investments would likely support them for a while, before becoming self-sufficient. It would not likely be as lucrative, but it was obvious his lucrative business was reaching an end. He did not want to spend time in jail because he pushed too long into a dying industry.

THE MAJOR OBSTACLE

Two problems were determined from further satellite imagery based upon how the cartel operated in the locations that were destroyed. The six locations in Costa Rica and Nicaragua had much larger infrared readings in the laborers structure than the others. It meant if they operated in the same fashion as those destroyed, the fields were either considerably larger or there were multiple fields to harvest. In either case they did not have enough rockets to destroy the majority of those fields, which would allow the cartel to resume operation, although on a smaller scale. The point of the assignment was to put them out of business entirely. They would also need visual confirmation to insure they did not damage anything more than the fields, especially in Costa Rica which was known for its lush environment and beautiful beach resorts, as well as unique wildlife. They only wanted to destroy the cocaine fields, not the beautiful country. It could not be accomplished with armed transporters traveling through half of Central America from South America. The distance was too far not to need refueling. As a result, the cargo plane would need to make a return trip to the DC area, for an extended time period. The time would depend on how quickly another set of forged acquisition forms could be made, and an additional 200 rockets obtained, as well as three jeeps from their own already acquired.

Half a dozen people including Jackson Frye, departed for DC on the second morning after the destruction of the first two fields. The team decided the best approach to take from this point forward was to go for the farthest locations from the Peru airfield, and work their way back to closer areas. No matter how they went about the large distance to cover and the number of locations, they were here for a long stretch of time. How long could not be determined to less than a year and half. Too much had to have closer observations in order to have a plan of attack for the different locations, and the cartels were now on alert, it would make things more complicated than they already were.

It took two weeks for the cargo plane to return with three jeeps and an additional 200 rockets for the helicopters rocket launchers. Once everyone was back and rested up from the trip, the plans for the next phase were set up with the input of the entire team. For the close support for the locations in Costa Rica and Nicaragua, Zoe was going to be used to get the attention of the armed guards as only a woman of her beauty could perform. She would not need to be involved in the actual killing, but to coerce some of the armed guards of the cartel to move out of position, for another close quarter's expert to dispatch. It was something she knew very well how to accomplish, and there were no other women in the group who could pull it off. Besides she was quite familiar with using her body and beauty as a weapon. It was only because she added this into the conversation of the planning, that it was going to become a part of the plan. There were no other opportunities with so many present at any location, for her to go into solo work and she wanted to make her contributions to the team.

Prior to the cargo plane leaving for DC, the tally of the four strongboxes was determined to be 2 billion in US currency in three boxes for a total of 6 billion dollars in gold. Two were taken to DC, with the very heavy three boxes containing gold bars. Zoe estimated at current value it was worth another 6 billion dollars, and took the pair of behemoths to load and unload so they were members of the departing DC crew.

15

The Major Obstacle Phase Two

The observation groups to Nicaragua and Costa Rica were sent in the three jeeps and provided with some currency, from the two billion in the strong box to establish sleeping and eating arrangements, while performing their observations of the six locations.

They reported their findings through burner phones as the communications earpieces were too distant in range to be useful, with the base in Peru's airfield being used for their operations. They did not have enough satellite communications equipment to use to avoid any security issues, so burner phones were the only option. The group would be gone for a month to observe the six locations, and as the reports came back, it was determined that there were 300 or more children used in each location for harvesting the cocaine. Each location had three separate fields, all similar in size to the others. It presented another issue for the helicopter, since it only had enough rockets for two fields at any given time. Even to reload would require the helicopter setting down to reload the rocket launchers for a third assault, on fields that were already going to be on high alert, with the first two being destroyed. Even at that the risk, it was decided to be acceptable with the helicopter, still having a heavy automatic weapon front mounted. It should keep the small automatic weapons users at bay, with time to dispatch the last of the fields.

Once the group was back, whether it attracted attention or not, the armed transporters were sent with the close quarter's experts, as well as those selected to do the closer follow up, to insure no survivors, and the condition of the children used as slave labor. With the way the helicopter had to operate, a closer refueling location needed to be used, and Costa Rica provided no resistance to aiding in a plague upon their territory that only existed, as a result of the number of poor people, who made up the majority of the population. The government was not financially capable of taking action against it, but by no means contributed to its existence either. The government stated if any officials were corrupted by the cartels, it would be only at a local level and not national. Also due to the fact, the locations were spread out enough not to allow multiple field strikes in a timely manner, they would be addressed individually.

It would take the transporters two days before getting into a position to be of any assistance in a timely fashion, to the taking out the armed guards, within the laborers structure, enticing the outer guards into a position of compromise, and sending in two helicopter rocket waves.

With everyone in place, the helicopter fully loaded including enough extra rockets in the cargo area securely in place a total of 144 including the sixteen loaded, was off for its first of three refueling, the last being in Costa Rica, where it would await word for the first strike. Those on the ground and in the helicopter, could utilize the earpiece communications gear, and all the team members had them. Two people of the thirty-five total sent, stayed at the Peruvian airfield location for intelligence gathering and communications from the team to relay to DC. The helicopter waited until dusk, before the communications were sent to make for the first location, which was predetermined before the teams left, as to the order the events would take place. The close quarter's experts were already near the laborers structure, and about the property that the armed guards were patrolling. The 10 guards inside the structure housing the children, required two people to remove with the use of poisoned darts. There was no reason to keep a single survivor

THE MAJOR OBSTACLE PHASE TWO

of the cartel members. Those guards were downed before the helicopter completed its liftoff. Next, Zoe went to work on the first of a dozen guards outside patrolling the grounds. She made it quite irresistible, and enticed one after another into their demise, as a close quarter's experts came up from behind to slit their throats without even suspecting they were in peril. After the ten guards in the structure had been dispatched, the children inside were again told to stay on the ground until the noise stopped. With the twelfth guard outside dispatched, the entire team moved farther from the location as the helicopter was supposed to be approaching soon.

The helicopter provided the team a seven minute window of distancing themselves from possible harm. The rockets took out two fields quite quickly, which got the remainder of the guards running in the direction of the field. Several cartel members got off small weapons fire toward the helicopter, which shifted directly toward them and removed them with much larger fire power from the heavy automatic weapon. The helicopter did not sustain any serious damage, had spotted a clearing 1100 yards away from the first field, but it would take fifteen to twenty minutes to reload the rocket launchers. That was enough time for the transporters to go in, and clear the processing location structure and any guards who were silly enough to think their small weapon would produce any harm. They did manage to get lucky, before six other guards were killed by the second transporter sent to finish what the first started in a timed fashion. The first transporter had the member of the team who operated the mounted heavy automatic weapon, got hit by a round of small arms fire, which went through the upper leg. It hurt and it bled a lot, but was not life threatening, it would require some first aid once the team was reassembled, after the last of the fields was destroyed. In the meantime, he kept pressure on it to keep the blood loss to as minimal as possible.

The helicopter made its third strike five minutes after the transporter had their run, and moved a little farther out of the way to wait for the last rocket before the whole team would converge on the location. The team found three guards trying to leave the area and dispatched them by whatever means necessary, and made a pass through of the processing structure, four of 100 people in the processing structure remained alive and single gun shots to the head ended their misery. Seven strongboxes were located in the structure, six were US currency and the seventh was equally proportioned Costa Rican and Nicaraguan. It was first divided into three equal portions for each currency. One portion was distributed to the children held against their will to return home. It was discovered all of those held in the first location, were all Costa Rican and the money received would not only get them home, it would be enough to feed the family well for two or three months. They were all more than happy to go home, and all 320 children ages 13 to 16 all departed for their homes and families. The helicopter set down near the two structures, and the currency strongboxes were all loaded on board for it to return for more fuel and the Costa Rican airfield. The wounded member went along and would require medical attention, hopefully available near the airfield.

Once the helicopter landed at the airfield, refueling was scheduled and the wounded member was taken to a nearby hospital. Being an airfield of a reasonable amount of traffic and use, injuries were frequent enough to have a close medical treatment facility. Initial examinations of the wounded member, indicated the bullet had passed through his leg but his pain was a result of it did nick the bone enough to cause some stress fracturing, and he would be out of action for a month to allow for proper healing, and prevent the fracturing from become more severe. The fracturing would recover without surgery, but it required less mobility than his duties were going to permit. He was stitched up after the examination, and provided a walking cane for the purpose of keeping weight off the leg, for at least two weeks, at which time he would need to be reexamined, to verify his fracturing was solving itself without a surgical procedure.

The helicopter returned with a full load of rockets loaded, but again would require a set down to complete the location. The transporters were already in place for the second location of the six, and the armed personnel around the location were definitely on a heightened state of awareness to potential problems. The good thing was there was nobody from the first location to tell them about Zoe Dubois, who was the type

THE MAJOR OBSTACLE PHASE TWO

of woman that a man on his death bed would attempt to have a final hurrah, before the lights went out for good.

The team was waiting for the soon to arrive dusk period for the initial removal of the slave laborers structure armed guards, with a Zoe encore afterwards. One less team member and a more alert cartel with arms of their own, only made things riskier, but not impossible, since this location had no information concerning how the attack was staged. To this point all the cartel knew was the amount of devastation inflicted upon them and their industry as they viewed it.

At the moment of dusk, the close quarter's experts selected for the laborers structure went into place at the same time the helicopter started to rise from the airfield. It would be at the fields of this location in twenty five minutes, giving the team including Zoe, twenty minutes to work before a small retreat for safer ground.

The team on the ground at the target location found a few variations from the first. There were fifteen armed guards within the children's structure, and only fifteen wandering the property. There were an additional dozen within the processing structure, but they did not appear to be there for the processing workers who all carried hand guns as well. Little did they know the first strike was considerably silent, and they would get no prior warning to the rockets, since the team would have neutralized all the guards within and outside the laborer's structure. The kids inside were provided the identical warning, and it allowed enough time for the transporters to neutralize the processing structure, before the first rockets were heard. The helicopter finding the structures were already neutralized, allowing the cleanup team to insure no survivors, while the helicopter landed in the location clearing, to reload rockets for the final field. It was off to finish and the team found no one alive inside the processing makeshift building. Arms were gathered as well as ammunition, to be loaded into the helicopter when it landed the second time. The strong box here was a single one with only Costa Rican and Nicaraguan currency. All of the Costa Rican currency was gathered and dispersed equally to the 300 surviving children, to return to their Costa Rican homes and family. There was one child, a female found dead among the child slaves. She was not a casualty from their attack, but appeared to have been beaten raped and sodomized repeatedly and returned to the structure nearly dead, to die among the others the night previously. She was used and abused by the cartel members responsible for guarding the children, and the team was told they were upset with her because she had been ill and unable to work the previous day.

The team would have liked to have burned the structures after the attacks, but the Costa Rican landscape surrounding was too precious to the people of the country, to have a fire destroy a single leaf of tropical foliage. So, they agreed not to do so with any of the three locations. They had not yet made a trip to Nicaragua, and did not know if the same were to apply there.

There were no wounded from this outing, and Zoe was a true art form when it came to distracting the unsuspecting armed guards, making the job of the close quarter's expert quite simple and easy. None of them felt they wished to encounter Zoe in a position they would not return from.

It took another month to complete the remaining four locations, although the Nicaraguans were not so concerned about their landscape, if it meant the end of the drug plagued villages. Only two other location had any US currency or gold, but it was quite a haul. Every location had a strong box of the two local currencies, so they distributed it among all those held against their will to allow them to return home and be with their families again. Not a single child found in any of the six location had surpassed the age of sixteen. Once all the team members were back to the Costa Rican airfield, they had the wonderful trek back to Peru, so they rested for two days, before making the trip by the different means of vehicles. The currency found between the two locations amounted to an additional 14 billion US dollars, and another strong box of gold but a little lighter than the others found. Zoe did not even provide an estimated value, and another cargo plane trip to DC would be necessary to lessen the load for a final trip home.

It meant after three months in Central and South America, they had cut down on the cartels operations of 26 locations by eight, leaving 14 more to go. The other places in South America were going

THE MAJOR OBSTACLE PHASE TWO

to take another month each of observation, before the attack could be performed, and there had to be a means to change up the tactics to keep the cartel guessing. To this date, outside of no survivors, the cartel cooperative had no real clue how to determine anything in advance of the attack. Without a single survivor to tell the story, the cartel knew only they were under attack but from whom and why, they were clueless. The news would still travel quickly to the remaining locations, and they would be more and more on guard and erratic in their behavior, if they had an inkling they were under attack as it was happening. Admittedly the close quarter's people in conjunction with Zoe Dubois as a decoy, were very efficient and it did provide far less resistance to the subsequent stages to the attack. The most effective was the nights where more guards were within structures, than outside. By the same token at some point one of the guards had to be wise enough to consider Zoe suspicious, and that would put her in grave danger, although she seldom did anything without a means to bring it to a quick end, she simply did not deal with small automatic weapons in her normal profession.

After two days of rest, it took another two and half days for all the teams' members to reassembled in the Peruvian airfield location. First order of business was to have the team well rested, before sending out an observation team to the next location, which would be in the southern region of South America. The most distant were the ones in Uruguay which had one, and three in Argentina, closest to it. It was not known how many fields were involved or the number of children slaves held in the locations. The original plan was to go to the furthest reaches north and south of Columbia, and then work back to finish off Columbia. It might make better sense to alter that a little after the first two most southern regions were destroyed.

It would take one month for two separate observation teams to get a better idea of how the cartel was taking their mounting losses. Having lost over 800 people was not an easy thing to recover from, much less the large amount of product that was never going to be distributed. Add to that, the team had removed approximately 16 billion dollars of currency and gold, from their possession, and with any luck they were not done yet. Although, it was possible that if gold and currency were in the remaining locations, it was going to be transported to a more secure location for the cartels. The team had hoped with the amount of losses already inflicted, that infighting and reconsiderations into a cooperative were taking place. To this point, there was no indication of any such activity, but they only knew of the product and processing locations used. The team had no way of finding the base locations of any of the eight cartels, and in all likelihood, they would be in more populated regions, and more likely cities where the cartel bosses lived like kings and queens. With the losses, the quality of life was definitely on a downhill slide. They were now at the best reduced to prince and princess in quality of life. Unfortunately, that was still quite acceptable to the vast majority of people in the world today. Especially since it would be at a level of luxury none of them ever experienced. Truth be known, most of them would find how the team lived at times, deplorable. It was unfortunately a matter of surviving under whatever conditions you had to work with, for any given assignment. Romero Trap's people were not above living on bugs as a food source, no matter how disgusting it may seem to most people. Zoe Dubois may be the sole exception, but the Black Widow had talents none of the others possessed, or could even dream to possess.

After the five days of travel to get to the location over less than perfect roads, the first reports were sent back through the use of the burner phones. It was decided since burner phone were to be destroyed after they had performed their service to the team, they would be dropped in mass from the cargo plane over the mountain regions of South America on the return trip. Even if they were found after the drop, the weather alone should make them entirely unusable. It was unlikely any of them would remain intact, but stranger things have occurred.

The first report was that the number of armed guards had significantly increased from three dozen or less to nearly twice the amount. This presented a numbers issue for the team, but it was hardly unusual or insurmountable. It meant more precautions needed to be put into the tactics to make it a less difficult situation. Zoe would not be used for the distraction, as marvelous as it was to watch and observe,

THE MAJOR OBSTACLE PHASE TWO

and use as an advantage, too many guards put her in jeopardy, and that was not a part of any deal with her or Romero Trap. It was also possible the cartel reinforced this area, because they were being a little bit too predictable. It meant the original plan was definitely in need of alterations, to see if they had any opportunity to catch the cartels off guard, because they did something unexpected.

The Peruvian cartel boss was asked when seen, of a safe place in the surrounding countries, which they could use for refueling the helicopter, for the Uruguay and Argentina locations. He informed them he had cooperation from most all of Brazil which covered a large portion of the territory between Peru and Uruguay. He did not have any such cooperation from Bolivia, and it would be best to keep to a minimal amount of time over their borders. His assistance was most appreciated, and the plan for the helicopter was at least in place for the time when it would be put to use. It would require two refueling stops to reach the target area, and it would likely need another refueling before getting to the second target location. The information over the next weeks was that two locations were quite similar to the first two, with roughly one hundred children slaves as harvesters, and a processing structure. Only two growing fields each location. Once the observation team had finished their reports, they were asked to remain in place until the transporter for each location arrived with the remaining crew members split between them, but they might need to converge on one before all going to the next.

The plan this time was to see how many they could draw out of the woodwork with the fields being attacked first. The transporters would need to be in close proximity to cut off any returning to the structures, and the helicopter would remain ready in a hover position with heavy automatic weapon at the ready. This was to cut down the armed guards from front and rear as the transporters would cut off a retreat option. The other team members would be positioned to prevent any from escaping, if all went well.

It took another five days to get the transporters in to the separate locations and another day to get the second transporter with support people, to the first of the two locations. A small group remained in place to keep eyes on the second location, and await the transporters and rest of the team to converge on the second location. With everything in place, the helicopter was already at the last Brazilian refueling location with enough fuel to hit the first location.

When the rockets started, the cartels had fifty armed people rushing to the field in the hopes of bringing down the helicopter. They were not prepared to have it waiting for them with heavy automatic weapons, and those that tried to retreat were cut down by the transporters closing the distance between them and the structures. The cleanup crew was standing ready, to take out any who tried to exit the processing structure. And some were watching the area where vehicles were located. The close quarter's experts were in place, but heard the automatic weapons open fire before fifteen additional guards tried to get to a vehicle to warn the other locations, how the attack was done. The close quarter's experts eliminate five of the fifteen and the other ten were finished by the cleanup crew awaiting any to get to their vehicles. The three who managed to get to the vehicle and start it up and move out, did not get far. One burst in to flames and it started a chain reaction among all the vehicles, and the team cleared away from the exploding fuel tanks and flying car parts.

The results were not what the team was hoping for, as all 100 of the child slaves were shot down in their structure and none survived the bullets of fifteen small automatic weapons used by the cartel guards. Without a doubt, this was not the way to perform at any of the remaining locations. The transporters returned to take out the processing center, although three people tried to leave and were shot just as they tried to leave, which kept the remaining occupants inside. The cleanup crew went into the structure after the transporters completed their work and finished off the five surviving people of one hundred, in the same fashion previously employed. The only strong box in this location had only local currency, which was no use to anyone, since none of the children remained among the living. Everything was set ablaze and the team departed for location two, while the helicopter returned for refueling, and reloading of the rocket launchers.

THE MAJOR OBSTACLE PHASE TWO

The second location would not be done in the same fashion. It was obvious the only way the children abducted and used as slave labor, would survive, was to first clear the structure of armed guards. The one thing noticeable during the rocket attack was not a single guard in the laborers structure, attempted to go aid in the rocket attack on the fields. It seemed their secondary task was to evacuate after killing the slave laborers, and attempt to report to the cartel, how the attacks were being staged. At least they learned from their error, and now knew in all cases to first remove the guards watching over the children, before any other form of attack took place. The massive blaze of the location would also serve as an old time funeral pyre, although there would not be any pageantry in how it was done. The team was highly disappointed in the outcome of this attack method, and would not incorporate it again in this assignment. The helicopter would have 29 hours on the ground to reload the rocket launchers, fill the tanks to capacity, and allow for the pilot to get rest at the airfield in some fashion or another. If there was a hotel on the grounds it was an option. The rest of the team needed the day to travel to the other location to start the second part of the operation, as it was done previously. First eliminate the guards within the children's haphazardly constructed building. Then the rockets could come into play to draw out the remaining guards.

The ground team would be a little less attentive with lack of sleep, but it was something they all knew how to overcome with so many years of practice. All but the driver could try to rest on the trip. In the travel, the driver could be relieved to allow that person some rest time. They were after all a team, and a team did whatever was necessary to accomplish the assignment. On top of all that, they were Romero Trap's team, and they knew what was required of them to get an assignment completed. None of them felt good about the outcome of the last tactics alteration, but they also knew occasionally collateral damage did occur. They would simply use it as a lesson learned and not permit it to affect their next job. Guilt was not a welcomed emotion to their profession, and it would only make them less effective or useless to the assignment. All of them fully understood this from the time they worked with Romero Trap, and they would put it out of their minds, knowing things did not always work out as planned. In all honesty, they were doing pretty good in keeping the innocent alive, in all of the previous eight locations.

They did also take into account that cartels were using location that were accessible only by roads less traveled, if you could call them roads at all. They also could not take their vehicles directly into the location and had to leave roads altogether to get into striking position. They had vehicles quite capable of traversing almost any type of terrain, but they also had to be concerned about the wildlife found within these regions as well. The biggest concern were the reptilian variety, largely the number of venomous snakes found in the region. They all wore some form of boots with ankle protection, but some snake could get quite far up on a human body for a coiled strike. Anywhere above the shins they were all vulnerable, and keep constant vigilance concerning the reptiles that might bring an end to the assignment permanently. They had to be aware with the regions they were conducting their trade, and not all snakes had warnings such as the rattlesnakes found in the US. The ones in this region, were deadly quiet and could be under or above, but body armor would aid from the above attacks, unless it managed to strike at the face.

The close quarter's specialists were the first ones in position for the second location, although all support personnel and transporters were relatively nearby. This was planned to the precise minute, and since it was already dark, it could commence as soon as the close quarter's experts were in place around the laborer's structure. They found once again fifteen armed cartel guards, watching over the 100 hundred young people used for harvesting their crops of cocaine. In this case there were five experts armed with the poisoned darts, to permit each to eliminate three apiece. The poison used was discovered by a British scientist of the eighteen hundreds. The asp it belonged to was a modestly size snake, reaching only 6 feet in length and maybe two inches in diameter. The scientist in exploring Africa was curious about observing an elephant appear to just topple over. When he got closer, he found the elephant landed upon the snake, which was his undoing. The snake was dead from the elephant, but it provided enough venom for the scientist to

THE MAJOR OBSTACLE PHASE TWO

develop a serum that would allow him to search out and capture other identical asps. His expedition to Africa was never disclosed as to what purpose he went there for, but the results, were both a serum and a poison of great effect. The asp protected itself with a venom that both paralyzed instantly, and then depending on the size of his target, killed it through the venom. It was not the size of snake that could consume such large prey, but it was a very effective defense mechanism against so many far greater sized beasts in its surroundings. The elephant or rhinoceros, took a little more than two hours after the bite to succumb to death, whereas as a human was a matter of minutes, after the paralysis took effect instantaneously. This was the poison used in the blow darts of the team. The instant paralysis, prevented anyone struck with the dart to give any warning or even squeeze the trigger of their weapon. Once they fell, it was only moments later that they were dead. A most effective poison for covert people to utilize in the dangerous profession of killer for hire. A total of fifteen darts from the five close quarter's expert quickly and effectively neutralized the makeshift building of the child laborer's guards. The young teenagers were given the same verbal message hoping the language used, remained unchanged. It would only take one or two of the hundred to react properly, to get the others to mimic the first one or two.

Five minutes later, the helicopter was destroying the cocaine fields in the first of the Argentinian locations, and the results of the rockets exploding this time brought 55 other guards running towards the trap that would be their end. None so much as flinched in the direction of the children's structure. The helicopter finished, with its rockets and poised to fire at those guards running towards it. The pilot was certain he would see muzzle flashes before the silhouettes of any human form in the darkness. The transporters were falling in from behind on the guards in pursuit of a helicopter. The close quarter's experts moved closer to the processing structure, to determine if any guards remained inside, and the cleanup crew was poised in their positions to prevent any from leaving it, or reaching their vehicles. The whole process took less than five minutes from the time the first rocket exploded until the guards running towards the fields, with transporters cutting off their retreat were all down. The transporters then turned their attention to the processing structure, as none attempted to leave and no guards were still within. The cleanup crew and close quarter's experts insured the number of survivors were zero. The team did the normal inspection to find only a strongbox of Argentinian currency, but this time in getting a verified head count all pockets were searched of the guards, and processing people and keys to vehicles were obtained.

The young teenage children held in the harvesting laborers building were gathered, and with the aid of the team members who could speak best in the language understood by most, inquired to how many had any experience operating a vehicle. Half of the one hundred indicated they had done it before, and with that the currency was equally divided among the hundred, and keys given to the fifty who claimed they had driven. The team was not concerned about how well they drove, just be able to leave in some fashion. Those that could not drive, were told to go with someone who did and whether they could drive all the way home, and get the other home as well, or at least to a place of public transportation and go home that way. There was very little time wasted beyond seeing what keys went to what vehicle. Most knew the identification on the key matched that of the vehicle, but since all of them were vehicles of all terrain or rugged terrain, the options were not so many to have only one key of a vehicle match the only vehicle. Among the vehicles were half a dozen range rovers, a dozen higher model jeeps and a variety of other four wheel or all-wheel drive vehicles of US and European manufacturers.

The children departed with fifty of the sixty-five vehicles that were seen. The number of people from the cartel who were no longer in need of the vehicles, numbered one hundred and seventy. Either they did share rides, or some lived in reasonable walking distance, which seem unlikely, or there were more vehicles somewhere else. The team was not going on a seek and find mission, but the vehicles were used to get everyone back to the Peruvian airbase, along with the two transporters. Seventeen vehicles and 32 people allow for more comfortable means for return.

THE MAJOR OBSTACLE PHASE TWO

The vehicles obtained would be used while in the region, and it was possible one or two, would be taken back to the DC operation base, to use for traveling about the area, where the jeeps they did use, were a little out of place. The rest would be left for the Peruvian cartel boss to decide on what he wanted to do with them. None of the vehicles were all that old and abused, and the majority were less than two years of age, the oldest being four years on the road. With the transporters and running more like a convoy, it took three days to get back to the Peruvian airfield. The diesel fuel used by the transporters was not found at every place that sold petrol for vehicles, more commonly used. Although like all places in the world today, large trucks were used to move products of every type around the regions. The driving was done in eight hour shifts, but two people would need to do a sixteen hour stretch, with each changeover because there were more vehicles than pairs. It still shortened the time and with the higher end models and luxury models, seats could be folded down to allow for a more relaxed sleep position for most.

Prior to everyone going off to get some well-deserved rest in a real bed with a place to have a breakfast, lunch and or dinner nearby, the strategy change was discussed. To possibly throw off the cartels anticipation of the next location, they were going to a more random approach. The first would be closer to home for the Columbians by removing the two in the neighboring borders of Venezuela, which would leave a single location in Columbia, owned by the cartels who formed a cooperative. Other locations in Columbia and neighboring Peru were considered to belong to those cartels, who refused to take part in the activities used by the cooperative; but it did not rule out the Columbian cooperative performing hostile takeovers, to recover some of the growing losses. That bridge would only be crossed if the cooperative made the move and the team's Peruvian cartel boss would know if that was taking place. The mounting number of cartel cooperative members not among the living any longer, should have weakened efforts to take over anything, unless they had some magical pool of waiting talent to replace the losses. Due to the volatile nature of their business, most required a high level of loyalty and trust that you did not get by wandering around asking people looking for work, if they wanted a new career. Aside from the fact they required job skills of using weapons, was not found on a resume in too many businesses. With the decision to go next to Venezuela, everyone went to get a bite to eat and then some sleep. The team still had over 1 billion seven hundred thousand dollars in US currency, and had not a single problem using it anywhere they had been. It was a welcomed currency in most of Central and South America for many small businesses, who offered fair exchange rates kept up to date, since the value fluctuated regularly, but if kept long enough, it was worth more than when first obtained. It was for some, the only form of investment they could afford.

After a forty-eight hour break in all activities concerning the assignment that was still ongoing, the team met to discuss how to best proceed, since they had been in the region for six months. The assignment was not yet completed, but tactics to keep the cartel members feeling a little less concerned over what was left of their businesses were now in place. Venezuela had two location in fairly close proximity, at least for the type of business it was. They were only 50 miles apart, and it would take two separate helicopter runs for destroying the fields. That was due to having to reload the missile launchers between locations, and assuming there were only two fields per location. The first decision unanimously determined by the team, was to take a one month break from attacks on the Columbian locations remaining. They had reduced the number of locations in operation from 26 to 14 in six months' time. With the production losses, the product destroyed and the lives lost, the cartels could not possibly have the resources to just rebuild and accept the losses. It would take them far more than a month to regroup, but the break might make them believe the worst was over, and the rebuilding could be planned. With planning they would have to relax the number of people in production locations to be available for planning, and possibly moving to yet another new location for startup business. With that and the wheels already in motion from the team, the next strike of two fields in Venezuela would be an even more difficult setback for the cartels.

THE MAJOR OBSTACLE PHASE TWO

An observation team would still be needed to insure the cartel had reduced personnel in those two location, and with any good fortune, the two locations could be destroyed without heavy automatic weapons, which would also be a new tactic employed by the team. The rockets were still the most and only effective means to destroy the growing fields. As of now, the team had acquired over 100 hundred small automatic weapons and enough ammunition to keep them loaded for the remainder of the locations. There were plenty more destroyed, and the cartels losses were far more reaching than product. This did not even account for the nearly 16 billion dollars and gold confiscated and returned to DC. In addition, in the satellite communications, countries now free of the Columbian drug cartels had paid up their portions of the bounty, and have tried to incorporate a better policing effort to prevent it reoccurring. The world was slowly turning into to better place, although it would be many years for it to be financial fulfilling for many countries.

During the one month break all the acquired cartel vehicles were put to use to see what Peru had to offer, besides an airfield and hotel with restaurant. None of the team members intended to be gone for more than a day at a given time, but it was something to take a break from long road trips packed like sardines into transporters for too long of a duration, and to spend time doing something other than killing the enemy. The cartel from all of their viewpoints were the enemy, and that was simply the mindset that they looked at any assignment. It was largely what kept most of them guilt-free of what they did professionally.

At the conclusion of the month, the observation team departed in a Range Rover to observe the two locations. There were all of four people, and the hope was they would know all they needed within three days' time. Burner phones were still used for communications. The trip to Venezuela was not that terribly long. They found at the first location a large amount of activity from the children used as slave laborers. First the field had been recently harvested, and the activity was replanting the cocaine crop for the next harvest. There were only a total of fifteen guards at the first location, and the number of processing people was down to 70. It was like they had to redistribute the people they had to the remaining locations for the product to be made into street value commodity. The second location had the same number of guards and processing people, but the fields were still in growth. They did not work after dark in the first location as far as the laborers were concerned.

In three days, all that was needed to determine the readiness of the cartel, was determined and the rest of the team was dispatched to the second location first, since that was where the observers were. The team was now at 34 strong with only one person remaining behind to communicate back and forth to DC, as well as the burner phone input from the team.

The transporters were brought, but only on standby mode for these two locations. First, at dusk the close quarter's specialists removed the three guards watching over the teenaged slaves. After the message in Spanish was quietly delivered, they spread out to remove the remaining dozen cartel guards at the location. Those guards were wandering about the location up to a perimeter from the buildings, and one by one the dozen silently fell to well-placed blades. In this particular location, they decide to go into the processing structure without any indication the cartel people were under attack to use the small automatic weapons to eliminate any returning to the cartel bosses with information concerning the attacks. Five minutes later the helicopter destroyed both fields and returned to the airfield to refuel.

Again, the team asked about those who could drive and handed out enough keys from the vehicles to get all the young teenagers on their way home, after distributing the local currency from a strong box. It was the only one for this location. They set everything ablaze after all the children were away, and immediately set out to cover the 50 miles to the second location before light might appear. They wanted both locations out by dawn. It took 90 minutes to cover the fifty miles, although not the most comfortable ride, the team got into closer position to perform the encore performance of the first strike.

Everything went exactly as the first, except it took a little longer for the helicopter to return to finish off the fields and retreat back to the airfield. Upon close inspection this location which had clean fields, had obviously done a recent distribution transaction had five strong boxes, four with US currency. Another 8 billion dollars removed from the control of the cartels of Columbia, and they were down to 12 location still operating. It had to hurt going from 26 locations to 12 in seven plus months' time, and severely hamper the way they had been doing business, to minimize losses to the crack down on drug trafficking. The vehicles and local currency were distributed among those exiting the slave labor of the Columbian cartel. With 140 processers no longer able to aid the cartel and 30 enforcers removed from their ranks as well, also eight billion dollars in US currency, the team felt they were progressing along nicely.

The cartels cooperative had to be feeling the strains internally to continue with this practice, and return to their separated means previously used. They did not have anywhere near the loss of people with seizure of product, which was the whole point of the cooperative.

Over the next eleven months with the team in Peru, the Columbian cooperative broke up to separate cartels as they had started. None were any longer large enough to defend against what the team had in the plans for what was left of them. The remaining twelve location were completely removed, and there were no more children lost in the events. All of the teenagers used as slave labor were able to return to the homes they were abducted from and rejoin the families, which had lost hope of them returning. Many families now had late model vehicles that they never could have afforded on their own. Most of the teenagers returned with enough currency to feed their families for two to three months, far above what was a normal meal consisted of on a daily basis.

The team with three jeeps and one Range Rover and one Porsche Cayenne returned on the first of the two cargo plane shuttle trips performed by Jackson Frye. During their time in Central and South America over seventeen months, they used one billion nine hundred thousand dollars of the two billion they kept for expenses, but that did include all the refueling stops for everything to be brought back to the base of operations in the DC area. The second trip retrieved the two transporters, and additional weapons while the cartel boss of Peru had fifteen vehicles to use as desired. Romero Trap in his final contact with the Peruvian cartel boss, said all business was concluded and if they were to meet again, it would not be under the best of conditions. He made certain that if in two years he had not gone from drug trafficking to more legitimate businesses, Romero Trap's team would bring it to an end for the betterment of the world. He did say it was nothing personal, but it was to bring his President's vision to reality, and that was what he had committed to from the very beginning. The Peruvian cartel boss informed Trap he had no intentions of still being in that profession after seeing what his team could do with far more potent people in the same trade.

While the team was away, Romero Trap had to endure yet another State of the Union address and the sheer boredom of the entire day among politicians. Even though there was a new breed of members to the House of Representatives, they all learned how to spend inordinate amounts of time saying the smallest amount on topic. Trap not being political, had always practiced using as few words as necessary to get his point out. It was largely why his portion of the State of the Union took all of five minutes, although he did not have to cover all the topics the President did over the prior year in office. Even at that, Thomas Hardesty was not one to overindulge the vocabulary, to see how much wind he could expel before getting to the point of the topic.

Romero Trap also informed the team the Central and South American bounty totaled 120 billion dollars, and as different countries were freed of the Columbian drug cartels, the bounty was paid and they had already received a large portion of the total bounty. Additionally, as those countries were free of the drug cartels, they entered the world governing council, and as of now seventy-five percent of all nations were on board the program. The world governing council was not meant to be an overseer of the world's governments or practices. The council was to be a diplomatic solution for all countries, to find a more peaceful approach to resolving difference with their neighboring countries. There was always going to be some infractions that would put one country at odds with another; but the world governing council was to be formed to find better ways than war, to resolve those problems. Its primary function was to be creating a more harmonious world, where all people could find ways to accept the other in peaceful means. Even it

THE MAJOR OBSTACLE PHASE TWO

if was merely tolerance of the fact that there would always be differences between cultures.

Upon return of all the equipment and supplies from Peru, Jackson Frye had the helicopter grounded until a maintenance procedure could be completed. The helicopter from the cartels had no maintenance records on board, and the team would need to locate the military maintenance standards and procedures for the type of helicopter they obtained. If it was a little early or late, a maintenance record could be kept with the first one performed by the people on the team who had experience with maintaining aircraft. The type of helicopter they obtained was not the most common of the military, but it was used as ground support for troops in a hostile area. The helicopter had distinct advantages and disadvantages as a support to troops. It was capable of flying in much lower to a target area. It was also capable of using cover while deploying its weapons in a hover mode. The biggest disadvantage was, although smaller than many other aircraft of its type, it could be brought down by smaller weapons. It was quick enough and agile enough to maneuver in tighter quarters, but it had no armor plating to prevent a vulnerable location being struck by return fire. Regardless of the advantages and disadvantages, it was not useful to anyone if it had a malfunction due to failing to perform routine maintenance. There was no reason to risk having it falling out the air because of maintenance issues.

It took the team about one week to locate all the specific documentation and procedures on the helicopter, and based upon the hours flown indicator, it was due for its first routine maintenance. It would take the team of five people, who had aircraft maintenance experience, another two weeks to go over every inch of the helicopter and obtain the necessary replacement items and proper lubricants, since they were quite different from the cargo plane. Since the helicopter was subjected to some small weapons return fire, it was thoroughly inspected for any damage it may have sustained. It had a single bullet lodged in the outer skin, and required a little patch work, but most of the other damage was from bullets that simply grazed it sufficiently to require some additional paint. All and all it held up quite well under the conditions it had been subjected to during the assignment.

The President had informed Romero Trap of half of a dozen countries that were trying to avoid the formation of the world governing council. He was trying to go through diplomatic process to sway their ignorance as to the purpose of the council. Unfortunately, these leaders held influence over a number of other countries within their immediate surroundings which was the holdup point for the remaining 25 percent to join. The world governing council to be an effective negotiating collectively, required 100 percent of all nations to be members. It was intended to be a place of bargaining and diplomacy among all nations. Those who objected were under the impression it would serve as a dictatorship over all nations. President Thomas Hardesty was having a difficult time convincing the leaders, who objected to the council forming, they had the wrong impression. He was going to continue trying to work it from a diplomatic solution before involving Romero Trap and his team. Should it come to an impasse, the President would not need a major assault to eliminate the individual leaders. It would be single individuals, and the most effective means of resolve, would be just the person who was the impasse point for half a dozen nations. He had hoped to find diplomatic solutions prior to going that extra step. It would only be done with six months left on his final term, and there would likely be no bounty to collect to keep it as quiet as possible for the advancement of the world governing council.

Romero Trap was not overly concerned any longer about additional profits as he had amassed nearly 310 billion with bounty and earnings and it would likely be the earnings alone, would serve as seed money for the assignments if that came to pass.

He did inform his team that the countdown was beginning for the end of their assignment, but the possibility existed of a final assignment consisting of six long range shooters at the most, to finalize the President's commitment to a world governing council taking place. Romero Trap could not provide them any additional details, since President Thomas Hardesty had not given him the locations or countries involved. He had his ideas as to where they would be going, but again he had to allow for the President to run the diplomacy to its fullest measure. The one thing he knew for certain, was Thomas Hardesty would give it his best effort,

THE MAJOR OBSTACLE PHASE TWO

and he was a man who was quite convincing in his approach to the situation. He could not however determine the extent of stubbornness he faced from those opposed to the world governing council, or the ignorance they may present to the issue at hand.

Romero Trap used one of the evenings at home to obtain a few more burner phones, since the stock was depleted from the return from Central and South America. In trying not to overdo the amount he would require, he figured less than a dozen if all six team members were required to leave for parts unknown. He needed three others, one to keep in touch with his team members, and two for different posts he had to place on the internet, although one was to a dedicated website, that only six people among all those who he had within his team were made aware of.

His second evening after being at the operations base, was to place the two different posts. It was his time to remove himself from the business he had been a part of for so many years. The first post was quite simple, it stated "Lost lease, going out of business." It had a phone number from the first of two burner phones, which would result in numerous calls from his team members, who were not a part of this mission of eight years.

He did expect at least enough time to place his second entry into the dedicated website, but he was wrong in that assumption. He still had over 120 people who had from time to time been members of his teams of elite professional, many were independent, and could select from a group of assignment providers, the jobs they wished to be a part of for a duration, typically less than six months. He hardly finished with the first post to the internet, when the calls started coming in. As each call hit his phone, he was asked what the deal was. Romero Trap explained that once his current assignment was completed, he would be sixty-four years of age and spent 43 of those years in his profession. It was time for new blood, and he had done more than enough killing in the duty of his country. He had neglected to have married, have children and it was time to at least find a more peaceful means to live, before he ran out of days to do it.

He got to repeat himself for nearly 40 calls that evening, before turning it off to get some sleep. While he slept, he had an additional 20 messages left for him, but he did not reply to any or turn his phone back on until he completed his half day session in the oval office, and arrived at the base of operations after his White House luncheon.

He spent most of his time among the team simply responding to his twenty messages, most all were answered by the incoming party to give them the identical speech he had for the previous forty. With already having heard from half of the people who had worked for him over the last 27 years as an independent contractor for hire. The calls subsided to the point when he returned home, he was able to make the website post. Fortunately, only six people had the website and one of them was currently among his team. Romero Trap did not expect Jackson Frye to want to take over his business affairs, after eight years on the current assignment. Jackson although a fine tactician, was still young enough to have a family life, and all the things Romero Trap had foregone for the sake of serving his country.

Over the next five days, all 123 people of his first post had checked into the post and Romero Trap repeated his same message to all of them. He did not have any calls concerning his website posting, which simply stated "Business for Sale." He really was not selling anything, but was willing to turn over all the business to a potential member, to take over the reins of his established business. He was willing to do that for any of the six, who were more than capable of making the same decisions he made in accepting or decline any assignment, turn over the property and equipment under the shell corporation name. It would also include a 1 billion dollar fund for assignments accepted, as the initial startup money. All six of the people he had on this list, were quite familiar with how Romero Trap had operated for more than twenty years, and would follow exactly in his footsteps. He truly expected one of the five people not on his team would like to find a way to retire much earlier than Trap was able to. He would be sixty-five years of age, when his Vice Presidency came to an end. He would like to accomplish a few things before reaching his end of days. He had never learned to cook a single thing for himself, and did not even own any of the utensils associated with that function. He never owned a home to call his own. He had probably spent enough money on other people's food, to feed the state of California for a whole month, under the means he did not know how to do. It was time to find companionship for the rest of his days. He did not believe it had to lead to marriage or having children, since he was far too old to consider having a child put him in the grave, earlier than he anticipated. Somebody to talk to and spend time with was a whole different perspective, than raising a family. Whether that person was interested in sharing in a life together, or simply seeing each other, and keep it that way, he really did not care how it worked out. It just seemed to him, for as much as he gave to his country to die alone and forgotten, was not how he wanted it to end.

16

Winding Down

It took 30 days for Romero Trap to get a nibble on his website post, although Jackson Frye had inquired in person concerning what Romero Trap was offering. Romero Trap said in all honesty that Jackson was ready to leave the business behind him, and make a life for himself, which did not involve killing people for a profession. Jackson had pretty much confirmed Romero Trap's insight, and merely wondered how he was going to accomplish it without his profession. In confidence, which meant Jackson was not to inform any other member of his team, the retirement plan of 500 million dollars per member, was how they were all going to finish the work they did for their country. It was far better than anything the government would have ever provided a single one of them, and it provided options none had ever had previously. Considering the team members were all younger than Romero Trap, they had the opportunity to have families, and live out life in relative comfort, without having to work another day in service to anybody, but themselves.

It did not rule out any of them continuing in the profession they had been a part of for a long time, but it opened avenues none would have had before. He did not believe Zoe would entirely abandon her profession, but she could be more selective in her options. The sum of money they would all receive, would go far beyond all their lifetimes as long as they were not overly excessive. Throwing money away on gambling or an abundance of extrangance, would certainly present a problem in having the funds last a lifetime and then some, but he could not prevent it either. Jackson Frye could not see it within himself to be any such person, but could see how that much of a retirement fund, could make his life much simpler, and more ordinary in respect to what he currently did for a means of making a living.

The team members from past assignments was not within his team currently in use, and was not subject to a percentage of the retirement fund Romero Trap had established for his present team members. The person who responded was a fine tactician, and would make an excellent leader in continuing operations. He followed Romero Trap's exact approach in planning assignments, but he did lack experience in obtaining them. His offer to the person in question required him coming to the base of operations, to see what was being offered in order to make a wise decision. It would take a month before he could be in a position to come to the DC area, as he was in the finishing stages of his assignment. Romero Trap had no hurry for him to view the property, so he did not push for a quicker time frame. He felt what he was offering was well worth this person's time for a number of vehicles, a cargo plane and helicopter with armaments, the billion dollars in seed money, as well as all the weapons and ammunition in the storage locker that had been built. It also provided a good deal of room for people to be a part of his team in future events, although he did foresee the need of their profession to drastically reduce. It was the way the President currently wanted to envision the world to become. Romero Trap had lived up to his expectations as a Vice President, and would see it to the end of his term in the White House. He was grateful there would be no additional time permitted to him as a government office holder, it was the most meaningless part of his profession, which was coming to a close.

With his team all back in base operations, he allowed for all of them to take the next 60 days away from having any work to perform, and after six years and seven months it was a well-deserved break from the rigors of the duties of their profession. All who had families could spend time with them, those who did not, could make the attempt to move forward in having one person of meaning in their lives, although none but Jackson Frye knew just how well they would be in such a position.

Zoe Dubois was still the youngest member of the team, and providing she was not so badly damaged from her early years of sexual abuse to have children of her own, had the most to gain from retirement. It also depended largely upon her and her ability to get over her dislike of the opposite gender, to move beyond it, and find a person she felt was good for her. She had a lot of hatred as a result of her youth, and it was what made her such a professional in her line of work. It was time to reach that crossroad in her life and move beyond it, but it was far more whether she was mentally capable of crossing the bridge to a more normal life, if she wished it. Romero Trap was considering letting her in on the secret of her retirement fund to aid in that, but thought it would be best to wait until the 60 days had come to pass. He hoped she would have crossed her bridge without his pushing toward a better life, than he could ever have.

Before the team departed, the last detail Jackson Frye took care of pertained to acquiring an additional 3 dozen plates for vehicles that had not expired, while he was in another country for eighteen months. The vast majority of plates had surpassed the time frame of being useable, and the most he could expect was a two year plate endorsement. It was highly unlike he would find plates replaced the day prior to his obtaining them, to get the full two years, and most people still worked in the annual option for the mere cost factor involved. Romero Trap figured by the President's own admission, it would be at least nine months, before anything would be decided on the half dozen leaders holding up the completion of nations joining the world governing council. There was no reason to keep his people sitting around and waiting for the time to expire. Even with 60 days away, it would still leave them looking for things to do for another six months.

With the team away, it did leave the window of opportunity for his potential replacement to thoroughly examine what was available. For many people in this profession, Romero Trap was making an offer that was beyond any expectations, especially since he was not looking for an exchange of funds, from the potential party to take over operations, and he was also offering ten time the seed money he currently kept on hand. He did take all the currency and gold, and put it into the numbered accounts to have a future growth in earnings. It had reached with his last deposit in excess of three hundred and ninety-five billion dollars. Even with nineteen billion paid out in retirement, there was plenty left for the extremely high earnings to grow the fund, should he ever have a change of heart in his profession. He may find retirement did not suite him, or cooking was beyond his skill set, or it was possible he could not find anyone he felt trustworthy to share his remaining life with. That was all variables that would require time to determine what was best for him, although he did not have much experience in worrying about that over the last forty plus years of his profession. His trade has always put the need of his country forefront in how he conducted his own daily affairs.

Romero Trap spent the next twenty three days performing his half day sessions at the White House, and doing a daily check on the base of operations in Maryland, just outside of the DC city limits. It did not take a long time to look over the property to determine nobody had infringed upon their domain. Considering the locked gates and the lights to deter those intent upon taking from the rich to care for the poor, usually those who did the taking, he would return to his small apartment. He received no other calls concerning his business for sale, which truly did not surprise him, the two most likely candidates were accounted for, and one was going to go into retirement when he did. On the twenty fourth day of the sixty day time off for his team, the other party made his second call to expect his arrival the following day, and a time was set for him to survey what was being offered. The time was set for after his half day session at the White House concluded, including the luncheon of course. Romero Trap had indulged in the White House luncheon long enough to formally miss such marvelous meals when his time to leave arrived. It was the only high point to most of his days as Vice President. He did not much appreciate the long winded politicians who imposed upon his time, because the President was too busy with other functions of his daily agenda. He was grateful he did not have to go through the day being planned for ten to twelve hours of everyday meetings, and agendas as Vice President. He merely looked into the people who could not be put into the agenda for the day. All politicians thought whatever they had to present to the President, was the most important and did not require setting up an appointment. Were they ever wrong when it came to the President's staff in overseeing his daily business affairs?

On the afternoon of the twenty fifth day of the sixty days' time off for the team, he met with his former associate who had proven himself to be a leader of his people, the meeting took place. He was shown first the two different barracks building used for housing for the team members. Romero trap pointed out, since he had utilized both female and male members of his team, the reason behind having two separate buildings for both genders. It was a matter of comfort level for his people, although he had employed females who were accustomed to having shared arrangements with the opposite gender, they seemed to appreciate having gender specific sleeping quarters.

The base had been in operation for nearly eight years, so it was well established as home for many of his team members. The property had been purchased from the local government to insure there was no questions of ownership, although the true business purpose was never disclosed. It was purchased under a long forgotten CIA shell corporation, and the CIA was none the wiser of the shell corporation. The CIA did not know they had such a shell corporation established, as he personally put it into their system in anticipation of going independent. The CIA never made the discovery and after nearly twenty years, he put it to use under their noses, and they did not ever need to know about it. After that, he took one of the jeeps to the airfield to show him the hanger which now housed the cargo plane and the attack helicopter. Romero Trap explained the airfield had been abandoned with the other airfield being used as a replacement. It was more capable of large planes and had refueling services, as well as maintenance available for those inbound, and away from their normal service people, which did occur from time to time under commercial flight guidelines.

Romero Trap also pointed out that although each plane had numbers, they were fictitious and in reality, the aircraft did not exist. His team currently in use, had maintenance skills among themselves, so all maintenance had been performed in house, but recorded under standard military procedures, and the records were kept on the aircraft. This was an important factor to Romero Trap's possible replacement in his independent contractor service continuing into the future. From the airfield, housing the cargo plane and the helicopter, he made the potential replacement aware he did not own the airfield in any way shape or form, but typically it took a very long time for cities to restore such facilities to accommodate more modern aircraft, which historical only got larger and required more runway. This particular airfield, had no expansion room without going through the government red tape to obtain lands owned by others. It was a long and difficult process, as most people these day had access to lawyers, who knew all the loopholes to prevent eminent domain from working for the government to utilize, since the biggest loophole was for the owner to receive a fair market value to their property, and the government seldom followed anything fair. The farther down the chain from Federal, the worse it became as budgets were simply too stretched for such additional expenses.

Once they arrived back to the base property, he showed his potential replacement the main building which was also used as the common room, housing the large flat screen video system, that like all the utilities were tapped into in untraceable fashion, and no payment was anticipated on a monthly basis. Keeping operating expenses minimal was a large part of conducting business in their profession, and every little bit could make the difference in a completed or failed assignment. Nobody wanted to fail because they ran out of money for the tank of gas that made it to the point of where the ultimate target was located. It was not something that Romero Trap had ever experienced, because of how he set up his business, but he had heard of numerous assignments that failed from such circumstances, when he was in the CIA. It was also the very reason, the CIA and other agencies offered assignments to multiple teams, and although that was never disclosed to the assignment takers, only one would fulfill the assignment and as such, only one got paid.

Having more than one contingency was also within the government's policies when getting contract help. Considering first who the contract was with, and the line of business that was being requested, there was no place to turn when you were one of the alternatives that did not complete the assignment.

Romero Trap knew this going into any assignment he accepted from the government agencies, and made certain his team pulled off the assignment and had proof of kill or completion, if it was something not involving loss of life to the target. He did not receive many requests from the government that did not require ending the existence of at least one person. Collateral killings were not included in the assignment bounty paid with proof of completion. One thing about Romero Trap was he was very thorough in his profession, and not only lost a bounty to a quicker person than himself, but he wasn't ever expected to complete the assignment first. He truly preferred working for other governments, or even individual businesses over his own government, but most of the assignments were his government, as they also liked to meddle into other countries affairs. What President Thomas Hardesty was doing over his first six and half years may be construed as such, but Romero Trap knew it was nothing like what agencies did as a protagonist to those considered enemies.

From the main common room, his potential replacement was shown the other facilities in the main building, which started with the bathrooms that had been cosmetically updated by outside contractors. Although the showers were still in the lower main area with the other two buildings now used as separate men and women buildings and sleeping arrangements, they had remained for emergency use only. Working on various things over the last six and one half years, a means to wash down quickly due to somebody coming in contact with a material that should not have been there, was kept in the precautionary procedures. His potential replacement was actually impressed with what he had seen to that point, seeing that unlike other times he worked short term assignments with Trap, he was far more prepared for the long run than any person he had dealt with. Trap admitted with his acceptance to his current position in the government, he never dealt with long term assignments, and knew he could not go with a four year to eight year assignment using his past methods, which were not going to cut it. The locations were actually selected by his team, based on what he could find readily available. The airfield that was abandoned was not originally put to use when the property was first put into use. The property was not even under their ownership, it was simply abandoned, and it took a few bounties and assignments to decide to obtain it outright, but the local government was making if difficult not to obtain, stating that all the structure were so far out of code they held no value, and it was just the acreage he purchased, and the buildings were free. They walked to the door and Trap pointed out to the fence lining the perimeter of the property, and told his potential replacement the property included every inch to the fence as far as he could see, which was somewhere like 45 acres. Although when they first got into the place, it was largely litter and used as a trash dump, but they did work it pretty well with the purchase making it officially theirs. The next stop was to the locked storage area, where the team's arsenal was kept with all the spare ammunition. He did point out that the two heavy automatic weapons used by two of his team members, did not belong to the property. His replacement was more than welcome to talk them into trying to sell them to him, but the fact of the matter was, few people could carry such a weapon to be used without a tripod mount.

His replacement knew exactly what Romero Trap was talking about, and none of the people he knew currently, were capable of lifting it solo, much less using it like an automatic weapon. He did ask if he ever worked with the two people Trap was referring to, and Trap did not believe he had, since their skill set was not typically needed when his replacement was on one of Trap's teams. He did believe he worked with a least fifty percent of those he currently had, maybe more, but his secret femme fatale was not known to him. Trap continued with telling his potential replacement, since all of his team would have been eight years into this assignment, it was highly unlikely any of them were going to refuse the retirement pay to continue with the profession they chose to follow. His potential replacement asked Trap why on earth he would take an assignment for such a length of time. Trap told him it was a part of his other job in political office, and contingent upon his acceptance of the role in government. His replacement seemed to be a little out of touch with current events, as Trap told him, he was President Thomas Hardesty's Vice President. His potential replacement said it never occurred to him to put one and one together, thinking Trap was a rather common name. He seldom paid that close of attention to political news coverage, unless it pertained to potential assignments to anticipate. Romero Trap had a good laugh, saying it was exactly the way he did things prior to Hardesty requesting him to join him. He told his replacement, whatever he did in the future, not to make the same mistake and take any political office, no matter how much respect or admiration he might have of the requestor. Trap told his potential replacement; it definitely cramped his way of performing assignments. He had not been involved with but a single assignment in the Middle East, and it was hardly like he got to perform anything beyond insure everything went according to plans. This planning idea was something he was quite familiar with, since you could never count on perfect conditions and backup plans, had to be understood also, for when it was less than perfect.

The final piece of the puzzle was to take his potential replacement to the buildings used as the garage. Inside were two transporters with mounted heavy automatic weapons. There were three more without, as well as a dozen jeeps for any terrain, although speed may be limited under those conditions, as any other vehicle would be as well. There were three other vehicles that Romero Trap did not believe would be included in the overall property, he though if he was going to retire, he might find use of the Porches Cayenne, Zoe liked the town car, and he was sure the Range Rover would be taken by Frye. Since the vehicles were confiscated, obtaining title and licensing may be an issue, unless it was addressed via military prior to the team fulfilling their commitment to this assignment. He would not look into that until the team had returned.

His final bit was more informational than visible to his potential replacement, first of all, Romero Trap said he could provide approximately 120 names of professionals his potential replacement could use for assignments, he had worked at one time or another with most of them. He could provide his replacement with the means to offer assignments, which he had used from the internet posts, as well as the site that only a few knew about, his potential replacement being one of them. Romero Trap stated, he still had one year and five months left on his current assignment, before he could turn over the property to his potential replacement, but he could conduct business with his other professionals, as long as he did not require use of the base of operations. His potential replacement was well aware of how Romero Trap functioned, and he did not plan to alter his methods, since they worked so well for the last twenty years. His final bit of information was at the time the property was turned over; Romero Trap was prepared to include one billion dollars in funds to cover the startup costs of any new assignment. Romero Trap also told him it was ten times more than he personally kept all these years, but he always made certain it was fully reimbursed by the end of the assignment. That insured he could accept additional assignments, as one was completed. He made sure his potential replacement understood exactly what he might face when accepting government agencies contracts, since they often gave the assignment to more than one, and only paid the group that completed it. If he got beat to the finish line, he had expenses without bounty, and that could be costly. His potential replacement was not fully aware of this fact, and had lost an assignment or two in the past, but never understood why until now.

    His potential replacement was no longer potential, he was more than willing to accept Romero Trap's generous offer, and foresaw no reason he could not operate without the base of operations until it was ready. There was no paperwork in this transaction, Romero Trap's replacement was made aware of the shell company the property was owned under, and also went over the additional communications gear and satellite imagery computers that were included in the deal. He also told his replacement about the use of military acquisition or requisition forms, since they periodically altered which was lease and which was not. It was important to have a good forgery member and a valid military commander's name to make it work. There were many different skills among those of his teams, which made assignments easier, even though those skills never were used for the target. This was all part of the planning and often a matter of who was available for each assignment posted. His replacement knew all the key words for postings on the internet for assignments, needing personnel to go about the assignment. It usually had to start up quickly, and planned in order to reach the objective first. Romero Trap would need to take his replacement back to his own apartment to transfer the computer information.

Romero Trap also went over the need for untraceable phones used for assignments, and how important it was to discard and preferably destroy them when the task was done. Trap said under active assignment conditions, he normally had one to two dozen available for the assignment. Between assignments, he never kept more than half a dozen. His source for burner phones had them available with 300 and 500 minutes. 500 hundred minute phones were only used for placing an internet assignment post. Once the job had all the team agreements, the phone was discarded. It would also be of no use when the minutes ran out.

They returned to Romero Trap's apartment where his replacement was surprised to see just how modestly Romero Trap existed. Romero Trap simply told his replacement, with his assignments having taking him out of the country for several months at a time, he did not need to worry about a home being left unattended. He did not require much, and until the last six and half years, was gone more than he was in his apartment. That was understandable from his replacement's viewpoint. All the pertinent information was exchanged by direct load to his replacement's computer laptop, he made sure he brought with him. It took a mere ten minutes and Romero Trap told his replacement if he had other associates, he wished to include into the list of 123 professionals from Trap, he could do so. He should inform them of the means to utilize for finding assignments with him. The posting on the internet, was usually too vague for unwanted calls to his burner phone, but it did happen from time to time. It was easiest to explain by telling the party they reached the wrong number, or got the wrong number. Trap had never had a person call back a second time to inquire about the posting.

The website had a total of seven people that knew about it including Romero Trap and Jackson Frye, both of whom were going to retire. Since it was possible, retirement did not agree with either of them, they would not delete the site permanently.

Everything was concluded between Romero Trap and his replacement, and Trap let him return home or onto other business, whichever was most appropriate. Romero Trap was never one to pry into information concerning his team of professionals other businesses or assignments. They were after all, independent contractors like himself, and were never expected to accept an assignment from Trap, even if it would prove to be a better assignment. It was highly important to be considered a member of Trap's team, to have finished to completion an assignment, leaving in the middle of one, because of a better opportunity, was unprofessional, and Trap would drop any such person from his list of potential team members. That was largely why only those, who were available for assignment responded to a new posting. If they were just finishing up, they typically indicated that in the response call, as in some cases, speed of arrival to Trap's location could alter whether they could make the deadline for the assignment to go into effective operation.

After a replacement had been identified and was simply waiting for the property to be made fully available. Trap's replacement was also on his way to his next location, which he did not pry from him as was his normal demeanor towards any and all who ever worked on his assignments. He went to the computer and made first a visit to the website, and typed in a single word. SOLD. He then went to his internet posting and typed in an advertisement he only expected to get responses from his 123 people. His advertisement was again simple, it read, change in leadership, and he added one of the burner phone numbers. The phone calls would take a little longer, but not terribly much, but he intended to inform everyone who was now going to be arranging assignments, and placing the internet posts, and that their name had been given to the new leader, if they wanted off the list to let him know now. Most of the 123 people had worked with the new leader at least once, although he would have largely held second in command under Trap at that time.

Again, he spent a good deal of time over the next four days responding to his burner phone, this time since the White House activity was not breaking down his office door, he kept the burner phone active while in his office, and only off for the time in the Oval Office. That normal equated to sixty minutes immediately upon arrival. At least three-fourth of the time was before formal hours of the White House, for staff and politicians to interrupt the President's Day, or just to give him his daily schedule of meetings or events. The President did manage to diplomatically persuade one of the six leaders who were holding up the world governing council, whose biggest concerns were his less than cooperative neighbors. It was a southern Asian country, although there was a second in the region with more influence over the rest, and he was not budging. It brought the loose ends down to five from six, but Romero Trap was under the impression the leader he persuaded was not one who held a great deal of influence over his neighbors.

Over the phone for four days, he talked to every member on the list, and since the new leader had Romero Trap's full approval, none wished to depart unless an assignment proved to be less than expected from Trap himself. He made sure they all understood his replacement was not his clone, and had his own personality, but from a planning perspective, he would be very much like Trap had planned it. Most had worked under him as second in command, and had no real issues, although he could be a little more demanding at times, when it was not necessary. Romero Trap did not expect his replacement to have his exact demeanor, just that he could have a prepared plan of action quickly, to work out the finer details with the crew.

After the fifth day, and the half way point of his team's returning to the base of operations, Romero Trap started using his office time to research things he never considered before this time in his life. He started looking into homes available and thinking he was likely done with Washington DC; it could be farther outside the city. Even with a five hundred million dollar payday coming, he was not looking at overly extravagant mansions, but nice maybe a little above average homes. There were all kinds of places listing homes from each individual real estate agency, to the local real estate organization that served over them.

There were also national real estate sites, but this was not what he was seeking, so as he found those, he made sure he put the names on a list to ignore returning to in the future. As he was looking into all the homes, he realized one crucial item he seemed to jump past. He had no idea how to take care of a home or apartment, cook, repair appliances, or even maintained simple things like heating routine procedures.

He decided to change gears and look into the local high schools and technical schools to see who offered evening basic cooking classes, and was surprised to find a high school not too far from his apartment, offered the classes. Romero Trap made a phone call from the White House, to inquire into when the next classes started, and explained outside of putting coffee into the filter collector, and dumping them afterwards, adding the water to the storage tank to make it give back coffee, he knew nothing about cooking, and did not even own a single utensil for the purpose. He was told the most basic classes started in one week, the classes were two nights each week, for eight weeks. It cost 10 dollars per class, and was paid upon entry to the class and a spot could be saved for him, if he just gave them his name. He gave them his name and made no reference to his current political position.

Romero Trap would have three weeks, or six two hour sessions of cooking classes completed before his team returned. Romero Trap's first class did not go at all the way he had hoped. It seemed too many people in the class, had nothing better to do than watch cable government broadcasts, and they all recognized him as the Vice President. They inquired what he did prior to becoming Vice President, and he tried to skirt the issue by saying he worked for the government, but was never in a prior political office. They all knew very little about his past, like it was supposed to be, but they wanted to know more about what he did. He told them most of the things he did were so classified, the documents could only be opened by the President, and he was simply under oath not to ever talk about them. That was insufficient for them, and he ended the discussion by saying if they knew their bible and he worked for God, he would have been an archangel. He hoped he did not have further explanation to the statement, but it did not work that way. So, he said according to some it is believed, whenever God needed a killing, he sent an archangel to do it.

From that point on, classes went about quite normally and the first thing Trap learned was he needed an awful lot of things in a kitchen to cook anything. On his third class after going over all types of utensils, pots and pans of various sizes they went through the first cooking assignment of potato salad. She had ingredients for a number of variations, since there were many, and most people all had favorite flavors, they preferred over others. Romero Trap did not think he was doing too terrible bad boiling potatoes and eggs, and mixing them with different ingredients. Spices were discussed, but until that evening, they were not out to examine to see how they differed, and in some cases, how much they appeared the same. His potato salad was finished off with a heathy sprinkling of Paprika for the color more than anything else. He sprinkled the first red spice bottle he found and it looked pretty good. The instructor was the taste tester for everyone completing their first assignment. Romero Trap could see immediately upon the first taste, he did something wrong, but had no clue what. It was quickly spit into a napkin, and discarded, and after recovering from her taste, asked if Trap had read the spice bottle, prior to using it. He said no, he just used the closest bottle that had the right color. She asked him if he could show her what bottle it was, and he grabbed it up and handed it to her, where she turned the label to face him, which read cayenne pepper. Even at that, Romero Trap had no idea Cayenne pepper was hot. She simply told him from this point forward, make sure you read what spice you are using before applying it, if you do not know about the spice, simply ask. She took it like a real trooper, but it had to be more than she expected when she tasted it.

Besides Romero Trap being a bit embarrassed by his lack of knowledge of kitchen spices and tools, he was starting to learn some very basic things about cooking, but he could see it would take quite a while in classes, before he would ever be ready to make his own meals at home. He completed his first six cooking classes at the high school by the time the team had returned to the operations base, from their 60 days of leave.

Romero Trap did his half day session at the White House, and a shortened visit to the operations base on the nights he had his cooking class. He did not disclose to his team his purpose of needing to leave on those two evenings, but simply stated he was taking up some much needed classes, to understand what he missed out on over the last 42 years of his life. Over the first week of his team returning, when not attending his cooking class, Romero Trap had met with each member of the team in a private face to face meeting. He did inform them that when the assignment for the President had run its course, he was retiring from the profession that had been his life, throughout his entire adult existence. He did not know for sure it would agree with him or not, having never done anything else his entire life, outside of serve his country in some fashion or another.

Romero Trap asked all of them about having military connections in order to obtain legal means for title and licensing of the three vehicles, which were not normally used within the military. He found half of a dozen people who could give Romero Trap a contact to make it possible. He also informed each of them what the retirement fund would be at the end of the assignment, and suggested each obtain a numbered account to make the large deposit. How they went about it from there, was entirely up to them, but the numbered accounts, still had better earning percentages than any US alternative. When asked what he would do, Romero Trap said he would keep it in a numbered account to keep the earnings, and tie it into a traditional account, to siphon off funds for his living expenses. He would need a fairly large amount in the beginning, if he followed through with his plans of owning his first home. He also informed each one of whom the replacement leader was, and at the end of this eight year assignment, the entire operations base and equipment would be turned over to him. They had the option of letting the other person know if they were going to remain available for additional assignments, or like him, take the time to retire to catch up on a life he missed out on as he served his country.

It took forty-five to sixty minutes for each individual, but confirmed from Zoe she would be happy to take the Lincoln Towne Car as her own, as Jackson Frye would with the Range Rover. Romero Trap got the impression initially due to the length of this assignment, everyone but Zoe was going to give retirement a good attempt. Zoe Dubois felt she still had a few more years of removing the opposite gender, before she would feel she could move on with her life. It would take a major effort for her to find her heart again, and deal with emotions she had put into a cold dark place. She did not know for sure she could ever get them back, to have a normal life like most women, but her life was never normal from a very young age, and the damage to her might not be reversible, from mental and emotional points of view. During the time of the individual meetings with each team member, Romero Trap had completed his first basic cooking class and signed up for the next sequence. He was informed with the advancement the first change he would discover, is each person would be their own taste tester, with the assignments, but the cooking classes were still concentrated on everyday meals served in the majority of homes. His second stage classes would teach him more about the various spices and other items used for preparing simple meals. None of the classes offered by the school were at gourmet or professional chef level, which was something taught outside of high school level cooking, at a much higher cost to participate. It also required being able to prepare some more exotic meals, without guidance prior to being accepted.

Romero Trap did not believe he wanted to go that far into cooking, and did not realize just how much work was involved in preparing and making meals. It did give him a little more understanding why the cost of restaurant prepared meals, were so much higher than making items for yourself. It largely involved the amount of labor involved for people paid to make meals for others.

During the next five months, Romero Trap continued his cooking classes and had learned enough to know what items he would need to obtain for his own home, which were rather extensive, including all the various spices and other items used in the cooking process. Different oils, flour, corn starch and bread crumbs were the most common although there were a few other grains substituted for breading, he found breading to be the easier of the choices. He learned about deep frying as a means for certain foods, but found it was a rather messy proposition, and required extensive clean up afterwards. He was unsure about using the method in his own home, but it did provide a better flavoring than simply pan frying the same type of foods. The President had convinced one other stubborn leader to join the world governing council, which brought the total number of countries committed to the program, to eighty-five percent. The remaining fifteen percent were hinged upon the other four leaders, who were obstinate, and refused to budge on their misunderstanding of the concept. No amount of diplomacy or persuasion swayed their opinion on the true purpose of the world governing council. The final State of the Union speeches were given by President Thomas Hardesty and Romero Trap. Once again it was an all-day bore fest, which wore Romero Trap out far more than any activity pertaining to his true professional calling.

The team had a relatively relaxing in home vacation. They traveled about the city often in pairs, for dinners and other entertainment. There was no more real improvements to make to the property, and with a change in ownership, they all felt it was money wasted. Largely because none of them planned on becoming members of the team after eight years of this assignment. The door was not entirely closed, as some like Romero Trap, did not know if they were suited for a life away from their professional trade. They were all willing to give it an attempt, especially those who had families and children they wanted to be a part of their lives, if it was not too late already.

It was not until seven months remained on the President's final term in office, which Thomas Hardesty requested Romero Trap and his team remove the final four leaders, who were preventing the formation of a unified world governing council. The biggest problem was in North Korea, and was keeping all but one of the surrounding nations, from committing to the formation of the council. A second was Germany, whose leader was desperately trying to revive a time long past, and preferably never to return to the planet.

A third was in eastern Europe, again within reach of the Russian borders and it appeared the replacement leader of the one in Belarus, was molded from the same cloth as the one eliminated previously. He held sway over many of his smaller neighboring countries.

The final piece to the puzzle was rather confusing, since the Canadians had always felt inclined to follow suit with the US and Britain in governing policies, but not this time. For some reason the Canadian leadership felt the world governing council would open the door for the US to absorb the entire nation, into one of their own. President Thomas Hardesty was not in the least bit interested in expanding the borders of the country, with a much smaller government, that was making good headway in reducing its deficit, which had been out of control for at least three decades.

Romero Trap only asked how this was to be done without a bounty, which did not really produce any difficulties financially with the team. His concern was if there was any expected collateral damage along with the leader who presented the problem to a world governing council. President Thomas Hardesty informed Romero Trap under no circumstance did he need to remove anyone one outside of the leader. His death ought to be more than sufficient for the message to make its point. He was certain, that the leaders of each country were receiving council from within, to change his course of action, since they saw greater benefits in a more unified means of countries to diplomatically discuss events pertaining to their own nation.

Romero Trap's only other question was whether this was the last assignment he and his team would need to undertake, while he and the President finished out the last of their term in office. President Thomas Hardesty foresaw no other obstacles to overcome over the remaining seven months, and said if Romero Trap liked, those he did not need for this final mission, could be released from his team, to go onto living their lives without government interference.

Romero Trap said he would discuss it with his team, and should have his answer within the next day or two at the most. Romero Trap already had an idea of who to select for each of the four assignments. The methods would be different for at least three of them. The Canadian leader had a long history of infidelity, which his wife only tolerated due to the life of luxury she was afforded by his position. He had a penchant for young women, and made no effort to hide his fondness for them. Zoe was the perfect candidate for just such a person, and it was merely a matter of how much it was going to cost him to have her take the assignment.

The North Korean leader was going to be somewhat different, by using a close quarter's expert, armed with merely a poisoned dart to take out his target. The poisoned dart was quite effective, he could disguise it being much closer than any other method, and regardless of where the dart struck its victim, the result were rapid for a human after the initial paralysis. Chu Fong (Dart) was the most likely candidate, as he would not be terribly out of place in a crowd in that region of the world.

Romero Trap had already contacted a military commander concerning obtaining title to seized property. It was the method that needed to be used in order to obtain a clear title of a vehicle. Regardless of which agency of the government seized the property, the process was time consuming. Although government had been streamlined with Thomas Hardesty, there were still areas within government, where the red tape was extensive and prolonged action being completed. Titles would be available for the three vehicles after at least three months, and before the base of operations had new ownership.

Susan Hobart (Hummer) would get the German assignment, as a long range shooter. She would require both a driver and a spotter, whereas Zoe would likely work solo, and Chu Fong would only require a driver. Romero Trap knew that Jackson Frye (Heartless) would be needed for the cargo plane trip one last time, to accommodate the movement of vehicles, and people to other parts of the world. Whether he remained on the ground, or planned to return to DC to make shuttle trips, was at his discretion.

The final choice was also going to long rifle, as Belarus was unlikely to get anyone close enough to the leader for another type of assassination. He decided that Shorty Johansen (Eyes) was the most effective person for that operation, and he would also need a driver and a spotter.

Upon his completion of the White House luncheon, Romero Trap went to the base of operation, and held a group meeting for what should be the final assignment for their eight year mission. It was never definite, so as a result until into the final month, the team would receive their retirement pension for a well-earned life away from the rigors of the profession, they all were members of for too long of a time. He laid out the general plan concept to the entire team, knowing he would likely have a lengthy conversation with Zoe Dubois (Black Widow) in more private surroundings. He asked the four primary selected team members to choose their own supporting members to accompany them, for the highest comfort level among the entire group, for each of the three assignments requiring support personnel. They had until the next day to give him a decision, equally agreeable to all the team members. At that point, he would give the President his final approval and acceptance of the mission. He made certain that no bounty was to be collected to try to keep it more confidential among the eighty-five percent of the countries, already committed to a world governing council. If they were not made aware of this program earlier, this was the ultimate goal of President Thomas Hardesty's legacy as a United States President, to go along with all his other achievement in his eight years as President. One of which, was regaining the confidence of the American people who were no longer anywhere close to another revolution within the country. With the Senator from Wyoming's removal, his confidence rating from the people grew to 95 percent, and maintained that percentage, since shortly after the Senator was eliminated.

With that completed, Romero Trap departed for his cooking lesson.

While Romero Trap was away for his cooking lesson, the team of selected people outside of Zoe, discussed among themselves who wished to be a part of the teams, and those who preferred to stay in DC to take care of communications and the other duties of a team being away, for an unknown duration. Satellite imagery was also being brought up into researching best locations for each job, and the times the satellite were in position. Belarus was the one most observed of the three, while Germany was lowest, outside of Canada which had virtually none. It was understandable, since Canada has always been far more ally than opposition, to the direction the US went in government policies.

The volunteers were limitless, as everyone wanted to be involved in the final mission if in fact, it were. As a result, those selected as the mission's prime candidate, choose those who they were most comfortable with, as well as felt could be beneficial to the accomplishment of the assignment. With Cho Fong who only require a driver but needed another team member who would not be out of place in North Korea, chose Shaq Lee (Stealth) for two reasons. He was a good driver, and in the event that Chu Fong could not accomplish the assignment, Shaq might be able to if they did a double team at the point of making the hit of the target.

Shorty Johansen (Eyes) selected Lacy Louis (Pricker) for his spotter, largely because she had never experienced a long range rifle kill. It would provide her with a number of different perspectives to her own skills. First, would be the precision involved with figuring out where to target a person from a distance where wind, velocity, humidity and wind direction, all played a role in pulling the trigger, and Murray Golic (Cyclone) as his driver. He figured nobody in their right mind would try anything abnormal with Murray.

Trap Johnson, who at the start of the assignment wanted nothing to do with Hummer, volunteered to be her spotter and she accepted. He found Hummer to be rather modest, considering her impressive accomplishments in long range shooting. He expected far more of a braggart than she was in reality, and thought he might try to learn something from someone, considered to be the very best in her and his trade. It may be of no consequence, if he retired never to return, but he like many others, wondered if he and retirement would be in agreement, so he kept the option open. Hummer thought in going to Germany, she would follow up with the concept started by Eyes, and have her driver be the other behemoth Feliz Ramirez (Turmoil), like Murray, few people in the world would make any attempt to make him mad. Turmoil was shorter in height, but more massive in muscular girth. He would also not be so out of place in Germany, as Spanish and Portuguese people were not as rare as in Belarus.

The departing teams were decided upon before Romero Trap returned the following day.

17

The Final Assignment

The following afternoon Romero Trap arrived at his normal time, having completed a half day White House session, including the wonderful luncheons served everyday by the more than adequate Presidential chef of the White House kitchen. The team provided him with the members who were going to go on the assignment's four locations, although Romero Trap still needed to have his private conversation with the Black Widow. The rest of the team were already looking into the satellite imagery available for the three locations, although it appeared Germany only had a one hour window over a twenty-four hour period. The good thing was, it was during daylight hours and they did not need to use infrared to determine anything pertaining to Germany. Belarus had nearly twelve hours coverage at a fifty percent mix of daylight and infrared. North Korea was largely outside of daylight hours, but it did provide one hour for more specific identification of locations the leader randomly visited. Both Belarus and North Korea's leaders spent a good amount of time in open air rally speeches. To generate more support and to get the people behind what their leader was trying to do for their country, although it was slanted to his own perceptions of the world, which were largely in total error.

All this had taken place in the past twenty two hours, and was on going with obtaining the best and most current information concerning the three targets, outside of this continent. Germany, North Korea, and Belarus would all require additional surveillance once people were in place, to insure a best time and location, to accomplish the mission. Jackson Frye had guaranteed all the aircraft were flight ready, and would be ready to go when it was decided on the time for departure. Jackson Frye stated considering the fact the duration from each separate assignment was considerably variable in duration, he would take all three in the departing flight, to their closest drop off point, and return to DC, when he had an idea of when to return for who and where. Romero Trap did not argue his input, realizing he would have to cover more fuel costs, but such was the case in this type of profession. He figured it would cost no more than 250 million dollars for all the expenses, include lodging and food for his people away from the base of operations.

After his update, he finally got to have his conversation with Zoe Dubois. Once they were away from everyone else, Romero Trap went right to the point and asked Zoe how much it was going to cost him for her part in this assignment. Zoe Dubois said, she had taken many factors into consideration, normally for such a high profile political figure her normal fee was 50 million dollars. She only paused momentarily to say, but considering the generous pension plan promised, she decided to do it for her nominal 15 million dollar fee for every assignment that required her special abilities. Romero Trap was fully prepared to pay the 50 million dollar fee, as he included that and a little more in his estimate to Frye. He said he did not really care which method she employed, whether it was by one of her favored poisons, or preferred method of the syringe up close and personal, but the requirements were definite, concerning how her target should be discovered. He should be fully disrobed, whether after or in anticipation he did not care, but it needed to appear he died trying to indulge in his favorite vice. It would work out best for his wife, that way she was not really a part of the collateral damages of this assassination. It would be highly preferable, if it was at somewhere other than his home, to avoid that possibility altogether. Zoe Dubois confirmed she understood all the requirements, and asked

THE FINAL ASSIGNMENT

when she was expected to leave and specifically where, Canada was a large amount of ground.

Trap said her target was largely in Montreal, which was common for the government to remain in areas more French Canadian, than where Canadians in favor of the English speaking people of the country were located. It was one of the closer targets and she could take the Lincoln, unless she preferred a driver to accompany her. She said she could drive without a chauffeur, and it would probably work better that way; if she appeared to be too pampered, the Canadian leader might feel out of his league. Trap certainly was out of his element when taking Zoe's observations into consideration for an assignment. Most of his assignments prior to becoming the independent team manager, was fairly straight forward and gender played no part in it. It was a mission that normally ended with his objective dead in some fashion or another, but Trap had his own methods, as did Zoe Dubois. She did have more of a specialty in her profession than Trap did himself, but he also understood why she was, what she was.

After the private meeting with Zoe Dubois, she took the Lincoln out of the building used as the garage, and went on a little shopping excursion. In order for a woman such as Zoe Dubois to accomplish her assignment, she always found she had to look the part as well. To be an enticing vixen to the male population, she had to dress the part to go along with her exotic beauty. It was simply how it worked for her line of work, she could not be a provocateur in baggy and unrevealing clothing, and her assignments often resulted in a few more dresses that caught the eyes of the opposite gender. If she walked out of an apparel store with a new dress, and immediately got the attention of the opposite gender with her emergence, she knew she made a wise selection for her intended target. Since the requirements for her profession were considerably different than most of the team, it was why she had to set a rather high fee for her assignments.

She had, like everyone else collected her weekly one thousand dollar salary over the nearly seven and a half years, but she had to hold herself to higher standards for the tasks, she was one of few people who could accomplish them. She also learned long before Romero Trap brought up numbered accounts, due to the nature of her income, it was best to keep it somewhere more difficult to trace to her. From her earnings over the last 18 years as the Black Widow, she owned her own home, bought and paid for before she ever entered it and furnished it. It was a home, people with money would purchase, and although it was not considered a mansion, it was quite large and had manicured landscaping. Everything was done for her. She had a housekeeper, cook and landscaper take care of everything she needed done, whether she was in the home or not. Even without the pension from Romero Trap, she had from her profession amassed nearly 2 billion dollars in two numbered accounts. Both had good earnings, and she only transferred so much into a normal account to take care of day to day expenses, which included payment to those who took care of the house.

She returned later that afternoon almost evening, with her packages and was preparing for her departure for Montreal. Trap had not given her any timeline, but thought since she was operating this assignment entirely solo, it was at her discretion, and planned to depart the day after next. The other assignments were still gathering intelligence, but she only needed to find her target in a public place, and entice him into a compromising position. It was something she had plenty of experience with, and could easily convince the target to get a suite or hotel room to see where it might lead.

Romero Trap had finished up his day with the team, and departed for his evening meal to take home to his apartment in order to perform a little work on the computer. With time for the team to be paid their retirement pensions, it was time to organize the six numbered accounts. He also thought in order to make it a nice round number with 36 team members and himself, he would give President Thomas Hardesty an equal amount to bring the total pension outgoing to nineteen billion dollars. He would place the largest amount of the remainder of 392 billion dollars, into two of the six accounts and leave one billion dollars in each of the other four. He also had to transfer one billion to his replacement or hand over one account to him. He was not decided, but thought since his accounting was sequential it would be wiser to transfer

THE FINAL ASSIGNMENT

it to his replacement to prevent anyone unwittingly finding the other accounts.

After eating his dinner from the local delicatessen and small restaurant, he went about rearranging the accounts leaving 2 billion in one, one billion in two, 20 billion in the account to be use for pension payouts. That left over 150 billion for the two primary accounts to gain earnings, which over the next 6 months should cover all the expenses without any additional losses to the accounts. He only was keeping the accounts in the event retirement and he did not agree with one another.

Having never really thought much about retirement until this last year or so, he had no idea what to expect, or whether he could find ways to occupy his free time, since it was not something he ever had previously. He only thought his time in the profession of removing obstacles had reached its end. He wanted to retire, before he gained a conscience that would interfere with the profession he had so long been involved with.

After addressing the team's finances, Romero Trap poured himself a nice bourbon, and used it to for the purpose of relaxing to go and get some sleep.

Over the next week, every one of the other three assignments had gathered as much intelligence as they could, without being in their specific regions. Jackson Frye was put on notice to be ready for departure, although the German team would be using the Range Rover, since it would not be as out of place as a military issue jeep. Both North Korea and Belarus teams could, it would not draw attention to the jeeps, as they were relatively common vehicles in both regions. They may not have been the same manufacturer as those in the region, but the similarities would not be considered so abnormal. The following day, the cargo plane was loaded with three vehicles and eight people for the three teams with Jackson piloting the cargo plane. One additional person went along to act as co-pilot, but the team of ten could easily unload vehicles and equipment to make stops as quick as possible. The longest part of some stops would be the refueling time which worked at the speed of the airfield or airport they used. From Washington DC the first stop was in neutral Switzerland, for a refueling stop only, to go onto

Germany for the first team to disembark, and set up closer surveillance on their target. From there it was near Belarus, but not within the borders as there would be far too many suspicious people in the airfield. It was also the second refueling, so it took a bit longer to disembark the team members leaving, although the largest delay was refueling.

The final leg of the journey for Jackson Frye and co-pilot was Korea, and once again they had to disembark in more neutral grounds. The travel for the vehicles was not excessively longer, but there was no reason to raise suspicions of the country that held their target. It was decided that refueling would be wise, since the distance was father than it appeared in flight plans. That was more a result of no fly zones than the actual distance between countries, but the detour consumed more fuel than Jackson anticipated. With his last group of the team leaving the cargo plane, it was decided to retrace their flight plan and stop at all the same locations returning. It made things simpler by not having to check for other location to safely land for refueling. It would entail one extra stop at the nearby airfield for refueling, before returning to the DC base hanger in the abandoned airfield.

During the week of surveillance and the dispatch of the three teams, Zoe had completed her assignment. The Canadian leader was easy prey to entice into a possible bedroom performance for the Canadian leader. Zoe was prepared to take action by both poison and syringe, but the Canadian leader was easiest to dispatch with poison. He had no problems in anticipation of the rewards to follow in having room service bring a bottle of fine French Champaign, to make the activity to follow a little more pleasant, at least in his mind. Zoe had the opportunity to place a small amount of poison in the Canadian leader's glass of Champaign, so she could actually partake of the fine sparkling wine, to give the leader no clue of what was to unfold.

She went through her little tease of slowing undressing in front of the Canadian leader, after he had drank some of his poisoned beverage, Zoe knew she only had so much time to get the Canadian leader to also prepare for more to follow, and she encouraged him to get ready by the time she had finished her little dance. Five minutes before she was finished, with the Canadian leader fully expecting to partake in the pleasures of Zoe's companionship, he drop over dead on the bed. Zoe did not so much as need to reposition him, and she quickly redressed herself, and departed the hotel suite to leave the Canadian leader to be discovered in the morning by housekeeping.

Zoe Dubois (Black Widow) was back to the DC base of operations, before any other team had finished up surveillance of their target for the best opportunity. The other teams were still gathering intelligence on their targets, but the Belarus and North Korea made frequent public appearance speeches, in the open forum arrangements to get support and encourage the people to believe in their leadership. Both were a little more random about where the events took place. They had identified locations to expect their victim to appear, and Chu Fong with the aid of Shaq Lee had gotten themselves into position for an open forum meeting, with neither standing more than fifty feet from where the North Korean leader was expected to give his speech. They were not out of place, since they had the correct physical features of the vast majority, even though they were of a different nationality. The best line of the poison dart was available to Chu Fong, and once the speech started, he waited for a duration where applause would seem imminent, before bringing his small tube and dart into place, and once fired he feigned a sneeze to disguise his weapon, and return it to his pocket as he reached for a handkerchief, to cover his face from the faked actions. The North Korean leader was immobilized immediately, the small dart stuck center mass in his torso, and it would take close observation to find it. The expected ensuing panic of the crowd quickly followed, and they got lost in the crowd, to return to the vehicle they left for their departure.

They were the first to call using the burner phone for a time to meet for returning to base.

Belarus was not much more complicated, and Shorty Johansen (Eyes) had pinpointed a location from where to take his long rifle shot, with the aid of Lacy Louis (Pricker) as his spotter. She learned quickly how to read the digital device to give Eyes the information most necessary for him to make a precise shot. It was only the day after Chu Fong completed his mission, although he did not know that. He was waiting for the Belarus leader to make his appearance, and from 1200 yards, it should not be terribly difficult, but the wind was a little brisker than he would have liked, but he learned well from Hummer how to make the adjustments for distance, humidity and wind velocity and direction. He had it all dialed in, waiting for the moment the Belarus leader would take his position and start his speech. Fortunately, he could not understand a word of the local language, or else he might have gotten upset with the speech that was only about how the West was meddling in affairs they had no business in, and spent a large amount of time bad mouthing President Thomas Hardesty. This was the leader's response to his people for the efforts President Hardesty employed, to bring them into the fold of a world governing council.

Ten minutes into his speech, Shorty Johansen (Eyes) took his shot, which was clean entering the Belarus leader's forehead just above the eyes, and the ordeal for the Belarus leader was a done deal. He quickly dismantled his rifle after returning all the adjustments back to normal, and the pair on the roof 1,200 yards from the panic area, quickly left the building to the awaiting jeep and driver. He used his burner phone to confirm the assignment completed, and was told the plane would be there the next morning after making the pickup for the North Korean team.

The team would return within one month of the assignment being accepted and intelligence gathered. The only person not done at that point was Hummer, who had a more reclusive target and like the other teams out, did not understand a single word of the local language. It was nearly six weeks into her futile surveillance attempts, before she found the local government channel on her hotel video system. It has alternative languages available, and although she had to read at the bottom of the screen what was being said, she learned in two weeks, the German leader was giving a speech at a specific location. The following morning, she tried to get an idea of where the German leader would be and could see from the location given, that her opportunities would be limited. The leader would exit his vehicle, walk the half dozen steps to the building the speech was given, and enter the building after the short top level from the steps to the entrance. At best she had 30 seconds from a precise location, to take her shot.

THE FINAL ASSIGNMENT

From that point, she checked the surroundings and spotted a building that would be able to allow clean visibility to the entrance point, as well as all the steps. It would be best to take the shot the precise moment he cleared the final step. Movement by her target would be less erratic. She and her team members made their way to the building location, which appeared to be nearly 1500 yards away. At a higher elevation from the ground, the difference should be nominal since projectiles from such a weapon, did not consider elevation an obstacle but more of an aid.

The team found three access points to the roof, first and easiest was the elevator to the top floor with the hall and half stairway to the roof exit. This would make egress faster and easier, but with a weapon in hand, it was not wise to use this means to enter the building. There was both an internal stairway and fire escape, with all doors unlocked, this was a very important factor in using a building, and locked doors meant wasted efforts if you get to the top, and cannot open the door. A large percentage of US public access buildings, used the stairway as a fire escape, and made each floor an exit only, once the door closed, you had no option but to descend to the lowest level to reenter the building through the standard methods, often the elevator. It meant the problem that caused the use of emergency evacuation, had to be resolved before people were allowed to enter the building again. The most common cause was a fire, whether real or not was not always determined by the emergency crews responding. A defective smoke alarm, could just as easily be the source of a fire alarm as a real fire, but cautionary measures were always taken first, especially in taller buildings.

Hummer found many foreign building structures were not locked, and not used as evacuation methods only. It made her wonder at times, how security conscience building owners really were, but since she did not live there, it was not much of a concern. For what was required of her as a professional, it only made the job easier to complete, and that was her foremost objective.

Before her opportunity arrived to complete her assignment, all the other team members had already returned to the DC area base of operations. It was not that she was slow in completing her assignment, as much as it was the others had targets who were far more predictable. It was all a portion of how the assignments worked out, and she felt not in the least bit guilty, that she would be the last to return. Romero Trap applied absolute zero pressure in completing the assignment, this was largely in part that with the President of the United States being the sole person to choose assignments, he did not have alternate teams of independent contractors trying to complete the identical mission. He had complete faith that Romero Trap would get the job completed in the timeliest fashion allowable. Since Romero Trap always allowed for some flexibility in his assignments, not a single person ever assigned to his team disappointed him. Romero Trap fully understood not all circumstance were ideal when it came to their professional trade. Romero Trap never concerned himself with it, largely because he made sure he had only the very best and treated them as if they were.

With the location decided upon by Hummer, it was now only a matter of waiting for the time to arrive. Almost two weeks could cause a change in schedule or even a cancellation, if something more imminent raised its head. It was the chance Hummer and her team would be forced to take, since this was the soonest possible public appearance by the German leader. As a result, they took turns keeping an eye on the local government news channel. They knew fully well, if something occurred while the three went to have dinner or something, it would be repeated more than the single first occurrence to the change in plans.

Meanwhile back at the ranch, or Washington DC, with only five months remaining on the President and Vice-Presidents term in office. There were all sorts of demand being placed upon them for endorsing successors. Since Thomas Hardesty was forced to leave his party due to lack of support; to run as an independent candidate, and Romero Trap had no previous party ties whatsoever, they solved the entire issue by placing internet posts to that effect, and added they believed the people were now more capable of making the best decision, for someone to continue in the path set by Thomas Hardesty, than at any time in the past.

Thomas Hardesty did put an addendum into his policy on length of term, that any person currently holding office between term lengths,

THE FINAL ASSIGNMENT

could maintain the position until all members of politics were in the same four year term lengths. It meant virtually none of the people currently in the House of Representatives could run for President, since they were between six and eight years. The next round of incoming political candidates would all be newcomers to a political office. It would limit how much damage a new member to office could inflict upon the people, who had the right now, to use the powers given them by the Constitution, and fire any politician not performing in the best interest of the people they represented. That included the President and his Vice President, who were the only matched set in the office structure. The representatives worked on behalf of half of the state they represented, and therefore were not considered a matched set. It was unlikely any state would remove both representatives simultaneously. The only way that could occur, was if the pair worked in conjunction with one another while holding office. Not inconceivable, but also not highly probable. President Thomas Hardesty had put a good deal of thought and preparation into the bills he presented to the people, to bypass the government bureaucracy at the time he took office. He did an excellent job according to the people of the country he was asked to represent. It was also something his predecessors had forgotten. They had spent far too many years taking advantage of the people, who put them into the office in the beginning of their careers.

Politics according to the Constitution and Bill of Rights, were never meant to be lifelong careers, they were meant to serve the country in ways otherwise unobtainable. It was never intended to be a means to make a comfortable living, by taking advantage of the very people you were supposed to represent as their political voice. When Thomas Hardesty first took office, this was the mindset of the vast majority of people, who held office from President to Congress.

Also, While Hummer was still trying to complete her assignment, and the other teams had returned, the President informed Romero Trap with Korea and Belarus leaders removed, the country and its surrounding neighbors, although not formally entered into the world governing council had committed to joining. It brought the world governing council to 98 percent of all the world's nations, either formally members or committed to joining the council. That left Germany, and the neighboring countries it held influence over, as well as Canada, but that was expected anytime soon.

Hummer was as patient as any in the world in long range rifle assassinations, but waiting around in a hotel room, and watching the local government news broadcast, she was reaching her breaking point in that department. She would rather be perched in a tree or awaiting her target to emerge, while sitting atop a roof top of a commercial style building. The difference being, that most commercial buildings had flat roofing to accommodate other equipment associated with the building, many residential structures had too much slant to the roofline, to get into a stable position. At least a tree had branches capable of lying on while in wait. Not all trees, but the older and larger variety had branches nearly as wide as the trunk.

In her state of agitation from waiting, she had to get out of the hotel room and simply go for a walk, to get some form of exercise. She actually considered making it a jog like when she was in the military, where everywhere was at a quicker pace with up to 70 pounds of gear strapped on. She did not miss the extra weight of the gear, but admitted to herself, it did make one a little more prepared for a long night of sleep. Susan Hobart took a walk that lasted for one hour, although without 70 pounds of extra weight she was hardly ready for some sleep, she at least felt less like a chicken in a small wire pen. Hummer returned to the waiting room, known as her hotel room, checked with whether anything had changed, since tomorrow would be the morning to go get into position for an expected arrival of the German leader at near noon. It was best for Hummer and her spotter to be in place a full hour or more ahead of the target, to minimize any errors and to be absolutely certain of weather conditions. Weather conditions could be stable or variable, but the factors needed to be known, and if possible, to have a duration for alterations especially with wind speed and direction. Going from a calm sunny day to a torrential downpour with gusty winds, was about the only thing that could prevent Hummer from getting her shot.

She did feel more herself after her walk, and not being cooped up for nearly two weeks outside of a relatively nice dinner with her other team members. Lunch and breakfast were brought to the rooms through room service, and all three of them had spent far too much time sitting, watching and waiting. The news broadcast brought no change in the expected speech of the German leader. The team went to bed in their separate rooms, and Hummer got a good night's rest, something needed, to be fully prepared and alert for the following day.

Most everyone was up by seven in the morning, and after a quick check into the news, they all went to the hotel restaurant for a better breakfast than could be obtained through room service. The entire team had a breakfast large enough to skip lunch and maybe even dinner, but it was necessary for Hummer to maintain a high energy level and be on ultimate alert level physically and even higher mentally. People who never waited two hours for a split second opportunity to take a kill shot, had no idea how much energy a person used while spilling over weather condition information and understanding exactly what to expect from the weapon used. Every shooter made some modifications to their weapon that made it unique. Hummer knew, she could not just pick up someone else's weapon and expect the identical results and reactions as her own. She knew every inch of her own, the feel of the stock, the weight distribution from one end to the tip of barrel, including the difference with the barrel extension in place. Breakfast took the team nearly one hour from taking their seat, until taking care of the charges. Rather than have things put on their room charges, they took care of things individually, knowing they all had a final checkout charge to deal with, although they should have enough money from expenses provided, to take care of them. Hummer did not think she would be in Germany quite as long as the team had been. It was never an easy single day trip when surveillance was required.

From the hotel restaurant they went to their SUV, and headed to the building that was selected for the shot to take place from. It was still fifteen hundred yards away from the location the German leader would enter, and under such typical conditions for any person of importance, security for a trip from a limousine to a building entrance, seldom went beyond 300 yards for the perimeter people. They arrived at the building an hour and forty five minutes before the leader was anticipated to arrive.

It took nearly twenty minutes to take the two bags, and make the climb from the ground level floor to the roof, using the fire escape. It was not the easiest climb, but it was the one that would most likely go unnoticed by people who happened to pass by after making it up the first two levels. Stopping during the climb was the biggest factor in why it took so long, they did not stop because they were tired, they stopped not to attract attention of people below on the street. Once in the best visibility location, Hummer took her weapon from the bag, and assembled it in a matter of ten minutes, taking care to make certain every piece was fully locked into place. Breakdown of the same weapon could be done in less than a minute. It was far more important to make sure the weapon was ready upon assembly, would not malfunction due to a single piece not properly locked into place.

Once in position, the pair, spotter and Hummer, had a little over an hour before the German leader was expected to arrive in front of the targeted building. Hummer had her spotter start taking reading with the digital device that instantly determined all the variables that needed to be adjusted for. The day was sunny and very calm, the humidity was low enough to be a non-factor for taking the shot. The wind if any was barely perceptible making in so the only adjustment Hummer needed to make was for the distance from the end of the barrel, to the point of impact on the target. Under the conditions and the distance, she only needed to make a single click up for the projectile to penetrate her intended target. As the pair waited, Hummer had the spotter taking continuous readings as was precautionary, but it seemed unnecessary to her spotter. The spotter asked why she needed to keep track of so many readings. She informed him it was simply to insure nothing had changed to cause any additional adjustment for the single bullet rifle. Missing was never an option, and only resulted in people getting caught or unable to complete the assignment. You could never have too much information even if it appeared to be the same every time you took the readings. Trap Johnson now understood what made Hummer so much better than most anyone else in the long range rifle profession.

He had learned his most valuable lesson since the first day he became a part of a military sniper team. He was never told to take readings continuously while he was waiting, conditions could change in a moment's notice, and be the difference between a clean kill and a missed assignment. Hummer had taken the time to explain that to him, although he was considered pretty good with the long range rifle, she was deservedly the best. He felt now he had the potential to be as good as Hummer.

The wait included additional weather checks every minute, and nothing had changed for the entire hour they were waiting for the German leader to make his appearance. Trap Johnson had spotted the lights of the arriving escort in front of the leader's limousine, and informed Hummer to be on her toes. She thanked him and asked for one last weather reading that again proved no changes.

The limousine pulled up in front of the building as indicated on the local government news broadcast. Hummer took her position at the fullest state of readiness and using her sights, watching for the German leader to exit the vehicle. Before he got out there were half of a dozen security people posted around the limousine, but only one at the door to open it for the German leader. Once the door opened, the next closest security detail member joined the one opening the door, and they walked on each side of the leader to go from the limousine to the front entrance door. Hummer watched carefully to time the gait the German leader took with the steps. As his head reach the last step which was entrance level, she squeezed the trigger ever so gently. The bullet impacted the back of the German leader's head center mass, which was a clean kill from that angle. There was a good deal of blood splatter and brain tissue exiting the front of the head that was once a face. Hummer saw all she needed to see to know a confirmed kill when she saw one, and Trap Johnson could make no argument against it either. Hummer quickly reset the single click back to fully normal, and dismantled her weapon to place inside the small bag, until the next time. Trap Johnson and Susan Hobart quickly made their way to the roof top exit door, and went down the steps from the inside of the building this time, to reach ground level in two and one half minutes from the time the trigger was squeezed. The SUV was ready to go, the driver heard the shot, and had it started and ready when they got in.

They left the building in the appearance of no particular hurry; it was essential to keep from receiving attention they did not want. They returned to the hotel room to make the burner phone communication back to base, to confirm the assignment had been completed, and told the following afternoon the cargo plane would be in Switzerland at the airfield they landed at. A specific time was not given, it did mean they could go through checkout in the morning, pack up everything after dinner, and be ready to leave by 11 AM to get to the airfield.

The Germany team enjoyed two very good meals in the hotel restaurant, since they had no additional details hovering over their heads with the assignment being completed. The room video systems did not have any more government news broadcast to watch, which each and every one of the team members enjoyed, since the government news was boring and tedious. While they packed up their belongings in each of their own room, the video had a movie each wished to watch while they packed up their articles to return to base. They all got a good night's sleep, and had breakfast the following morning before going through check out at the hotel, to finalize their charges.

As planned, they were in the SUV at 11 AM, and started making the trip to the Switzerland airfield where the cargo plane landed to drop them off. Traffic was a bit heavier than expected, but did not keep them from arriving at the airfield, at 12:30 PM local time. They knew the time was different in Washington DC area, but none were concerned about what time it was there, they would find out when they arrived. The cargo plane did not touch down until 1:30 PM, and needed a full load of fuel for the return trip, as well as a refueling close to the DC area hanger they kept the aircraft. It would not be ready until 2:30 PM, so once Jackson Frye located them, the four went for a quick lunch, nothing too exotic, since the airfield did not offer fine cuisine, more of a cafeteria style eating area. For the majority of the time, the people most likely to have meals in the cafeteria were employed in some fashion at the airfield. Some were airfield employees such as the refueling personnel and tanker drivers. They did have a few luggage people for smaller commercial aircraft, although it was mostly commuter planes. They did have some buildings for cargo planes that brought in goods from other areas to be distributed locally. It was largely a temporary holding area for commercial delivery companies to pick up, and take to their own distribution centers, occasionally packages for individuals that required personal pick up in a limited time frame. There were also commercial services that had hangers and employees for their own maintenance and shops. It was fairly simple food available, but it was edible.

The cargo plane was loaded after refueling, and left the airfield at 3:15 PM in route to the DC area airfield for refueling, before the short hop to the hanger at the abandoned airfield. It was roughly a six hour flight mostly over the Atlantic Ocean and the cargo plane was stretching the airtime to near maximum, to accomplish it in a single fuel run. Only Jackson Frye was aware of that fact, as he did not inform others of the fuel situation when he was pilot. With a co-pilot, he let the other person read the gauges themselves, he did not need to point it out to him or her. Jackson Frye had encounter a few rather panicked co-pilots in his past, so he decided not to draw attention to the fuel situation anytime during the flight. Like a vehicle, as he grew more and more familiar with it, he pushed it to its limits. The trip from DC to Switzerland and the same on the return flight, were about as far as the plane could go and remain airborne. The wrong type of wind or weather, could change that with no options truly available.

At the DC airfield, it took another 45 minutes for refueling, but it was rather late for the airfield to be excessively busy. It was barely more than taking off and landing to get to the hanger at the abandoned airfield, to unload the single vehicle on board, and the three team members all taking their luggage. Jackson Frye had a regular jeep and it was simply easier to toss the luggage in the rear, while both vehicles made the short trip to the operations base. It was fairly late in the DC area, but the latest and last of the team members to return from their assignment, were not overly tired. With the last of the group back to the base of operations, there was only a mere four months left before Romero Trap and Thomas Hardesty would have replacements elected. The pair would still need to go through the formality of turning over the office keys to the next President and Vice President, whomever they might be.

With the team having everyone back, Romero Trap went over the accounts once again to find 4 had a base of 1 billion dollars, but had some earnings to up the ante a little bit. The other two accounts, had in excess of 150 billion dollars and Romero Trap was debating over an additional five hundred million for each team member, but he and the President would remain unchanged. He still had time to decide, while he was still attending basic cooking classes at the high school, and learned to at least have an understanding of what he needed to do in a kitchen. He learned the spices he liked and those he did not, but there were so many, that it took much more time than he really thought it would. He still did not do any fancy meals in the kitchen, and really did not know if he ever would. He could survive with what he knew, but it would not be meals guests would be dying to try. Not that he had many guests, but he was far enough along in his cooking learning that he could start finding the utensils he would need, once he had a home of his own. It was pointless to get them while in the apartment, just to move them later. It did mean his only cooking experience was while in class, unlike many others who went home to practice on what they learned and try new things.

He did not hide the fact from the very beginning he only knew how to put grounds and water into his coffee maker, which had a storage tank to keep the wait time nominal. He really did not like to wait half an hour for it to drip.

18

Short Timing

With four months left to the election to bring in new faces to the Presidency, Romero Trap though the old military terminology of a member on his way out, due for retirement, was an appropriate way to go about his remaining four months as Vice President. The general concept here, was to do as little as humanly possible in anticipation of being officially retired. Another way to look at it was to merely take up space until the moment arrived. President Thomas Hardesty was looking over his list of things to do as President from the very first day, and found he did not miss a single thing he intended to accomplish as President. He had taken the people from near revolution to content and happy, although it did not take place overnight. He reduced the size of government considerably, and turned a fair amount into a much more businesslike manner than ever existed previously. He completely removed some parts of government that contributed more towards the deficit, than towards a profit margin. He reduced the size of Senate and Congress to simply 100 state representatives at two members per state. He also made politicians, who were not already eligible toward a retirement program under the previous means, equal to the people in how they would be paid outside of a working career. He reduced time in office to a maximum of twelve years, once all those who spent careers in politics, left office. He transferred the extra funds of political retirement programs to the general fund for all people, why not the politicians as well. His crowning achievement would be the formal formation of a world governing council, where every country or nation had a say in the proceedings.

He for all intents and purposes, had met every goal he wished to achieve while holding the office of the President of the United States. Romero Trap told him that was way too much to put down for his epitaph, and hoped former President of the United States would suffice. If nothing else, it achieved a good laugh from President Thomas Hardesty, who also had to say that although Romero Trap's contributions to making it possible, would go unrecognized, he had as large of a part in it happening, as anyone else in the government. In all reality, Hardesty said, Trap was more vital in his role, than even himself.

Romero Trap simple felt he had served his President in the best way he could, but realized his time for duty to his country was coming to a closure, after forty two years. He had reach an age where he could no longer perform at the level he would expect from his team, and it was time for a change in leadership, which was already arranged. The rest of his team members for this eight year assignment in large part, had time left to do something beyond service to their country. It was time for families, and life away from removing obstacles in the path of the government. His best wish was none had developed a guilt trip from the things they had done for their country. As far as he was concerned, it would be better to go through post-traumatic stress disorder, than to get a guilt complex. And in facing the reality of things, what they did for the good of the country were not things to brag about. Probably a good reason the documents of government agencies were classified. Also, it was why many did not wish to have a conversation with anybody concerning the things they had done, whether considered an accomplishment or merely a completed assignment.

These were the issues of retirement for an assassin, and some dealt with it without any issues, and others could not live with themselves in looking back upon what they did for a living. Romero Trap only hoped the coping mechanism for while they did it, would stay active after they left the trade. Like so many other things in life, it was an individual that had the controls of what happened afterwards. Romero Trap only wished the best for the people who worked with and for him over the last twenty some years, although the numbers were fewer than when he first went independent.

Romero Trap only had a few more classes in cooking at the high school level remaining, before he had to determine whether he needed to move forward with it, which was largely costly if he proved he was worthy, which he did not feel he accomplished that in his basic cooking skills. He was able to make a large number of basic meals that would not result in his immediate death. To him, that was an accomplishment, since he never cooked anything prior to going basic classes. He had not spent an unreasonable amount of money to get the training, but he would not reach gourmet chef status at high school level cooking either. He could make himself breakfast, lunch and dinner, which was far more than he could prior to his lessons. And to be honest with himself, he had lived on things most people would be repulsed at the thought of eating. By the same token, he did not live a pampered life, and did what was necessary to survive in many cases. So, in his viewpoint, the worst thing he had done in his life, was to eat at the White House luncheon meal, which had done its job in spoiling him to some degree.

The days in an office of political value were winding down for both Romero Trap and Thomas Hardesty, and were much more relaxing than during the previous seven years and nine months. With many office holders also reaching the limits of how long they could hold office, things in the oval office had reached a calm, not felt in forty years. All the political activity was concentrated on the people of the United States to have someone else in office, other than the vast majority of those currently in the position. The good thing for the representatives, was there was no time involved in informing the next member of things they needed to know before assuming the office. It was only the President and Vice President, who had to endure that additional ordeal. More so for Thomas Hardesty than Romero Trap.

Time in office was getting short, and Romero Trap also knew time for any other assignments was running out as well. If something came to his attention from the President, he barely had enough time to plan and execute a plan, before the time to close operations for his team came upon them.

He brought the subject up with the President, who could only say he foresaw nothing more requiring of the talents of Romero and his team of experts. Romero Trap did not want to turn them loose too soon, and need to try to reassemble another group of specialists for a single mission. This exact conversation took place each day until there were only 90 days left, before a new president would be elected to office, that president would nominate his own vice president. Romero Trap never figured out why exactly all of the representative positions and the president, were elected by the people and the vice president was selected by the president alone. It was the second highest office in the nation, and yet it was filled by the decision of a single individual, over all the voices of the people in the nation.

Romero Trap in the 89th remaining day, asked President Thomas Hardesty the exact question concerning the vice president selection. Thomas Hardesty explained it was because the President had to have the utmost faith in his right hand man to follow through with the plans set in motion, by the president should anything make the president incapable of fulfilling his duties as the nation's leader. History had people die in office, either by natural causes or assassination, a couple had debilitating illnesses that made them unfit for the demands of the highest office in the land. To his knowledge, that was the sole reason for the vice president being handpicked by the president.

Romero Trap also made all of his cooking lessons, and daily trips to the base of operations. His trips to the base were largely to see how his team members were coping with no assignments, and the high probability there were no more. Additionally, time was running out for an assignment to have sufficient time to complete, before he and the president were no longer holding office.

On the evening of the 61st day remaining to Romero Trap and Thomas Hardesty's eight-year run in the Oval Office. Romero Trap decided to transfer not 500 million dollars to each team members numbered accounts, but 1 billion dollars to each for a total of 36 billion dollars, plus one half billion to his own and one provided to Thomas Hardesty. The total of 37 billion dollars now left three funds with about 1.5 billion left in the account for the original amount, with the earnings and investment continuing to accrue as well as 130 billion dollars in each of the two major accounts. Somewhere buried deep in the CIA archive records, was the name of the shell company used by Romero Trap and his team, as well as the sequential file records on the numbered accounts, which also got the investment earnings shown in the records, all they ever had to do was figure out the shell company was used, and had numbered accounts affiliates with it. Since they were not formally informed of it when he worked in the CIA, he felt no obligation to let them become aware of it now. They were going to have to dig through all of their own archived information to find it, and it was something while he was there, was all but forgotten about with more current and pressing issues. In addition, Thomas Hardesty had combined all the agencies under the single title of the Marshall's Services.

The following afternoon upon his arrival, he informed everyone their pension payments were sent to the numbered account, they each had provided, and they could pack their belongings, and go onto a new life away from this profession, if they so desired. He wished them all the very best and told them it had been a pleasure to work with such professionals, but at nearly 65 years of age, his days in this profession had reached its end, at least as far as being able to perform at the same level he expected from his team members. That being said, it was unfair to any of them to expect more than he himself could do any longer, and should leave the game behind him.

He did tell the team he made the deposits a little more than he originally told them, because of the wonderful job they all did, and how they helped shape the world to open the potential for a world governing council, and maybe some form of peace among the peoples of all nations.

Two week prior, the titles to the three vehicle arrived, and with the exception of Romero Trap, the other two planned to get temporary license plates, until the vehicle was in the state they lived. With the short notice of departure, both Zoe and Jackson Frye left in a jeep, to go get the item needed to drive to their respective homes the following morning. Romero Trap on the other hand, was allowed to get Government Issue plates, being one of the few benefits of being a former Vice President of the United States he could take advantage of, he got his to read simply VP 48 since government plates never expired, or required annual renewal fees. His plates arrived the same day as the titles did, and he still knew how to use hand tools to put them on the Porches Cayenne. He handed the keys to his other vehicle, which had seen its years, but was still kept in top form mechanically, to Lacy Louis in the event she would like to drive home, instead of fly and get a taxi.

Of the thirty six team members, all but Zoe would go into a life of retirement and never return to the profession, which was more than demanding at times. Jackson Frye would return to his family, and enjoy being around while his children finished growing up, and he felt he had missed out on enough of it already. He would never look back and totally forgot he was the only other person to know about the numbered accounts used for the team. It was not all that difficult to not think about the accounts, since during the entire eight years, only Romero Trap took care of them. He was only told early about them in the event Romero Trap could not be there when funds were needed for an assignment. Something they had found numerous ways to work around, including military acquisition/requisition for a large portion of what they needed. It was by far cheaper than doing it through the black market.

Romero Trap used his burner phone to contact his replacement for the property, who was just finishing an assignment in Virginia, and could be at the location by the following afternoon. With all the arrangements in place, most of the team was busy packing things up that belonged to them, although both Feliz Ramirez and Murray Golic told him the weapons they used, were not going to leave, since they would never get through security at an airport, which they would need to use to return to their own places. Romero Trap did not figure they would, but still left it to those departing to take whatever weapons they brought. A large number of people for that reason went and reserved one way rental vehicles, to drive home with their belongings, most of them kept their preferred weapons of choice, among their own possessions,

SHORT TIMING

instead of the secured area for armaments. The secured location in the main building had enough weapons and ammunition to start a small scale war, although that was never the purpose of Trap or his team of professionals. The armaments storage was for the primary purpose of removing obstacles that came from assignments, depending on the nature of the assignment, often decided on how much was required to complete the assignment, and have everyone return home safely. During the eight years of working behind the scenes of President Thomas Hardesty, his team of thirty-six experts were all accounted for, although four were wounded during the various assignments. They were out of action for a period of time for recovery purposes, but at no point, was any of the members in danger of dying. They made full recoveries, and were back into the operations of the team.

Since almost everyone brought their own body armor, the armament storage room had none to offer his replacement. His replacement having been a part of a number of assignments with Romero Trap, was one to know this, but he would give him a reminder just in case.

None of the team members had checked their numbered accounts prior to Romero Trap departing in his Porches Cayenne for the evening. Most of them would be gone before Romero Trap returned the following afternoon after his White House session including the luncheon meal in the White House dining area. There were two such dining areas, but only one was for the first family and Vice President. The other was for larger political gatherings, typical of a number of foreign delegates invited for some conference or discussion concerning problems around the world. During Romero Trap's eight years, there was only one such gathering, which took place shortly after his commitment to joining the world governing council. That evening was spent largely in learning how to proceed and to insure it was not a supreme power over all the nations of the globe.

The following day while Romero Trap was at the White House, his last detail in reference to his unseen duties as Vice President, dealt with the six people working the secret service detail for the president and his family. Thomas Hardesty was not a difficult man to work with and neither was his wife any more of a problem. Both members of the six in the White House detail, decided to stay on as secret service to the President Thomas Hardesty, and the first lady. Both of them liked having a continuing paycheck coming in, something as independent consultants, was not often the case since their skills were not needed for every assignment. Also, none of them really worked for anyone other than Romero Trap, it was a trust issue, and insured they were never involved in mercenary type activities during their careers. The primary leader of the group of six, told Romero Trap, since the president would soon be leaving office, his two children had the option to continuing with secret service assigned to them, or have them relieved of their assignment. At no point during the nearly eight years were either of them threatened or ever in danger. Both were long done with school, and the President's daughter had her own family, which at last report, included three grandchildren to the president and first lady.

Thomas Hardesty's son on the other hand, had managed to get three different paternity suits filed against him in his last years in school. Upon his son telling him of the first, Thomas Hardesty informed his son that it was not his father's responsibility to solve his problem financially, and expected his son of taking responsible for his actions, or the consequence that resulted from those actions. Thomas Hardesty's son managed to take care of the first two, by working jobs while in school, and reaching a settlement before going to court. His son did call him again concerning the third, which was going to be far more costly, and even though at that point his son had completed school and gone on to find a decent means of employment, it would leave him destitute. His son provided his father with the option and thought, marriage was the only thing that would allow him some form of a life, not living out of his car. His father did inform his son that was a viable option, but if he did not remain loyal and treat the woman with respect, the divorce she would file would be his end as well. He pointed out if the woman was willing to go court for fathering their child, infidelity would lead to much worse.

Thomas Hardesty's son said he understood the potential issues, and went ahead with marriage and the intentions of being with one woman for the rest of his life, he just hoped at some point, love would become a factor in their relationship.

Both of Thomas Hardesty's children declined the continuing efforts of the secret service, since they preferred to have less attention brought to them by having armed guards in close proximity of everywhere they went. Romero Trap said he would give his replacement their names as well, to allow them possible assignments in the future. The primary leader of the group involved with the secret service told Romero Trap that was unnecessary, all four had enough advanced notice, they had made arrangements to become bodyguards for some of the more visible high profile business people in the country. Being former secret service had distinct advantages in that type of employment, and they would all be paid substantially more as private body guards to their respective employers.

The other highlight that Romero Trap had learned from the President, was the Middle East. Ali bin Uddin had read the bible sent to him by the President in a language he could understand. The results of Ali bin Uddin's finding were that what he was told by Zoe Dubois were largely true. The similarities were considerable between both books. Ali bin Uddin had to admit that the wording of the bible was much more concise, and left little room to doubt, that warring and killing were not ever the intentions of either book. Using his group as an example of how the different religious factions of Islam were all based upon the same book, there was no reason for so much variation in the meaning of it. All the governments of the Middle East eventually found Ali bin Uddin's group were the best option for prevention of border incursions among their group of nations. All the governments provided him with support, and the border group grew to five times the original size. During the time since the group formed, and Ali bin Uddin had read and understood the bible, there were three incursions that were attempted. Ali bin Uddin's primary weapons at the start of each, were a bible in one hand and the Koran in the other. His religious understanding prevented all three incursion attempts from becoming more than attempts, which resulted in no nation losing any territory to another. The team of border people accomplished it without a single shot taking place from both sides, and the mere fact that his group were from multiple factions of religious followings, they were all brothers in arms for a greater cause. That cause was not so much peace among all nations within the Middle East, but tolerance among all people regardless of their religious beliefs. Ali bin Uddin was wise enough to realize, until there was at least tolerance, there would never be a chance for peace.

Romero Trap found a good consolation in the fact, his group of non-government sanctioned professionals, had accomplished more than any government with use of military might had ever done. His team had managed to get the Middle East to take it upon themselves to find the way to work from within, than from outside interference. It was the first step in the right direction, since before Romero Trap was born, and in all likelihood, many centuries prior to that. What he found in his recollection of this single event, was the person who accomplished it, was the least likely to have considered such an option. Zoe Dubois (Black Widow) was a highly proficient assassin, which possessed a unique set of skills, and seemed void of any moral fiber in her veins after her childhood, that led to untold horrors for most women at her young age. She had overcome those, but her hatred for one person fueled her desire to remove all such men from the planet. It was partially what made her so unique, but the psychological aftermath was something only she could resolve in whatever timeframe it would take. That was provided there was any resolution possible. If there was, it had to start with her and her determination to have a more fruitful life afterwards. As of the day she left the team, she was just barely 33 years of age, and still had time to find a person she was comfortable with and possibly have a family, if she was not permanently damaged from the intrusion she was subjected to as a young girl. There was a large amount that Romero Trap did not know concerning Zoe Dubois, he did not know if she had any brothers or sisters, although he did know her parents, both worked two full time jobs, to simply keep a roof over their heads and food on the table, with little left over each month. She was hardly the spoiled child of some well to do family that could provide her with everything she ever desired.

When Romero Trap arrived at the base location, there were only a few people still remaining, awaiting the arrival of either a taxi or rental car being delivered. They did inform Romero Trap that they had all seen the deposit into their accounts, and although many had already departed, the entire team wanted to give him their thanks for such a generous retirement pension. Not a single one felt they would live long enough to deplete all the funds he had provided them. He responded with it was his duty to insure they were all well cared for once leaving, and it was with the hopes none of them ever needed to return to the profession they had endured for long enough. Romero Trap was the first to admit, it was not the ideal life to have, and in some case led to psychological issues that had to be dealt with. He more than anyone, wanted the team to have the resources available to them, to receive the proper care if that did occur.

An hour after his arrival, his replacement arrived for the final look around to see what he was getting for the next group of people, to perform duties for their country. Romero Trap had no additional names to give his replacement for possible members to the elite teams that would operate out of this very location. Romero Trap also did not inquire from his replacement what other names he included in his own list of professionals. He did point out that there was absolutely no body armor within the secured area for armaments. Everything else was his for his replacements options for weapons required for assignments he might try to take on for his team. Romero Trap could not provide his replacement with who might be his predecessor as VP, but his replacement could stay in contact with the news to make that discovery for himself. He suggested to his replacement to find somewhere local, to consider his home while having the property, as it was a good idea to perform a daily check of the property. He provided his replacement with keys to all the various locks and told him what each was used for. They went to the large commercial kitchen area, to see what was left in both the refrigerator and the walk in freezer. Romero Trap had not really kept track of the stocks since he did not live within the main building, or any of the other buildings. He did point out to his replacement that was a possibility for him, if he already had a home and family elsewhere, although Romero Trap had his doubts concerning that. He did not push for, or expect an answer in that regard. The pair did go over all the other buildings and all the vehicles left, were a part of the changeover in control of the property. If nothing else, his replacement could have a new assignment in matter of days as long as he had a team ready to move in, with all the equipment that was available to him. The next to the last thing was to go to the nearby abandoned airfield to see the aircraft available to his replacement. His replacement was informed that both were flight ready and the maintenance records were on board each aircraft, as required under military standards. His replacement was also informed that maintenance on both had been performed under those standards, and within a small little office area were the copies of the military standard maintenance procedures and information material regarding each aircraft.

At the conclusion of the final walk around the entire property, Romero Trap had brought his laptop computer to make the one billion dollar startup fund for his replacement. His replacement provide a numbered account, and the transfer was concluded in less than 30 seconds. His replacement using his own laptop, confirmed the transfer and said he would be looking into a place to live until he reached the same point in his career that Romero Trap had reached. There were a few additional pleasantries exchange between the two, as both had nothing but good things to say regarding each other. With the keys handed over to the gate, and the understanding to prevent unwanted visitors it was kept locked at all times, when not in use, Romero Trap left, never to return while he was still holding office as Vice President.

There was only 58 days left before the elections would decide on who his replacement would be. Although each candidate had announce whom it would be, if they were elected President, the election had not decided just whom that would be. Romero Trap used his last fifty eight days to once again view what homes were available in a more suburban area to Washington DC. Since it did involve two different states, each state had their own real estate sites to visit. Romero Trap had lived in the DC area for so long, he could not fathom leaving it entirely. Although he knew of many places in the United States that offered homes, and different attractions, he had never had time to visit, DC area was what he knew to be home ground.

The following days in the offices at the White House were largely spent in anticipation of who was taking over for the next four years at least, unless the President did such a poor job, the people of the country removed him from office. If the President was fired, so was his Vice President, since they were considered a matched set. It would leave the house speaker in charge, until a new leader was elected by the people. It did not really make the house speaker President, unless he was also a candidate for the position. Although the formal documentation would indicate the House speaker served as President, for the duration. There were some things in government, which even Thomas Hardesty could not get around with his streamlined government in place. His most impressive accomplishment in eight years, was the deficit was reduced by more than 50 percent, and if all went well, under the same plan as currently being done in government, it would be eliminated altogether in less than eight years from the time Thomas Hardesty left office. In his six weeks of time with the incoming President, he would stress that single most important issue to keep the people of the country on a more positive mind set nationally. He would point out to his replacement that the nation was on the verge of revolution when he first obtained office. The plan he put into effect not only brought about a more profitable people, the revolution had gone into the bit bucket. He would also point out that his predecessor had three attempts of violent behavior towards the White House as well as himself, while he had none, and would prefer to keep it that way.

Thomas Hardesty from Romero Trap's point of view, was an easy man to like and admire. He did not force his views upon anyone, but made them available to people by their own choice. He was not a vindictive man; he made every possible move for people to express their own opinions concerning the direction the country should take to move forward. He just wanted it to move forward, and not descend into a revolutionary state, which would for all intents and purposes, nullify the proud reputation of the country having the longest running successful republic in the world. Without that, the country would be no different than any other, and leave it open to greater threats than ever before in the history of the country.

As each day passed for President Thomas Hardesty and Vice President Romero Trap, it was that much closer to both leaving politics behind them, and move forward with the life that either had established or wished to pursue. Romero Trap spent an enormous amount of his time both in the office and at the apartment, looking at homes available for purchase. Romero Trap had definitely decided he wanted an existing home as opposed to a home built for him. He was eliminating far more than wishing to see, as he truly wanted something that was move in ready, instead having to wait an undetermined amount of time for it to take place. The selections were numerous, but the conditions of homes were far more work than he desired to invest in for the purpose of moving in. After 30 days of viewing, he only had three homes, which truly interested him. They had all the right options for what he desired to consider on a home, and he did take into consideration if it were ever to be sold again, it would be in demand among a larger percentage of people. He was not looking into outrageously large homes for the highly wealthy people of the country, as those homes, often went a much longer time period before sold or forgotten about. He was looking at homes in the 290,000 – 350,000 dollar range, that would be considered better than average homes for most citizens of the area. It would have three or four large bedrooms, and well-appointed kitchen and sufficient space for the common areas of any home. It would be preferable to have a lower level, whether finished or unfinished was not a major concern, as long as it was home to some of the standard appliances of all houses of a residential purpose.

He did find a number of homes that he felt were way too overpriced for what was offered, and felt it was a result of people taking advantage of the President making homes affordable to all, and not a select percentage of the population. He was more than aware that this would take place when the President remove housing controlled by a government agency from the hands of government. He was also seeing it was not overly abused, but a select group of people, were set on having high profits from offering it to the public. Romero Trap also took into consideration, that some people would always try to take advantage of others, and he feared that human capacity would never truly be eliminated the world over. It was not something unique to the United States, it was either instinctive by some, or simply a capacity to get more than it was worth to maximize profits. Like businesses the world over, the profit margin was what justified every decision made. It did not matter where on the planet you lived, there were some peoples whose mindset only worked within those parameters of profit margin. Losses were not within their formula or genetic make-up.

In the last 30 days of the President and Vice President holding office solo, every day was a short discussion over the items that the next office holder needed to be made aware of once holding office. President Thomas Hardesty made Romero Trap aware of the fact the first week at a minimum, would be a conversation without any other people present, between him and the newly elected president. There were national secrets that only the President was to know about, and it had to remain that way for the security of the office, as well as the country. President Thomas Hardesty did say one of the most important factors was to make the next president aware of the handwritten book of secrets as it was called, since George Washington first took office. There were entries dating back to the first President, and the information within was never to be discussed outside of one president to another. It was hidden, and only to be accessed by a president. Some of things within were considered tales and other simply secrets to be forever kept by the leader of this nation. Thomas Hardesty was careful not to reveal anything within those pages, except for his only entry which Romero Trap was made aware of when he agreed to take his position in the government. Romero Trap had a good idea that the entry made by the president pertained to his activities in serving his country. He did put in into words for the President to get confirmation, and that from Hardesty until the end of time, only the President would know what was in the documents that concerned what Romero Trap did for the sake of his country. Thomas Hardesty did not want the public to ever know that his Vice President, was a highly trained assassin, who had done nothing beyond serving his country to his fullest potential. It would also change the public opinion of all the good that both of them did for the people of the nation.

Over the last 30 days, as they dwindled down to zero, the Oval Office was no longer interrupted by staff or other people. There was no longer a daily schedule of events and appearances for the president, as the public focus was solely on who would take his place.

The presidential campaign included three people, one from each party, the republicans and the democrats and an independent. The independent based his entire campaign on continuing the good works of the 48th President, Thomas Hardesty.

On Election Day, which would consume most of it, the polls at the start indicated the independent candidate had a fair lead between the three candidates. It was still considered too close to make a determination by the news networks, a clear front runner and anticipated winner in the election process. That was not determined until 50 percent of the votes had been tallied, with the independent candidate holding 58 percent of the votes tallied, and the other pair pretty much equal in the difference of forty-two percent split between them. The final tally and clear and decisive winner was not formally announced until the following morning, with the independent having a sixty percent margin over his competitor holding nearly equal 20 percent each. It was not considered a landslide victory for the independent, but it was by a large majority percentage.

Since the time Thomas Hardesty took housing out of the government's control, the housing market nationwide had seen vast improvements. With his flat tax program, people and businesses had far more than prior to when he first took office. As a result, the nation took giant steps forward in the standing among all nations going from near the bottom to the top ten, and the improvements to the standards of living were up considerably. Seventy five percent of all Americans with families, were once again owners of housing, while there would always be a percentage of families and largely singles who were still working their way to homes ownership and having families. It was once again the American dream, to own your own home, and raise a family for a next generation. Thomas Hardesty wanted to see the percentage reach

80 to 85 percent of all families, but he had returned the country to a far more pleasant mind set from when he first took office eight years prior.

It was not until the third day after the election results were confirmed, that the newly elected President and Vice President made their first appearances to the White House. Romero Trap did not have so much wisdom to pass on to his replacement as Thomas Hardesty had for his. Romero Trap spent several days, just repeating largely the same advice over and over again, just in different words. He made his replacement aware of the two most crucial portions of his position to the president. First his primary function was his utmost support to the man in the Oval Office, who selected him above any other potential person to choose from for the position. Second, it was his duty to keep abreast of all the plans his President had detailed to make the nation a better place for all the people. This was largely in the event, something unexpected occurred to the President while he was second in command of the nation, to step in and complete those plans. Outside of those two things, his duties were rather limited to whatever the president might like him to do on his behalf. That could be, depending on his skill set, have diplomatic meetings that the President was unable to perform himself, due to his schedule, or public appearances on the President's behalf, but even his additional duties were in support of his President.

Thomas Hardesty needed ten days with his replacement to insure he understood all the things only the President of the United States was to know about, including the book of secrets, and where it was kept, and the code to unlock it from its hiding place. It was not something kept out in the open, and whenever it was used, it was done only with the President completely alone, including his secret service people. NO ONE could know what was within those pages besides himself. He also pointed out to his replacement, in making any entry into the book of secrets, that if his handwriting was poor to use print instead, so the next president to replace him, would be able to read it. There were numerous such entries, and even Script used in the earliest entries as it was far more common in that day and age of the history of this country. Thomas Hardesty did tell his replacement, that although the book of secrets did exist, the movie that was made a number of years previously

A SELECT FEW

was largely fiction, and it did not reside in the Library of Congress. He also reiterated that the only time more than one person was in the room containing the book of secrets to be accessed, was an outgoing president showing the incoming president its location and access code. There remained only one exception to that rule, and that was in the event of a president dying while in office, and the vice president assuming the position. In that undesirable event, the Vice President would need to learn it from a former president still living, which has always been the case while the nation had a political history. There were several cases of that very event occurring, and typically it was handled by the former president, since the vice president assuming the presidency, did not likely know of its existence. Unless he got it from the President's deathbed, he would not know of the book of secrets.

Once the ten days of the Presidents incoming and outgoing had concluded all the details only to be known by a President, the Oval Office was a more of an open meeting to discuss other events. For this particular portion of Thomas Hardesty's hopes, he wanted both incoming office holders present.

During the last thirty days of Romero Trap spending more time in the White House, he not only went to the luncheon but the dinner served for the evening. He was impressed by the luncheon meals, but was overwhelmed by the foods served by the White House kitchen staff for dinner. He truly did not understand how the president and first lady had not gained 50 pounds each, indulging in such wonderful creations the chef prepared for the evening meal. He knew his cooking skills were never going to reach such potential, but he could see being spoiled considerably, with eight years of the type of meals served daily.

President Thomas Hardesty had one last closed door session, where not even the incoming president was permitted to enter, to insure this took place, his secret service people were posted at both entrances to the Oval Office. The meeting consisted of five people, one on which was the President, since he was the one to request the meeting. The other four members were the heads of each military branch of the four services of the government's national military groups. Once all five members were present and accounted for, Trap had the doors locked, barring any admittance once the meeting started. His only duty pertaining to those within the Oval Office.

President Thomas Hardesty started out by saying, "Gentlemen, I am aware of the fact that all of you probably feel I stepped on toes shortly after taking office, I am afraid if you are here anticipating an apology, this I will not do. I did what was necessary to insure the nation was kept stable, before I could get plans ready to present to the people, to change their minds from where they were when first taking office. I kept all military personnel within domestic territory, because whether you were aware of it or not, this nation was on the very edge of starting a revolution, and that would have been our ultimate undoing, as a nation to look up to by other nations. We served as the longest successful democracy in the world, and we provide an example to other nations of what can be accomplished, when people are entitled to certain rights, living in a democracy. You presence was required within our own nation, if something did not work out in a proper timeframe. I hope all of you can agree this was the only course of action considering the pendulum of balance between a united nation, and one in revolution. I realize that most of you spend far more of your day, looking into problems around the world, than at your own front door." This received four affirmative head nods.

"Our nation had to be considerably more stable within our borders, to allow you all to concentrate on problems of the world, which brings us to the next point. The contents of what I am going say within this room, is never to be uttered to another living soul. I faced a dilemma on multiple fronts, and all of them needed to be addressed. I do not believe for a single minute, any of you are so young, as to not have any idea what the Vice President did for over thirty years prior to becoming my Vice President. His service to this country was exactly what made him the ideal candidate for some things that were put into operation, from this very office, and I am the one who requested them. Many things, that were news worthy were accomplished by the mere fact, it was not done by a show of strength by this government's military. What was accomplished with a small team of experts, are totally on account of the Vice President's abilities to plan and execute in ways nobody else could. He did these things without a shred of evidence pointing at the heart of this country. His removal of the Mexican and Columbian cartels brought stability to the countries around them, and increased the world's programs to combat and eradicate drug problems. He did all this with a team of no more than 36 people at any given point in his many assignments. His most prized accomplishment, from my own viewpoint, was bringing the Middle East to the most peaceful times I have experienced in my lifetime. Admittedly, it is more a point of tolerance for all the people within those nations, but without tolerance, peace would never exist, and for the first time in a long time, they are doing this all from within, without anyone interfering with them. It seems completely unfair for Romero Trap to have done so much in the aid of his country, and not get any single minute of recognition for his accomplishments." Thomas Hardesty went about informing the four generals of every branch of military all of the thing Romero Trap and his elite team accomplished over the last eight years, as instigated by the President. The President could not take credit for any of how it was planned or accomplished, that was solely a result of his Vice President's understanding of what he faced, and what needed to be done with the tools he had available.

The four pentagon members were impressed by the President's foresight into the world's problems, and walked away with a good deal more admiration for the man they thought, was only concerned about the nation he was made leader of by the people's choice. For eight years, they only has their suspicions he and Romero Trap, were working together in a less conspicuous nature, to get better results than military might ever achieved, and even they saw the wisdom of how well it worked. They also admitted to themselves, if they were made aware of it, they would have argued amongst themselves on which group would get to partake in the actions. The president's parting statement to the four leaders from the Pentagon struck nerves on each of them.

The president said that there was nothing wrong with having a prepared military force ready to go to action when called upon by their commander in chief. It was the honorary title by the military to whoever was President. He said it was totally unnecessary to bother

SHORT TIMING

the president over every time more than two people from two different nations starting shooting at each other. It would do them well to keep that in mind for the next president, and to also remember, a number of people informed the president daily, of activities both domestic and global. A President would know well before the Pentagon told him, of a possible reason to exercise military might. With any good fortune, the world governing council, would make for less and less military actions, and find diplomacy a more useful tool.

When the four generals returned to the Pentagon, they immediately went into their own closed door session, to discuss what they learned from the president. Past deeds were not on that agenda. That kept Romero Trap's name out of the discussion, besides they each knew enough about Romero Trap, that if any of them inadvertently disclosed any of his assignments, it would likely be the last words they ever got to speak. Romero Trap's reputation as an assassin, was too impressive to discount by any of them.

The conversation between the four military branch leaders were what to anticipate with a world governing council. Also discussed was how to restore some faith in the Pentagon concerning the next and subsequent presidents to follow. They agreed that Thomas Hardesty's point was well thought out, and they should have a truly valid reason for suggesting the use of military, under any circumstances. For the last twenty five years, it was a matter of the Pentagon trying to find something to do for the people they commanded under them. That would likely change a good deal with the formation of the world governing council. They all did agree, it would not be the end of the military although, it would most certainly be much leaner in personnel. It might mean the military choosing allies among the other nations, if aid was needed or required elsewhere. Another issue would be how much effect would be felt in the defense budget for obtaining the latest technology in various pieces of equipment. Aircraft and ship were without a doubt the costliest of them all, but tanks and ATV's (All-Terrain Vehicles) were no single dollar items either, although the ground forced used far more ATV's than the flyboys or surfers. Jeeps, also being members of the ATV class, were used by all for security around their various installations. Even the Navy had ground bases around docking stations for training, and living quarters for those not on a floating artillery or aircraft carrier. The meeting lasted for two hours with many things agreed upon, which was something unusual in itself, as the four had spent many more hours arguing in the past over who was better at what.

Each general had a great deal of pride in his own branch of the military, and in most conversations if their pride was hurt, it was common to lash out against the others. It was not unique to any single branch; it was shared equally. Additionally, anybody who ever wore a uniform beyond the initial first enlistment period with a military unit the world over, shared a common quality of one upmanship. To a man, there was no greater unit in existence, than the one they belonged to during their career. Words of that pride were often shared among other military units and branches, and when one upmanship was beyond words, it turned into a brawl. To the four generals, they could only recall three military members if not the highest, at least of high rank to become President. First President of the United States, George Washington, was the commander in chief of the continental army. The naval member was sure there was in likelihood the equivalent rank in the continental navy, but whether they had ships capable of traveling the ocean or merely the rivers he was unsure. If they had ocean capable ships, the British would likely have made sure they were destroyed upon entering the waters, of the revolutionary people from the colonies. With the way things were done then, it was unlikely they had sufficient time to get the ships to sea, out of harm's way.

Next known was Ulysses S. Grant, and last confirmed was Dwight D. Eisenhower. Although a large number of past presidents served in the military, most did not make it a lifelong career in order to enter into politics.

The Oval Office was now officially an open door room again for the four people who would spend the most time in it over the next month. At the end of the month, it would be time for Thomas Hardesty and Romero Trap to walk away, with the hopes of seldom, if ever, returning.

The first meeting among all four members present was to inform the incoming president of the formation of the world governing council. He and his vice president were both present, and this was to insure if anything came to be that brought the vice president into the office of president, he would be able to follow through with what Hardesty hoped it would become. He went on to tell them, although Romero Trap knew all the details, he was present for his wise council if needed, it was not to become an ultimate power ever. The primary purpose of the world governing council, was first to insure the world worked for the betterment of all people and nations. It was intended to be a place where every nation in the world represented itself, and was used to find a diplomatic solution to any problems among the nations of the world. One thing that needed to be mentioned, was the world governing council would not have members or delegates elected to offices. Each nation's leader, would represent their own nation with the world council. The wisdom behind this was the world was not going to support yet another governing body. Although each nation would be required to make annual contributions for an office complex sufficient to have a council meeting of all the nations of the world, and a small support staff. Whose primary duties were to be able to meet the needs of the nation's attending, as well as things like coffee, tea, water and maybe meals brought in for really long sessions. Not having had a single meeting, without a building, the one meeting he did have with those behind this idea, was within the White House. The only agenda he knew of currently unfolding is the use of a world currency that would make all countries, equal in the currency value of the world. Granted smaller and poorer nations, would have less compensation for similar jobs elsewhere in the world, but with the currency would hopefully become standards of living equally among all countries. "The one thing I found to be extremely wise in the use of a world currency was the group did a great deal of research into their concept. The United States, still uses the most difficult currency paper to reproduce, it is not impossible, but takes far more skill than most people and countries are willing to exert into counterfeit currency. Also, the group though it absolute best not to use any figures of national leaders on any currency value that it produced. That means, things of beauty such as woodland forests or tropical paradises and such items, would be incorporated to prevent it to appear any favoritism to any specific nation.

The people with the idea over money brought into play two very important factors to deter as much as possible for counterfeiting to become a major problem. First the money denominations will be colorful, and the most difficult colors to reproduce, will be utilized. The second deterrent, will be each denomination would be replaced every six months of production, with a new version. Money will be able to be circulated for up to two years, making it so no more than four versions of each denomination, would be in circulation at any one time. For a person who holds a real but expired version of any denomination, they will merely need to go to any banking institution, have it validated as none counterfeit, and get the current replacement denomination for it. I saw a good deal of wisdom behind this plan, and as a result volunteered our treasury department that has four printing location across this great nation, and knows how to have the paper stock manufactured. We will have nothing to do with the color section, or the engraving, and no country will know more than one major ingredient into the production of the money. Once all the nations of the world agreed to this, it will take approximately six months to start exchanging currency from one type to another on an exchange rate based on equality to the value of currencies currently used around the globe. From my understanding, almost every nation will have something to obtain for making the new world currency. One final note on the world currency, each denomination will have a total of four water stamps, it is an old and archaic term, but they will only be visible in a dark room under a black light. It is something that can only be done by a financial institution that handles currency, and it is supposed to be done without any people from the lobby able to view the process. It does not completely prevent counterfeiting, but it sure ought to make it a good deal more difficult. If everyone in every shop could verify it for real or counterfeit, it would not make it such a difficult ordeal in counterfeiting."

Any questions asked Thomas Hardesty. Romero Trap only one, when is this anticipated to become a reality?

Thomas Hardesty could give not a firm answer, as it first needed the approval of every country. Which was a mere formality in the paperwork, but only one country had not joined but submitted. It is a mere matter of how long the paperwork takes which seems to be a sticking point to every government the world over, including the world governing council, but admittedly, they are keeping staff levels to as little as possible to spare nations the burden of more taxes. "The last things I need are two promises from the next president.

First, I listened occasionally to your campaign and repeatedly heard you only wanted to continue my good work. If that is true, you will know the size of government had been drastically reduced from 75 percent of working people to 30 percent. A much more reasonable percentage, and those working are running like a fine-tuned business machine, as opposed to the old way of seeing how many people it took to change a light bulb. I had thought that statement was exaggerated, until I witnessed it here in this very office, when one of the overhead lights quit working. It took 15 electrical technicians to determine if it was the light or the ballast, and it was totally unnecessary. In business a single technician brings a light tube with him, and it works or it does not. If it does not, he swaps it with the one that does, and if it works there, he knows to bring a ballast for the light fixture. That is how this government is currently operating, and everyone seems content about the work. I need your promise there will be no increase in the size of government which ties directly into the second promise.

Since the flat tax program for individuals went into effect, this country had been able to keep from borrowing any money to operate. With the business flat tax incorporated and the government downsized, the operating surplus had been applied to the massive deficit left by my predecessors. As of now, that deficit is less than 50 percent of what it was, and we still make our payments on time every time. The monthly payment is set at 110 billion dollars each month. If you promise to continue both of these programs as they are, you will fulfill your campaign promise, and if you get reelected and continue these two program as they are right now, you will see a deficit at zero, and it will add even more funds to the black at the end of the rainbow, because there will be no more payments to make. At its current course, that should be somewhere between six and one half to no more than seven years from now. I realize it is a long time for those still employed within this government, to have to wait for a well-earned raise, but it has to be that way. This country needs to be self-sufficient, and to never become another country's territory or colony ever again. When there are no payments to make, if you are still here, all your employees should get a 10 to 12 percent increase for the outstanding job they performed in returning the country to standing on its own feet. And if memory serves me correctly, all of their raises combined will not equal half the payment amount we have to send each month. Leaving all the funds used for the deficit to show the country in the black for the first time in at least 30 years. Your promises to these two things, will make your presidency a far easier burden to hold on your shoulders."

After that, the conversation between the incoming president and the outgoing one was concentrated on how Thomas Hardesty had managed to accomplish so much in such a short time. He said he did it with the aid of the people, as the first thing he did was use a website for presenting bills to be voted on, afterwards submitting the formal Supreme Court version. Since he was an economist as a businessman, the last thing he cared about was the proper legal mumble jumble required by the Supreme Court, but his staff was paramount in putting his proposals into the correct wording for them. They were also instrumental in putting the same proposals, to the people in the most straight forward and easiest terms possible. That was done to bypass the quagmire that was the Senate and Congress. "Any proposal to them, typically died in those very halls. As an independent, I had no chance of working with the people of those houses, and expect to accomplish anything, so I found a better approach, and instituted a few more rights to the people, which in reality they already had, but were never really made aware of it by career politicians. Pretty sure the rest is fairly well documented, what you may not be aware of, is when I first took office, this country was on the very doorstep of another revolution, and that fed the fires to prevent it from happening. The President before me who served two terms, had three attempts, by people to storm the White

House and they were armed for that intention. Fortunately, the White House guards who are all Marines, prevented it from taking place to a completion by the people."

The final day arrived in the White House to turn over the keys to the Oval Office and the Vice Presidential Office. In reality there were no keys to exchange, but the changing of the guard was already used in Great Britain.

On the fifth day after leaving the White House, Romero Trap had finally got a real estate agent to show him the five properties, that most interested him. The most intriguing was farther away in Virginia than had planned to go, at 70 miles from his apartment. He was to meet the agent at her office, and they would leave from there. A driver under the influence of either alcohol or drugs was traveling at rate of speed beyond the limit, and interpreted a parked car as someone who just pulled out in front of him. He swerved onto the sidewalk, missing all the cars, but lost control and at the precise moment Romero Trap opened the door from the apartment entrance and took half a step out, the car slammed into him and the front of the building. The metal framing around the door of the apartment sheared into jagged sharp edges tearing through a large portion of Romero Trap, and the impact pushed him farther over the jagged framing. What damage that did not do, was completed by the shattered plate glass window use as the viewing area for visitors to apartment tenants. His body had extensive and massive laceration on front and rear of his middle torso. The plate glass shards that dropped onto him perforated at least one artery, and in less than three minutes time, Romero Trap had bled out. He would not get to see a single home, was his last thoughts.

In the short time from impact until Romero Trap died, it was insufficient for any emergency vehicle to arrive in time to attempt to save the former Vice President. He was pronounced dead at the scene, and the driver was taken away in handcuffs, after minor medical attention. The news broadcasts went national to every station across the continent by the major networks. All made mention of the fact, after only five days after leaving office, he was the victim of a drunk driver leaving his apartment building.

The current President, having read the entry by Thomas Hardesty in the book of secrets, and all the eyes only to the president, classified documents pertaining to Romero Trap, at one point wondered, just how such a person could even hold the second highest office in the land. He realized, that Thomas Hardesty had sealed his documents before naming him Vice President, and that Thomas Hardesty was masterful in how he accomplished so much in eight years. Largely due to his Vice President's behind the scenes methods, and selecting a very skilled team of experts. His sealing the records made it appear that both were completely innocent in the events that took place, and even Houdini would be amazed at how it was all orchestrated. After that conclusion, the President made a single phone call to the Supreme Court, and asked if the drunk driver who killed Romero Trap, the 48th Vice President of the United States, could be tried as an act of treason. They said it was a bit unusual, but since it was Romero Trap, it was quite feasible. The President simply said, make it so. The headlines read: For the first time in the history of this nation, a stupid act of drunk driving, now has a person being tried for treason, as the death of a prominent former member of government, holding the office of Vice President for eight years, was the victim of his driving under the influence. Romero Trap was pronounced dead at the scene only five days following his last day in the White House, as the 48th Vice President.

With all the news broadcasts almost every member of his team teams past and present were saddened by the news. Thomas Hardesty and his wife were in total shock, having seen him less than a week ago, when he was rambling on about getting to see homes for the first time in his life. Such a tragic loss, was all either of them could say. Thomas Hardesty's secret service, as well as that of the first lady, asked their permission to be there for his funeral. Both said it was fine, because they had no intention of not going themselves.

There was no church service for Romero Trap, and all the arrangements were performed by the military, since Romero Trap had earned a spot in Arlington Cemetery right next to the two plots, reserved for Thomas Hardesty and his first lady. Thomas Hardest provided a short eulogy after confirming with the honor guard, which for all Romero

SHORT TIMING

Trap had done for his country, he deserved twenty one guns, more than any President ever did. The honor guard gave Thomas Hardesty his request, although normally a Vice President only received 18 guns as 21 was reserved only for Presidents. The eulogy was short, saying Romero Trap had done more for his country than any man he knew, and it was an absolute shame his accomplished cannot be told since, it was act of treason. Here's to the 48th Vice President of the United States. 250 former team members of Romero Trap had made the trip to pay their final respects. It included all 36 members of his eight year assignment recently completed, as well as the half dozen people who accepted secret service detail. His replacement, as well as all 123 names he was given were present, and the remainder were people who had left the business, but once worked with Romero Trap. As tribute to Romero Trap, each former team member placed a single bullet with RT engraved on it, except for Zoe Dubois, who left a single syringe.

Romero Trap would never learn that after three more years of premier assignments, Zoe Dubois met a man who at first, she simply responded to his statement while going into to her fitness club for her four hour workout. After she had completed her work out and emerged from the building, that very same man had waited all that time, to say he knew it was not for long, but he had enjoyed talking with her, and asked if she would like to go for drinks, and he did not care if it was alcoholic or not.

After four hours in the fitness center, all Zoe Dubois wanted to do was rehydrate herself, and that could be accomplished at any convenience store. She told him as much, but for some reason she felt at ease with this perfect stranger. They went to the closest convenience store and she got a fairly large bottle of a sports drink, to replenish the fluids and mineral she expended in her four hour work out, although the finishing half hour swim did help a good deal, but only externally. He got a coke, and paid for them, and they walked and talked for about thirty minutes before returning to her Lincoln to head home. During the time, the man who made no advancements upon her or lewd remarks, he accomplished one thing no man had ever done in her entire life. He made Zoe feel good about herself. She could not explain it to herself, much less anyone else, this man was slightly overweight, a very plain face, neither handsome nor ugly. He was by no means an Adonis to go with the Venus, many considered Zoe to be. If anything was best used to describe him, he was 100 percent ordinary in features, appearance and stature. But they did exchange phone numbers. It took Zoe nearly one and half years to give in to herself, she had feeling for the man who made her feel good about herself. After three years of premium assignment, which were at 50 million per assignment, and 36 assignments after finishing her assignment with Romero Trap, Zoe retired from the profession, as a result of one stranger, she met in front of the Fitness Club.

CPSIA information can be obtained
at www.ICGtesting.com
Printed in the USA
BVHW032253090323
660087BV00005B/119